Windows® 8 FOR DUMMIES®

by Andy Rathbone

WILEY

John Wiley & Sons, Inc.

Windows® 8 For Dummies®

Published by
John Wiley & Sons, Inc.
111 River Street
Hoboken, NJ 07030-5774

www.wiley.com

Copyright © 2012 by John Wiley & Sons, Inc., Hoboken, New Jersey

Published by John Wiley & Sons, Inc., Hoboken, New Jersey

Published simultaneously in Canada

No part of this publication may be reproduced, stored in a retrieval system or transmitted in any form or by any means, electronic, mechanical, photocopying, recording, scanning or otherwise, except as permitted under Sections 107 or 108 of the 1976 United States Copyright Act, without either the prior written permission of the Publisher, or authorization through payment of the appropriate per-copy fee to the Copyright Clearance Center, 222 Rosewood Drive, Danvers, MA 01923, (978) 750-8400, fax (978) 646-8600. Requests to the Publisher for permission should be addressed to the Permissions Department, John Wiley & Sons, Inc., 111 River Street, Hoboken, NJ 07030, (201) 748-6011, fax (201) 748-6008, or online at http://www.wiley.com/go/permissions.

Trademarks: Wiley, the Wiley logo, For Dummies, the Dummies Man logo, A Reference for the Rest of Us!, The Dummies Way, Dummies Daily, The Fun and Easy Way, Dummies.com, Making Everything Easier, and related trade dress are trademarks or registered trademarks of John Wiley & Sons, Inc. and/or its affiliates in the United States and other countries, and may not be used without written permission. Windows is a registered trademark of Microsoft Corporation. All other trademarks are the property of their respective owners. John Wiley & Sons, Inc. is not associated with any product or vendor mentioned in this book.

For general information on our other products and services, please contact our Customer Care Department within the U.S. at 877-762-2974, outside the U.S. at 317-572-3993, or fax 317-572-4002.

For technical support, please visit www.wiley.com/techsupport.

Wiley publishes in a variety of print and electronic formats and by print-on-demand. Some material included with standard print versions of this book may not be included in e-books or in print-on-demand. If this book refers to media such as a CD or DVD that is not included in the version you purchased, you may download this material at http://booksupport.wiley.com. For more information about Wiley products, visit www.wiley.com.

Library of Congress Control Number is available from the publisher.

ISBN 978-1-118-13461-0 (pbk); ISBN 978-1-118-22513-4 (ebk); ISBN 978-1-118-23871-4 (ebk); ISBN 978-1-118-26331-0 (ebk)

Manufactured in the United States of America

10 9 8 7 6 5 4 3 2 1

WILEY

About the Author

Andy Rathbone started geeking around with computers in 1985 when he bought a 26-pound portable CP/M Kaypro 2X. Like other nerds of the day, he soon began playing with null-modem adapters, dialing computer bulletin boards, and working part-time at Radio Shack.

He wrote articles for various techie publications before moving to computer books in 1992. He's written the *Windows For Dummies* series, *Upgrading and Fixing PCs For Dummies, TiVo For Dummies, PCs: The Missing Manual,* and many other computer books.

Today, he has more than 15 million copies of his books in print, and they've been translated into more than 30 languages. You can reach Andy at his website, www.andyrathbone.com.

Author's Acknowledgments

Special thanks to Dan Gookin, Matt Wagner, Tina Rathbone, Steve Hayes, Nicole Sholly, Virginia Sanders, and Russ Mullen.

Thanks also to all the folks I never meet in editorial, sales, marketing, proof-reading, layout, graphics, and manufacturing who work hard to bring you this book.

Publisher's Acknowledgments

We're proud of this book; please send us your comments at http://dummies.custhelp.com. For other comments, please contact our Customer Care Department within the U.S. at 877-762-2974, outside the U.S. at 317-572-3993, or fax 317-572-4002.

Some of the people who helped bring this book to market include the following:

Acquisitions and Editorial

Senior Project Editor: Nicole Sholly

Executive Editor: Steve Hayes

Copy Editor: Virginia Sanders

Technical Editor: Russ Mullen

Editorial Manager: Kevin Kirschner

Editorial Assistant: Leslie Saxman

Sr. Editorial Assistant: Cherie Case

Cover Photo: © Yin Yang/Getty Images

Cartoons: Rich Tennant
(www.the5thwave.com)

Composition Services

Project Coordinator: Katherine Crocker

Layout and Graphics: Jennifer Creasey, Corrie Niehaus, Julie Trippetti

Proofreaders: Lindsay Amones, ConText Editorial Services, Inc.

Indexer: BIM Indexing & Proofreading Services

Publishing and Editorial for Technology Dummies

  Richard Swadley, Vice President and Executive Group Publisher

  Andy Cummings, Vice President and Publisher

  Mary Bednarek, Executive Acquisitions Director

  Mary C. Corder, Editorial Director

Publishing for Consumer Dummies

  Kathleen Nebenhaus, Vice President and Executive Publisher

Composition Services

  Debbie Stailey, Director of Composition Services

Contents at a Glance

Table of Contents

Part II: Working with Programs, Apps, and Files 117

Chapter 6: Playing with Programs, Apps, and Documents 119

Chapter 7: Finding the Lost 139

Chapter 8: Printing Your Work 153

Introduction

Welcome to *Windows 8 For Dummies,* the world's best-selling book about Windows 8!

This book's popularity probably boils down to this simple fact: Some people want to be Windows whizzes. They love interacting with dialog boxes. Some randomly press keys in the hope of discovering hidden, undocumented features. A few memorize long strings of computer commands while washing their hair.

And you? Well, you're no dummy, that's for sure. But when it comes to Windows and computers, the fascination just isn't there. You want to get your work done, stop, and move on to something more important. You have no intention of changing, and there's nothing wrong with that.

That's where this book comes in handy. Instead of making you a whiz at Windows, it merely dishes out chunks of useful computing information when you need them. Instead of becoming a Windows 8 expert, you'll know just enough to get by quickly, cleanly, and with a minimum of pain so that you can move on to the more pleasant things in life.

And you'll be able to do that whether you're dealing with a touchscreen, laptop, or desktop computer.

About This Book

Don't try to read this book in one sitting; there's no need. Instead, treat this book like a dictionary or an encyclopedia. Turn to the page with the information you need and say, "Ah, so that's what they're talking about." Then put down the book and move on.

Don't bother trying to memorize all the Windows 8 jargon, such as Select the Menu Item from the Drop-Down List Box. Leave that stuff for the computer enthusiasts. In fact, if anything technical comes up in a chapter, a road sign warns you well in advance. Depending on your mood, you can either slow down to read it or speed on around it.

Instead of fancy computer jargon, this book covers subjects like these, all discussed in plain English:

- ✔ Keeping your computer safe and secure
- ✔ Making sense of the new Start screen
- ✔ Finding, starting, and closing programs and apps
- ✔ Locating the file you saved or downloaded yesterday
- ✔ Setting up a computer for the whole family to use
- ✔ Copying information to and from a CD or DVD
- ✔ Saving and sharing photos from your digital camera
- ✔ Printing your work
- ✔ Creating a network between computers to share an Internet connection or printer
- ✔ Fixing Windows 8 when it's misbehaving

There's nothing to memorize and nothing to learn. Just turn to the right page, read the brief explanation, and get back to work. Unlike other books, this one enables you to bypass the technical hoopla and still get your work done.

How to Use This Book

Windows 8 will most definitely leave you scratching your head at some point. It's the most confusing version of Windows ever released to the public, so take pride in the fact that you're strong enough to persevere.

When something in Windows 8 leaves you stumped, use this book as a reference. Find the troublesome topic in this book's table of contents or index. The table of contents lists chapter and section titles and page numbers. The index lists topics and page numbers. Page through the table of contents or index to the spot that deals with that particular bit of computer obscurity, read only what you have to, close the book, and apply what you've read.

If you're feeling adventurous and want to find out more, read a little further in the bulleted items below each section. You can find a few completely voluntary extra details, tips, or cross-references to check out. There's no pressure, though. You aren't forced to discover anything that you don't want to or that you simply don't have time for.

If you have to type something into the computer, you'll see easy-to-follow bold text like this:

Type **Media Player** into the Search box.

In the preceding example, you type the words *Media Player* and then press the keyboard's Enter key. Typing words into a computer can be confusing, so a description follows that explains what you should be seeing on the screen.

When I describe a key combination you should press, I describe it like this:

Press Ctrl+B.

That means to hold down your keyboard's Control key while pressing your keyboard's B key. (That's the shortcut key combination that applies bold formatting to selected text.)

Whenever I describe an email address or filename, I present it this way:

```
notepad.exe
```

And website addresses appear like this:

```
www.andyrathbone.com
```

This book doesn't wimp out by saying, "For further information, consult your manual." Windows 8 doesn't even *come* with a manual. This book also doesn't contain information about running specific Windows software packages, such as Microsoft Office. Windows 8 is complicated enough on its own! Luckily, other *For Dummies* books mercifully explain most popular software packages.

Don't feel abandoned, though. This book covers Windows in plenty of detail for you to get the job done. Plus, if you have questions or comments about *Windows 8 For Dummies,* feel free to drop me a line on my website at `www.andyrathbone.com`. I answer a reader's question on my website each week.

Finally, keep in mind that this book is a *reference.* It's not designed to teach you how to use Windows 8 like an expert, heaven forbid. Instead, this book dishes out enough bite-sized chunks of information so that you don't *have* to learn Windows.

Tablet Owners Aren't Left Out

Although Windows 8 comes preinstalled on all new Windows computers, Microsoft not-so-secretly aims this bold new version of Windows at owners of *touchscreens.* Tablets, as well as some laptops and desktop monitors, come with screens you can control by touching them with your fingers.

If you're a new touchscreen owner, don't worry. This book explains where you need to touch, slide, or tap your fingers in all the appropriate places.

If you find yourself scratching your head over explanations aimed at mouse owners, remember these three touchscreen rules:

- **When told to *click,* you should *tap.*** Quickly touching and releasing your finger on a button is the same as clicking it with a mouse.

- **When told to double-click, *tap twice.*** Two touches in rapid succession does the trick.

- **When told to *right-click* something, *hold down your finger on the item.* Then, when a little menu pops up, *lift your finger.*** The menu stays put onscreen. (That's exactly what would have happened if you'd right-clicked the item with a mouse.) While you're looking at the pop-up menu, tap any of its listed items to have Windows carry out your bidding.

If you find touchscreens to be cumbersome while you're sitting at a desk, you can always plug a mouse and keyboard into your touchscreen tablet. They'll work just fine. In fact, they usually work better when working on the Windows desktop rather than the Start screen.

And What about You?

Chances are good that you already own Windows 8 or are thinking about upgrading. You know what *you* want to do with your computer. The problem lies in making the *computer* do what you want it to do. You've gotten by one way or another, perhaps with the help of a computer guru — either a friend at the office, somebody down the street, or your fourth-grader.

But when your computer guru isn't around, this book can be a substitute during your times of need. (Keep a doughnut nearby in case you need a quick bribe.)

How This Book Is Organized

The information in this book has been well sifted. This book contains seven parts, and I divide each part into chapters relating to the part's theme. With an even finer knife, I divide each chapter into short sections to help you figure out a bit of Windows 8 weirdness. Sometimes, you may find what you're looking for in a small, boxed sidebar. Other times, you may need to cruise through an entire section or chapter. It's up to you and the particular task at hand.

Here are the categories (the envelope, please).

Part I: Windows 8 Stuff Everybody Thinks You Already Know

This part dissects the backbone of Windows 8: its new Start screen, where you load apps and programs. It also explains how to find the traditional Windows desktop — the background found in every version of Windows for the past decade. It explains how to move windows around and click the right buttons at the right time. It explains the Windows 8 stuff that everybody thinks you already know.

Part II: Working with Programs, Apps, and Files

Windows 8 comes with bunches of free programs. Finding and starting the programs, however, often proves to be a chore. This part of the book shows you how to prod programs into action. If an important file or program has vanished from the radar, you discover how to make Windows 8 dredge your computer's crowded cupboards and bring it back. It also explains how to move your work from the computer screen onto paper through your printer.

Part III: Getting Things Done on the Internet

Turn here for a crash course in today's computing playground, the Internet. This part explains how to send e-mail and globetrot across websites. Best yet, an entire chapter explains how to do it all safely.

A section explains Internet Explorer's built-in security tools. They stop evil phishing sites from tricking you and keep parasites from attaching themselves to your computer as you move from one website to another.

Part IV: Customizing and Upgrading Windows 8

When Windows 8 needs a jolt, fix it by flipping one of the switches hidden in its Control Panel, described here. Another chapter explains computer maintenance you can easily perform yourself, reducing your repair bills. You discover how to share your computer with several people in your family or in a shared apartment — without letting anybody peek into anybody else's information.

And when you're ready to add a second computer, head to the networking chapter for quick instructions on linking computers to share an Internet connection, files, and a printer, as well.

Part V: Music, Photos, and Movies

Turn here for information on playing music CDs, digital music, and movies. Buy some cheap CDs and create your own greatest hits CDs from your favorite tunes. (Or just copy a CD so that your favorite one doesn't get scratched in the car.)

Digital camera owners should visit the chapter on transferring pictures from your camera to your computer, organizing the pictures, and e-mailing them to friends.

Part VI: Help!

Although glass doesn't shatter when Windows crashes, it still hurts. In this part, you find some soothing salves for the most painful irritations. Plus, you find ways to unleash the Windows 8 program's team of troubleshooters.

Stuck with the problem of moving your files from an old computer to a new one? You can find help here, as well. (If you're ready to upgrade your Windows XP, or Windows Vista, or Windows 7 computer to Windows 8, check out `www.dummies.com/go/windows8` for instructions.)

Part VII: The Part of Tens

Everybody loves lists (except during tax time). This part contains lists of Windows-related trivia, such as ten aggravating things about Windows 8 (and how to fix them). As a bonus for the tablet and laptop crowd, I've collected the most useful portability tips for Windows 8 and placed them into one chapter. You can find step-by-step instructions for the most frequently used tasks while traveling, whether you're moving across the world or across the street.

Icons Used in This Book

It just takes a glance at Windows 8 to notice its *icons,* which are little push-button pictures for starting various programs. The icons in this book fit right in. They're even a little easier to figure out.

Watch out! This signpost warns you that pointless technical information is coming around the bend. Swerve away from this icon to stay safe from awful technical drivel.

This icon alerts you about juicy information that makes computing easier: a method for keeping the cat from sleeping on top of your tablet, for example.

Don't forget to remember these important points. (Or at least dog-ear the pages so that you can look them up again a few days later.)

The computer won't explode while you're performing the delicate operations associated with this icon. Still, wearing gloves and proceeding with caution is a good idea.

Are you moving to Windows 8 from an older Windows version? This icon alerts you to areas where Windows 8 works significantly differently from its predecessors.

Controlled by fingertips rather than mice and keyboards, touchscreens are standard fare on tablets, as well as some laptops and desktop computer monitors. This icon appears next to information aimed directly at the touchy feely crowd.

Where to Go from Here

Now, you're ready for action. Give the pages a quick flip and scan a section or two that you know you'll need later. Please remember, this is *your* book — your weapon against the computer nerds who've inflicted this whole complicated computer concept on you. Please circle any paragraphs you find useful, highlight key concepts, add your own sticky notes, and doodle in the margins next to the complicated stuff.

The more you mark up your book, the easier it will be for you to find all the good stuff again.

To access additional Windows 8 content, go to www.dummies.com/go/windows8. Occasionally, we have updates to our technology books. If this book does have technical updates, they will be posted at www.dummies.com/go/windows8fdupdates.

Part I

Windows 8 Stuff Everybody Thinks You Already Know

In this part . . .

Most people are dragged into Windows 8 without a choice. Their new computers probably came with Windows 8 already installed. Or maybe the office switched to Windows 8, and everyone has to learn it except for the boss, who still doesn't have a computer. Or maybe Microsoft's marketing hype pushed you into it.

Whatever your situation, this part explains the bizarre new Start screen in Windows 8. It shows how to find the traditional Windows desktop and then gives a refresher on Windows basics and buzzwords such as dragging and dropping, cutting and pasting, and even tapping a touchscreen.

This part explains how Windows 8 has changed things for the better, and it warns you when Windows 8 has messed things up completely.

Chapter 1

What Is Windows 8?

Chances are good that you've heard about *Windows:* the boxes and windows that greet you whenever you turn on your computer. In fact, millions of people worldwide are puzzling over Windows as you read this book. Almost every new computer and laptop sold today comes with Windows preinstalled, ready to toss colorful boxes onto the screen.

This chapter helps you understand why Windows lives inside your computer, and I introduce Microsoft's latest Windows version, called *Windows 8.* I explain how Windows 8 differs from previous Windows versions, whether you should upgrade to Windows 8, and how well your faithful old PC and programs will weather the upgrade.

What Is Windows 8, and Why Are You Using It?

Created and sold by a company called Microsoft, Windows isn't like your usual software that lets you calculate income taxes or send angry e-mails to mail-order companies. No, Windows is an *operating system,* meaning it controls the way you work with your computer. It's been around for nearly 30 years, and the latest incarnation is called *Windows 8,* shown in Figure 1-1.

Figure 1-1:
The newest
version of
Windows,
Windows 8,
comes pre-
installed on
most new
PCs today.

The name *Windows* comes from all the little windows it places on your computer screen. Each window shows information, such as a picture, a program, or a baffling technical reprimand. You can place several windows onscreen simultaneously and jump from window to window, visiting different programs. Or, you can enlarge one window to fill the entire screen.

When you turn on your computer, Windows jumps onto the screen and begins supervising any running programs. When everything goes well, you don't really notice Windows; you simply see your programs or your work. When things don't go well, though, Windows often leaves you scratching your head over a perplexing error message.

In addition to controlling your computer and bossing around your programs, Windows 8 comes with a bunch of free programs and *apps* — mini-programs. These programs and apps let you do different things, such as write and print letters, browse the Internet, play music, and send your friends dimly lit photos of your latest meal.

And why are you using Windows 8? Well, you probably didn't have much choice. Nearly every computer sold since October 2012 comes with Windows 8 pre-installed. A few people escaped Windows by buying Apple computers (those nicer-looking computers that cost a lot more). But chances are good that you, your neighbors, your boss, and millions of other people around the world are using Windows.

Separating the ads from the features

Microsoft touts Windows as a helpful companion that always keeps your best interests in mind, but that description isn't really true. Windows always keeps *Microsoft's* interests in mind. You'll find that out as soon as you call Microsoft for help with a Windows problem. Microsoft charges $100 an hour for phone support.

Microsoft also uses Windows to plug its own products and services. Internet Explorer opens to Microsoft's own MSN.com website, for example. The browser's Favorites area, a place

for you to add *your* favorite web destinations, comes stocked with *Microsoft* websites.

The Maps app uses the Microsoft Bing mapping service, rather than Google Maps or another competitor. The list goes on.

Simply put, Windows not only controls your computer, but also serves as a huge Microsoft advertising vehicle. Treat these built-in advertising flyers as a salesperson's knock on your door.

✔ Windows 8 introduces a radical new full-screen–sized Start menu that's designed for *touchscreens* — displays controlled with your fingertips. Now called a *Start screen,* it also appears on desktop PCs, oddly enough. Be prepared for some initial mouse awkwardness as you try to mimic a fingertip with your mouse pointer.

✔ The new automatic backup program in Windows 8, *File History,* greatly simplifies what you should have been doing all along: creating copies of your important files for safekeeping. Because Microsoft leaves it turned off, I explain how to turn it on in Chapter 13.

What's New in Windows 8?

You may have worked with earlier versions of Microsoft Windows. If so, toss away that hard-earned knowledge because Windows 8 starts from scratch. Why? Because Windows 8 tries to please two camps of computer owners.

See, some people are mostly *consumers.* They read e-mail, watch videos, listen to music, and browse the web, often while away from their desktop PC. Whether on the go or on the couch, they're consuming media (and popcorn).

Other people are mostly *creators.* They write papers, prepare tax returns, update blogs, edit videos, or, quite often, tap whichever keys their boss requires that day.

To please both markets, Microsoft broke Windows 8 into two very different sections:

- **Start screen:** For the on-the-go information grabbers, the Windows 8 Start screen fills the entire screen with large, colorful tiles that constantly update to show the latest stock prices, weather, e-mail, Facebook updates, and other tidbits. Shown earlier in Figure 1-1, that information appears before you touch a button. And *touch* is a keyword: The Start screen works best with a touchscreen monitor or tablet.

- **Desktop tile:** When it's time for work, head for the Start screen's *desktop* tile. The traditional Windows desktop appears, shown in Figure 1-2, bringing all its power — as well as its detailed, cumbersome menus.

Some people like the convenience of having both types of computers built into one. Others find the two experiences to be oddly disjointed.

- In a way, Windows 8 offers the best of both worlds: You can stay on the Start screen for quick, on-the-go browsing. And when work beckons, you can head for the desktop, where your traditional Windows programs await.

Figure 1-2:
The
Windows 8
desktop
works much
as it did in
Windows 7,
but without
a Start
button.

✔ The catch is that the Windows desktop no longer contains the traditional Start button and the Start menu that sprouted from the corner. Instead, you must retreat to the new, Start *screen.* To open a program, click or tap a program's tile from the Start screen, and Windows shuffles you back to the desktop, where the newly opened program awaits.

✔ Welcome to the split personality awaiting you in Windows 8! I explain the Start screen in Chapter 2; the Windows desktop awaits your attention in Chapter 3.

Should I Bother Switching to Windows 8?

In a word, no. Most people stick with the Windows version that came installed on their computers. That way they avoid the chore of figuring out a new version of Windows. Also, Windows 8 comes with a particularly steep learning curve because it's quite different from earlier Windows versions.

Also, many of the biggest changes in Windows 8 work best with *touchscreens* — those fingertip-controlled screens found on expensive cellphones, tablets, and some of the latest laptops. No matter what device it runs on, Windows 8 looks and behaves the same, whether it's controlled by fingers on a touchscreen tablet or by a mouse and keyboard on a desktop PC.

On the positive side, if you manage to figure out Windows 8 once, you'll know how to run it on *all* of your Windows devices: a tablet, Windows phone, a laptop, a desktop PC, and perhaps even a touchscreen television. On the negative side, being designed for so many different things makes Windows 8 behave a little awkwardly on *all* of them.

Instead of upgrading, stick with the masses and stay with your current computer. When you're ready to buy a new computer, the latest version of Windows will be installed and waiting for you. (But if you've bought Windows 8 on a DVD, you can install Windows 8 onto a computer you own that's currently running Windows 7, Windows Vista, or Windows XP; find out how at www.dummies.com/go/windows8. There, you'll also find a plethora of other helpful Windows 8 tidbits.)

Windows 8 doesn't support *Windows XP mode,* a popular way to run a Windows XP desktop inside its own window within Windows 7. If you needed Windows XP mode in Windows 7, don't upgrade to Windows 8.

Can My Current PC Still Run Windows 8?

If you want to upgrade to Windows 8, your computer probably won't complain. Windows 8 should run without problem on any PC currently running Windows 7 or Windows Vista. In fact, Windows 8 may run faster on your old PC than Windows Vista did, especially on laptops.

If your PC runs Windows XP, it may still run Windows 8, but probably not at its best.

If you have a technogeek in your family, have him or her translate Table 1-1, which shows the Windows 8 hardware requirements.

Table 1-1	The Windows 8 Hardware Requirements	
Architecture	*x86 (32-bit)*	*x86 (64-bit)*
Processor	1 GHz	1 GHz
Memory (RAM)	1GB	2GB
Graphics Card	DirectX 9 graphics device with WDDM 1.0 or higher driver	
HDD free space	16GB	20GB

In common language, Table 1-1 simply says that nearly any computer sold in the past five years can be upgraded to Windows 8 with little problem.

Windows 8 runs nearly any program that runs on Windows 7 and Windows Vista. It even runs some Windows XP programs, as well. Some older programs, however, won't work, including most security-based programs, such as antivirus, firewall, and security suites. You'll need to contact the program's manufacturer for an upgraded version.

Shopping for a new PC to run Windows 8? To see how well a particular showroom PC can handle Windows 8, point your mouse at any screen's bottom-left corner and click the right mouse button. When the menu appears, choose System. The Windows Experience Index appears. It has already tested the PC and given it a grade ranging from 1 (terrible) to 9.9 (extraordinary).

Don't know what version of Windows runs on your current PC? Go to the Start menu, right-click Computer, and choose Properties. The screen that appears lists your Windows version. (If your Start menu fills the screen with a bunch of colorful tiles, you're already running Windows 8. If so, right-click in the bottom-left corner, choose System from the pop-up menu, and the System window's Windows Edition section says which version of Windows 8 is running.)

The Four Flavors of Windows 8

Microsoft offers four main versions of Windows 8, but you'll probably want only one: the aptly titled "Windows 8" version.

Small businesses will choose Windows 8 Pro, and larger businesses will want Windows 8 Enterprise. Still, to clear up the confusion, I describe all the versions in Table 1-2.

Table 1-2	The Four Flavors of Windows 8
The Version of Windows 8	*What It Does*
Windows RT	Designed for long-battery life, this version only comes preinstalled, mostly on touchscreen tablets and laptops. It runs the Start screen and apps, but its limited desktop won't run your own Windows programs. To compensate, Windows RT includes versions of Microsoft Word, Excel, PowerPoint, and OneNote.
Windows 8	Aimed at consumers, this version includes the Start screen, apps, and a full-featured Windows desktop that can run most Windows programs.
Windows 8 Pro	Aimed at the small business market, this version features everything from the Windows 8 version, as well as tools used by small businesses: encryption, extra networking features, and similar tools. If you buy a Media Center Pack upgrade, Windows 8 Pro can record TV shows through a TV tuner with Windows Media Center, as well as play DVDs. (To upgrade Windows 8 to Media Center, buy a Windows 8 Pro Pack.)
Windows 8 Enterprise	Microsoft sells this large business version in bulk to large businesses.

Each version in the table contains all the features of the versions preceding it. Windows 8 Pro contains everything found in Windows 8, for example.

Here are some guidelines for choosing the version you need:

- ✔ If you're considering a tablet with **Windows RT**, make sure you realize that it *can't run regular Windows programs*. You're limited to its bundled Office programs and any apps you download from the Windows Store.

- ✔ If you'll be using your PC at home, pick up **Windows 8** or **Windows 8 Pro.**

- ✔ If you need to connect to a domain through a work network — and you'll know if you're doing it — you want **Windows 8 Pro.**

  Want to play DVDs or record TV shows with Windows Media Center in Windows 8 Pro? Then pull out your credit card and upgrade online for the Media Center Pack. (To upgrade the consumer-oriented Windows 8 with Windows Media Center, buy the Windows 8 Pro Pack.)

- ✔ If you're a computer tech who works for businesses, go ahead and argue with your boss over whether you need **Windows 8 Pro** or **Windows 8 Enterprise.** The boss will make the decision based on whether it's a small company (Windows 8 Pro) or a large company (Windows Enterprise).

Most computers let you upgrade to a more powerful version of Windows 8 from the desktop Control Panel's System area. (Reach for your credit card before clicking the Get More Features with a New Edition of Windows link.)

Chapter 2

The Mysterious New Start Screen

*W*indows 8 comes with the traditional Windows desktop, but the new Start screen creates all the excitement. The Start screen's large, colorful tiles offer quick stepping stones for checking e-mail, watching videos, and sampling Internet fare.

On a touchscreen tablet, you could spend all day working within the Start screen's world of full-screen apps, deftly maneuvering through them with your fingertips.

On a desktop computer, however, armed with only a mouse and keyboard, you could spend all day trying to *avoid* the Start screen and find the traditional Windows desktop.

But love it or hate it, the new Start screen plays an integral role in Windows 8. This chapter explains how to make the most of it, whether you want to enjoy it or avoid it as much as possible.

When you stare glumly at the confusing new Start screen, try these tricks: Right-click a blank spot, or point at any screen corner with your mouse. Those actions fetch hidden menus, bringing you a glimmer of navigational hope.

If you're using a touchscreen computer, substitute the word *tap* when you read the word *click.* Tapping twice works like *double-clicking.* And when you see the term *right-click,* touch and hold your finger on the glass; lift your finger when the right-click menu appears.

Being Welcomed to the World of Windows 8

Starting Windows 8 is as easy as turning on your computer — Windows 8 leaps onto the screen automatically with a flourish. But before you can begin working, Windows 8 stops you cold: It displays a locked screen, shown in Figure 2-1, with no entrance key dangling nearby.

Figure 2-1:
To move past this lock screen, drag up on the screen with your mouse or finger, or press a key on the keyboard.

Previous versions of Windows let you sign in as soon as you turned on your computer. Windows 8, by contrast, makes you unlock a screen before moving to the sign in page, where you type in your name and password.

How do you unlock the lock screen? The answer depends on whether you're using a mouse, keyboard, or touchscreen:

- ✔ **Mouse:** On a desktop PC or laptop, click any mouse button.

- ✔ **Keyboard:** Press any key, and the lock screen slides away. Easy!

- ✔ **Touch:** Touch the screen with your finger and then slide your finger *up* the glass. A quick flick of the finger will do.

When you're in the door, Windows wants you to *sign in,* as shown in Figure 2-2, by clicking your name and typing in a password.

Figure 2-2: Click your user account name and then type your name and password on the next screen.

I've customized my Sign In screen. Yours will look different. If you don't see an account listed for you on the Sign In screen, you have several options:

- ✔ **If you see your name and e-mail address listed, type your password.** Windows 8 lets you in and displays your Start screen, just as you last left it.

- ✔ **If you don't see your name, but you have an account on the computer, click the left-pointing arrow shown in the margin.** Windows 8 displays a list of *all* the account holders. You may see the computer owner's name, as well as an account for Administrator and one for Guest.

- ✔ **If you just bought the computer, use the account named Administrator.** Designed to give the owner full power over the computer, the Administrator account user can set up new accounts for other people, install programs, start an Internet connection, and access *all* the files on the computer — even those belonging to other people. Windows 8 needs at least one person to act as administrator.

- ✔ **Use the Guest account.** Designed for household visitors, this account lets guests, such as the babysitter or visiting relatives, use the computer temporarily.

- ✔ **No Guest account?** Then find out who owns the computer and beg that person to set up an account for you or to turn on the Guest account.

If you need more information about user accounts, including creating new ones, managing old ones, or turning on the Guest account, flip ahead to Chapter 14.

Don't *want* to sign in at the Sign In screen? The screen's two bottom-corner buttons offer these other options:

- ✔ **The little wheelchair-shaped button in the screen's bottom-left corner,** shown in Figure 2-2 and the margin, customizes Windows 8 for people with physical challenges in hearing, sight, or manual dexterity, all covered in Chapter 12. If you choose this button by mistake, click or touch on a different part of the screen to avoid changing any settings.

- ✔ **The little button in the screen's bottom-right corner,** shown in Figure 2-2 and the margin, lets you shut down or restart your PC. (If you've accidentally clicked it and shut down your PC, don't panic. Press your PC's power button, and your PC will return to this screen.)

Even while locked, as shown in Figure 2-1, your computer's screen displays current information in its bottom-left corner. Depending on how it's configured, you can see the time and date; your wireless Internet signal strength (the more bars, the better); battery strength (the more colorful the icon, the better); your next scheduled appointment; a count of unread e-mail; and other items.

Understanding user accounts

Windows 8 allows several people to work on the same computer, yet it keeps everybody's work separate. To do that, it needs to know who's currently sitting in front of the keyboard. When you *sign in* — introduce yourself — by clicking your *username,* as shown in Figure 2-2, Windows 8 presents your personalized Start screen, ready for you to make your own personalized mess.

When you're through working or just feel like taking a break, sign out (explained at this chapter's end) so that somebody else can use the computer. Later, when you sign back in, your *own* files will be waiting for you.

Although you may turn your work area into a mess, it's your *own* mess. When you return to the computer, your letters will be just as you saved them. Jerry hasn't accidentally deleted your files or folders while playing Angry Birds. Tina's Start screen still contains links to her favorite quilting websites. And nobody will be able to read your e-mail.

Until you customize your username picture, you'll be a silhouette, like the Guest account in Figure 2-2. To add a photo to your user account, click your username in the screen's corner and choose Change Account Picture. Click the Webcam button to take a quick shot with your computer's built-in webcam. No webcam? Then choose Browse to peek through existing photos. Hint: Click the word Files and choose Pictures to see all the photos on your PC.

Keeping your account private with a password

Because Windows 8 lets many people use the same computer, how do you stop Rob from reading Diane's love letters to Jason Bieber? How can Josh keep Grace from deleting his *Star Wars* movie trailers? Using a *password* solves some of those problems.

In fact, a password is more important than ever in Windows 8 because some accounts can be tied to a credit card. By typing a secret password when signing in, as shown in Figure 2-3, you enable your computer to recognize *you* and nobody else. If you protect your username with a password, nobody can access your files. And nobody can rack up charges for computer games while you're away from home.

Running Windows 8 for the first time

If you've worked with Windows previously, you may not recognize Windows 8. When you first turn on your computer, you won't see the familiar desktop. Instead, you'll be awash in a screen of brightly colored tiles. Adding to the confusion, some tiles resemble a marquee, changing their words and pictures as you watch.

But if you click on a tile named *Desktop*, the familiar Windows desktop appears.

Although these two very different worlds — the Start screen and the desktop — seem completely insulated from each other, they're actually connected in a variety of ways. It's hard to find the connections, however, because they're all hidden.

So, when you're running Windows 8 for the first time, try the following tricks to lure the menus from their hiding places. You can summon these hidden menus from both the Start screen and the desktop:

✔ **Point your mouse cursor at the corners.** When working with a mouse, start by pointing at each corner. Point at the top and bottom-right corners, for example, and you'll see the Charms bar, a special menu covered in this chapter. Point at the top-left corner, and you'll see a thumbnail of your last-used application, ready to run again with a click. And if you point at the bottom-left corner, you'll find a thumbnail of the Start screen, also ready to be summoned with a click. Move the mouse away from any corner, and the menus withdraw, hiding once again.

✔ **Right-click a Start screen app.** Whenever you're on the Start screen or running one of its apps, all the corner tricks still work. But there's one more: Right-click anywhere inside

the Start screen or an app to summon the App bar. The App bar, a strip along the screen's bottom, contains menus for whatever happens to be onscreen at the time. Right-click again, and the App bar disappears.

These mouse tricks work whether your mouse is connected to a desktop PC, laptop, or tablet.

If you're running Windows 8 on a tablet, you can find the same menus by using your fingers:

✔ **Slide your finger inward from the screen's right edge.** This summons the Charms bar from anyplace within Windows 8. To close the Charms bar, touch the screen away from the Charms bar.

✔ **Slide your finger from the top edge to the bottom edge.** As you slide your finger downward, the currently used app follows the motion, eventually shrinking to a tile. When your finger reaches the screen's bottom, the app disappears. You've successfully closed it. Repeat the process, closing other apps, and you'll eventually reach the only screen that can't be closed: the Start screen.

✔ **Slide your finger inward from the left edge.** As you slide your finger inward, it drags your last used app or program onto the screen, ready for use. Repeat the process, and you'll eventually cycle through *all* of your open programs and apps, including the desktop itself.

Don't be afraid to experiment with the screen's corners and sides, pointing, clicking, tapping, or sliding your way around. Finding all the hidden menus is the first step in understanding the brave new world of Windows 8.

To set up or change your password, follow these steps:

1. Summon the Charms bar and click the Settings icon.

I cover the *Charms bar*, a shortcut-filled strip of icons — sometimes called *charms* — that hug every screen's right edge, later in this chapter.

You fetch the Charms bar differently depending on whether you're using a mouse, keyboard, or touchscreen:

- *Mouse:* Move the mouse pointer to the top-right or bottom-right corners of your screen.

- *Keyboard:* Hold down the key and press the letter C.

- *Touchscreens:* Slide your finger from the screen's right edge inward.

When the Charms bar appears, click the Settings icon. The Settings screen appears.

2. **Click the words Change PC Settings at the very bottom of the Settings screen.**

   The PC Settings screen appears.

3. **Click the Users category on the left and then click the Change Your Password button. Or, to create a password, click the Create a Password button.**

   You may need to type your existing password to gain entrance.

4. **Type a password that will be easy to remember.**

   Choose something like the name of your favorite vegetable, for example, or your dental floss brand. To beef up its security level, capitalize some letters and embed a number in the password, like **Glide2** or **Ask4More**. (Don't use these exact two examples, though, because they've probably been added to every password cracker's arsenal by now.)

5. **If asked, type that same password into the Retype Password box, so Windows knows you're spelling it correctly.**

6. **In the Password Hint box, type a hint that reminds you — and only you — of your password.**

   Windows won't let you type in your exact password as a hint. You have to be a bit more creative.

7. **Click the Next button, and click Finish.**

   Suspect you've botched something during this process? Click Cancel to return to Step 3 and either start over or exit.

After you've created the password, Windows 8 begins asking for your password whenever you sign in.

- ✔ Passwords are *case-sensitive.* The words *Caviar* and *caviar* are considered two different passwords.

- ✔ Afraid that you'll forget your password someday? Protect yourself now: Flip ahead to Chapter 14, where I describe how to make a *Password Reset Disk*: a special way of resetting forgotten passwords.

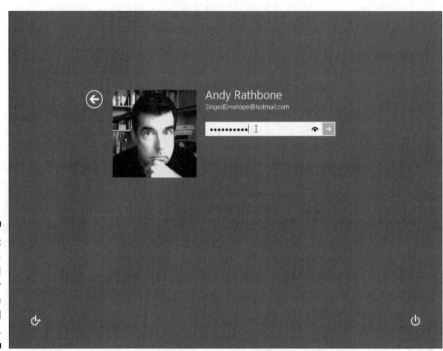

Figure 2-3:
Using a
password
keeps your
private
material
private.

✔ Windows also offers to Create a Picture Password in Step 3, where you drag a finger or mouse over a photo in a certain sequence. Then, instead of entering a password, you redraw that sequence on the sign-in picture. (Picture passwords work much better on touchscreen tablets than desktop monitors.)

✔ Another new option in Step 3 is Create a PIN. A *PIN* is a four-digit code like the ones punched into Automated Teller Machines (ATMs). The disadvantage of a PIN? There's no password hint to a four-digit password.

✔ Forgotten your password *already?* When you type a password that doesn't work, Windows 8 automatically displays your hint — if you created one — which should help to remind you of your password. Careful, though — anybody can read your hint, so make sure that it's something that makes sense only to you. As a last resort, insert your Password Reset Disk, a job I cover in Chapter 14.

I explain lots more about user accounts in Chapter 14.

Make Windows stop asking me for a password!

Windows asks for your name and password only when it needs to know who's tapping on its keys. And it needs that information for any of these four reasons:

✔ Your computer is part of a network, and your identity determines what goodies you can access.

✔ The computer's owner wants to limit what you can do on the computer.

✔ You share your computer with other people and want to keep others from signing in with your name and changing your files and settings.

✔ You own a Microsoft account, with is required for some Start screen apps.

If these concerns don't apply to you, purge the password by selecting Change My Password in Step 3 in the section "Keeping your account private with a password." In the next step, leave the New Password box blank and click Next.

Without that password, though, anybody can sign in, use your user account, and view (or destroy) your files. If you're working in an office setting, this setup can be serious trouble. If you've been assigned a password, it's better to simply get used to it.

Signing up for a Microsoft account

Whether you're signing in to Windows 8 for the first time, trying to access some Start screen apps, or just trying to change a setting, you'll eventually see a screen similar to the one in Figure 2-4.

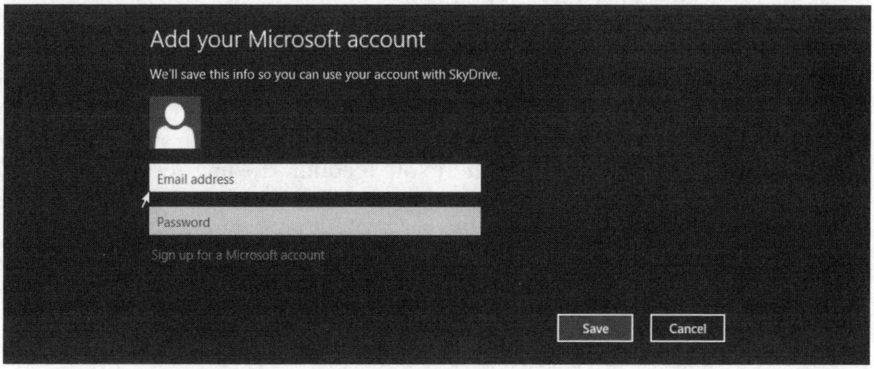

Figure 2-4:
You need a Microsoft account to access many of the Windows 8 features.

Add your Microsoft account

We'll save this info so you can use your account with SkyDrive.

Email address

Password

Sign up for a Microsoft account

Save   Cancel

That screen appears because Windows 8 introduces a new type of user account. You can sign in with either a *Microsoft* account or a *Local* account. Each serves different needs:

- ✔ **Local account:** This account works fine for people working with traditional Windows programs on the Windows desktop. Local account holders can't run many of the Start screen apps bundled with Windows 8, including the Mail app. Nor can they download new apps from the Windows Store.

- ✔ **Microsoft account:** Consisting of an e-mail address and a password, this lets you download apps from the Windows Store and run all the bundled apps in Windows 8. You can link a Microsoft account with your social media accounts, automatically stocking your address book with your friends from Facebook, Twitter, and other sites. (Plus, you can access both your own and your friends' Facebook photos.)

You can sign in with a Microsoft account in either of two ways, ranked according to simplicity:

- ✔ **Use an existing Microsoft account.** If you already use Hotmail, Xbox Live, or Windows Messenger, you already have a Microsoft account and password. Type in that e-mail address and password at the screen shown in Figure 2-4 and then click the Sign In button.

- ✔ **Sign up for a new Microsoft account.** Click the Sign Up for a Microsoft Account link, shown in Figure 2-4, and Microsoft takes you to a website where you can turn your existing e-mail address into a Microsoft account. (Signing up for a new Microsoft e-mail address is a better option, however, because it lets you use the Windows 8 built-in Mail app.)

If you're signing into Windows 8 for the first time, and you don't want a Microsoft account, you'll see a Cancel button. Click Cancel, and the next screen shows a button that lets you sign in with a Local account instead.

But until you create a Microsoft account, the nag screen in Figure 2-4 will haunt you whenever you try to access a Windows 8 feature that requires a Microsoft account.

Figuring Out the New Start Screen in Windows 8

The new Start screen in Windows 8 whisks you away from traditional Windows desktop and drops you into a foreign land with no helpful translator at your side. That's right: Windows 8 no longer has a Start button *or* a Start menu.

Instead, the new Windows 8 Start *screen,* shown in Figure 2-5, appears whenever you turn on your computer. Whereas older Windows versions had a small Start menu on a desktop, the Windows 8 Start screen fills the entire screen with large tiles stretching beyond the right edge. Each tile represents a program installed on your computer.

As you work, you'll constantly switch between the screen-filling Start screen and the traditional screen-filling desktop, covered in the next chapter.

Despite the drastic remodel, the Start screen still offers a way to start programs; adjust Windows settings; find help for sticky situations; or, thankfully, shut down Windows and get away from the computer for a while.

Some Start screen tiles needn't be opened to see their contents. For example, the Calendar tile constantly updates to show the current date and day, as well as your next few appointments. The Mail tile cycles through the first words of your latest e-mails.

Your Start screen will change as you add more programs and apps to your computer. That's why the Start screen on your friend's computer, as well as in this book, is probably arranged differently than your computer's Start screen.

Figure 2-5:
Click a Start screen tile to start a program.

Try the following tricks to make the Start screen feel a little more like home:

✔ See the Start screen's tile named Desktop? Click that one to fetch the familiar Windows desktop. Whew! (I cover the desktop in Chapter 3.)

✔ If you prefer to avoid the Start screen and stay on the traditional Windows desktop as much as possible, I explain that in Chapter 3, as well.

✔ Does your mouse have a little wheel embedded in its back? Spin the wheel, and the Start screen moves to the left or right, accordingly. It's a handy way to move quickly across the entire Start screen, from left to right.

✔ As you move your mouse pointer, the Start screen follows along. When the pointer reaches the screen's right edge, for example, the Start screen brings the offscreen portions into view.

✔ See the little bar along the Start screen's bottom edge? That's a *scroll bar*. Drag the scroll bar's light-colored portion to the left or right: As you move that portion, the Start screen moves along with it, letting you see items living off the screen's right edge.

✔ On a touchscreen, navigate the Start screen with your finger: Pretend the Start screen is a piece of paper lying on a table. As you move your finger, the Start screen moves along with it.

✔ On a keyboard, press the right- or left-arrow keys, and the Start screen's tiles move accordingly. Press the keyboard's End key to move to the end of the Start screen; the Home key moves you back to the Start screen's front.

✔ Windows 8 contains hidden doorways tucked away in its corners, as well as secret passages enabled by pressing certain key combinations. Table 2-1 reveals unlabeled ways to fetch the Start screen and switch among your apps, whether you're using a mouse, keyboard, or touchscreen.

Table 2-1	Finding Hidden Hotspots in Windows 8	
To Do This . . .	*. . . With This . . .*	*. . . Do This*
Fetch the Start screen	Mouse	Point to the screen's lower-left corner. When the Start screen icon appears, click the mouse.
	Keyboard	Press the Windows key, ⊞, found near the spacebar on most keyboards.
	Touchscreen	Press the ⊞ key below your tablet's screen.

To Do This . . .	. . . With This . . .	. . . Do This
Switch to another currently running app	Mouse	Point to the screen's upper-left corner and then slide the mouse pointer downward. When thumbnails of your running apps appear, click the one you want to see full screen.
	Keyboard	Hold down Alt and press Tab to switch between currently opened apps; let go of the Alt key when you highlight your desired app.
	Touchscreen	Slide your finger inward from the screen's left edge, then back. Then tap the thumbnail of your desired app.

Launching a Start screen program or app

Windows 8 stocks your Start screen with *apps* — small programs for performing simple tasks. In fact, Windows 8 now refers to *all* Windows programs as apps. (It even refers to your once almighty desktop as the *Desktop app.*)

Each tile on the Start screen is a button for starting an app or traditional Windows program. Click the button, and the program or app jumps into action. Windows 8 complicates matters, as it offers several ways to push a button:

- ✔ **Mouse:** Point at the tile and click the left mouse button.
- ✔ **Keyboard:** Press the arrow keys until a box surrounds the desired tile. Then press the Enter key.
- ✔ **Touchscreens:** Tap the tile with your finger.

No matter which item you've chosen, it fills the screen, ready to inform you, entertain you, or maybe even do both.

I explain the Start screen's built-in apps later in this chapter. If you feel like digging in, you can begin downloading and installing your own by clicking the Start screen's Store tile. (I explain how to download apps in Chapter 6.)

What's an app?

Short for *application*, apps herald from the world of *smartphones:* cellphones powerful enough to run small programs, as well as make phone calls. The Windows 8 apps differ from traditional windows programs in several ways:

✔ Windows apps come from only one place: the Windows Store. Available as its own app, the Store app lets you download apps from Microsoft; once downloaded, they're automatically installed on your computer. Many apps are free, but others cost money.

✔ Only *Windows* apps can run on Windows. Apps found on iPhones and Android phones aren't designed to run on your Windows 8 computer. Creators of some popular apps create versions for each platform, but they sometimes differ slightly. Have you bought apps for your Android or iPhone? You'll have to pay again to buy the apps' Windows versions.

✔ Apps, by nature, fill the entire screen when running, although Windows 8 does offer an awkward way to "snap" two apps together, covered later in this chapter.

✔ Apps are usually fairly simple to use, but simplicity brings limitations. Many apps don't let you copy words, photos, or links. There's often no way to share an app's contents with a friend or to leave public comments. Most apps lack the power of traditional desktop programs.

Although Windows 8 refers to traditional desktop programs as apps, there's a big difference: Windows programs run only atop your Windows 8 desktop, whereas apps run only in the new world of the Start screen.

Viewing or closing your open apps

Start screen apps, by nature, consume the entire screen, with no visible menus. That makes it difficult not only to control them but also to switch among them. The same holds true when you're working in the separate world of the traditional Windows desktop.

How do you switch between recently used programs and apps? Windows 8 makes it fairly easy to switch between them by following these steps:

1. **Point the mouse pointer at the screen's bottommost-left corner.**

   A thumbnail of your last used app appears. You can click to bring that app to the screen. Or, if you want to revisit other apps running in the background, move to the next step.

2. **When the desktop icon appears, raise your mouse pointer along the screen's left edge.**

   As you move it up the screen, shown in Figure 2-6, a bar appears alongside the screen's left edge, showing thumbnails of your open apps.

To switch to any recently used app, click its thumbnail.

Figure 2-6:
Point in the
bottom-left
corner of
the Start
screen.
Slide your
mouse up
the edge to
see a list of
currently
running
Start screen
apps.

To see your last-used app, point in this corner; when the
app's thumbnail appears, click it to switch to the app.

To see other recently used apps, point in the bottom-left corner.
Then slide your mouse up the screen's left edge, and these
thumbnails of your recently used apps appear.

3. **To return to an app, click its thumbnail.**

4. **To close an app, right-click its thumbnail and choose Close.**

These tips can help you keep track of your running apps, as well as close
down the ones you no longer want open:

✔ To cycle through your currently running apps, hold down the ⊞ key
and press Tab: The same bar you see in Figure 2-6 appears along the left
edge. Each time you press Tab, you select another app. When you select
the app you want, let go of the ⊞ key, and the app fills the screen.

✔ You can view your most-recently-used apps whether you're working on the Windows desktop or on the new Start screen. From the desktop, point your mouse at the screen's bottom-left corner, slide the mouse up the screen's left edge, and then click the app you want to revisit. On a touchscreen, slide your finger inward and then back from the screen's left edge. When the list of apps cling to the screen's left edge, touch the one you want to revisit.

✔ After you close an app in Step 4, the bar listing your running apps stays onscreen. You can then close other apps by right-clicking them and choosing Close, as well.

✔ To close an app you're currently working on, point your mouse or finger at the screen's top edge. When the mouse pointer turns into a hand (shown in the margin), hold down your mouse button (or slide your finger) and drag the app toward the screen's bottom. When your mouse reaches the screen's bottom edge, you've closed the app. (This trick works to close the Desktop app, as well.)

Finding a Start screen app or program

You can scroll through the Start screen until your eagle-eyes spot the tile you need, and then you can pounce on it with a quick mouse click or finger tap. But when the thrill of the hunt wanes, Windows 8 offers several shortcuts for finding apps and programs hidden inside a tile-stuffed Start screen.

When searching for a particularly elusive app or program, try these tricks:

✔ Mouse users can right-click on a blank portion of the Start screen. A bar rises from the screen's bottom showing an icon named All Apps (shown in the margin). Click the All Apps icon to see an alphabetical listing of *all* your computer's apps and programs. Click the desired app or program to open it.

✔ While looking at the Start screen, keyboard owners can simply begin typing the name of their desired app or program, like this: **facebook**. As you type, Windows 8 lists all the apps matching what you've typed so far, eventually narrowing down the search to the runaway.

✔ On a touchscreen, slide your finger up from the screen's bottom. When the bottom menu appears, tap the All Apps icon to see an alphabetical list of all your apps and programs.

Adding or removing Start screen items

Removing something from the Start screen is easy, so you can begin there. To remove an unwanted or unused tile from the Start screen, right-click it and choose Unpin from Start from the pop-up menu along the screen's bottom. The unloved tile slides away without fuss.

But you'll probably want to spend more time *adding* items to the Start screen, and here's why: It's easy to escape the Start screen by clicking the Desktop app. But once you're safely on the desktop, how do you start a program without heading back to the Start screen?

To escape this recursive conundrum, stock your Start screen with icons for your favorite desktop destinations, such as programs, folders, and settings. Then, instead of loading the desktop and looking lost, you can head to your final destination straight from the Start screen.

After you've stuffed your Start screen with your favorite desktop joints, head to this chapter's "Customizing the Start screen" section to place them in orderly groups. When you finish, you're caught up with where you started with in previous Windows versions: a fully stocked Start screen.

To add programs or apps to the Start screen, follow these steps:

1. **Press the Start screen's All Apps button.**

   Right-click a blank portion of the Start screen (or press ■ +Z) and then choose the All Apps button along the screen's bottom.

   On a touchscreen, slide your finger upward from the screen's bottom edge and then tap the All Apps icon.

   No matter which route you take, the Start screen alphabetically lists all your installed apps and programs.

2. **Right-click the item you want to appear on the Start screen and choose Pin to Start.**

3. **Repeat Step 2 for every item you want to add.**

   Unfortunately, you can't select and add several items simultaneously.

4. **Choose the Desktop app.**

   The desktop appears.

5. **Right-click desired items and choose Pin to Start.**

   Right-click a library, folder, file, or other item you want added to the Start screen; when the pop-up menu appears, choose Pin to Start.

When you're through, your Start screen will have grown considerably with all your newly added destinations.

The Charms bar and its hidden shortcuts

The Charms bar is simply a menu, one of a million in Windows 8. But the Microsoft marketing department, eager to impart a little humanity to your computer, calls it a *Charms bar.*

Shown in Figure 2-7, the Charms bar's five icons, or *charms,* list things you can do with your currently viewed screen. For example, when you're gazing at a website you want a friend to see, fetch the Charms bar, choose Share, and choose the friend who should see it. Off it goes to your friend's eyeballs.

Figure 2-7: The Charms bar in Windows 8 contains handy icons for performing common tasks.

The Charms bar can be summoned from *anywhere* within Windows 8, whether you're on the Start screen, the Windows desktop, and even from within apps and desktop programs.

But no matter what part of Windows 8 you're working with, you can summon the Charms bar using a mouse, keyboard, or touchscreen by following these steps:

✔ **Mouse:** Point at the top- or bottom-right corners.

✔ **Keyboard:** Press ⊞+C.

✔ **Touchscreen:** Slide your finger inward from the screen's right edge.

When the Charms bar appears, lingering along your screen's right edge, it sports five icons, ready to be either clicked or touched. Here's what each icon does:

✔ **Search:** Choose this, and Windows assumes you want to search through what you're currently seeing onscreen. To expand your search, choose one of the other search locations: Apps, Settings, or Files. (I cover Search in Chapter 7.)

✔ **Share:** This fetches options for sharing what's currently on your screen. When viewing a web page, for example, a click of the Share button lets you choose Mail to e-mail the page's link to a friend. (I cover e-mail in Chapter 10.)

✔ **Start:** This simply takes you back to the Start screen. The ⊞ key on your keyboard or tablet also whisks you back there.

✔ **Devices:** Choose this to send your current screen's information to another device, such as a printer, second monitor, or perhaps a phone. (The Devices option lists only devices that are currently connected with your computer and able to receive the screen's information.)

✔ **Settings:** This lets you quickly tweak your computer's six major settings: WiFi/Network, Volume, Screen, Notifications, Power, and Keyboard/Language. Not enough? Then choose the words Change PC Settings along the bottom to open the Start screen's mini-Control Panel, covered in Chapter 12.

Tap a Charms bar icon, and Windows gives a hint as to its purpose. For example, tapping the Settings pane's Screen icon on a tablet presents a sliding bar for adjusting the screen's brightness. Sitting atop the sliding bar is a lock icon that keeps the screen from rotating, which is handy for reading e-books.

Table 2-2 shows some keyboard shortcuts to bypass the Charms bar and head straight to one of its icons.

Table 2-2	The Charms Bar's Keyboard Shortcut Keys
To Do This . . .	*. . . Press This*
Open the Charms bar	⊞+C
Search for apps, files or settings	⊞+Q
Share what you see onscreen	⊞+H
Return to the Start screen	⊞
Interact with attached devices	⊞+K
Change settings	⊞+I

Introducing your free apps

The Windows 8 Start screen comes stocked with several free apps, each living on its own square or rectangular tile. Every tile is labeled, so you know what's what.

The tiles for some apps, known as *live tiles,* change constantly. The Finance app tile, for example, constantly updates with the stock market's latest swings; the Weather tile always tells you what to expect when you walk outdoors.

The Windows 8 Start screen shows only some of your apps; to see them all, right-click a blank portion of the Start screen and choose All Apps from the screen's bottom.

You may spot some or all of the following apps on the list, ready to be launched at the click of a mouse or touch of a finger:

✔ **Calendar:** This lets you add your appointments or grab them automatically from calendars already created through accounts with Google or Hotmail.

✔ **Camera:** Covered in Chapter 17, this lets you snap photos with your computer's built-in camera or webcam.

✔ **Desktop:** Choose this to fetch the traditional Windows desktop, which runs the Windows programs you've used for the past decade. I cover the desktop in Chapter 3.

✔ **Finance:** A live tile, this shows a 30-minute delay of the Dow, NASDAQ, and S&P. Choose Finance to see the usual charts and graphs of fear and uncertainty.

✔ **Games:** Designed mostly for Xbox 360 owners, this app lets you see your friends and gaming achievements. You can explore new games, watch game trailers, and buy new games for your console.

✔ **Internet Explorer:** Covered in Chapter 9, this miniversion of Internet Explorer browses the web full screen, with nothing to get in the way: no menus, no tabs; just you and the current page. (When you're through, press the ▤ key on your keyboard to return to the Start screen.)

✔ **Mail:** Covered in Chapter 10, this lets you send and receive e-mail. If you enter a Hotmail or Google account, the Mail app sets itself up automatically, stocking your People list, as well.

✔ **Maps:** Handy for trip planning, the Maps app brings up a version of Microsoft Bing Maps.

✔ **Messaging:** Covered in Chapter 10, this app lets you send text messages to friends through Facebook, Microsoft's Instant Messenger, and other systems.

✔ **Music:** Covered in Chapter 16, this plays music stored on your PC. But Microsoft hopes you'll buy music from its store, as well.

✔ **News:** Visit here to read the news of the day, compiled from news services.

✔ **People:** The beauty of the People app, covered in Chapter 10, comes from its openness. Once you enter your accounts — Facebook, Twitter, Google, and others — the People app grabs all your contacts, as well as their information, and stocks itself automatically.

✔ **Photos:** Covered in Chapter 17, the Photos app displays photos stored in your computer, as well as on accounts you may have on Facebook, Flickr, or SkyDrive.

✔ **Reader:** This handy app reads documents stored in the Adobe Portable Document Format (PDF). It jumps into action when you try to open any file stored in that document. (Most manuals available on websites come in PDF format; you can also find them attached to some e-mails.)

✔ **SkyDrive:** This term describes the Microsoft Internet cubbyhole where you can store your files. By storing them online in SkyDrive, covered in Chapter 5, you can access them from any Internet-connected computer.

✔ **Sports:** You can find sports news and scores here, as well as a way to add listings for your favorite sports teams.

✔ **Store:** Covered in Chapter 6, the Windows Store is the only way to add more apps on your Start screen. (Programs you install through your Windows desktop, covered in Chapter 3, also add shortcuts to the Start screen.)

✔ **Travel:** Resembling a travel agent's billboard, this app lists travel hotspots, complete with maps, panoramic photos, reviews, and links for booking flights and hotels.

✔ **Video:** Covered in Chapter 17, this works more like a video rental store, with a small button that lets you watch videos stored on your computer.

✔ **Weather:** This weather station forecasts a week's worth of weather in your area, but only if you grant it permission to access your location information. (Unless your computer has a GPS — Global Positioning System — the app narrows down your location by closest city rather than street address.)

The bundled Windows 8 apps work well within the confines of the Start screen. Unfortunately, Microsoft configured the Windows 8 desktop to use some of these Start screen apps rather than standard desktop programs.

I explain in Chapter 3 how to choose which apps and programs handle which tasks, but here's a hint: On the desktop, right-click a file and choose Open With. A menu appears, letting you choose which program should handle the job.

Customizing the Start screen

The Start screen behaves much like a grocery list, growing longer and longer as you add more items. That lack of organization comes at a cost, though. How can you find the important things inside a sprawling list of randomly colored tiles?

Give yourself a fighting chance by organizing your Start screen. The following steps begin with a small dose of organization: purging unwanted tiles and adding tiles for your favorites.

Keep following these steps, and you'll eventually reach organizational nirvana: A screen full of neatly labeled *groups* — collections of related tiles — that match *your* interests.

You can organize the tiles any way you want, into any number of groups with any names. For example, you may want to organize the Start screen tiles into four groups: Work, Play, Web, and People. (For a quick peek at what organized and labeled groups look like, page ahead to Figure 2-11.)

But no matter how organized you want to be, follow these steps to begin turning that haphazard Start screen into your *own* piles o' tiles:

1. Remove tiles you don't need.

Spot a tile you don't need? Right-click it and choose Unpin from Start. Repeat until you've removed all the tiles you don't use.

Choosing Unpin from Start doesn't *uninstall* the app or program; removing the tile merely removes that item's "start" button from the screen. In fact, if you accidentally remove the tile for a favorite app or program, you can easily put it back in Step 3.

2. Move related tiles next to each other.

As an example, you might want to keep your people-oriented apps — Mail, People, and Calendar — next to each other. To move an app to a new location, drag its tile to the desired spot. As you drag the tile, other tiles automatically move out of the way to make room for newcomer.

When you've dragged an app's tile to the desired spot, drop the tile to set the tile into its new place.

To conserve screen real estate, shrink a wide tile from a rectangle to a square: Right-click the wide tile and click the Smaller button.

3. Add tiles for apps, programs, folders, and files you need.

I explain how to add tiles for apps, programs, folders, and files earlier, in this chapter's "Adding or removing Start screen items" section.

After you've purged any unwanted tiles, rearranged the remaining tiles, and added new tiles for items you need, your Start screen may meet your needs. If so, *stop.* You're done!

But if your Start screen still sprawls off the screen's right edge and you can't find important items, keep reading.

Still here? Okay. When first installed, the Windows 8 Start screen includes two unlabelled groups of tiles, with a narrow space between the two groups. Windows 8 didn't even bother to name the two groups. And, if you're like most people, you probably didn't notice the slightly wider space that separates those two groups. And that brings you to the next step.

4. **Find the gap between the Start screen's existing groups of tiles.**

   Keep scrolling to the Start screen's right edge, and you'll eventually notice a place where one group of tiles breaks away from the rest, leaving a slightly wider gap between the two groups. Shown in Figure 2-8, that wider gap separates each of your Start screen's groups.

5. **To create a new group, drag and drop a tile into the gap between two existing groups.**

   Drag and hold any tile in the blank space between two groups. A vertical bar will appear, shown in Figure 2-9, widening the space to make room for your incoming tile. Drop the tile, and the tile forms a *new* group of one lonely tile, located between the two other groups.

A gap separating the tile groups

Figure 2-8: A wider gap separates tiles into groups.

A group of tiles

A second group of tiles

6. **To add more tiles to your newly created group, drag and drop additional tiles into the group.**

   Drag and drop new tiles next to your new group's first tile. After you drop a tile into a group, you can drag the tile around to a new position within the group.

   Want to create yet another group? Then repeat Steps 4 and 5, dragging and dropping a tile between two more groups to create yet another group.

   You might find groups of related tiles to be enough organization for you. If so, stop. But if you want to label the groups or move the groups to different positions on the Start screen, go to the next step.

7. **Click in the screen's bottommost-right corner to switch to a view of your groups. Then drag the groups into your preferred order.**

   Now that you've created groups of tiles to match your interests, you can shuffle them into any order you want. For example, you can move your favorite group to the screen's far left, where it's always visible.

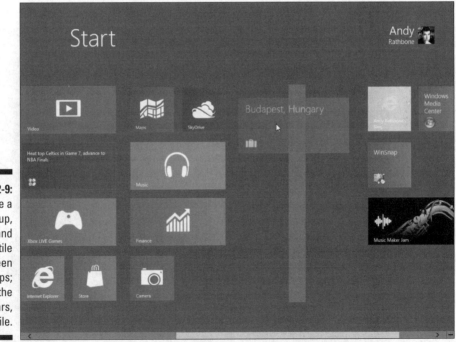

Figure 2-9: To create a new group, drag and hold a tile between two groups; when the bar appears, drop the tile.

To begin rearranging your groups, click the minus sign (–) icon (shown in the margin) in the Start screen's bottommost-right corner: The Start screen changes to show all your tiles as little clumps, shown in Figure 2-10, with each clump representing one group.

Drag and drop the groups into the order you want them to appear on your Start screen.

8. Name the groups.

While still looking at your clumped groups in Figure 2-10, add the final layer of order by placing a name atop each group.

Right-click the group you want to name and click the Name Group icon that appears along the screen's bottom. When the Name box appears, type a name and then click the Name button.

9. Return to the Start screen.

Click any place but on the groups in the shrunken Start screen, shown in Figure 2-10, and the shrunken groups expand to their normal size, letting you bask in your organizational prowess, as shown in Figure 2-11.

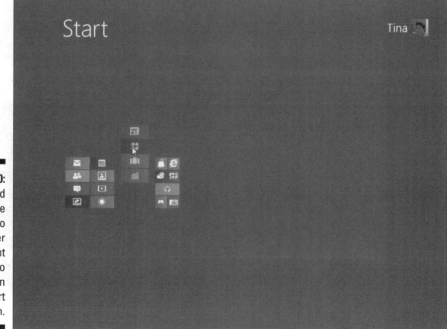

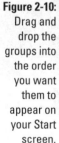

Figure 2-10: Drag and drop the groups into the order you want them to appear on your Start screen.

✔ There's no right or wrong way to organize the Start screen. Just as in real life, be as organized or as messy as you want.

✔ As you install additional apps and desktop programs, you'll once again find a hodgepodge of tiles piling up along the Start screen's right edge. To keep things organized, drag and drop the newcomers into your existing groups or make new groups for the new tiles.

✔ Feel free to create a group for your favorite websites, as well, making it easy to visit them in the Start screen's browser.

✔ If you find it jarring to switch from the Start screen to the desktop, change your desktop's background color to match your Start screen's background color. I explain how to change your desktop background in Chapter 12.

Figure 2-11:
Your Start screen is easier to work with when organized into labeled groups of related tiles.

Exiting from Windows

Ah! The most pleasant thing you'll do with Windows 8 all day could very well be to stop using it. Exiting Windows brings a new hurdle to the process, however: You must decide whether to Lock, Sign Out, Shut Down, Restart, or Sleep your computer.

The answer depends on how long you're abandoning your computer. Are you simply stepping away from the computer for few moments, or are you through working for the day?

I cover both scenarios — a temporary sojourn and leaving your computer for the day — in the next two sections.

But if you don't want to trudge through a manual in order to turn off your PC, here's the quickest way to turn it off:

1. **Move your mouse pointer to the bottom-right corner to fetch the Charms bar. (On a touchscreen, swipe inward from the right edge.)**

2. **Click the Settings icon and then click the Power icon.**

3. **Choose Shut Down.**

4. **If the computer protests, saying you'll lose unsaved work, choose Sleep instead.**

The following two sections deal with the finer points of what's become an alarmingly complex chore.

Temporarily leaving your computer

Windows 8 offers three options when you're leaving your computer temporarily, perhaps to reheat some fish in the office microwave and sneak back to your cubicle before anybody notices. To make the right choice among the three "temporary leave" scenarios in Windows 8, follow these steps:

1. **Return to the Start screen.**

     Press the ▦ key or summon the Charms bar and click the Start icon.

2. **Click your user account picture in the Start screen's upper-right corner.**

    There, shown in Figure 2-12, you can choose one of three options:

Figure 2-12:
Click your
account
name in
the Start
screen's
top-right
corner to
choose
from these
options.

- **Lock:** Meant to add privacy while you take short trips to the water cooler, this option locks your PC, veiling your screen with the Lock screen picture. When you return, unlock the screen and type your password; Windows quickly displays your work, just as you left it.

- **Sign Out:** Choose this when you're through working at the PC and somebody else wants to have a go at it. Windows saves your work and your settings and then returns to the Lock screen, ready for the next person to log on.

- **Another account:** Below your name, as shown earlier in Figure 2-10, Windows lists names of other accounts on the computer. If one of those people wants to borrow the computer for a few minutes, let him choose his name from the list. When he types in his password, his customized screen appears, ready for him to work. When he signs out and you log back in, all your work reappears, just as you left it.

Each of the three options lets you give up your computer for a little while, but leaves it waiting for your return.

If you're finished for the day, though, you're ready for the next section.

Leaving your computer for the day

When you're done computing for the day — or perhaps you just want to shut down the laptop while on the subway or that flight to Rome — Windows 8 offers three ways to handle the situation.

You can find each option by following these steps:

1. **Summon the Charms bar.**

2. **Click the Settings icon.**

   This icon, shaped like a gear, is clearly labeled. Finally!

3. **Click the Power icon.**

   The Power icon's pop-up menu offers three settings, shown in Figure 2-13.

Figure 2-13: Choosing Sleep makes your computer wake up more quickly when turned back on; choosing Shut Down turns off the power completely.

Here's the rundown on your options:

- **Sleep:** The most popular choice, this saves your work in your PC's memory *and* on its hard drive and then lets your PC slumber in a low-power state. Later, when you return to your PC, Windows quickly presents everything — even your unsaved work — as if you'd never left. And if the power goes out, your PC will still wake up with everything saved, but it will take a few more seconds.

- **Restart:** Choose this option as a first cure when something weird happens (a program crashes, for example, or Windows seems dazed and confused). Windows turns off your computer and then starts itself anew, hopefully feeling better. (Newly installed programs sometimes ask you to restart your PC.)

- **Shut Down:** This turns your computer off completely. It's just like Restart but without turning back on again.

That should be enough to wade through. But if you have a little more time, here are some other facts to consider:

You don't *have* to shut down your computer each night. In fact, some experts leave their computers turned on all the time, saying it's better for their computer's health. Other experts say that their computers are healthier if they're turned *off* each day. Still others say the Sleep mode gives them the best of both worlds. However, *everybody* says to turn off your monitor when you're done working. Monitors definitely enjoy cooling down when not in use.

Older computers without much extra memory don't offer a Sleep option. Without enough memory, they can't store your work until you return. Unless you pony up for a memory upgrade, you're stuck with the Shut Down or Restart options.

Don't just press your PC's Off button to turn off your PC, or you might lose unsaved work. Instead, be sure to shut down through one of its official options: Sleep or Shut Down. Otherwise, your computer can't properly prepare itself for the dramatic event, which can lead to future troubles.

Want your laptop or tablet to wake up in Airplane mode, cut off from Internet access? Then switch to Airplane mode and use Sleep rather than Shut Down. When your laptop or tablet wakes back up, it stays in Airplane mode, disconnected from the Internet. (I cover Airplane mode in Chapter 23.)

Chapter 3

The Traditional Desktop

*T*he app-filled world of Windows 8 works fine for couch-top computing. Without leaving your Start screen, you can listen to music, check your e-mail, watch the latest funny cat videos, and see whether anything particularly embarrassing has surfaced on Facebook.

But when Monday morning inevitably rolls around, it's time to switch gears. Working usually requires ditching the Start screen simple apps and firing up more full-featured programs. Employers prefer that you work with spreadsheets and word processors rather than play Angry Birds.

That's when the second half of Windows 8, the *desktop,* comes into play. The desktop works like a *real* desktop, a place where you arrange your work and make things happen.

Thankfully, the desktop lives on in Windows 8, ready for those inevitable Monday mornings. This chapter shows you how to turn your computer from an entertainment device into a workhorse.

NEW IN WINDOWS 8

Where's the Start button?

Windows 8 dropped something integral to every version of Windows for more than a decade: the Start button. That little round button that lived in your screen's bottom-left corner lives no more.

Although the button has disappeared, the Start menu of old lives on as the new tile-filled Start *screen,* as I describe in Chapter 2. So, instead of clicking the Start button to summon a menu and launch programs, summon the Windows 8 Start screen with these tricks:

✔ **Mouse:** Point in the screen's bottom-left corner, and a thumbnail image of the Start screen appears. Click that thumbnail image, and the Start screen fills the screen.

✔ **Keyboard:** Press the Windows (⊞) key. Most keyboards have two of them, one near each side of the spacebar.

✔ **Touchscreen:** All Windows 8 tablets come with a built-in Windows button, usually centered just below the screen. (Look for the Windows logo on it.) Push that button with your finger to return to the Start screen. (Press it again to return to your previous screen.)

Choose any of the preceding methods, and the Start screen emerges, filling the entire screen. To return to the desktop, click the Start screen's Desktop tile. (You can also head for the Start screen from the Charms bar, a new Windows 8 feature I cover in Chapter 2.)

Finding the Desktop and the Start Screen

The Windows 8 Start screen treats the desktop as just another *app:* a small, single-purpose program. So, you open the desktop just as you'd open any other app: Click the Start screen's Desktop tile.

The Desktop tile looks like a miniature version of your *real* desktop, complete with your current desktop background.

When summoned, the desktop pushes aside the Start screen and fills the screen, ready to run your traditional Windows programs.

The Windows 8 desktop works much like the desktop found in previous Windows versions. Shown in Figure 3-1, the Windows 8 desktop is almost indistinguishable from the one in the previous version, Windows 7.

The desktop, with its tiny buttons and thin bars, works best with a keyboard and mouse. If you're using Windows on a touchscreen tablet, you'll probably want to buy a portable mouse and keyboard for desktop work.

Point and click here to return to your last-used app.

Recycle Bin

Hover the mouse in either of these two corners to see the Charms bar and click its icons.

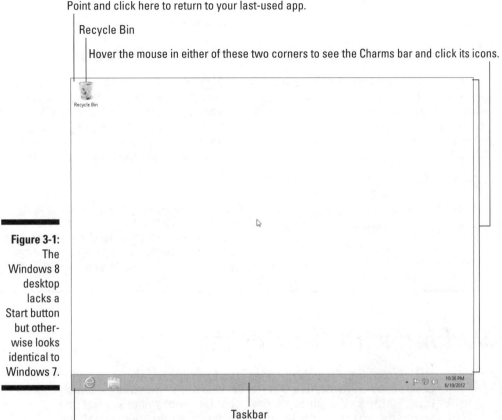

Figure 3-1:
The
Windows 8
desktop
lacks a
Start button
but other-
wise looks
identical to
Windows 7.

Taskbar

Point and click here to return to the Start screen.

The Windows 8 desktop will run nearly all the Windows programs that ran on your old Windows XP, Windows Vista, or Windows 7 computer. Exceptions are antivirus programs, security suites, and some utility programs. Those don't usually transfer well from one Windows version to another.

Still addicted to apps? You can "snap" an app to the right or left side of your desktop, which gives you the best of both worlds. I describe how in this chapter's "Snapping an app alongside the Desktop" section.

Touching the desktop on a touchscreen

Fingers work well for tapping the Start screen's extra-large tiles. And if you grimace enough, your touchscreen's touch controls will still work on the desktop's tiny buttons and thin borders. Here's how to control the desktop with your fingers:

✔ **Select:** To select something on the desktop, tap it with a fingertip; the pad of your finger may be too large.

✔ **Double-click:** To double-click something, tap it twice. Again, your fingertip works best.

✔ **Right-click:** To right-click an item, press your fingertip gently on it and wait for a small square to appear onscreen. When the square appears, remove your finger, and the pop-up menu stays on the screen. Then you can tap your desired option on the menu.

If your fingertip seems too wide for delicate desktop window maneuvers, buy a Bluetooth mouse and keyboard for your tablet. They turn your tablet into two computers: the lightweight Start screen apps for casual computing and the full Windows desktop for doing some *real* work.

Working with the Desktop

Start screen apps hog the entire screen, making it difficult to multitask. The desktop, by contrast, lets you run several programs simultaneously, each living within its own little *window.* That lets you spread several programs across the screen, easily sharing bits of information between them.

Windows 8 starts with the freshly scrubbed, nearly empty desktop shown earlier in Figure 3-1. After you've been working for a while, your desktop will fill up with *icons* — little buttons that load your files with a quick double-click. Many people leave their desktops strewn with icons for easy access.

Others organize their work: When they finish working on something, they store their files in a *folder,* a task covered in Chapter 4.

But no matter how you use the desktop, it comes with four main parts, labeled earlier in Figure 3-1:

✔ **Start screen:** Although hidden, you can fetch the Start screen by pointing your mouse at the very bottom-left corner and clicking the Start screen thumbnail. (A press of the ▦ key returns you to the Start screen, as well.) When summoned, the Start screen still lets you choose programs to run on your desktop.

I cover the new Start screen and all its quirks in Chapter 2.

- ✔ **Taskbar:** Resting lazily along the desktop's bottom edge, the taskbar lists the desktop programs and files you currently have open, as well as icons for a few favored programs. (Point at a program's icon on the taskbar to see the program's name or perhaps a thumbnail photo of that program in action.)

- ✔ **Recycle Bin:** The desktop's *Recycle Bin,* that wastebasket-shaped icon, stores your recently deleted files for easy retrieval. Whew!

- ✔ **Charms bar:** Technically, the shortcut-filled Charms bar isn't part of the desktop; it lives *everywhere* in Windows 8, hidden beyond every screen's right edge. To summon the Charms bar with a mouse, point at your desktop's top- or bottom-right corners. I cover the Charms bar and its five icons (Search, Share, Start, Devices, and Settings) in Chapter 2.

I cover those items later in this chapter and throughout the book, but these tricks will help you until you page ahead:

- ✔ You can start new projects directly from your desktop: Right-click a blank part of the desktop, choose New, and choose the project of your dreams from the pop-up menu, be it loading a favorite program or creating a folder to store new files. (The New menu lists most of your computer's programs, allowing you to avoid a laborious journey back to the Start screen.)

- ✔ Are you befuddled about some desktop object's reason for being? Timidly rest the pointer over the mysterious doodad, and Windows pops up a little box explaining what that thing is or does. Right-click the object, and the ever-helpful Windows 8 usually tosses up a menu listing nearly everything you can do with that particular object. This trick works on most icons and buttons found on your desktop and its programs.

- ✔ All the icons on your desktop may suddenly disappear, leaving it completely empty. Chances are good that Windows 8 hid them in a misguided attempt to be helpful. To bring your work back to life, right-click your empty desktop and choose View from the pop-up menu. Finally, make sure the Show Desktop Icons menu option has a check mark so everything stays visible.

Summoning the Start screen and open apps

The Start button no longer lives in the desktop's bottom-left corner. Now, simply pointing and clicking at that little corner of desktop real estate fetches the new Windows 8 Start *screen.* When the Start screen appears, you click the app or program you'd like to run. (I cover the new Start screen in Chapter 2.)

To visit the Start screen from the desktop, as well as to revisit any recently opened apps, follow these steps:

1. **Point the mouse cursor at your screen's bottom-left corner.**

   A tiny thumbnail-sized Start screen icon rears its head, shown in the bottom-left corner of Figure 3-2. Click it to return to the Start screen.

   Or, if you want to return to any currently running apps, move to the next step.

2. **When the Start screen icon appears, slowly raise your mouse pointer along the screen's left edge.**

   As you move the pointer up the screen's edge, thumbnails of your open apps appear, leaving you with several choices:

   • To return to an open app, click its thumbnail. The desktop disappears, and the app fills the screen, looking just as you last left it. Return to the Internet Explorer app, for example, and you'll see the web page you last visited.

   • To return to the desktop from any app, head for the Start screen and click the Desktop tile. Or, if you spot a Desktop thumbnail among the list of recently used apps, click the Desktop thumbnail to return to the desktop.

Figure 3-2:
Point at the bottommost left corner to reveal an icon that takes you to the Start screen.

- To close an open app, right-click its thumbnail and choose Close. The app disappears from the screen, leaving you at the desktop.

You can also fetch the Start screen by pressing the ⊞ key on your keyboard or tablet.

I explain more about apps, and returning to recently used apps (including the desktop), in Chapter 2.

Jazzing up the desktop's background

To jazz up your desktop, Windows 8 covers it with a pretty picture known as a *background*. (Many people refer to the background simply as *wallpaper*.)

When you tire of the built-in scenery, feel free to replace it with a picture stored on your computer:

1. **Right-click a blank part of the desktop, choose Personalize, and click the Desktop Background option in the window's bottom-left corner.**

2. **Click any one of the pictures, shown in Figure 3-3, and Windows 8 quickly places it onto your desktop's background.**

   Found a keeper? Click the Save Changes button to keep it on your desktop. Or, if you're still searching, move to the next step.

Figure 3-3: Try different backgrounds by clicking them; click the Browse button to see pictures from different folders.

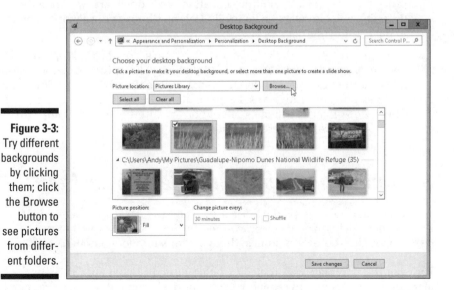

3. Click the Browse button to see photos inside your Pictures library or My Pictures folder.

Most people store their digital photos in their Pictures library or My Pictures folder. (I explain browsing folders and libraries in Chapter 4.)

4. Click different pictures to see how they look as your desktop's background.

When you find a background you like, you're done. Exit the program with a click in its upper-right corner, and your chosen photo drapes across your desktop.

Here are some tips on changing your desktop's background:

✔ Options listed in the Picture Position section let you choose whether the image should be *tiled* repeatedly across the screen, *centered* directly in the middle, or *stretched* to fill the entire screen. The Tile, Fill, and Fit options work best with small photos, such as those taken with cellphones, by repeating or enlarging them to fit the screen's borders.

✔ The desktop's Internet Explorer web browser can easily borrow any picture found on the Internet for a background. Right-click on the website's picture and choose Set as Background from the pop-up menu. Microsoft sneakily copies the image onto your desktop as its new background.

✔ If a background photograph makes your desktop icons too difficult to see, splash your desktop with a single color instead: After Step 1 of the preceding list, click the Picture Location box's down arrow. When the drop-down list appears, select Solid Colors. Choose your favorite color to have it fill your desktop.

✔ To change the entire *look* of Windows 8, right-click on the desktop, choose Personalize, and select a theme. Aimed at heavy-duty procrastinators, different themes splash different colors across the various Windows buttons, borders, and boxes. I explain more about themes in Chapter 12. (If you download any themes offered on the Internet, check them with antivirus software, covered in Chapter 11.)

Snapping an app alongside the desktop

Windows 8 normally keeps the Start screen and the desktop separated into two distinct worlds. You can work within the Start screen or within the desktop, but not both. Sometimes, though, that's not good enough.

For example, you may want to see the Start screen's Calendar app resting alongside your desktop to remind you of your day's commitments. Or perhaps you need your Messenger app open while you work, so you can consult a friend on a name for your latest jazz band.

The solution is to *snap* your app alongside the desktop: The app consumes less than one quarter of the screen, while the desktop fills the rest, as shown in Figure 3-4. Or, you can give your app the larger screen portion, shrinking the desktop.

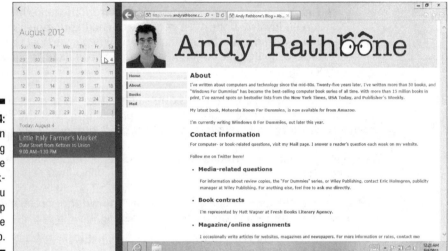

Figure 3-4:
Snapping an app (placing it alongside your desktop) lets you view an app from the desktop.

To snap an app on your desktop, follow these steps:

1. **Open any Start screen app.**

   To reach the Start screen, press the ⊞ key. Or, using a mouse, point at the bottom-left corner of your desktop and click when the Start screen icon appears. Then open an app you want to snap alongside the desktop.

   If you're using a mouse or touchscreen, jump ahead to Step 3.

2. **If you're using a keyboard, hold down the ⊞ key and press the period key.**

   The app snaps to the left of your screen. (Press ⊞+. [period] again to snap the app to the screen's *right* edge, instead.) If you don't see the desktop along the app's side, move to Step 3; the desktop will open alongside the docked app.

3. **Switch back to the desktop.**

   To return to the desktop, hold down the ⊞ key and press D, or click the Start screen's Desktop tile.

4. **Snap the app of your choosing against your desktop.**

These steps are much simpler to *do* than read. But here goes:

- **Mouse:** Point at the screen's top- or bottom-left corner until a thumbnail of your most recently used app appears. Right-click the desired app and, from the pop-up menu, choose Snap Left or Snap Right to snap the app to the screen side of your choosing.

- **Touchscreen:** Slowly drag your finger from the left edge of the screen inward; your most recently opened app appears, following along with the motion of your finger. When a vertical strip appears onscreen, lift your finger, and the app snaps itself to the screen's left edge.

When the app snaps against the desktop's edge, it leaves a vertical bar separating it from your desktop. When the app snaps against the desktop's edge, it stays there, even if you switch to the Start screen or load other apps.

Although app snapping works well for a few tasks, it comes with more rules than a librarian:

- ✔ To *unsnap* the app, drag that vertical bar toward the screen's edge. Or press ■+. (period) until the app disappears.

- ✔ When the app sticks to the side, you can drag the vertical bar inward, making the app fill most of the screen and turning the desktop into a rather useless little strip.

- ✔ To toggle the app from one edge to another, press ■+. (period); the app switches sides. Press ■+. (period) again, and the app unsnaps from the edge.

- ✔ You can't snap an app to the side of the Start screen. The Start screen *always* consumes the entire screen. But when you switch away from the Start screen, the previously snapped app will still be in place, clinging to its same edge.

- ✔ You can only snap *one* app at a time. For example, you can't snap an app onto each side of your desktop.

- ✔ You can snap apps only on a screen with a resolution of at least 1366 x 768. In human language, that means an *extra-wide* computer screen, which you won't find on most netbooks or older laptops. You *will* find that resolution, however, on all Windows 8 tablets.

- ✔ To see your screen's resolution, open the desktop by pressing ■+D. Right-click a blank part of your desktop and choose Screen Resolution from the pop-up menu. You can select your resolution from the Resolution drop-down scroll bar. (You should usually choose the highest resolution offered.)

Dumpster diving in the Recycle Bin

Recycle Bin

The Recycle Bin, that glass wastebasket icon in the corner of your desktop, works much like a *real* recycle bin. Shown in the margin, it lets you retrieve the discarded files you thought you'd never need.

You can dump something from the desktop — a file or folder, for example — into the Windows 8 Recycle Bin in either of these ways:

- Simply right-click on the unwanted item and choose Delete from the menu. Windows 8 asks cautiously if you're *sure* that you want to delete the item. Click Yes, and Windows 8 dumps it into the Recycle Bin, just as if you'd dragged it there. Whoosh!

- For a quick deletion rush, click the unwanted object and poke your Delete key.

Want something back? Double-click the Recycle Bin icon to see your recently deleted items. Right-click the item you want and choose Restore. The handy little Recycle Bin returns your precious item to the same spot where you deleted it. (You can also resuscitate deleted items by dragging them to your desktop or any other folder; drag 'em back into the Recycle Bin to delete them again.)

The Recycle Bin can get pretty crowded. If you're searching frantically for a recently deleted file, tell the Recycle Bin to sort everything by the date and time you deleted it: Right-click an empty area inside the Recycle Bin and choose Sort By. Then choose Date Deleted from the pop-up menu.

To delete something *permanently,* just delete it from inside the Recycle Bin: Click it and press the Delete key. To delete *everything* in the Recycle Bin, right-click the Recycle Bin icon and choose Empty Recycle Bin.

To bypass the Recycle Bin completely when deleting files, hold down Shift while pressing Delete. Poof! The deleted object disappears, ne'er to be seen again — a handy trick when dealing with sensitive items, such as credit-card numbers or late-night love letters meant for a nearby cubicle dweller.

- The Recycle Bin icon changes from an empty wastepaper basket to a full one as soon as it's holding any deleted file or files.

- Your Recycle Bin keeps your deleted files until the garbage consumes about 5 percent of your hard drive space. Then it purges your oldest deleted files to make room for the new. If you're low on hard drive space, shrink the bin's size by right-clicking the Recycle Bin and choosing Properties. Decrease the Custom Size number to purge the bin more quickly; increase the number, and the Recycle Bin hangs onto files a little longer.

- ✔ The Recycle Bin saves only items deleted from your *own* computer's drives. That means it won't save anything deleted from a CD, memory card, MP3 player, flash drive, or digital camera.

- ✔ Already emptied the Recycle Bin? You might still be able to retrieve the then-trashed-now-treasured item from the new File History backup in Windows 8, covered in Chapter 13.

- ✔ If you delete something from somebody else's computer over a network, it can't be retrieved. The Recycle Bin holds only items deleted from your *own* computer, not somebody else's computer. (For some awful reason, the Recycle Bin on the other person's computer doesn't save the item, either.) Be careful.

Bellying Up to the Taskbar

Whenever more than one window sits across your desktop, you face a logistics problem: Programs and windows tend to overlap, making them difficult to spot. To make matters worse, programs such as Internet Explorer and Microsoft Word can each contain several windows apiece. How do you keep track of all the windows?

The Windows 8 solution is the *taskbar* — a special area that keeps track of your currently running programs and their windows. Shown in Figure 3-5, the taskbar lives along the bottom of your desktop, constantly updating itself to show an icon for every currently running program.

The taskbar also serves as a place to launch your favorite programs. By keeping them in sight and one quick click away, you're spared a detour to the Start screen.

Figure 3-5: Click buttons for currently running programs on the taskbar.

Not sure what a taskbar icon does? Rest your mouse pointer over any of the taskbar's icons to see either the program's name or a thumbnail image of the program's contents, as shown in Figure 3-5. In that figure, for example, you can see that Internet Explorer contains two web pages.

From the taskbar, you can perform powerful magic, as described in the following list:

✔ To play with a program listed on the taskbar, click its icon. The window rises to the surface and rests atop any other open windows, ready for action. Clicking the taskbar icon yet again minimizes that same window.

✔ Whenever you load a program on the desktop, its icon automatically appears on the taskbar. If one of your open windows ever gets lost on your desktop, click its icon on the taskbar to bring it to the forefront.

✔ To close a window listed on the taskbar, *right-click* its icon and choose Close from the pop-up menu. The program quits, just as if you'd chosen its Exit command from within its own window. (The departing program thoughtfully gives you a chance to save your work before it quits and walks off the screen.)

✔ Traditionally, the taskbar lives along your desktop's bottom edge, but you can move it to any edge you want, a handy space saver on extra-wide monitors. (**Hint:** Try dragging it to your screen's side. If it doesn't move, right-click the taskbar and click Lock the Taskbar to remove the check mark by that option.)

✔ If the taskbar keeps hiding below the screen's bottom edge, point the mouse at the screen's bottom edge until the taskbar surfaces. Then right-click the taskbar, choose Properties, and remove the check mark from Auto-Hide the Taskbar.

✔ You can add your favorite programs directly to the taskbar: From the Start screen, right-click the favored program's tile and choose Pin to Taskbar. The program's icon then lives on the taskbar for easy access, just as if it were running. Tired of the program hogging space on your taskbar? Right-click it and choose Unpin This Program from Taskbar.

Shrinking windows to the taskbar and retrieving them

Windows spawn windows. You start with one window to write a letter of praise to your local taco shop. You open another window to check an address, for example, and then yet another to ogle online reviews. Before you know it, four more windows are crowded across the desktop.

To combat the clutter, Windows 8 provides a simple means of window control: You can transform a window from a screen-cluttering square into a tiny button on the taskbar, which sits along the bottom of the screen. The solution is the Minimize button.

See the three buttons lurking in just about every window's top-right corner? Click the *Minimize button* — the button with the little line in it, shown in the margin. Whoosh! The window disappears, represented by its little button on the taskbar at your screen's bottom.

To make a minimized program on the taskbar revert to a regular, onscreen window, just click its icon on the taskbar. Pretty simple, huh?

✔ Can't find the taskbar icon for the window you want to minimize or maximize? If you hover your mouse pointer over the taskbar button, Windows 8 displays a thumbnail photo of that program or the program's name.

✔ When you minimize a window, you neither destroy its contents nor close the program. And when you click the window's name on the taskbar, it reopens to the same size you left it, showing its same contents.

Switching to different tasks from the taskbar's Jump Lists

The Windows 8 taskbar doesn't limit you to opening programs and switching between windows. You can jump to other tasks, as well, by right-clicking the taskbar's icons. As shown in Figure 3-6, right-clicking the Internet Explorer icon brings up a quick list of your recently visited websites. Click any site on the list to make a quick return visit.

Figure 3-6:
Jump Lists,
from left
to right:
Internet
Explorer,
File
Explorer,
and
Windows
Media
Center.

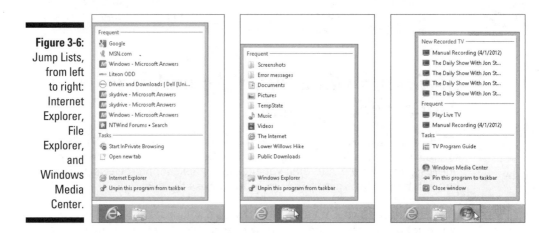

Called *Jump Lists,* these pop-up menus add a new trick to the taskbar: They let you jump quickly to previously visited locations, letting you work more quickly.

Clicking the taskbar's sensitive areas

Like a crafty card player, the taskbar comes with a few tips and tricks. For example, here's the lowdown on the icons near the taskbar's right edge, shown in Figure 3-7, known as the *notification area*. Different items appear in the notification area depending on your PC and programs, but you'll probably encounter some of these:

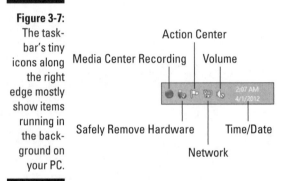

Figure 3-7:
The taskbar's tiny icons along the right edge mostly show items running in the background on your PC.

✔ **Minimize Windows:** This small strip hidden against the taskbar's far-right edge instantly minimizes all open windows when you click it. (Click it again to put the windows back in place.)

✔ **Time/Date:** Click the time and date to fetch a handy monthly calendar and clock. If you want to change the time or date, or even add a second time zone, click the Time/Date area and choose Change Date and Time Settings, a task I cover in Chapter 12.

✔ **Windows Media Center Recording:** The glowing red circle means Windows Media Center, available separately as an add-on, is currently recording something off the television.

✔ **Media Center Guide Listings:** Media Center is downloading the latest TV listings.

✔ **Safely Remove Hardware:** Before unplugging a storage device, be it a tiny flash drive, a portable music player, or a portable hard drive, click here. That tells Windows to prepare the gadget for unplugging.

✔ **Action Center:** Windows wants you to do something, be it to click a permission window, install an antivirus program, check your last backup, or perform some other important task.

✔ **Wired Network:** This appears when you're connected to the Internet or other PCs through a wired network. Not connected? A red X appears over the icon.

✔ **Wireless Network:** Your PC is wirelessly connected to the Internet or other network. When all five bars show, you have a very strong signal.

✔ **Volume:** Click or tap this ever-so-handy little speaker icon to adjust your PC's volume, as shown in Figure 3-8. (Or double-click the word Mixer to bring up a mixing panel. *Mixers* let you adjust separate volume levels for each program, letting you keep Media Player's volume louder than your other programs' annoying beeps.)

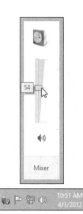

Figure 3-8:
Slide the
lever to
adjust the
volume.

✔ **Windows Problem Reporting:** When Windows runs into trouble, this icon appears; click it to see possible solutions.

✔ **Windows Automatic Updates:** This icon appears when Windows downloads *updates,* usually small programs designed to fix your PC, from Microsoft's website at Windows Update.

✔ **Task Manager:** Coveted by computer technicians, this little program can end misbehaving programs, monitor background tasks, monitor performance, and do other stuff of techie dreams.

✔ **Windows Host Process:** This dismally named icon delivers an even worse message: Your newly plugged-in gadget won't work, be it your printer, scanner, music player, or other item. Try unplugging the device, running its installation software again, and plugging it back in.

✔ **Explorer:** Older PCs come with two types of USB ports: fast and slow. This icon means you've plugged a speedy gadget into your slow port. Try unplugging it and plugging it into a different port. (The USB ports on a desktop computer's back side are often the faster ones.)

✔ **Power, Outlet:** This shows that your laptop is plugged into an electrical outlet and is charging its battery.

✔ **Power, Battery:** Your laptop or tablet is running on batteries only. (Rest your mouse pointer over the icon to see how much power remains.)

✔ **Arrow:** Sometimes the taskbar hides things. If you see a tiny upward-pointing arrow at the start of the taskbar's notification area, click it to see a few hidden icons slide out. (Check out the "Customizing the taskbar" section for tips and tricks on whether icons should hide.)

Customizing the taskbar

Windows 8 brings a whirlwind of options for the lowly taskbar, letting you play with it in more ways than a strand of spaghetti and a fork.

And that's especially important in Windows 8: By stocking the taskbar with icons for oft-used programs, you can avoid unnecessary trips to the Start screen.

First, the taskbar comes preloaded with two icons on its far left: Internet Explorer (your full-featured web browser) and File Explorer (your file browser). Like all your taskbar icons, they're movable, so feel free to drag them to any order you want.

If you spot a favored program's icon on your Start screen, right-click the icon and choose Pin to Taskbar from the pop-up menu. You can drag and drop a desktop program's icon directly onto the taskbar, as well.

For even more customization, right-click a blank part of the taskbar and choose Properties. The Taskbar Properties dialog box appears, as shown in Figure 3-9.

Figure 3-9:
Click the
Taskbar
tab to cus-
tomize the
taskbar's
appearance
and
behavior.

Taskbar Properties

Taskbar | Jump Lists | Toolbars

☐ Lock the taskbar
☐ Auto-hide the taskbar
☐ Use small taskbar buttons

Taskbar location on screen: Bottom

Taskbar buttons: Always combine, hide labels

Notification area: Customize...

☑ Use Peek to preview the desktop when you move your mouse to the Show desktop button at the end of the taskbar

How do I customize taskbars?

OK   Cancel   Apply

Table 3-1 explains the dialog box's options, as well as my recommendations for them. (You need to remove the check mark by Lock the Taskbar before some of these options will work.)

Table 3-1	Customizing the Taskbar
Setting	**My Recommendations**
Lock the Taskbar	Selecting this check box locks the taskbar in place, keeping you from changing its appearance. Keep it locked to protect from accidental changes, but lock the taskbar only after you've set it up to suit your needs.
Auto-Hide the Taskbar	Handy mostly for small screens, this option makes the taskbar *automatically* hide itself when you're not near it. (Point your cursor at the screen's bottom edge to bring it back up.) I leave this option deselected to keep the taskbar always in view.
Use Small Taskbar Buttons	Another helper for small screens, this shrinks the taskbar to half-height, letting you pack in a few extra tiny icons.
Taskbar Location On Screen	Your taskbar can live on any edge of your desktop, not just the bottom. Choose any of the four edges here.
Taskbar Buttons	When you open lots of windows and programs, Windows accommodates the crowd by grouping similar windows under one button: All open Microsoft Word documents stack atop one Microsoft Word button, for example. To protect the taskbar from overcrowding, select the option called Always Combine, Hide Labels.
Notification Area	This section's Customize button lets you decide which icons should appear in the notification area. I choose Always Show All Icons and Notifications On the Taskbar.
Use Peek to Preview the Desktop	When you activate this feature, pointing at the strip on the taskbar's far-right edge makes the windows transparent, letting you peek at your underlying desktop. (Clicking it minimizes all open windows.) Select this check box to activate that strip.

Feel free to experiment with the taskbar until it looks right for you. After you've changed an option, see the changes immediately by clicking the Apply button. Don't like the change? Reverse your decision and click Apply to return to normal.

After you set up the taskbar just the way you want it, select the Lock the Taskbar check box, described in Table 3-1.

The Jump Lists tab of the Taskbar Properties dialog box, shown earlier in Figure 3-9, placates privacy seekers. It lets you prevent Jump Lists (described earlier in this chapter) from remembering where you've been, so others don't see those places in your Jump Lists. (I cover Jump Lists earlier in this chapter.)

Making Programs Easier to Find

After you've found your way to the desktop on a desktop PC, you'll probably want to stay there and avoid the Start screen's over-stretching conglomeration of clunky tiles.

Avoid that time-wasting trip to the Start screen by stocking your desktop with shortcuts to your favorite programs and places. This section explains how to set up camp on the desktop and stay there as long as possible.

If the Start screen feels more like home to you, Chapter 2 explains how to hang your hat in that hallway, instead, and avoid the desktop.

Add five helpful icons to your desktop

When first opened, the desktop contains only three icons: the Recycle Bin lives in the top corner; the taskbar's left corner offers File Explorer (for browsing your own files) and Internet Explorer (for browsing the world's offerings on the web).

Everything else requires a trip to the Start screen. Until you follow these steps, that is:

1. **Right-click a blank portion of your desktop and choose Personalize.**

   The Personalization window appears.

2. **On the Personalization window's left side, click the Change Desktop Icons link.**

   The Desktop Icon Settings window appears.

3. **Put a check mark in the top five boxes: Computer, User's Files, Network, Recycle Bin, and Control Panel. Then click Apply.**

   Shortcuts for those five icons appear on your desktop for quick and easy access.

4. **Remove the check mark from the option labeled Allow Themes to Change Desktop Icons.**

   That ensures that those icons will stay put, even if you drape your desktop with a decorative theme. (I describe themes in Chapter 12.)

After those icons appear on your desktop, feel free to drag and drop them any place you'd like. Chances are good that they'll save you quite a few trips to the Start screen.

Creating taskbar shortcuts for your favorite programs

Whenever you install a new program on your computer, the program usually asks way too many obtuse questions. But perk up your ears when you see this question: "Would you like a shortcut icon placed on your desktop or taskbar?"

Say yes, please, as that will save you from dashing out to the Start screen to find the program's tile.

But if your favorite programs don't yet have icons on the desktop or taskbar, put them there by following these steps:

1. **Head to the Start screen and open its menu bar.**

   Right-click a blank portion of the Start screen (or press ⊞+Z) to reveal the Start screen's menu bar along the screen's bottom edge. (Or, if you're a touchscreen owner, reveal the bar by sliding your finger up from the Start screen's bottom edge.) I cover the Start screen and its menus in Chapter 2.

2. **From the bottom menu, click the All Apps icon (shown in the margin) to see a list of all your available apps and programs.**

3. **On the Start screen, right-click any app or program you want to appear on the desktop and choose Pin to Taskbar.**

   In an odd break in protocol, touchscreens can't right-click on the Start screen. Instead, *select* a Start screen tile: Hold your finger down on the tile and slide your finger down a fraction of an inch. When a check mark appears in the tile's upper-right corner, lift your finger. The menu bar appears below, letting you tap the Pin to Taskbar option (shown in the margin).

   To *deselect* the tile, slide your finger down on it, just as before. This time, though, the check mark disappears.

4. **Repeat Step 3 for every app or program you want to add.**

   Unfortunately, you can't select several simultaneously.

   When you're through, your taskbar will have sprouted new icons for your favorite programs.

Now, instead of heading to the Start screen, you can launch them straight from the taskbar.

After you've stocked your taskbar with icons, pretend they're numbered, from left to right. Pressing ⊞+1 from the desktop opens the first program; ⊞+2 opens the second, and so on. You've created automatic shortcuts!

Chapter 4

Basic Desktop Window Mechanics

. . . .

In This Chapter

▶ Understanding a window's parts

▶ Manipulating buttons, bars, and boxes

▶ Finding commands on the Ribbon

▶ Understanding the Navigation and Preview Panes

▶ Paging through a document in a window

▶ Filling out forms

▶ Moving windows and changing their size

. . . .

*T*he simplistic Windows 8 Start screen comes with bold, oversized buttons, large letters, and bright colors that shout from the screen. The Windows desktop, by contrast, comes with miniscule, monochrome buttons, tiny lettering, and windows with pencil-thin borders.

And in another contrast, every Start screen app fills the entire screen for easy viewing. On the crowded desktop, through, dozens of windows can overlap.

To help you maneuver through this messy maze of desktop windows, this chapter provides a windows anatomy and navigation lesson.

This chapter tosses an ordinary window onto the dissection table. I've yanked out each part for thorough labeling and explanation — the terminology you can find listed in Windows programs, manuals, and menus. You find out the theory behind each window part and the required procedures for making each part do your bidding.

A standard field guide follows, identifying and explaining the buttons, boxes, windows, bars, lists, and other oddities you may encounter when you're trying to make the Windows 8 desktop do something useful.

By all means, use this book's margins to scribble notes as you move from the simplistic Start screen to the powerful yet complicated Windows desktop.

Dissecting a Typical Desktop Window

Figure 4-1 places a typical window on the slab, with all its parts labeled. You might recognize the window as your Documents library, that storage tank for most of your work.

Ribbon menu

Ribbon menu tabs

Quick Access toolbar

Backward

Forward

Home tab

Share tab

View tab Manage tab Title bar Minimize Maximize Close

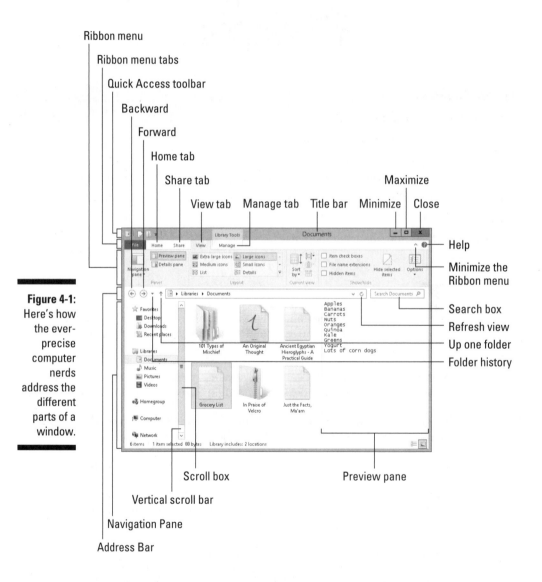

Help

Minimize the Ribbon menu

Search box

Refresh view

Up one folder

Folder history

Figure 4-1: Here's how the ever-precise computer nerds address the different parts of a window.

Scroll box Preview pane

Vertical scroll bar

Navigation Pane

Address Bar

Just as boxers grimace differently depending on where they've been punched, windows behave differently depending on where they've been clicked. The next few sections describe the main parts of the Documents library window in Figure 4-1, how to click them, and how Windows jerks in response.

✔ Windows XP veterans remember their My Documents folder: that stash for all their files. Windows Vista dropped the word *My* to create the Documents folder; Windows 7 and Windows 8 put the word *My* back in place. (No matter what it's called, you're still supposed to stash your files inside it.)

✔ In a break from the past, Windows 8 places a thick, control-filled panel called the *Ribbon* to the top of your folders. Some people like the Ribbon's larger buttons and menus; others preferred the older menu system. But like it or not, the Ribbon is here to stay.

✔ Windows 8 places your My Documents folder inside your Documents *library* — a type of super folder described in Chapter 5. The Documents library displays both your My Documents folder and the Public Documents folder. (Everybody who uses your PC sees the same Public Documents folder, making it a handy folder for sharing files.)

✔ Windows 8 is full of little oddly shaped buttons, borders, and boxes. You don't need to remember all their names, although that would give you a leg up on figuring out the scholarly Windows Help menus. When you spot an odd portion of a window, just return to this chapter, look up its name in Figure 4-1, and read its explanation.

✔ You can deal with most things in Windows by clicking, double-clicking, or right-clicking. **Hint:** When in doubt, always right-click.

✔ Navigating the desktop on a touchscreen computer? For some touching tips, drop by the sidebar in Chapter 3 on touching the desktop on a Windows 8 tablet.

✔ After you click a few windows a few times, you realize how easy it is to boss them around. The hard part is finding the right controls for the *first* time, like figuring out the dashboard on that rental car.

Tugging on a window's title bar

Found atop nearly every window (see examples in Figure 4-2), the title bar usually lists the program name and the file it's currently working on. For example, Figure 4-2 shows the title bars from the Windows 8 WordPad (top) and Notepad (bottom) programs. The WordPad title bar lists the file's name as Document because you haven't had a chance to save and name the file yet.

Figure 4-2:
A title
bar from
WordPad
(top) and
Notepad
(bottom).

Although mild-mannered, the mundane title bar holds hidden powers, described in the following tips:

✔ Title bars make convenient handles for moving windows around your desktop. Point at a blank part of the title bar, hold down the mouse button, and move the mouse around: The window follows along as you move your mouse. Found the right location? Let go of the mouse button, and the window sets up camp in its new spot.

✔ Double-click a blank portion of the title bar, and the window leaps to fill the entire screen. Double-click it again, and the window retreats to its original size.

✔ See the cluster of little icons in the WordPad program's top-left corner? Those icons form the Quick Access Toolbar, which is part of what Microsoft calls a *Ribbon interface*. The icons offer one-click access to common tasks such as saving a file.

✔ The right end of the title bar contains three square buttons. From left to right, they let you Minimize, Restore (or Maximize), or Close a window, topics all covered in the "Maneuvering Windows Around the Desktop" section, later in this chapter.

✔ To find the window you're currently working on, look for a darker title bar sporting a red Close button in its top-right corner (Figure 4-2, top). Those colors distinguish that window from windows you *aren't* working on (Figure 4-2, bottom). By glancing at all the title bars on the screen, you can tell which window is awake and accepting anything you type.

Dragging, dropping, and running

Although the phrase *drag and drop* sounds as if it's straight out of a Mafia guidebook, it's really a nonviolent mouse trick used throughout Windows. Dragging and dropping is a way of moving something — say, an icon on your desktop — from one place to another.

To *drag*, put the mouse pointer over the icon and *hold down* the left or right mouse button. (I prefer the right mouse button.) As you move the mouse across your desk, the pointer drags the icon across the screen. Place the pointer/icon where you want it and release the mouse button. The icon *drops,* unharmed.

Holding down the *right* mouse button while dragging and dropping makes Windows toss up a helpful little menu, asking whether you want to *copy* or *move* the icon.

Helpful Tip Department: Did you start dragging something and realize midstream that you're dragging the wrong item? Don't let go of the mouse button — instead, press Esc to cancel the action. Whew! (If you've dragged with your right mouse button and already let go of the button, there's another exit: Choose Cancel from the pop-up menu.)

Navigating folders with a window's Address Bar

Directly beneath every folder's title bar lives the *Address Bar,* shown atop the Documents library in Figure 4-3. Internet Explorer veterans will experience déjà vu: The Windows 8 Address Bar is lifted straight from the top of Internet Explorer and glued atop every folder.

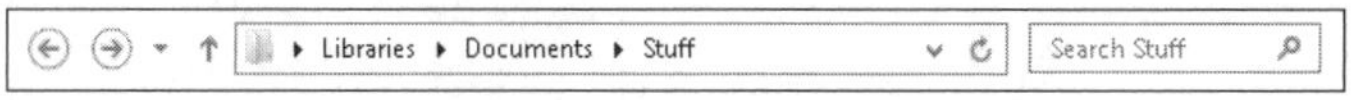

Figure 4-3: An Address Bar.

The Address Bar's four main parts, described from left to right in the following list, perform four different duties:

✔ **Backward and Forward buttons:** These two arrows keep track as you forage through your PC's folders. The Backward button backtracks to the folder you just visited. The Forward button brings you back. (Click the miniscule arrow to the right of the Forward arrow to see a list of places you've visited previously; click any entry to zoom right there.)

- ✔ **Up Arrow button:** Removed from Windows 7, the Up Arrow button triumphantly returns to Windows 8. Click it to move up one folder from your current folder. For example, if you've been sorting files in your Documents library's "Stuff" folder, click the Up arrow to return to your Documents library.

- ✔ **Address Bar:** Just as the Internet Explorer Address Bar lists a website's address, the Windows 8 Address Bar displays your current folder's address — its location inside your PC. For example, the Address Bar shown in Figure 4-3 shows three words: *Libraries, Documents,* and *Stuff.* Those words tell you that you're looking inside the *Stuff* folder inside the *Documents* library of your *Libraries.* Yes, addresses are complicated enough to warrant an entire chapter: Chapter 5.

- ✔ **Search box:** In another rip-off from Internet Explorer, every Windows 8 folder sports a Search box. Instead of searching the Internet, though, it rummages through your folder's contents. For example, type the word **carrot** into a folder's Search box: Windows 8 digs through that folder's contents and retrieves every file or folder mentioning *carrot.*

In the Address Bar, notice the little arrows between the words *Libraries, Documents,* and *Stuff.* The arrows offer quick trips to other folders. Click any arrow — the one to the right of the word *Documents,* for example. A little menu drops down from the arrow, letting you jump to any other folder inside your Documents library.

Finding commands on the Ribbon

The Windows desktop has more menu items than an Asian restaurant. To keep everybody's minds on computer commands instead of seaweed salad, Windows 8 places menus inside a new tab-filled *Ribbon* that lives atop every folder and library. (See Figure 4-4.)

Figure 4-4:
The
Ribbon's
tabs.

| File | Home | Share | View | Manage | Play | | ⌃ ❷ |

The Ribbon's tabs each offer different options. To reveal the secret options, click any tab — Share, for example. The Ribbon quickly changes, as shown in Figure 4-5, presenting all your options related to *sharing* a file.

Figure 4-5:
Click any
Ribbon tab
to see its
associated
commands.

Just as restaurants sometimes run out of specials, a window sometimes isn't capable of offering all its menu items. Any unavailable options are *grayed out,* like the Print option in Figure 4-5. (Because you can't print music files, that option is grayed out.)

If you accidentally click the wrong tab on the Ribbon, causing the wrong commands to leap onto the screen, simply click the tab you *really* wanted. A forgiving soul, Windows displays your newly chosen tab's contents, instead.

You needn't know much about the Ribbon because Windows 8 automatically places the correct buttons atop each window. Open your Music library, for example, and the Ribbon quickly spouts a new Play tab for listening sessions.

If a button's meaning isn't immediately obvious, hover your mouse pointer over it; a little message explains the button's *raison d'être.* My own translations for the most common tabs and buttons are in the following list:

✔ **File:** Found along every Ribbon's left edge, this handy shortcut offers little in rewards: basically, opening new windows.

✔ **Home:** Found on every folder's Ribbon, the Home tab usually brings pay dirt, so every folder opens showing this tab's options. The Home tab offers tools to select, cut, copy, paste, move, delete, or rename a folder's items.

✔ **Share:** As the name implies, this offers ways to let you share a folder's contents with other people using your computer. More important, by clicking a name and clicking the Stop Sharing button, you can cut off access to mistakenly shared documents. (I cover sharing more in Chapter 14.)

✔ **View:** Click here to change how files appear in the window. In your Pictures library, for example, choose Extra Large Icons to see larger thumbnails of your photos.

✔ **Manage:** This general-purpose tab shows customized ways to handle your folder's items. Atop the Pictures library, for example, it offers a Slide Show button, as well as buttons to rotate skewed photos or turn them into desktop backgrounds.

Don't like that thick Ribbon hogging an inch of space atop your window? If you're pressed for space, axe the ribbon by clicking the little upward-pointing arrow next to the blue question mark icon in the upper-right corner. Click it again to bring back the Ribbon. (Or hold down the Ctrl key and press F1 to toggle it on and off again, which is often more fun than doing something productive.)

Quick shortcuts with the Navigation Pane

Look at most "real" desktops, and you'll see the most-used items sitting within arm's reach: the coffee cup, the stapler, and perhaps a few crumbs from the coffee room snacks. Similarly, Windows 8 gathers your PC's most frequently used items and places them in the Navigation Pane, shown in Figure 4-6.

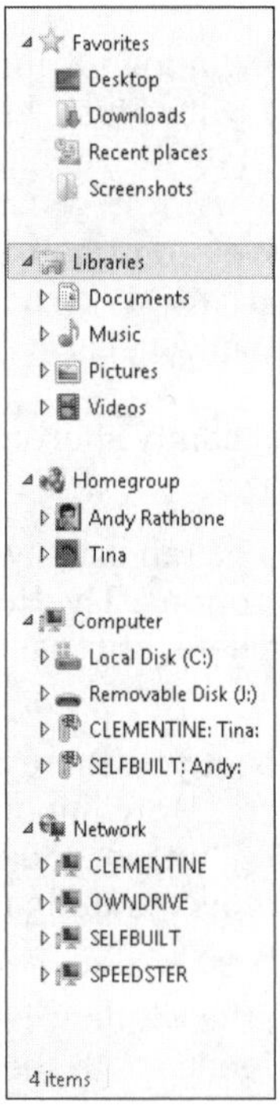

Figure 4-6:
The
Navigation
Pane offers
shortcuts to
places you
visit most
frequently.

▲ ☆ Favorites
   ■ Desktop
   🔽 Downloads
   📖 Recent places
   📷 Screenshots

▲ 📚 Libraries
   ▷ 📄 Documents
   ▷ 🎵 Music
   ▷ 🖼 Pictures
   ▷ 🎬 Videos

▲ 🏠 Homegroup
   ▷ 👤 Andy Rathbone
   ▷ 👤 Tina

▲ 💻 Computer
   ▷ 💾 Local Disk (C:)
   ▷ 💾 Removable Disk (J:)
   ▷ 💽 CLEMENTINE: Tina:
   ▷ 💽 SELFBUILT: Andy:

▲ 🖧 Network
   ▷ 💻 CLEMENTINE
   ▷ 💻 OWNDRIVE
   ▷ 💻 SELFBUILT
   ▷ 💻 SPEEDSTER

4 items

Found along the left edge of every folder, the Navigation Pane contains five main sections: Favorites, Libraries, Homegroup, Computer, and Network. Click any of those sections — Favorites, for example — and the window's right side shows you the contents of what you've clicked.

Here's a more detailed description of each part of the Navigation Pane:

- ✔ **Favorites:** Not to be confused with your favorite websites in Internet Explorer (covered in Chapter 9), the Favorites in the Navigation Pane are words serving as clickable shortcuts to your most frequently accessed locations in Windows:

  - • **Desktop:** Your Windows desktop, believe it or not, is actually a folder that's always spread open across your screen. Clicking Desktop under Favorites quickly shows you the contents of your desktop.

  - • **Downloads:** Click this shortcut to find the files you've downloaded with Internet Explorer while browsing the Internet. Ah, that's where they ended up!

  - • **Recent Places:** You guessed it: Clicking this shortcut lists every folder or setting you've recently visited.

  - • **Recorded TV:** If you've ponied up the extra cash to buy the Windows 8 Media Pack for recording TV shows, you can find your shows waiting in here.

- ✔ **Libraries:** Unlike normal folders, libraries show you the contents of several folders, all collected in one place for easy viewing. Windows' libraries begin by showing the contents of two folders: your *own* folder and its *public* equivalent, which is available to anyone with an account on your PC. (I explain Public folders in Chapter 14.)

  - • **Documents:** This opens the Documents library, which immediately displays your My Documents and Public Documents folders.

  - • **Music:** Yep, this shortcut jumps straight to your Music library, where a double-click on a song starts it playing through your PC's speakers.

  - • **Pictures:** This shortcut opens your Pictures library, the living quarters for all your digital photos.

  - • **Videos:** Similarly, this shortcut jumps straight to your Videos library, where a double-click on a video opens it for immediate viewing.

- ✔ **Homegroup:** A convenient way of sharing information between several household computers, Homegroups are two or more PCs that share information through a simple network. Click Homegroup in the Navigation Pane to see folders shared by other networked PCs in your Homegroup. (I cover Homegroups and other networks in Chapter 15.)

- ✔ **Computer:** Opened mainly by PC techies, this button lets you browse through your PC's folders and disks. Other than a quick click to see what lives on a recently inserted flash drive or portable hard drive, you probably won't visit here much.

✔ **Network:** Although Homegroups simplify file sharing, old-school networks still work in Windows 8, and any networked PCs — including your Homegroup buddies — appear here.

Here are a few tips for making the most of your Navigation Pane:

✔ To avoid treks back to the Start screen, add your own favorite places to the Navigation Pane's Favorites area: Drag and drop folders onto the word Favorites, and they turn into clickable shortcuts.

✔ Messed up your Favorites or Libraries area? Tell Windows 8 to repair the damage by right-clicking the problem child and choosing Restore Favorite Links or Restore Default Libraries.

Moving inside a window with its scroll bar

The scroll bar, which resembles a cutaway of an elevator shaft (see Figure 4-7), rests along the edge of all overstuffed windows. You can even find a scroll bar along the bottom of the Start screen.

Inside the shaft, a little elevator (technically, the *scroll box*) rides along as you move through the window's contents. In fact, by glancing at the box's position in the scroll bar, you can tell whether you're viewing items in the window's beginning, middle, or end.

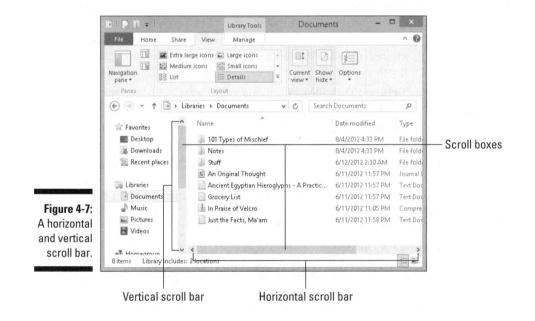

Figure 4-7:
A horizontal and vertical scroll bar.

Scroll boxes

Vertical scroll bar   Horizontal scroll bar

By clicking in various places on the scroll bar, you can quickly view different parts of things. Here's the dirt:

✔ Click inside the scroll bar in the direction you want to view. On a *vertical* scroll bar, for example, click above the scroll box to move your view up one page; similarly, click below the scroll box to move your view down a page.

✔ Clicking the scroll bar along the bottom of the Start screen lets you view any shy apps hiding beyond the screen's right edge.

✔ Don't see a scroll box in the bar? Then you're already seeing all that the window has to offer; there's nothing to scroll.

✔ To move around in a hurry, drag the scroll box inside the scroll bar. As you drag, you see the window's contents race past. When you see the spot you want, let go of the mouse button to stay at that viewing position.

✔ Are you using a mouse that has a little wheel embedded in the poor critter's back? Spin the wheel, and the elevator moves quickly inside the scroll bar, shifting your view accordingly. It's a handy way to explore the Start screen, long documents, and file-filled folders.

Boring borders

A *border* is that thin edge surrounding a window. Compared with a bar, it's really tiny.

When one just isn't enough

Normally, you can select only one thing at a time in Windows. When you click another item, Windows deselects the first in order to select the second. When you want to select several things simultaneously, try these tricks:

✔ To select more than one item, hold down the Ctrl key and click each item you want. Each item stays highlighted.

✔ To select a bunch of adjacent items from a list box, click the first item you want. Then hold down Shift and click the last item you want. Windows 8 immediately highlights the first item, last item, and every item in between. Pretty sneaky, huh? (To weed out a few unwanted items from the middle, hold down Ctrl and click them; Windows unhighlights them, leaving the rest highlighted.)

✔ Finally, when grabbing bunches of items, try using the "lasso" trick: Point at an area of the screen next to one item and, while holding down the mouse button, move the mouse until you've drawn a lasso around all the items. After you've highlighted the items you want, let go of the mouse button, and they remain highlighted.

To change a window's size, drag the border in or out. (Dragging by a corner gives the best results.) Some windows, oddly enough, don't have borders. Stuck in limbo, their size can't be changed — even if they're an awkward size.

Except for tugging on them with the mouse, you won't be using borders much.

Maneuvering Windows Around the Desktop

A terrible dealer at the poker table, Windows 8 tosses windows around your desktop in a seemingly random way. Programs cover each other or sometimes dangle off the desktop. This section shows you how to gather all your windows into a neat pile, placing your favorite window on the top of the stack. If you prefer, lay them all down like a poker hand. As an added bonus, you can change their size, making them open to any size you want, automatically.

Moving a window to the top of the pile

Windows 8 says the window atop the pile that getting all the attention is called the *active* window. Being the active window means that it receives any keystrokes you or your cat happen to type.

You can move a window to the top of the pile so that it's active in any of several ways:

✔ Move the mouse pointer until it hovers over any portion of your desired window; then click the mouse button. Windows 8 immediately brings the window to the top of the pile.

✔ On the taskbar along the desktop's bottom, click the button for the window you want. Chapter 3 explains what the taskbar can do in more detail.

✔ Hold down the Alt key and keep tapping the Tab key. A small window pops up, displaying a thumbnail of each open window on your desktop. When your press of the Tab key highlights your favorite window, let go of the Alt key: Your window leaps to the forefront.

✔ Hold down the Windows key (■) and keep tapping the Tab key. A bar appears along your screen's left edge, showing thumbnails of all your running apps and programs. When your tap of the Tab key highlights your desired window, let go of the ■ key.

Repeat the process when necessary to bring other windows to the front. (And if you want to put two windows on the screen at the same time, read the "Placing two windows side by side" section, later in this chapter.)

Is your desktop too cluttered for you to work comfortably in your current window? Then hold down your mouse pointer on the window's title bar and give it a few quick shakes; Windows 8 drops the other windows down to the taskbar, leaving your main window resting alone on an empty desktop.

Moving a window from here to there

Sometimes you want to move a window to a different place on the desktop. Perhaps part of the window hangs off the edge, and you want it centered. Or maybe you want one window closer to another.

In either case, you can move a window by dragging and dropping its *title bar,* that thick bar along its top. (If you're not sure how dragging and dropping works, see the sidebar "Dragging, dropping, and running," earlier in this chapter.) When you *drop* the window in place, the window not only remains where you've dragged and dropped it but it also stays on top of the pile — until you click another window, that is, which brings *that* window to the pile's top.

Making a window fill the whole screen

Sooner or later, you'll grow tired of all this multiwindow mumbo jumbo. Why can't you just make one window fill the screen, like Start screen apps? Well, you can.

To make any desktop window grow as large as possible, double-click its *title bar,* that bar along the window's topmost edge. The window leaps up to fill the screen, covering up all the other windows.

To bring the pumped-up window back to its former size, double-click its title bar once again. The window quickly shrinks to its former size, and you can see things that it covered.

✔ If you're morally opposed to double-clicking a window's title bar to expand it, you can click the little Maximize button. Shown in the margin, it's the middle of the three buttons in the upper-right corner of every window.

✔ When a window is maximized to fill the screen, the Maximize button turns into a Restore button, shown in the margin. Click the Restore button, and the window returns to its smaller size.

✔ Need a brute force method? Then drag a window's top edge until it butts against the top edge of your desktop. The shadow of the window's borders will expand to fill the screen; let of the mouse button, and the window's borders fill the screen. (Yes, simply double-clicking the title bar is faster, but this method impresses any onlookers from neighboring cubicles.)

✔ Too busy to reach for the mouse? Maximize the current window by holding down the ⊞ key and pressing the Up Arrow key.

Closing a window

When you're through working in a window, close it: Click the little X in its upper-right corner. Zap! You're back to an empty desktop.

If you try to close your window before finishing your work, be it a game of Solitaire or a report for the boss, Windows cautiously asks whether you'd like to save your work. Take it up on its offer by clicking Yes and, if necessary, typing in a filename so that you can find your work later.

Making a window bigger or smaller

Like big lazy dogs, windows tend to flop on top of one another. To space your windows more evenly, you can resize them by *dragging and dropping* their edges inward or outward. It works like this:

1. **Point at any corner with the mouse arrow. When the arrow turns into a two-headed arrow, pointing in the two directions, you can hold down the mouse button and drag the corner in or out to change the window's size.**

2. **When you're happy with the window's new size, release the mouse button.**

   As the yoga master says, the window assumes the new position.

Placing two windows side by side

The longer you use Windows, the more likely you are to want to see two windows side by side. For example, you may want to copy things from one window into another, or compare two versions of the same file. By spending a few hours with the mouse, you can drag and drop the windows' corners until they're in perfect juxtaposition.

If you're impatient, Windows lets you speed up this handy side-by-side placement several ways:

✔ For the quickest solution, drag a window's title bar against one side of your screen; when your mouse pointer touches the screen's edge, let go of the mouse button. Repeat these same steps with the second window, dragging it to the opposite side of the monitor.

✔ Right-click on a blank part of the taskbar (even the clock will do) and choose Show Windows Side by Side. The windows align next to each other, like pillars. To align them in horizontal rows, choose Show Windows Stacked. (If you have more than three open windows, Show Windows Stacked tiles them across your screen, handy for seeing just a bit of each one.)

✔ If you have more than two windows open, click the Minimize button (the leftmost icon in every window's top-right corner) to minimize the windows you *don't* want tiled. Then use the Show Windows Side by Side from the preceding bullet to align the two remaining windows.

✔ To make the current window fill the screen's right half, hold the ⊞ key and press the → key. To fill the screen's left half, hold the ⊞ key and press the ← key.

Making windows open to the same darn size

Sometimes a window opens to a small square; other times, it opens to fill the entire screen. But windows rarely open to the exact size you want. Until you discover this trick, that is: When you *manually* adjust the size and placement of a window, Windows memorizes that size and always reopens the window to that same size. Follow these three steps to see how it works:

1. **Open your window.**

   The window opens to its usual unwanted size.

2. **Drag the window's corners until the window is the exact size and in the exact location you want. Let go of the mouse to drop the corner into its new position.**

   Be sure to resize the window *manually* by dragging its corners or edges with the mouse. Simply clicking the Maximize button won't work.

3. **Immediately close the window.**

Windows memorizes the size and placement of a window at the time it was last closed. When you open that window again, it should open to the same size you last left it. But the changes you make apply only to the program you made them in. For example, changes made to the Internet Explorer window will be remembered only for *Internet Explorer,* not for other programs you open.

Most windows follow these sizing rules, but a few renegades from other programs may misbehave, unfortunately.

Chapter 5

Storage: Internal, External, and in the Sky

*E*verybody hoped the new Start screen would simplify their work, finally transcending the complicated world of files and folders. Unfortunately, that's not the case.

Insert a flash drive or portable hard drive into your Windows 8 computer, and the Start screen dumps you onto the Windows desktop. There, File Explorer — Windows' age-old digital filing cabinet — rears its head.

Because the Start screen lacks a file manager, you're stuck with File Explorer whenever you need to find folders inside your computer, *outside* your computer on plug-in drives, and even in most storage spots on the Internet.

Whether you're using a touchscreen tablet, a laptop, or a desktop PC, files and folders still rule the computing world. And unless you grasp the Windows folder metaphor, you may not find your information very easily.

This chapter explains how to use the Windows 8 filing program, called *File Explorer*. (You'll recognize it as *Windows Explorer*, its name from previous Windows versions.) Along the way, you ingest a big enough dose of Windows file management for you to get your work done.

Browsing the File Explorer File Cabinets

To keep your programs and files neatly arranged, Windows cleaned up the squeaky old file cabinet metaphor with whisper-quiet Windows icons. Inside File Explorer, the icons represent your computer's storage areas, allowing you to copy, move, rename, or delete your files before the investigators arrive.

To see your computer's file cabinets — called *drives* or *disks* in computer lingo — open the Start screen's Desktop app. The Start screen vanishes, and the Windows desktop appears, showing the File Explorer tile to the right of the taskbar's Internet Explorer icon.

Open the File Explorer tile with a double-click or finger tap, and you quickly see your files and folders listed in File Explorer. File Explorer can display its contents in many ways. To see your computer's storage areas, click the word Computer from the pane along the left edge.

The File Explorer image shown in Figure 5-1 will look slightly different from the one on your PC, but you'll still see the same basic sections, each described in the upcoming list.

The File Explorer window comes with these main parts:

- **Navigation Pane:** The handy Navigation Pane, that strip along the left edge, lists shortcuts to special folders called *libraries* that hold your most valuable computerized possessions: your Documents, Music, Pictures, and Videos. (It tosses in a few other convenient items, covered in Chapter 4.)

- **Hard Disk Drives: Shown** in Figure 5-1, this area lists your PC's *hard drives* — your biggest storage areas. Every computer has at least one hard drive. Double-clicking a hard drive icon displays its files and folders, but you'll rarely find much useful information when probing that way. No, your most important files live in your Documents, Music, Pictures, and Videos libraries, which live one click away on the Navigation Pane.

Notice the hard drive bearing the little Windows icon (shown in the margin)? That means Windows 8 lives on that drive. And see the multicolored line next to each hard drives' icon in Figure 5-1? The more colored space you see in the line, the more files you've stuffed onto your drive. When the line turns red, your drive is almost full, and you should think about upgrading to a larger drive.

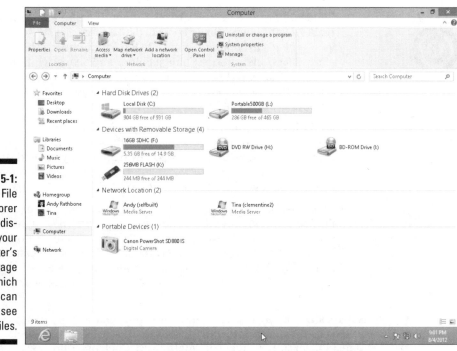

Figure 5-1:
The File
Explorer
window dis-
plays your
computer's
storage
areas, which
you can
open to see
your files.

✔ **Devices with Removable Storage:** This area shows detachable storage gadgetry attached to your computer. Here are some of the more common ones:

- **CD, DVD, and Blu-ray drives:** As shown in Figure 5-1, Windows 8 places a short description next to each drive's icon. For example, *CD-RW* means the drive can write to *CDs* but not DVDs. *DVD-RW* means that it can both read and write to DVDs *and* CDs. A *BD-ROM* drive can read Blu-ray discs, but it can write only to CDs and DVDs. And the ever-so-versatile *BD-RE* and *BD-R* drives can read and write to Blu-ray discs, DVDs, *and* CDs.

  Writing information to a disc is called *burning.*

- **Memory card reader and flash drives:** Memory card readers add a little slot to your PC for inserting memory cards from your camera, MP3 player, or similar gadget. Their icon, shown in the margin, looks like an empty slot — even after you insert the memory card. And oddly enough, the icon for some flash drive brands resembles a flash drive (refer to Figure 5-1); other flash drives show an icon like the one in the margin.

Windows 8 doesn't display icons for your computer's memory card readers until you've inserted a card into them. To see icons for your *empty* card readers, open File Explorer, choose the View tab, choose Options, choose Change Folder and Search Options, click the View tab, and then pause to catch your breath. Finally, click to remove the check mark next to the Hide Empty Drives in the Computer option and then click OK.

- **MP3 players:** Although Windows 8 displays an icon for a few MP3 players, it coughs up a generic thumbdrive or hard drive icon for most iPods and cellphones. If you own an iPod, you need the Apple iTunes software; Windows 8 can't copy songs to and from an iPod by itself. (I cover MP3 players in Chapter 16.)

- **Cameras:** Digital cameras usually appear as camera icons in the File Explorer window. To ensure success, turn on your camera and set it to its View Photos mode rather than its Take Photos mode. Then, to grab the camera's pictures, double-click the camera's icon. After Windows 8 walks you through the process of extracting the images (see Chapter 17), it places the photos in your Pictures library.

Windows Media Player

- ✔ **Network Location:** This icon in the margin, seen only by people who've linked groups of PCs into a *network* (see Chapter 15), represents the Media Player library living on another PC. Click one of these icons to access the music, photos, and video stored on those other PCs.

If you plug a digital camcorder, cellphone, or other gadget into your PC, the File Explorer window will often sprout a new icon representing your gadget. If Windows neglects to ask what you'd like to do with your newly plugged-in gadget, right-click the icon; you see a list of everything you can do with that item. No icon? Then you need to install a *driver* for your gadget, a precipitous journey detailed in Chapter 13.

Tip for tablets: When you read the word *click,* substitute *tap.* Similarly, *right-click* means *touch and hold.* And the term *drag and drop* means *slide your finger along the screen, as if your finger is the mouse pointer, and then lift the finger to drop the item.*

Getting the Lowdown on Folders and Libraries

This stuff is dreadfully boring, but if you don't read it, you'll be just as lost as your files.

A *folder* is a storage area on a drive, just like a real folder in a file cabinet. Windows 8 divides your computer's hard drives into many folders to separate your many projects. For example, you store all your music in your My Music folder and your pictures in your My Pictures folder. That lets both you and your programs find them easily.

A *library,* by contrast, is a super folder, if you will. Instead of showing the contents of a single folder, it shows the contents of *several* folders. For example, your Music library shows the tunes living in your *My* Music folder, as well as the tunes in your *Public* Music folder. (The Public Music folder contains music available to everyone who uses your PC.)

Windows 8 gives you four libraries for storing your files and folders. For easy access, they live in the Navigation Pane along the left side of every folder. Figure 5-2 shows your libraries: Documents, Music, Pictures, and Videos.

Figure 5-2:
Windows 8 provides every person with these same four libraries, but it keeps everybody's folders separate.

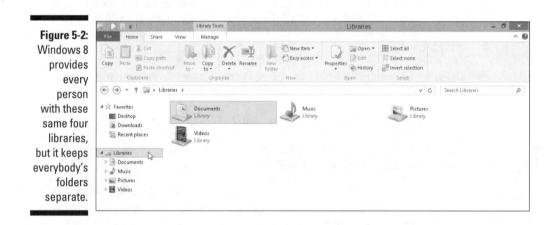

Keep these folder facts in mind when shuffling files in Windows 8:

✔ You can ignore folders and dump all your files onto the Windows 8 desktop. But that's like tossing everything into your car's back seat and pawing around to find your sunglasses a month later. Organized stuff is much easier to find.

✔ If you're eager to create a folder or two (and it's pretty easy), page ahead to this chapter's "Creating a New Folder" section.

✔ File Explorer folders use a *tree metaphor* as they branch out from one main folder (a disk drive) that contains folders which contain even more folders.

Peering into Your Drives, Folders, and Libraries

Knowing all this folder stuff not only impresses computer store employees but also helps you find the files you want. (See the preceding section for a lowdown on which folder holds what.) Put on your hard hat; go spelunking among your computer's drives, folders, and libraries; and use this section as your guide.

Seeing the files on a disk drive

Like everything else in Windows 8, disk drives are represented by buttons, or icons. The File Explorer program also shows information stored in other areas, such as MP3 players, digital cameras, or scanners. (I explain these icons in the section "Browsing the File Explorer File Cabinets," earlier in this chapter.)

Opening an icon usually lets you access the device's contents and move files back and forth, just as with any other folders in Windows 8.

When you double-click a hard drive icon in File Explorer, Windows 8 promptly opens the drive to show you the folders packed inside. But how should Windows react when you insert something new into your computer, such as a CD, DVD, or flash drive?

Earlier versions of Windows tried to second-guess you. When you inserted a music CD, for example, Windows automatically began playing the music. The more polite Windows 8, by contrast, asks how you prefer it to handle the situation, as shown in Figure 5-3. The same message appears whether you're working within the desktop or Start screen.

When that message appears, choose it with a click of the mouse; a second message appears, shown in Figure 5-4, listing everything you can do with that item.

Choose an option, and Windows 8 behaves the same way the next time you insert a similar item.

But what if you change your mind about how Windows 8 should treat a newly inserted item? Then you just need to change the Windows 8 reaction: In File Explorer, right-click the inserted item's icon and choose Open AutoPlay. Once again, Windows 8 shows the message from Figure 5-4, and asks you to plot the future course.

Figure 5-3:
Windows 8 asks how it should handle newly inserted items.

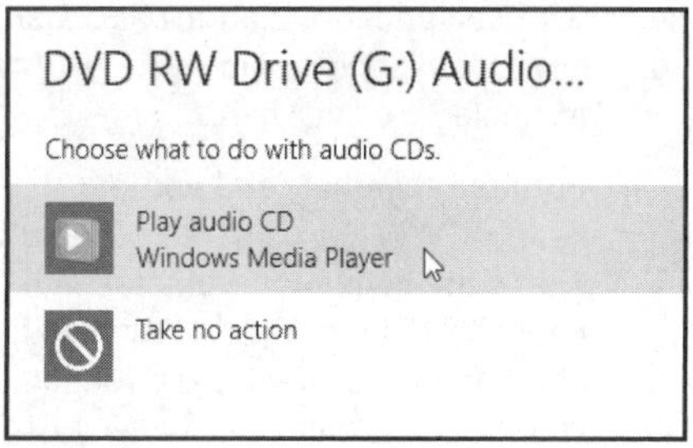

Figure 5-4:
Choose how Windows 8 should react the next time you insert that item.

TIP

Adjusting the AutoPlay settings comes in particularly handy for USB thumb-drives. If your flash drive carries a few songs, Windows 8 may want to play them, slowing your access to your flash drive's other files. To prevent that, select the AutoPlay option, Open Folder to View Files.

REMEMBER

✔ When in doubt as to what you can do with an icon in File Explorer, right-click it. Windows 8 presents a menu of all the things you can do to that object. (You can choose Open, for example, to see the files on a flash drive, making it simpler to copy them to your computer.)

✔ If you double-click an icon for a CD, DVD or Blu-ray drive when no disk is in the drive, Windows 8 stops you, gently suggesting that you insert a disk before proceeding further.

✔ Spot an icon under the heading Network Location? That's a little door-way for peering into other computers linked to your computer — if there are any. You find more network stuff in Chapter 15.

Seeing what's inside a folder

Because folders are really little storage compartments, Windows 8 uses a picture of a little folder to represent a place for storing files.

To see what's inside a folder, either in File Explorer or on the Windows 8 desktop, just double-click that folder's picture. A new window pops up, showing that folder's contents. Spot another folder inside that folder? Double-click that one to see what's inside. Keep clicking until you find what you want or reach a dead end.

What's all this path stuff?

A *path* is merely the file's address, similar to your own. When a letter is mailed to your house, for example, it travels to your country, state, city, street, and, hopefully, your apartment or house. A computer path does the same thing. It starts with the letter of the disk drive and ends with the file's name. In between, the path lists all the folders the computer must travel through to reach the file.

For example, look at the Downloads folder. For Windows 8 to find a file stored in my Downloads folder, it starts from the computer's C: drive, travels through the Users folder, and then goes through the Andy folder. From there, it goes into the Andy folder's Downloads folder. (Internet Explorer follows that path when saving your downloaded files.)

Take a deep breath and exhale slowly. Now add in the computer's ugly grammar: In a path, the Windows disk drive letter is referred to as **C:**. The disk drive letter and colon make up the first part of the path. All the other folders are inside the big C: folder, so they're listed after the C:

part. Windows separates these nested folders with something called a *backslash,* or \. The downloaded file's name — *Tax Form 3890,* for example — comes last.

Put it all together, and you get C:\Users\ Andy\Downloads\Tax Form 3890. That's my computer's official path to the Tax Form 3890 file in Andy's Downloads folder. Of course, on your computer, you can substitute your own username for *Andy.*

This stuff can be tricky, so here it is again: The letter for the drive comes first, followed by a colon and a backslash. Then come the names of all the folders leading to the file, separated by backslashes. Last comes the name of the file itself.

Windows 8 automatically puts together the path for you when you click folders — thankfully. But whenever you click the Browse button to look for a file, you're navigating through folders and traversing along the path leading to the file.

Reached a dead end? If you mistakenly end up in the wrong folder, back your way out as if you're browsing the web. Click the Back arrow at the window's top-left corner. (It's the same arrow that appears in the margin.) That closes the wrong folder and shows you the folder you just left. If you keep clicking the Back arrow, you end up right where you started.

The Address Bar provides another quick way to jump to different places in your PC. As you move from folder to folder, the folder's Address Bar — that little word-filled box at the folder's top — constantly keeps track of your trek.

Notice the little arrows between the folder names. Those little arrows provide quick shortcuts to other folders and windows. Try clicking any of the arrows; menus appear, listing the places you can jump to from that point. For example, click the arrow after Libraries, shown in Figure 5-5, and a menu drops down, letting you jump quickly to your other libraries.

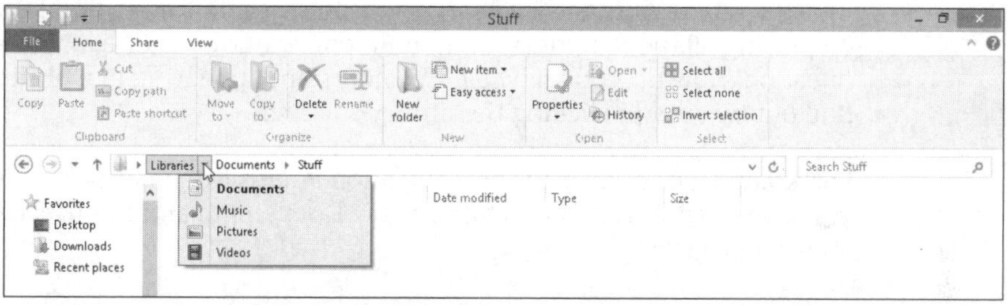

Figure 5-5:
Here, click the little arrow after Libraries to jump to any place that appears in the Libraries folder.

Here are some more tips for finding your way in and out of folders:

- ✔ Sometimes, a folder contains too many files or folders to fit in the window. To see more files, click that window's scroll bars along a window's bottom or right edges. (I cover scroll bars in your field guide, Chapter 4.)

- ✔ While burrowing deeply into folders, the Forward arrow (shown in the margin) provides yet another quick way to jump immediately to any folder you've plowed through: Click the little downward-pointing arrow next to the Forward arrow in the window's top-left corner. A menu drops down, listing the folders you've plowed past on your journey. Click any name to jump quickly to that folder.

- ✔ Removed from Windows 7 and Windows Vista, the Up Arrow button reappears in Windows 8. Click the Up Arrow button, located just to the right of the Address Bar, to move your view up one folder. Keep clicking it, and you'll eventually wind up at someplace recognizable: your desktop.

✔ Can't find a particular file or folder? Instead of aimlessly rummaging through folders, check out the Charms bar's Search command, which I describe in Chapter 7. Windows can automatically find your lost files, folders, e-mail, and nearly anything else hiding in your PC.

✔ When faced with a long list of alphabetically sorted files, click anywhere on the list. Then quickly type the first letter or two of the desired file's name. Windows immediately jumps up or down the list to the first name beginning with those letters.

Managing a library's folders

The Windows 8 library system may seem confusing, but you can safely ignore the mechanics behind it. Just treat a library like any other folder: a handy spot to store and grab similar types of files. But if you want to know the inner workings behind a library, hang around for this section.

Introduced in Windows 7, libraries constantly monitor several folders, displaying all those folders' content in one window. That leads to a nagging question: How do you know *which* folders are appearing in a library? You can find out by double-clicking the library's name.

For example, double-click the Navigation Pane's Documents library, and you'll see that library's two folders: My Documents and Public Documents, as shown in Figure 5-6.

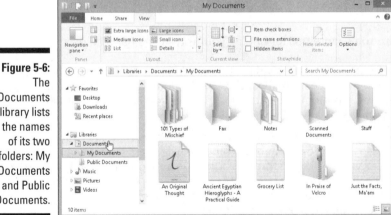

Figure 5-6:
The Documents library lists the names of its two folders: My Documents and Public Documents.

If you keep files in another location, perhaps a portable hard drive or even a networked PC, feel free to add them to the library of your choice by following these steps:

1. **Right-click the library you want to expand and choose Properties.**

   If you choose the Documents library, for example, the Documents Properties dialog box appears, as shown in Figure 5-7.

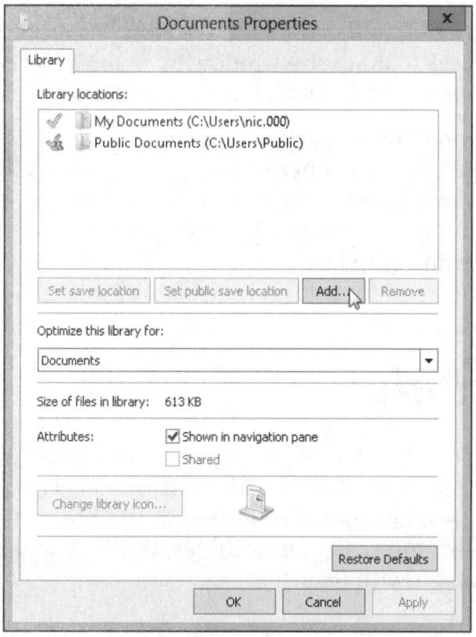

Figure 5-7:
The
Documents
Properties
dialog box
lists the
folders
visible
inside a
library.

2. **Click the Add button.**

   The Include Folder in Documents window appears.

3. **Navigate to the folder you want to add, click the folder, click the Include Folder button, and click OK.**

   The library automatically updates itself to display that folder's contents, sorting the contents into groups.

   ✔ You may add as many folders to a library as you want, which is handy when your music files are spread out across many places. The library automatically updates to show the folders' latest contents.

✔ To remove a folder from a library, follow the first step but click the folder to be removed and click the Remove button.

✔ So, when you drop a file into a library, which folder does that file *really* live in? It lives in the folder known as the *Default Save Location* — the folder that currently holds the honor of receiving incoming files. For example, when you drop a music file into your Music library, the file goes into your *My Music* folder. Similarly, documents end up in your *My Documents* folder, videos go into *My Videos,* and pictures go into *My Pictures.*

What if you want a *different* folder to receive a library's incoming files? To assign that noble task, call up the window in Figure 5-7, right-click the desired folder and choose Set As Default Save Location.

✔ You can create additional libraries to meet your own needs: Right-click Libraries in the Navigation Pane, choose New, and choose Library from the pop-up menu. A new Library icon appears, ready for you to type in a name. Then begin stocking your new library with folders by following Steps 1–3 in the preceding step list.

Creating a New Folder

To store new information in a file cabinet, you grab a manila folder, scrawl a name across the top, and start stuffing it with information. To store new information in Windows 8 — a new batch of letters to the hospital's billing department, for example — you create a new folder, think up a name for the new folder, and start stuffing it with files.

To create a new folder quickly, click Home from the folder's toolbar buttons and choose New Folder from the Ribbon menu. If you can't find the right menus, though, here's a quick and foolproof method:

1. **Right-click inside your folder (or on the desktop) and choose New.**

   The all-powerful right-click shoots a menu out the side.

2. **Select Folder.**

   When you choose Folder, shown in Figure 5-8, a new folder quickly appears, waiting for you to type a new name.

3. **Type a new name for the folder.**

   A newly created folder bears the boring name of New Folder. When you begin typing, Windows 8 quickly erases the old name and fills in your new name. Done? Save the new name by either pressing Enter or clicking somewhere away from the name you've just typed.

If you mess up the name and want to try again, right-click the folder, choose Rename, and start over.

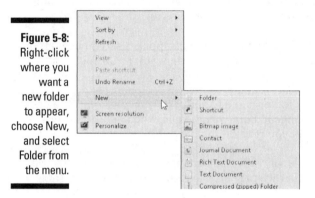

Figure 5-8:
Right-click where you want a new folder to appear, choose New, and select Folder from the menu.

🖝 Certain symbols are banned from folder (and file) names. The "Using legal folder names and filenames" sidebar spells out the details, but you never have trouble when using plain old letters and numbers for names.

🖝 Shrewd observers notice that in Figure 5-8 Windows offers to create many more things than just a folder when you click the New button. Right-click inside a folder anytime you want to create a new shortcut or other common items.

🖝 Cautious observers may remark that their right-click menu looks different than the one shown in Figure 5-8. There's nothing wrong; installed programs often add their own items to the right-click list, making the list look different on different PCs.

Using legal folder names and filenames

Windows is pretty picky about what you can and can't name a file or folder. If you stick to plain old letters and numbers, you're fine. But don't try to stick any of the following characters in there:

    : / \ * | < > ? "

If you try to use any of those characters, Windows 8 bounces an error message to the screen, and you have to try again. Here are some illegal filenames:

```
1/2 of my Homework
JOB:2
ONE<TWO
He's no "Gentleman"
```

These names are legal:

```
Half of my Term Paper
JOB=2
Two is Bigger than One
A #@$%) Scoundrel
```

Renaming a File or Folder

Sick of a file- or folder name? Then change it. Just right-click the offending icon and choose Rename from the menu that pops up.

Windows highlights the file's old name, which disappears as you begin typing the new one. Press Enter or click the desktop when you're through, and you're off.

Or you can click the file- or folder name to select it, wait a second, and click the file's name again to change it. Some people click the name and press F2; Windows automatically lets you rename the file or folder.

- ✔ When you rename a file, only its name changes. The contents are still the same, the file is still the same size, and the file is still in the same place.

- ✔ To rename large groups of files simultaneously, select them all, right-click the first one, and choose Rename. Type in the new name and press Enter; Windows 8 renames that file. However, it also renames all your *other* selected files to the new name, adding a number as it goes: cat, cat (2), cat (3), cat (4), and so on. It's a handy way to rename photographs.

- ✔ Renaming some folders confuses Windows, especially if those folders contain programs. And please don't rename these folders: My Documents, My Pictures, My Music, or My Videos.

- ✔ Windows won't let you rename a file or folder if one of your programs currently uses it. Sometimes closing the program fixes the problem. Other times, you need to restart your PC. That releases the program's clutches so you can rename it.

Selecting Bunches of Files or Folders

Although selecting a file, folder, or other object may seem particularly boring, it swings the doors wide open for further tasks: deleting, renaming, moving, copying, and performing other file-juggling tricks discussed in the rest of this chapter.

To select a single item, just click it. To select several files and folders, hold down the Ctrl key when you click the names or icons. Each name or icon stays highlighted when you click the next one.

To gather several files or folders sitting next to each other in a list, click the first one. Then hold down the Shift key as you click the last one. Those two items are highlighted, along with every file and folder sitting between them.

Windows 8 lets you *lasso* files and folders as well. Point slightly above the first file or folder you want; then, while holding down the mouse button, point at the last file or folder. The mouse creates a colored lasso to surround your files. Let go of the mouse button, and the lasso disappears, leaving all the surrounded files highlighted.

- ✔ You can drag and drop armfuls of files in the same way that you drag a single file.

- ✔ You can also simultaneously cut or copy and paste these armfuls into new locations using any of the methods described in the "Copying or Moving Files and Folders" section, later in this chapter.

- ✔ You can delete these armfuls of goods, too, with a press of the Delete key.

- ✔ To quickly select all the files in a folder, choose Select All from the folder's Edit menu. (No menu? Then select them by pressing Ctrl+A.) Here's another nifty trick: To grab all but a few files, press Ctrl+A, and while still holding down Ctrl, click the ones you don't want.

Getting Rid of a File or Folder

Sooner or later, you'll want to delete a file that's no longer important — yesterday's lottery picks, for example, or a particularly embarrassing digital photo. To delete a file or folder, right-click its name or icon. Then choose Delete from the pop-up menu. This surprisingly simple trick works for files, folders, shortcuts, and just about anything else in Windows.

To delete in a hurry, click the offending object and press the Delete key. Dragging and dropping a file or folder to the Recycle Bin does the same thing.

The Delete option deletes entire folders, including any files or folders stuffed *inside* those folders. Make sure that you select the correct folder before you choose Delete.

- ✔ After you choose Delete, Windows tosses a box in your face, asking whether you're *sure*. If you're sure, click Yes. If you're tired of Windows' cautious questioning, right-click the Recycle Bin, choose Properties, and remove the check mark next to Display Delete Confirmation Dialog. Windows now deletes any highlighted items whenever you — or an inadvertent brush of your shirt sleeve — press the Delete key.

Don't bother reading this hidden technical stuff

You're not the only one creating files on your computer. Programs often store their own information in a *data file*. They may need to store information about the way your computer is set up, for example. To keep people from confusing those files for trash and deleting them, Windows hides them.

You can view the names of these hidden files and folders; however, if you want to play voyeur:

1. **Open any folder and click the View tab from along the top edge.**

   The Ribbon changes to show different ways you can view that folder's files.

2. **Click in the box named Hidden Items.**

   Don't see the Hidden Items box? Make the window a little wider until that option appears.

That makes the formerly hidden files appear alongside the other filenames. Be sure not to delete them, however: The programs that created them will gag, possibly damaging them or Windows itself. To avoid trouble, click the Hidden Items box again to drape the veil of secrecy back over those important files.

✔ Be extra sure that you know what you're doing when deleting any file that has pictures of little gears in its icon. These files are usually sensitive hidden files, and the computer wants you to leave them alone. (Other than that, they're not particularly exciting, despite the action-oriented gears.)

✔ Icons with little arrows in their corner (like the one in the margin) are *shortcuts* — push buttons that merely load files. (I cover shortcuts in Chapter 6.) Deleting shortcuts deletes only a *button* that loads a file or program. The file or program itself remains undamaged and still lives inside your computer.

✔ As soon as you find out how to delete files, trot off to Chapter 3, which explains several ways to *un*delete them. (***Hint for the desperate:*** Open the Recycle Bin, right-click your file's name, and choose Restore.)

Copying or Moving Files and Folders

To copy or move files to different folders on your hard drive, it's sometimes easiest to use your mouse to *drag* them there. For example, here's how to move a file to a different folder on your desktop. In this case, I'm moving the Traveler file from the House folder to the Morocco folder.

1. **Align the two windows next to each other.**

I explain this in Chapter 4. If you skipped that chapter, try this: Click the first window and then hold the ⊞ key and press the → key. To fill the screen's left half, click the other window, hold the ⊞ key and press the ← key.

2. **Aim the mouse pointer at the file or folder you want to move.**

   In this case, point at the Traveler file.

3. **While holding down the right mouse button, move the mouse until it points at the destination folder.**

   As you see in Figure 5-9, the Traveler file is being dragged from the House folder to the Morocco folder.

Figure 5-9:
To move a file or folder from one window to another, drag it there while holding down the right mouse button.

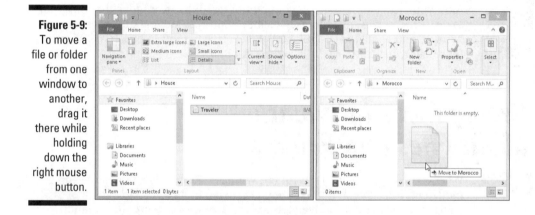

Moving the mouse drags the file along with it, and Windows 8 explains that you're moving the file, as shown in Figure 5-9. (Be sure to hold down the right mouse button the entire time.)

Always drag icons while holding down the *right* mouse button. Windows 8 is then gracious enough to give you a menu of options when you position the icon, and you can choose to copy, move, or create a shortcut. If you hold down the *left* mouse button, Windows 8 sometimes doesn't know whether you want to copy or move.

4. **Release the mouse button and choose Copy Here, Move Here, or Create Shortcuts Here from the pop-up menu.**

When dragging and dropping takes too much work, Windows offers a few other ways to copy or move files. Depending on your screen's current layout, some of the following onscreen tools may work more easily:

✔ **Right-click menus:** Right-click a file or folder and choose Cut or Copy, depending on whether you want to move or copy it. Then right-click your destination folder and choose Paste. It's simple, it always works, and you needn't bother placing any windows side by side.

✔ **Ribbon commands:** In File Explorer, click your file or folder; then click the Ribbon's Home tab and choose Copy To (or Move To). A menu drops down, listing some common locations. Don't spot the right spot? Then click Choose Location, click through the drive and folders to reach the destination folder, and Windows transports the file accordingly. Although a bit cumbersome, this method works if you know the exact location of the destination folder.

I explain more about the new Windows 8 Ribbon menus in Chapter 4.

✔ **Navigation Pane:** Described in Chapter 4, this panel along File Explorer's left edge lists popular locations: libraries, drives, and oft-used folders. That lets you drag and drop a file into a spot on the Navigation Pane, sparing you the hassle of opening a destination folder.

After you install a program on your computer, don't ever move that program's folder. Programs wedge themselves into Windows. Moving the program may break it, and you'll have to reinstall it. Feel free to move a program's *shortcut* (shortcut icons contain a little arrow), though.

Seeing More Information about Files and Folders

Whenever you create a file or folder, Windows 8 scrawls a bunch of secret hidden information on it: the date you created it, its size, and even more trivial stuff. Sometimes it even lets you add your own secret information: reviews for your music files, or thumbnail pictures for any of your folders.

You can safely ignore most of the information. Other times, tweaking that information is the only way to solve a problem.

To see what Windows 8 is calling your files and folders behind your back, right-click the item and choose Properties from the pop-up menu. Choosing Properties on a Jimi Hendrix song, for example, brings up bunches of details, as shown in Figure 5-10. Here's what each tab means:

✔ **General:** This first tab (far left in Figure 5-10) shows the file's *type* (an MP3 file of the song "Hey Joe"), its *size* (3.27MB), the program that *opens* it (in this case, the Start screen's Music app), and the file's *location*.

Want a different program to open your file? Right-click the file, choose Properties, and click the Change button on the General tab, shown in Figure 5-10. A list of music players appears, letting you choose your preferred program.

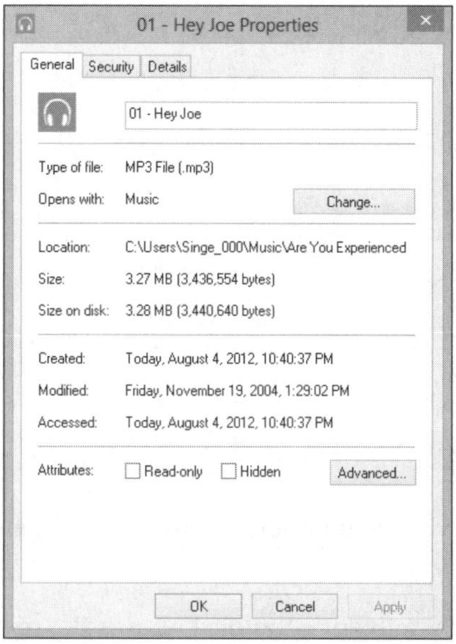

Figure 5-10:
A file's
Properties
dialog box
shows
which
program
automati-
cally opens
it, the
file's size,
and other
details.

```
┌─────────────────────────────────────────────┐
│ ⌂      01 - Hey Joe Properties            ✕  │
├─────────────────────────────────────────────┤
│ General │ Security │ Details                  │
│                                               │
│  ⌒    ┌─────────────────────────────┐       │
│  ∩    │ 01 - Hey Joe                │       │
│                                               │
│  Type of file:  MP3 File (.mp3)               │
│  Opens with:    Music         ┌──────────┐   │
│                               │ Change...│   │
│                               └──────────┘   │
│  Location:      C:\Users\Singe_000\Music\Are You Experienced │
│  Size:          3.27 MB (3,436,554 bytes)     │
│  Size on disk:  3.28 MB (3,440,640 bytes)     │
│                                               │
│  Created:       Today, August 4, 2012, 10:40:37 PM │
│  Modified:      Friday, November 19, 2004, 1:29:02 PM │
│  Accessed:      Today, August 4, 2012, 10:40:37 PM │
│                                               │
│  Attributes:   ☐ Read-only  ☐ Hidden  ┌─────────┐ │
│                                       │Advanced.│ │
│                                       └─────────┘ │
│                                               │
│         ┌────┐  ┌──────┐  ┌──────┐           │
│         │ OK │  │Cancel│  │Apply │           │
│         └────┘  └──────┘  └──────┘           │
└─────────────────────────────────────────────┘
```

✔ **Security:** On this tab, you control *permissions:* who can access the file and what they can do with it — details that become a chore only when Windows 8 won't let your friend (or even you) open the file. If this problem develops, copy the folder to your *Public* folder, which I cover in Chapter 14. That folder provides a haven where every account holder on your computer can access the file.

✔ **Details:** True to its name, this tab reveals arcane details about a file. On digital photos, for example, this tab lists EXIF (Exchangeable Image File Format) data: the camera model, F-stop, aperture, focal length, and other items loved by photographers. On songs, this tab displays the song's *ID3 tag* (IDentify MP3): the artist, album title, year, track number, genre, length, and similar information.

Normally, all these details remain hidden unless you right-click a file or folder and choose Properties. But what if you want to see details about all the files in a folder, perhaps to find pictures taken on a certain day? For that, switch your folder's view to Details:

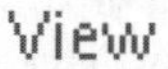

View

1. **Click the View tab on the Ribbon (shown in the margin.)**

   A menu appears, listing the umpteen ways a folder can display your files.

2. **In the Layout group, select Details, as shown in Figure 5-11.**

   The screen changes to show your file's names, with details about them stretching to the right in orderly columns.

Figure 5-11:
To see
details
about files
in a folder,
click the
View tab
and select
Details.

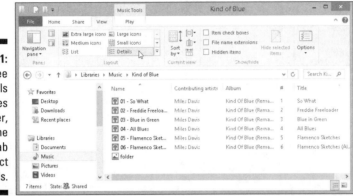

Try all the views to see which view you prefer. (Windows 8 remembers which views you prefer for different folders.)

✔ If you can't remember what a folder's toolbar buttons do, rest your mouse pointer over a button. Windows 8 displays a helpful box summing up the button's mission.

✔ Although some of the additional file information is handy, it can consume a lot of space, limiting the number of files you can see in the window. Displaying only the filename is often a better idea. Then, if you want to see more information about a file or folder, try the following tip.

✔ Folders usually display files sorted alphabetically. To sort them differently, right-click a blank spot inside the folder and choose Sort By. A pop-up menu lets you choose to sort items by size, name, type, and other details.

✔ When the excitement of the Sort By menu wears off, try clicking the words at the top of each sorted column. Click Size, for example, to reverse the order, placing the *largest* files at the list's top.

Writing to CDs and DVDs

Most computers today write information to CDs and DVDs using a flameless approach known as *burning.* To see whether you're stuck with an older drive that can't burn discs, remove any discs from inside the drive; then from the desktop, open the taskbar's File Explorer icon and look at the icon for your CD or DVD drive.

Because computers always speak in secret code, here's what you can do with the disc drives in your computer:

✔ **DVD-RW:** These drives both read and write to CDs *and* DVDs.

✔ **BD-ROM:** These can read and write to CDs and DVDs, plus they can read Blu-ray discs.

✔ **BD-RE:** These can read and write to CDs, DVDs, *and* Blu-ray discs.

If your PC has two CD or DVD burners, tell Windows 8 which drive you want to handle your disc-burning chores: Right-click the drive, choose Properties, and click the Recording tab. Then choose your favorite drive in the top box.

Buying the right kind of blank CDs and DVDs for burning

Stores sell two types of CDs: CD-R (short for CD-Recordable) and CD-RW (short for CD-ReWritable). Here's the difference:

✔ **CD-R:** Most people buy CD-R discs because they're very cheap and they work fine for storing music or files. You can write to them until they fill up; then you can't write to them anymore. But that's no problem because most people don't want to erase their CDs and start over. They want to stick their burned disc into the car's stereo or stash it as a backup.

✔ **CD-RW:** Techies sometimes buy CD-RW discs for making temporary backups of data. You can write information to them, just like CD-Rs. But when a CD-RW disc fills up, you can erase it and start over with a clean slate — something not possible with a CD-R. However, CD-RWs cost more money, so most people stick with the cheaper and faster CD-Rs.

DVDs come in both R and RW formats, just like CDs, so the preceding R and RW rules apply to them, as well. Most DVD burners sold in the past few years can write to any type of blank CD or DVD.

Buying blank DVDs for older drives is chaos: The manufacturers fought over which storage format to use, confusing things for everybody. To buy the right blank DVD, check your computer's receipt to see what formats its DVD burner needs: DVD-R, DVD-RW, DVD+R, or DVD+RW.

✔ Discs come rated by their speed. For faster disc burning, buy the largest number "x" speed you can find, usually 52x for CDs and 16x for DVDs.

- Blank CDs are cheap; borrow one from a neighbor's kid to see whether it works in your drive. If it works fine, buy some of the same type. Blank DVDs, by contrast, are more expensive. Ask the store whether you can return them if your DVD drive doesn't like them.

- Blank Blu-ray discs cost a lot more than CDs or DVDs. Luckily, Blu-ray drives aren't very picky, and just about any blank Blu-ray disc will work.

- For some odd reason, Compact Discs and Digital Video Discs are spelled as *discs,* not *disks.*

- Although Windows 8 can handle simple disc-burning tasks, it's extraordinarily awkward at *duplicating* discs. Most people give up quickly and buy third-party disc-burning software. I explain how Windows 8 creates music CDs in Chapter 16.

- It's currently illegal to make duplicates of movie DVDs in the United States — even to make a backup copy in case the kids scratch up the new Disney DVD. Windows 8 can't copy DVDs on its own, but some programs on websites from other countries can handle the job.

Copying files to or from a CD or DVD

CDs and DVDs once hailed from the school of simplicity: You simply slid them into your CD player or DVD player. But as soon as those discs graduated to PCs, the problems grew. When you create a CD or DVD, you must tell your PC *what* you're copying and *where* you intend to play it: Music for a CD player? Photo slideshows for a TV's DVD player? Or files to store on your computer?

If you choose the wrong answer, your disc won't work, and you've created yet another coaster.

Here are the Disc Creation rules:

- **Music:** To create a CD that plays music in your CD player or car stereo, flip ahead to Chapter 16. You need to fire up the Windows 8 Media Player program and burn an *audio CD.*

- **Photo slide shows:** Windows 8 no longer includes the Windows DVD Maker bundled with Windows Vista and Windows 7. To create photo slideshows, you now need a third-party program.

If you just want to copy *files* to a CD or DVD, perhaps to save as a backup or to give to a friend, stick around.

Follow these steps to write files to a new, blank CD or DVD. (If you're writing files to a CD or DVD that you've written to before, jump ahead to Step 4.)

1. **Insert the blank disc into your disc burner. Then click or tap the Notification box that appears in the screen's upper-right corner.**

2. **When the Notification box asks how you'd like to proceed, click the box's Burn Files to a Disc option.**

   Windows 8 displays a Burn a Disc dialog box and asks you to create a title for the disc.

3. **Type a name for the disc, describe how you want to use the disc, and click Next.**

   Unfortunately, Windows 8 limits your CD or DVD's title to 16 characters. Instead of typing **Family Picnic atop Orizaba in 2009**, stick to the facts: **Orizaba, 2009**. Or, just click Next to use the default name for the disc: the current date.

   Windows can burn the files to the disc two different ways. To decide which method works best for you, it offers you two options:

   • **Like a USB flash drive:** This method lets you read and write files to the disc many times, a handy way to use discs as portable file carriers. Unfortunately, that method isn't compatible with some CD or DVD players connected to home stereos or TVs.

   • **With a CD/DVD player:** If you plan to play your disc on a fairly new home stereo disc player that's smart enough to read files stored in several different formats, select this method.

   Armed with the disc's name, Windows 8 prepares the disc for incoming files.

4. **Tell Windows 8 which files to write to disc.**

   Now that your disc is ready to accept the files, tell Windows 8 what information to send its way. You can do this in any of several ways:

   • Right-click the item you want to copy, be it a single file, folder, or selected files and folders. When the pop-up menu appears, choose Send To and select your disc burner from the menu. (The pop-up menu will list the disc's title you chose in Step 2.)

   • Drag and drop files and/or folders on top of the burner's icon in File Explorer.

   • From your My Music, My Pictures, or My Documents folder, click the Share tab and then click Burn to Disc. This button copies all of that folder's files (or just the files you've selected) to the disc as files.

   • Tell your current program to save the information to the disc rather than to your hard drive.

Duplicating a CD or DVD

Windows 8 doesn't have a command to duplicate a CD, DVD, or Blu-ray disc. It can't even make a copy of a music CD. (That's why so many people buy CD-burning programs.)

But it can copy all of a CD's or DVD's files to a blank disc using this two-step process:

1. **Copy the files and folders from the CD or DVD to a folder on your PC.**

2. **Copy those same files and folders back to a blank CD or DVD.**

That gives you a duplicate CD or DVD, which is handy when you need a second copy of an essential backup disc.

You can try this process on a music CD or DVD movie, but it won't work. (I tried.) It works only when you're duplicating a disc containing computer programs or data files.

No matter which method you choose, Windows 8 dutifully looks over the information and copies it to the disc you inserted in the first step. A progress window appears, showing the disc burner's progress. When the progress window disappears, Windows has finished burning the disc.

5. **Close your disc-burning session by ejecting the disc.**

   When you're through copying files to the disc, push your drive's Eject button (or right-click the drive's icon in File Explorer and choose Eject). Windows 8 closes the session, adding a finishing touch to the disc that lets other PCs read it.

If you try to copy a large batch of files to a disc — more than will fit — Windows 8 complains immediately. Copy fewer files at a time, perhaps spacing them out over two discs.

Most programs let you save files directly to disc. Choose Save from the File menu and select your CD burner. Put a disc (preferably one that's not already filled) into your disc drive to start the process.

Working with Flash Drives and Memory Cards

Digital camera owners eventually become acquainted with *memory cards* — those little plastic squares that replaced the awkward rolls of film. Windows 8 can read digital photos directly from the camera after you find its cable and plug it into your PC. But Windows 8 can also grab photos straight off the memory card, a method praised by those who've lost their camera's cables.

The secret is a *memory card reader:* a little slot-filled box that stays plugged into your PC. Slide your memory card into the slot, and your PC can read the card's files, just like reading files from any other folder.

Most office supply and electronics stores sell memory card readers that accept most popular memory card formats: Compact Flash, SecureDigital, Micro-Secure Digital, SecureDigital High Capacity, and a host of other tongue twisters. Some computers even come with built-in card readers — tiny slots on the front of their case.

The beauty of card readers is that there's nothing new to figure out: Windows 8 treats your inserted card just like an ordinary folder. Insert your card, and a folder appears on your screen to show your digital camera photos. The same drag-and-drop and cut-and-paste rules covered earlier in this chapter still apply, letting you move the pictures or other files off the card and into a folder in your Pictures library.

Flash drives — also known as thumbdrives — work just like memory card readers. Plug the flash drive into one of your PC's USB ports, and the drive appears as an icon (shown in the margin) in File Explorer, ready to be opened with a double-click.

- ✔ First, the warning: Formatting a card or disk wipes out all its information. Never format a card or disk unless you don't care about the information it currently holds.

- ✔ Now, the procedure: If Windows complains that a newly inserted card isn't formatted, right-click its drive and choose Format. (This problem happens most often with brand-new or damaged cards.) Sometimes formatting also helps one gadget use a card designed for a different gadget — your digital camera may be able to use your MP3 player's card, for example.

SkyDrive: Your Cubbyhole in the Clouds

Storing files inside your computer works fine while you're at home or work. And when leaving your computer, you can tote files on flash drives, CDs, DVDs, and portable hard drives — if you remember to grab them on the way out.

But how can you access your files from *anywhere,* even if you've forgotten to pack them?

Microsoft's solution to that problem is called *SkyDrive.* Basically, it's your own private storage space on the Internet where you can dump your files and then retrieve them whenever you find an Internet connection. Romantic engineers refer to Internet-stashed files as *cloud storage.*

The Windows 8 Start screen comes with the free SkyDrive app, but you need a few extra things in order to use it:

- **Microsoft account:** You need a Microsoft account in order to upload or retrieve files to SkyDrive. Chances are, you created a Microsoft account when you first created your account on your Windows 8 PC. (I describe Microsoft accounts in Chapter 2.)

- **An Internet connection:** Without an Internet signal, either wireless or wired, your files stay floating in the clouds, away from you and your computer.

- **Patience:** Uploading files always takes longer than downloading files. Although you can upload small files fairly quickly, larger files like digital photos can take several minutes to upload.

For some people, SkyDrive offers a safe haven where they'll always find their most important files. For others, though, SkyDrive brings yet another possible hiding place for that file they were working on last night. If you don't care for SkyDrive, buy a flash drive, store your files there, and keep the flash drive in your pocket.

Accessing files with the SkyDrive app

To add, view, or download files you've stored on SkyDrive from the Start screen's SkyDrive app, as well as to add your own, follow these steps:

1. **From the Start screen, open the SkyDrive app.**

    When opened, the SkyDrive app (shown in Figure 5-12) may react any of several different ways:

    - If your Internet connection is working, the SkyDrive app appears onscreen. No Internet connection? Head for Chapter 9 to set one up.

    - If you've never used SkyDrive, the app will be empty: Until you add files, there's nothing to view or download.

    - If you've already uploaded files to SkyDrive, you'll see them waiting for you, just as if they were in a "real" folder.

    - If Windows tells you to sign in with a Microsoft account, visit Chapter 2, where I explain how to create one.

    When opened, SkyDrive lists your stored folders along the left edge and your files along the right.

2. **To copy files from your computer to SkyDrive, choose Upload and locate the desired files on your computer.**

To add files, right-click a blank part of the SkyDrive program; when the app's menu appears along the screen's bottom edge, choose Upload (shown in the margin). The Start screen's File Picker appears, shown in Figure 5-13, ready for you to choose the files you'd like to store in the clouds.

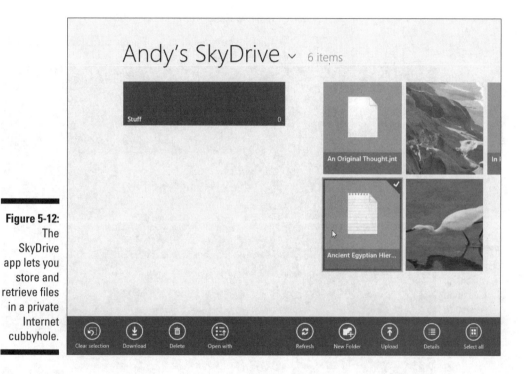

Figure 5-12:
The SkyDrive app lets you store and retrieve files in a private Internet cubbyhole.

Click a folder to see its contents; to move to other folders, click the Go Up button along the top. Click the Go Up button enough times, and you end up looking at four top-level folders: Libraries, Homegroups, your user account's folders, and Computer. From there, you can click back down to your desired folder.

When you spot the folder containing the files you want, click it to open it and see its files.

3. Choose the files you'd like to upload to SkyDrive.

Click the files you'd like to upload; if you click one by mistake, click it again to remove it from the upload list. Each time you click a file, SkyDrive adds the file to its upload list, shown along the app's bottom edge in Figure 5-13.

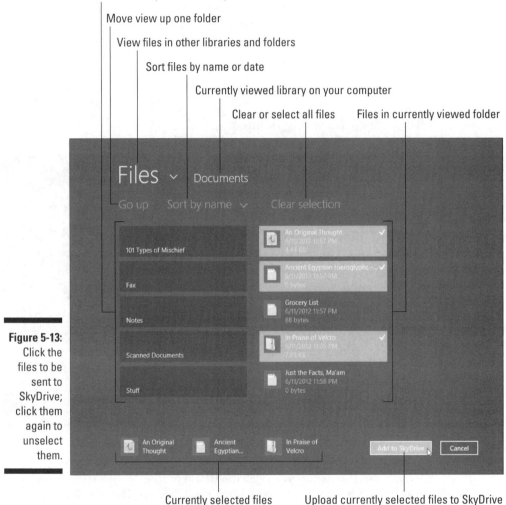

Folders in currently viewed library

Move view up one folder

View files in other libraries and folders

Sort files by name or date

Currently viewed library on your computer

Clear or select all files   Files in currently viewed folder

Figure 5-13:
Click the
files to be
sent to
SkyDrive;
click them
again to
unselect
them.

Currently selected files   Upload currently selected files to SkyDrive

Jump to another folder and click more files; SkyDrive adds those file to
the list along the bottom, as well.

4. **Click the Add to SkyDrive button.**

SkyDrive begins uploading your selected files to the sky. Documents float up there pretty quickly, but digital music and photos can take a lot of time.

The SkyDrive app makes it fairly easy to open files you've already uploaded to the cloud, but it offers little control. For more features, visit SkyDrive from your desktop's web browser, a chore described in the next section.

✔ To open a file from the SkyDrive app, click it: The file opens, just as if it still lived on your own computer.

 ✔ To copy a file from SkyDrive to your own computer, right-click the desired file. Then, when the menu appears along the app's bottom, choose Download (shown in the margin). The File Picker app appears, shown earlier in Figure 5-13, letting you choose one of your computer's folders to receive the incoming file.

✔ To delete a file from the SkyDrive app, right-click the unwanted file. When the bottom menu appears, click the button (shown in the margin).

Accessing SkyDrive from the desktop

If the Start screen's SkyDrive app is too simple for your needs, head for the Windows desktop and visit the SkyDrive website at `http://skydrive.live.com`.

Shown in Figure 5-14, the SkyDrive website offers much more control when shuttling files between your computer and the cloud. From the SkyDrive website, you can add, delete, move, and rename files, as well as create folders and move files between folders.

For best results, use the SkyDrive website to upload and manage your files. After you've stocked SkyDrive with your favorite files, use the Start screen's SkyDrive app to access the particular files you need.

 For even more control over SkyDrive and your files, download the SkyDrive for Windows program from `http://apps.live.com/skydrive`. The desktop program creates a special folder on your computer that mirrors what's stored on SkyDrive. That makes SkyDrive particularly easy to use: Whenever you change the contents of that special folder on your computer, Windows automatically updates SkyDrive, as well.

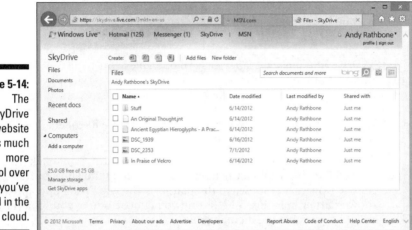

Figure 5-14:
The
SkyDrive
website
offers much
more
control over
files you've
stored in the
cloud.

Part II
Working with Programs, Apps, and Files

The 5th Wave   By Rich Tennant

"So far he's called up a cobra, 2 pythons, and a bunch of skinks, but not the file we're looking for."

In this part . . .

The first part of the book explains how to manipulate Windows 8 by poking and prodding its sensitive parts with the mouse or, on a touchscreen, your fingers.

This part of the book finally lets you get some work done. For example, here's where you find out how to run programs and Start screen apps, open existing files, create and save your own files, and print your work when you're through.

A primer details the Windows essentials: copying information from one window or program and pasting it into another.

And when some of your files wander (it's unavoidable), Chapter 7 explains how to unleash Windows's robotic search hounds to track them down and bring them within reach.

Chapter 6

Playing with Programs, Apps, and Documents

*1*n Windows, *programs* and *apps* are your tools: Load a program or app, and you can add numbers, arrange words, and shoot spaceships.

Documents, by contrast, are the things you create with apps and programs: tax forms, heartfelt apologies, and lists of high scores.

This chapter explains the basics of opening programs and apps from the new, tile-filled Start screen in Windows 8. It explains how to find and download a new app from the Start screen's Store app. It also shows you where to find an app's menus because Microsoft mysteriously hid them.

As you flip the chapter's pages, you figure out how to make your *preferred* program open your files. You also create desktop *shortcuts* — buttons that let you load desktop programs without visiting the tile-filled Start screen.

The chapter ends with the "Absolutely Essential Guide to Cutting, Copying, and Pasting." Put this one trick under your belt, and you'll be well on your way to dealing with nearly every situation Windows tosses your way.

Starting a Program or App

Windows 8 banished the Start button from its oft-clicked spot on the desktop's bottom-left corner. Microsoft prefers to say, however, that it has *expanded* the Start button, turning it into a full-screen launching pad for your programs.

I explain the giant new Start screen, shown in Figure 6-1, in Chapter 2, as well as how to customize it, adding or removing tiles to ensure you find things more easily.

Figure 6-1: From this Start screen, click the tile for the program you want to open.

But even though the Start screen lives in a new place, it still lets you launch programs or apps by following these steps:

1. Open the Start screen.

Because there's no longer a Start button, you can summon the Start screen any of these ways:

- **Mouse:** Point your mouse in the screen's bottom-left corner and then click when the Start icon appears.

- **Keyboard:** Press the Windows key (⊞).

• **Touchscreen:** Slide your finger inward from your screen's right edge and then tap the Start icon.

The Start screen appears, shown earlier in Figure 6-1, bringing a screen full of tiles representing many of your apps and programs. (I explain how to add or remove tiles to the Start screen in Chapter 2.)

2. **If you spot the tile for your program or app, choose it with a mouse click or, on a touchscreen, a tap of a finger.**

Don't see a tile for your sought-after program on the Start screen's list? Move to the next step.

3. **Scroll to the screen's right to see more tiles.**

The Start screen always opens to display the tiles on its farthest left edge. To see the apps and programs hiding from view, point at the screen's right edge with your mouse cursor; the rest of the Start screen's tiles begin scrolling into view.

If you're a touchscreen owner, you can view the tiles by sliding your finger across the screen to the left.

Still don't see your program or app listed? Head for Step 4.

4. **View *all* your apps.**

The Start screen shows apps first, followed by desktop programs. But to keep the list from stretching down the hallway, the Start screen doesn't list everything.

To reveal them *all*, right-click a blank part of the Start screen and then choose All Apps. All your apps appear listed by name and icon, followed by alphabetical lists of desktop programs, organized by categories. (Your most recently installed desktop programs always appear on the farthest right edge.)

To see all your apps on a touchscreen, slide your finger upward from the screen's bottom edge and click the All Apps icon.

If you *still* can't find your program on the admittedly crowded Start screen, follow these tips for other ways to open an app or program:

✔ While you view the Start screen, begin typing the missing program's name. As you type the first letter, the Start screen clears, presenting a list names beginning with that letter. Type a second or third letter, and the list of matches shrinks accordingly. When you spot the app or program you want, open it with a double-click (or a touch on a touchscreen.)

✔ Open File Explorer from the Start screen, choose Documents from the Navigation Pane along the window's left edge, and double-click the file you want to open. The correct program automatically opens with that file in tow. (And if the *wrong* program opens it, head to this chapter's "Choosing Which Program Should Open Which File" section.)

✔ Double-click a *shortcut* to the program. Shortcuts, which often sit on your desktop, are handy, disposable buttons for launching files and folders. (I explain more about shortcuts in this chapter's "Taking the Lazy Way with a Desktop Shortcut" section.)

✔ While you're on the desktop, you may spot the program's icon on the *taskbar* — a handy strip of icons lazily lounging along your desktop's bottom edge. If so, click the taskbar icon, and the program leaps into action. (I cover the desktop's taskbar, including how to customize its row of handy icons, in Chapter 3.)

✔ Right-click on the Windows desktop, choose New, and select the type of document you want to create. Windows 8 loads the right program for the job.

Windows offers other ways to open a program, but the preceding methods usually get the job done. (I cover the Start screen more extensively in Chapter 2; the desktop is the star of Chapter 3.)

Opening a Document

Like Tupperware, Windows 8 is a big fan of standardization. Almost all Windows programs load their documents — often called *files* — exactly the same way:

1. **Click the word File on the program's *menu bar,* that row of staid words along the program's top.**

   If your program hides its menu bar, pressing the Alt key often reveals it.

   Still no menu bar? Then your program might have a *Ribbon,* a thick strip of multicolored icons along the window's top. If you spot the Ribbon, click the tab or button in its leftmost corner to let the File menu tumble down.

2. **When the File menu drops down, choose Open.**

   Windows gives you a sense of déjà vu with the Open window, shown in Figure 6-2: It looks (and works) just like your Documents library, which I cover in Chapter 5.

   There's one big difference, however: This time, your folder displays only files that your particular program knows how to open — it filters out all the others.

3. **Point at your desired document, shown in Figure 6-2; click the mouse button; and click the Open button.**

On a touchscreen, tap the document to open it.

The program opens the file and displays it on the screen.

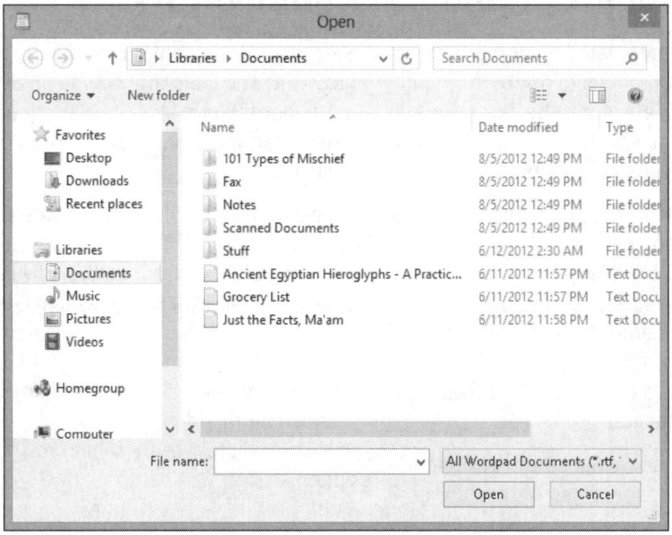

Figure 6-2:
Double-click
the filename
you want to
open.

Opening a file works this way in most Windows programs, whether written by Microsoft, its corporate partners, or the teenager down the street.

✔ To speed things up, double-click a desired file's name; that opens it immediately, automatically closing the Open window.

✔ If your file isn't listed by name, start browsing by clicking the buttons or words shown along the left side of Figure 6-2. Click the Documents library, for example, to see files stored inside.

✔ Humans store things in the garage, but computers store their files in neatly labeled compartments called *folders*. (Double-click a folder to see what's stored inside; if you spot your file, open it with a double-click.) If browsing folders gives you trouble, the folders section in Chapter 5 offers a refresher.

✔ Whenever you open a file and change it, even by accident, Windows 8 assumes that you've changed the file for the better. If you try to close the file, Windows 8 cautiously asks whether you want to save your changes. If you updated the file with masterful wit, click Yes. If you made a mess or opened the wrong file, click No or Cancel.

✔ Confused about any icons or commands along the Open window's top or left side? Rest your mouse pointer over the icons, and a little box announces their occupations.

When programmers fight over file types

When not fighting over fast food, programmers fight over *formats* — ways to pack information into a file. To tiptoe around the format wars, most programs let you open files stored in several different types of formats.

For example, look at the drop-down list box in the bottom-right corner of Figure 6-2. It currently lists All WordPad Documents (*.rtf), one of several formats used by WordPad. To see files stored in *other* formats, click in that box and choose a different format. The Open box quickly updates its list to show files from that new format, instead.

And how can you see a list of *all* your folder's files in that menu, regardless of their format?

Select All Documents from the drop-down list box. That switches the view to show all of that particular folder's files. Your program probably can't open them all, though, and it will choke while trying.

For example, WordPad may include some digital photos in its All Documents view. But if you try to open a photo, WordPad dutifully displays the photo as obscure coding symbols. (If you ever mistakenly open a photo in a program and *don't* see the photo, don't try to save what you've opened. If the program is like WordPad, saving the file will ruin the photo. Simply turn tail and exit immediately with a click on the Cancel button.)

Saving a Document

Saving means to send the work you've just created to a hard drive, flash drive, or disc for safekeeping. Unless you specifically save your work, your computer thinks that you've just been fiddling around for the past four hours. You must specifically tell the computer to save your work before it will safely store it.

Thanks to Microsoft snapping leather whips, a Save command appears in every Windows 8 program, no matter what programmer wrote it. Here are a few ways to save a file:

  ✔ Click File on the top menu, choose Save, and save your document in your Documents folder or to your desktop for easy retrieval later. (Pressing the Alt key, followed by the letter F and the letter S does the same thing.)

  ✔ Click the Save icon (shown in the margin).

  ✔ Hold down Ctrl and press S. (S stands for *Save.*)

What's the difference between Save and Save As?

Huh? Save as *what?* A chemical compound? Naw, the Save As command just gives you a chance to save your work with a different name and in a different location.

Suppose that you open the *Ode to Tina* file and change a few sentences. You want to save your new changes, but you don't want to lose the original words, either. Preserve *both* versions by selecting *Save As* and typing the new name, *Tentative Additions to Ode to Tina.*

When you're saving something for the *first* time, the Save and Save As commands are identical: Both make you choose a fresh name and location for your work.

The Save As command also lets you save a file in a different *format.* You can save your original copy in your favorite format, but save a copy in a different format for a friend clinging to older software that requires a format from yesteryear.

If you're saving something for the first time, Windows 8 asks you to think up a name for your document. Type something descriptive using only letters, numbers, and spaces between the words. (If you try to use one of the illegal characters I describe in Chapter 5, the Windows Police step in, politely requesting that you use a different name.)

✔ Choose descriptive filenames for your work. Windows 8 gives you 255 characters to work with. A file named *Report on June 2012 Squeegee Sales* is easier to locate than one named *Stuff.*

✔ You can save files to any folder, CD, DVD, or even a flash drive. But files are much easier to find down the road when they stay in one of Windows' four main libraries: Documents, Music, Pictures, or Videos. (Those four libraries are listed on the left of every folder.)

✔ Most programs can save files directly to a CD or DVD. Choose Save from the File menu and choose your preferred drive from the right-pane's Computer section. Put a disc (preferably one that's not already filled) into your disc-writing drive to start the process.

✔ If you're working on something important (and most things are), click the program's Save command every few minutes. Or use the Ctrl+S keyboard shortcut. (While holding down the Ctrl key, press the S key.) Programs make you choose a name and location for a file when you *first* save it; subsequent saves are much speedier.

Choosing Which Program Should Open Which File

Most of the time, Windows 8 automatically knows which program should open which file. Double-click a file, and Windows tells the correct program to jump in and let you view its contents.

But sometimes Windows doesn't choose your preferred program, and that holds especially true for Windows 8. For example, the app-loving Windows 8 tells the Start screen's Music app to play your music. You may prefer that the desktop's Windows Media Player handle the music-playing chores, instead.

When the wrong program opens your file, here's how to make the *right* program open it instead:

1. **Right-click your problematic file and choose Open With from the pop-up menu.**

   As shown in Figure 6-3, Windows lists a few capable programs, including ones you've used to open that file in the past.

   If a different window says, "Try an app on this PC" or "Look for an app in the Store," jump ahead to Step 4.

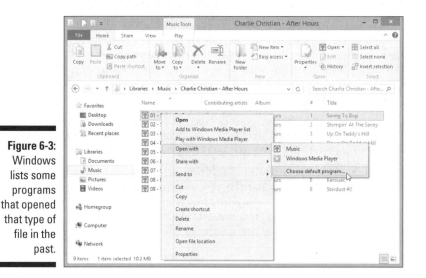

Figure 6-3: Windows lists some programs that opened that type of file in the past.

2. **Click Choose Default Program and select the program you want to open the file.**

   A window appears, shown in Figure 6-4, that lists more programs, with the currently assigned program appearing at the list's top. If you spot your favorite program, double-click to tell it to open your file. (Make sure the Use This App for All Files check box is selected; it's usually selected by default.)

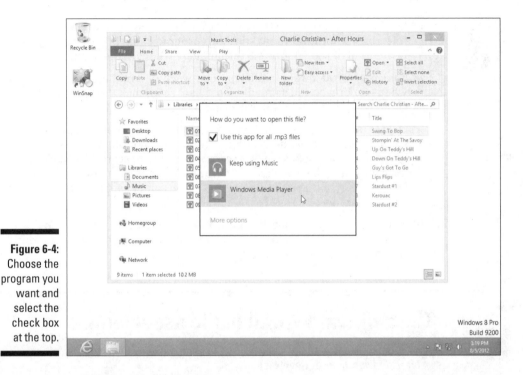

Figure 6-4:
Choose the program you want and select the check box at the top.

Don't see the program you want or need to open the file? Move to Step 3.

3. Click the More Options link at the bottom of the list in Figure 6-4.

In a bit of tomfoolery, Windows lists *all* of your programs — even ones that couldn't open the file if they tried. If you happen to spot your desired program, click it. Chances are good, though, that you'll move on to Step 4.

4. Choose an option.

Clicking the More Options link in the previous step reveals two more options at the bottom of the list:

- **Look for an App in the Store:** This opens the Store app, where you can search for an app to open your file. The Store app leaves you at a virtual shelf stocked with apps capable of opening the file.

- **Look for Another App on This PC:** A tidbit tossed in for techies, this option drops you into a File Explorer folder that lists all of your installed desktop programs by folder name. Choose this option *only* if you already know exactly where your desired program file lives. Otherwise, you'll be lost.

If you install a new program or app to open a particular file, the newcomer usually assigns itself the rights to open that type of file in the future. If it doesn't, head back to Step 1. This time, however, your newly installed program or app will appear on the list. Choose it, and you've *finally* finished.

✔ In a bit of revisionist history, Windows 8 uses the term *app* when referring to both traditional desktop programs and Start screen apps. Be mindful of the Windows 8 terminology when on the desktop.

✔ Sometimes you'll want to alternate between different apps or programs when working on the same file. To do so, right-click the file, choose Open With, and select the program you need at that time.

✔ Occasionally, you can't make your favorite program open a particular file because it simply doesn't know how. For example, Windows Media Player can play most videos, *except* when they're stored in QuickTime, a format used by Microsoft's competition. Your only solution is to install QuickTime (www.apple.com/quicktime) and use it to open that particular video.

✔ If somebody says something about "file associations," feel free to browse the technical sidebar, "The awkward world of file associations," which explains that awful subject.

The awkward world of file associations

Every Windows program slaps a secret code known as a *file extension* onto the name of every file it creates. The file extension works like a cattle brand: When you double-click the file, Windows 8 eyeballs the extension and automatically summons the proper program to open the file. Notepad, for example, tacks on the three-letter extension .txt to every file it creates. So, Windows associates the .txt extension with Notepad.

Windows 8 normally doesn't display these extensions, isolating users from Windows' inner mechanisms for safety reasons. If somebody accidentally changes or removes an extension, Windows won't know how to open that file.

If you're curious about what an extension looks like, sneak a peek by following these steps:

1. **Click the View tab from atop any folder.**

   The menu quickly changes across the folder's top, showing different ways to view that folder's contents.

2. **Select the File Name Extensions check box.**

   The files inside the folder immediately change to show their extensions — a handy thing to know in technical emergencies.

Now that you've peeked, hide the extensions again by repeating the steps, but deselect the File Name Extensions check box.

Warning: Don't change a file's extension unless you know exactly what you're doing; Windows 8 will forget what program to use for opening the file, leaving you holding an empty bag.

Navigating the Windows Store

Apps, which are miniprograms specialized for single tasks, come from the world of *smartphones*: computerized cellphones.

Apps differ from traditional desktop programs in several ways:

- ✔ Apps consume the entire screen; programs run within windows on the desktop.

- ✔ App are tied to your Microsoft account. That means you need a Microsoft account to download a free or paid app from the Store app.

- ✔ When you download an app from the Windows 8 Store app, you can run it on up to five PCs or devices — as long as you're signed in to those PCs or devices with your Windows account.

- ✔ When installed, programs tend to sprinkle several tiles onto your Start screen. Apps, by contrast, consume just one tile, reducing Start screen bloat.

Apps and programs can be created and sold by large companies, as well as by basement-dwelling hobbyists working in their spare time.

Although desktop programs and Start screen apps look and behave differently, Microsoft unfortunately refers to both as *apps* in Windows 8. You'll run across this terminology quirk when dealing with older programs, as well as newer programs created by companies not hip to Microsoft's new lingo.

Adding new apps from the Store app

When you're tired of the apps bundled with Windows 8 or you need a new app to fill a special need, follow these steps to bring one into your computer.

1. **Open the Store app from the Start screen.**

   Don't see the Start screen? Press your keyboard's ⊞ key to whisk your way there.

   The Store app fills the screen, as shown in Figure 6-5.

   The Store opens to show the Spotlight category, but scrolling to the right reveals many more categories, such as Games, Books and Reference, News and Weather, and others.

2. **To narrow your search, choose a category by clicking its name.**

   As you see more of the Store, you see several more ways to sort the available apps, as shown in Figure 6-6.

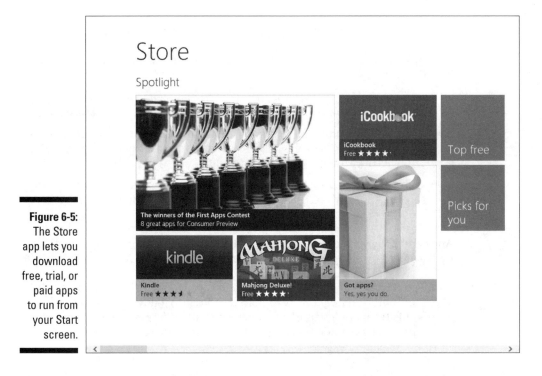

Figure 6-5:
The Store app lets you download free, trial, or paid apps to run from your Start screen.

3. **Sort by subcategory, price, and noteworthiness; and choose apps that look interesting.**

   For example, you can sort by subcategory, limiting the Games category to show only Card games.

   Some categories also let you sort by price, and you can choose Free, Paid, or Trial. And if you sort by noteworthiness, Microsoft shows you which apps are either Newest, have the Highest Rating, or Lowest Price. (Hedge fund managers may sort by Highest Price, as well.)

4. **Choose any app to read a more detailed description.**

   A page opens to show more detailed information, including its price tag, pictures of the app, reviews left by previous customers, and more technical information.

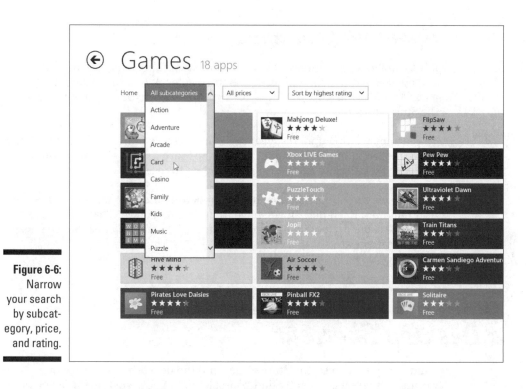

Figure 6-6:
Narrow
your search
by subcat-
egory, price,
and rating.

5. **Click Install, Buy, or Try button.**

   When you find a free app that you can't live without, click the Install button. Paid apps let you click either Buy or Try (a limited trial run). If you choose to install, try, or buy an app, its tile appears on your Start screen as quickly as your Internet connection speed allows.

   Newly downloaded apps appear in a group on the Start screen's far-right edge. I explain how to rearrange your Start screen in Chapter 2, bringing some order to the chaos.

Uninstalling apps

Downloaded a dud app? To uninstall any app from the Start screen, right-click its tile. When the menu bar rises up from the screen's bottom edge, click Uninstall (shown in the margin).

Uninstalling an app only removes that app from *your* account's Start screen. Your action won't affect other account holders who may have installed the app.

Updating your apps

Programmers constantly tweak their apps, smoothing over rough spots, adding new features, and plugging security holes. When the program releases an update for your app, the Store tells you about it by putting a number on the Store app's tile.

To grab any waiting updates, visit the Start screen's Store app. Then click the word Update(s) in the top-right corner. The Store lists all the apps requiring updates; click Update All to bring them all up-to-date.

Note: When you update an app, it's not updated for every account holder on the computer. Each person will have to update it, as well. That holds true for apps that came preinstalled on your computer, as well as ones you've chosen to install afterward.

Taking the Lazy Way with a Desktop Shortcut

Windows tries to keep the Start screen and the desktop in two separate worlds, but you'll constantly find yourself jumping between them. When you grow tired of meandering through the woods to find a program, folder, disk drive, document, or even a website, create a desktop *shortcut* — an icon that takes you directly to the object of your desires.

Calculator

Because a shortcut is a mere icon that launches something else, shortcuts are safe, convenient, and disposable. And they're easy to tell apart from the original, because they have a little arrow lodged in their bottom-left corner, such as the Calculator shortcut shown in the margin.

To skip the Start screen, follow these instructions to create desktop shortcuts to your oft-used items:

- ✔ **Folders or Documents:** On your desktop, right-click a favorite folder or document, choose Send To, and select the Desktop (Create Shortcut) option. The shortcut appears on your desktop.

- ✔ **Websites:** On the desktop version of Internet Explorer, see the little icon in front of the website's address in Internet Explorer's Address Bar? Drag and drop that little icon to your desktop for quick access later. You can also add websites to Internet Explorer's handy list of Favorites, which I describe in Chapter 9.

✔ **Control Panel:** Found a particularly helpful setting in the desktop's Control Panel, the mammoth switch box in Windows 8? Then drag that helpful setting's icon from the Control Panel onto your desktop, the Navigation Pane's Favorites area, or any other handy spot. The icon turns into a shortcut for easy access. (An easy way to access the Control Panel from the desktop is to right-click in the screen's bottom-left corner and choose Control Panel from the pop-up menu.)

✔ **Disk drives:** Open File Explorer from the Start screen. From the Navigation Pane along File Explorer's left side, right-click the drive you want and choose Create Shortcut. Windows immediately places a shortcut to that drive on your desktop.

Here are some more tips for desktop shortcuts:

✔ For quick CD or DVD burning, put a shortcut to your disc drive on your desktop. Burning files to disc becomes as simple as dragging and dropping them onto the disc drive's new shortcut. (Insert a blank disc into the disc drive's tray, confirm the settings, and begin burning your disc.)

Want to send a desktop shortcut to the Start screen? Right-click the desktop shortcut and choose Pin to Start; the item appears as a new Start screen tile. Click that tile on the Start screen to switch to the desktop, where your item awaits you.

✔ Feel free to move shortcuts from place to place but *don't* move the items they launch. If you do, the shortcut won't be able to find the item, causing Windows to panic, searching (usually vainly) for the moved goods.

✔ Want to see what program a shortcut will launch? Right-click the shortcut and click Open File Location (if available). The shortcut quickly takes you to its leader.

Absolutely Essential Guide to Cutting, Copying, and Pasting

Windows took a tip from the kindergartners and made *cut* and *paste* an integral part of computing life. You can electronically *cut* or *copy* just about anything and then *paste* it just about anyplace else with little fuss and even less mess.

For example, you can copy a photo and paste it onto your party invitation fliers. You can move files by cutting them from one folder and pasting them into another. And you can easily cut and paste paragraphs to different locations within a word processor.

The beauty of the Windows desktop is that, with all those windows onscreen at the same time, you can easily grab bits and pieces from any of them and paste all the parts into a brand-new window.

Don't overlook copying and pasting for the small stuff. Copying a name and an address is much quicker than typing them into your letter by hand. Or, when somebody e-mails you a web address, copy and paste it directly into Internet Explorer's Address Bar. It's easy to copy most items displayed on websites, too (much to the dismay of many professional photographers).

The quick 'n' dirty guide to cut 'n' paste

In compliance with the Don't Bore Me with Details Department, here's a quick guide to the three basic steps used for cutting, copying, and pasting:

1. **Select the item to cut or copy: a few words, a file, a web address, or any other item.**

2. **Right-click your selection and choose Cut or Copy from the menu, depending on your needs.**

   Use *Cut* when you want to *move* something. Use *Copy* when you want to *duplicate* something, leaving the original intact.

   Keyboard shortcut: Hold down Ctrl and press X to cut or C to copy.

3. **Right-click the item's destination and choose Paste.**

   You can right-click inside a document, folder, or nearly any other place.

   Keyboard shortcut: Hold down Ctrl and press V to paste.

The next three sections explain each of these three steps in more detail.

Selecting things to cut or copy

Before you can shuttle pieces of information to new places, you have to tell Windows 8 exactly what you want to grab. The easiest way to tell it is to *select* the information with a mouse. In most cases, selecting involves one swift trick with the mouse, which then highlights whatever you've selected.

✔ **To select text in a document, website, or spreadsheet:** Put the mouse arrow or cursor at the beginning of the information you want and hold down the mouse button. Then move the mouse to the end of the information and release the button. That's it! That selects all the stuff lying between where you clicked and released, as shown in Figure 6-7.

On a touchscreen, double-tap one word to select it. To extend your selection, touch the highlighted word again, keeping your finger pressed on the glass. Slide your finger along the glass until you've reached the area where the highlighting should stop. Done? Remove your finger to select that portion of text.

Be careful after you highlight a bunch of text. If you accidentally press the K key, for example, the program replaces your highlighted text with the letter *k*. To reverse that calamity, choose Undo from the program's Edit menu (or press Ctrl+Z, which is the keyboard shortcut for Undo).

Figure 6-7:
Windows
highlights
the selected
text,
changing
its color
for easy
visibility.

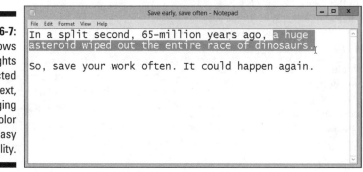

✔ **To select any files or folders:** Simply click a file or folder to select it. To select *several* items, try these tricks:

• **If all the files are in a row:** Click the first item in the bunch, hold down the Shift key, and then select the last item. Windows highlights the first and last items, as well as everything in between.

• **If the files *aren't* in a row:** Hold down the Ctrl key while clicking each file or folder you want to select.

Now that you've selected the item, the next section explains how to cut or copy it.

✔ After you've selected something, cut it or copy it *immediately.* If you absentmindedly click the mouse someplace else, your highlighted text or file reverts to its boring self, and you're forced to start over.

✔ To delete any selected item, be it a file, paragraph, or picture, press the Delete key. Or right-click the item and choose Delete from the pop-up menu.

Selecting individual letters, words, paragraphs, and more

When dealing with words in Windows, these shortcuts help you quickly select information:

✔ To select an individual *letter or character,* click in front of the character. Then while holding down the Shift key, press your → key. Keep holding down these two keys to keep selecting text in a line.

✔ To select a single *word,* point at it with the mouse and double-click. The word changes color, meaning it's highlighted. (In most word processors, you can hold down the button on its second click, and then by moving the mouse around, you can quickly highlight additional text word by word.)

✔ To select a single *line* of text, simply click next to it in the left margin. To highlight

additional text line by line, keep holding down the mouse button and move the mouse up or down. You can also keep selecting additional lines by holding down the Shift key and pressing the ↓ key or the ↑ key.

✔ To select a *paragraph,* just double-click next to it in the left margin. To highlight additional text paragraph by paragraph, keep holding down the mouse button on the second click and move the mouse.

✔ To select an entire *document,* hold down Ctrl and press A. (Or choose Select All from the Edit menu.)

Cutting or copying your selected goods

After you select some information (which I describe in the preceding section, in case you just arrived), you're ready to start playing with it. You can cut it or copy it. (Or just press Delete to delete it.)

This bears repeating. After selecting something, right-click it. (On a touchscreen, touch it and hold down your finger to fetch the pop-up menu.) When the menu appears, choose Cut or Copy, depending on your needs, as shown in Figure 6-8. Then right-click your destination and choose Paste.

The Cut and Copy options differ drastically. How do you know which one to choose?

> ✔ **Choose Cut to *move* information.** Cutting wipes the selected informa-
> tion off the screen, but you haven't lost anything: Windows stores the
> cut information in a hidden Windows storage tank called the *Clipboard,*
> waiting for you to paste it.

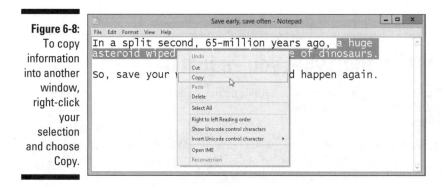

Figure 6-8: To copy information into another window, right-click your selection and choose Copy.

Feel free to cut and paste entire files to different folders. When you cut a file from a folder, the icon dims until you paste it. (Making the icon disappear would be too scary.) Changed your mind in mid-cut? Press Esc to cancel the cut, and the icon reverts to normal.

✓ **Choose Copy to make a copy of the information.** Compared with cutting, *copying* information is quite anticlimactic. Whereas cutting removes the item from view, copying the selected item leaves it in the window, seemingly untouched. Copied information also goes to the Clipboard until you paste it.

To save a picture of your entire screen, press ⊞+PrtScr. (Some keyboards call that key *Print Screen* or *PrintScr.*) Windows quickly saves the image in a file called Screenshot inside your Pictures library. Do it again, and the screenshot is named Screenshot (2). (You get the idea.)

Pasting information to another place

After you cut or copy information to the Windows Clipboard, it's checked in and ready for travel. You can *paste* that information nearly anyplace else.

Pasting is relatively straightforward:

1. **Open the destination window and move the mouse pointer or cursor to the spot where you want the stuff to appear.**

2. **Right-click the mouse and choose Paste from the pop-up menu.**

   Presto! The item you just cut or copied immediately leaps into its new spot.

Undoing what you've just done

Windows 8 offers a way for you to undo your last action, which quickly pours the spilled milk back into the carton:

Hold down the Ctrl key and press the Z key. The last mistake you made is reversed, sparing you from further shame. (Pressing a program's

Undo button, if you can find one, does the same thing.)

And, should you mistakenly undo something that really should have stayed in place, press Ctrl+Y. That undoes your last undo, putting it back in place.

Or, if you want to paste a file onto the desktop, right-click on the desktop and choose Paste. The cut or copied file appears where you've right-clicked.

✔ The Paste command inserts a *copy* of the information that's sitting on the Clipboard. The information stays on the Clipboard, so you can keep pasting the same thing into other places if you want.

✔ To paste on a touchscreen, hold down your finger where you'd like to paste the information. When the menu pops up, tap Paste.

✔ Some programs, including File Explorer, have toolbars along their tops, offering one-click access to the Cut, Copy, and Paste buttons, as shown in Figure 6-9. (Hint: Look on File Explorer's Home tab.)

Figure 6-9:
The Cut, Copy, and Paste commands in the new Ribbon menu (left) and traditional menu (right).

Chapter 7

Finding the Lost

*S*ooner or later, Windows 8 gives you that head-scratching feeling. "Golly," you say, as you drum nervous fingers, "that stuff was *right there* a second ago. Where did it go?"

When Windows 8 starts playing hide-and-seek, this chapter tells you where to search and how to make it stop playing foolish games.

Finding Currently Running Start Screen Apps

By nature, Start screen apps fill the screen. Switch to another app, and *it* fills the screen, shoving away the previous app. Because the Start screen shows only one app at a time, your other running apps remain hidden beneath an invisibility cloak.

When you switch to the desktop, you're in yet another world, away from the land of apps. How do you return to an app you just used?

To solve that problem, Windows 8 can reveal a list of your recently used apps, complete with thumbnail photos, as shown in Figure 7-1. The list conveniently includes your desktop, letting you shuffle easily between apps and the desktop.

Figure 7-1:
Windows 8
lists recently
used apps
in a strip
along the
screen's left
edge; click
an app's
thumbnail to
return to it.

The thumbnail-filled strip pops up along the screen's left edge, and it's
available whether you're on the Start screen *or* the desktop.

To see that list of your recently used apps (and to close unwanted apps, if
desired), employ any of these tricks:

✔ **Mouse:** Point in the screen's top-right corner; when a thumbnail of your
last-used app appears, slide the mouse down the screen: The list of your
most-recently used apps sticks to the screen's left side. To switch to an
app, click it. To close an app, right-click its thumbnail and choose Close.

✔ **Keyboard:** Press ⊞+Tab to see the list of your most recently used apps,
as shown in Figure 7-1. While still holding down the ⊞ key, press the
Tab key; each press of the Tab key highlights a different app on the list.
When you've highlighted your desired app, release the ⊞ key, and the
app fills the screen. (Highlighted an app you want to close? Then press
the Del key.)

✔ **Touchscreen:** Slide your finger gently inward from the screen's left edge. When the last-used app begins to appear, slide back toward the left edge; the list of recently used apps sticks to the left edge. Tap any app on the strip to make it fill the screen. To close an unwanted app, slide your finger from the screen's top to the screen's bottom until the app vanishes, like water off a cliff.

This trick reveals currently running *apps,* but not desktop *programs.* That's because Windows 8 treats your desktop as a single app: No matter how many desktop programs you may have running, the left strip shows only a single app for the desktop. (To find currently running programs, head for the next section.)

Finding Lost Windows on the Desktop

As opposed to the full-screen Start screen, the Windows 8 desktop works much like a spike memo holder. Every time you open a new window or program, you toss another piece of information onto the spike. The window on top is easy to spot, but how do you reach the windows lying beneath it?

If you can see any part of a buried window's edge or corner, a well-placed click will fetch it, bringing it to the top.

When your window is completely buried, look at the desktop's taskbar — that strip along your screen's bottom edge. Spot your missing window's name on the taskbar? Click it to dredge it back to the top. (See Chapter 3 for details about the taskbar.)

Still can't get at that missing window? Hold down the Alt key and press Tab. Shown in Figure 7-2, Windows 8 shows thumbnails of all your open windows, programs, *and* apps. While holding down the Alt key, repeatedly press Tab (or roll your mouse's scroll wheel); the highlighted app or window fills your screen with each press of the Tab key.

Spot your window? Let go of the Alt key, and that window appears atop your desktop.

If you're convinced a window is open but you still can't find it, spread all your windows across the desktop by right-clicking a blank spot on the task-bar along the desktop's bottom and choosing Show Windows Side By Side from the pop-up menu. It's a last resort, but perhaps you'll spot your missing window in the lineup.

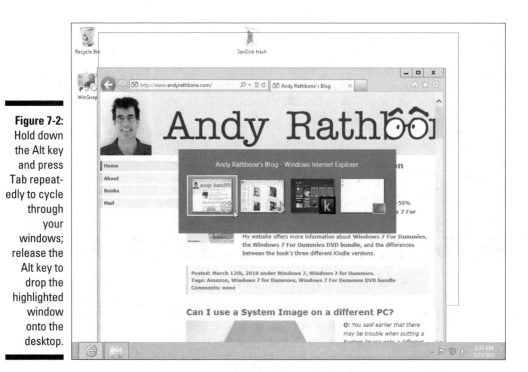

Figure 7-2:
Hold down the Alt key and press Tab repeatedly to cycle through your windows; release the Alt key to drop the highlighted window onto the desktop.

Locating a Missing App, Program, Setting, or File

The preceding two sections explain how to find *currently running* apps and programs. But what about things that you haven't looked at for a while?

To help you find lost apps, wandering files, hidden settings, or even things like missing e-mail, Windows 8 offers an easily searchable index. To begin searching, fetch the Charms bar's Search icon. You can do that any of three ways:

✔ **Mouse:** Move the mouse pointer to the screen's top- or bottom-right corner; when the Charms bar appears, click the Search icon.

✔ **Keyboard:** Press ⊞+Q to both summon the Charms bar *and* open the Charm bar's Search pane.

✔ **Touchscreen:** Slide your finger inward from the screen's right edge; when the Charms bar appears, tap the Search icon.

All those methods summon the Windows 8 Search pane, shown in Figure 7-3, so you can search your computer. To search for missing things, follow these steps:

1. **Click the category you'd like to search.**

   Unlike Windows 7, Windows 8 doesn't search your entire computer, subsequently listing every match. Instead, Windows 8 first makes you specify what *category* you want to search. Route your search to any one of the categories shown earlier in Figure 7-3 by clicking its name:

   - **Apps:** The default choice in Windows 8; this searches for both Start screen apps and desktop programs. Should you begin typing letters directly onto the Start screen, Windows 8 quickly chooses this option automatically and begins listing matching apps and programs.

   - **Settings:** This lets you search through the zillions of settings in both the desktop's Control Panel and the Start screen's PC Settings pane. It's a handy way to find settings dealing with only fonts, for example, keyboards, backups, or other technicalities.

   - **Files:** An oft-chosen option, choose this to locate a specific file on your computer's hard drive.

• **A Particular App:** Below the three main categories — Apps, Settings, and Files — the Search pane lists names of apps, shown earlier in Figure 7-3. To route a search to your mailbox, for example, choose the Mail app. The Mail app opens, and the Search pane continues to hug the screen's right edge, waiting for you to type in your search.

2. **Type your search term into the white box, shown earlier in Figure 7-3.**

Type a word or phrase that appears somewhere inside your chosen category.

As soon as you begin typing, the Start screen begins listing matches. With each letter you type, Windows 8 whittles down the list. After you type enough letters, your lost item floats alone to the top of the list.

For example, searching for the first few word of **Lester Young** in the File category, as shown in Figure 7-4, lists every mention of Lester Young on my PC.

Figure 7-4: Type the first few letters or words of what you're seeking, and Windows 8 lists possible matches.

No matches? Then Windows didn't find your lost item, unfortunately. Try searching for fewer words, or even portions of words.

3. **Click a match or press Enter after typing your word or phrase; and Windows shows all matching files, settings, or apps.**

Windows 8 lists detailed information about all the matching items, as shown in Figure 7-5. Click a match, and Windows brings it to the screen.

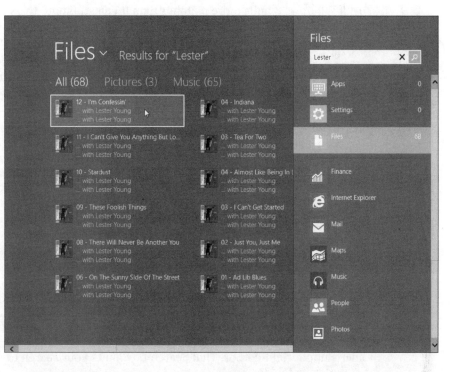

4. **Choose a matching item to open it, bringing it the screen.**

   Click a song, for example, and it begins playing. Click a Setting, and the Control Panel or PC Settings window appears, open to your setting's contents. Click a letter, and it opens in your word processor.

   ✔ The Windows 8 index includes every file in your Documents, Music, Pictures, and Videos libraries, which makes storing your files in those folders more important than ever. (Windows 8 doesn't let you search through private files stored in accounts of *other* people who may be using your PC.)

   ✔ The index *doesn't* include files stored in other places, such as flash drives or external drives. To add those places to your index, add them to your libraries. (I cover libraries in Chapter 5.)

   ✔ If you're searching for a common word and Windows 8 turns up too many files, limit your search by typing a short phrase from your sought-after file: **Shortly after the cat nibbled the bamboo**, for example. The more words you type, the better your chances of pinpointing a particular file.

✔ The search box ignores capital letters. It considers **Bee** and **bee** to be the same insect.

✔ If Windows 8 finds more matches than it can stuff onto the screen, the entries will scroll off to the right. Figure 7-5, for example, shows only the first few songs featuring Lester Young; to see the rest, scroll to the screen's right.

✔ Keyboard hounds can search only *Files* by pressing ⊞+F; search for *Settings* by pressing ⊞+W; and search through your *Apps* and programs by pressing ⊞+Q.

✔ Want to route your search to the entire Internet rather than your particular PC? Then choose Internet Explorer as your category in Step 1. The Search pane will route your search through Bing, Microsoft's search engine. (I describe how to choose your favorite search engine in Chapter 9.)

Finding a Missing File inside a Desktop Folder

The Start screen's Search pane probes the entire Windows 8 index, which includes a *lot* of information. But that's overkill when you're poking around inside a single desktop folder, looking for a missing file. To solve the "sea of files in a folder" problem, Windows 8 includes a Search box in every desktop folder's upper-right corner. That Search box limits your search to files within that *particular* folder.

To find a missing file within a specific folder, click inside that folder's Search box and begin typing a word or short phrase from your missing file. As you type letters and words, Windows 8 begins filtering out files that are missing your sought-after word or phrase. It keeps narrowing down the candidates until the folder displays only a few files, including, hopefully, your runaway file.

When a folder's Search box locates too many possible matches, bring in some other helping hands: the headers above each column. (For best results, select the Details option in the View tab's Layout group, which lines up your filenames in one column, as shown in Figure 7-6.) The first column, Name, lists the name of each file; the adjacent columns list specific details about each file.

See the column headers, such as Name, Date Modified, and Type, atop each column? Click any of those headers to sort your files by that term. Here's how to sort by some of the column headers in your Documents folder:

✔ **Name:** Know the first letter of your file's name? Then click here to sort your files alphabetically. You can then pluck your file from the list. (Click Name again to reverse the sort order.)

✔ **Date Modified:** When you remember the approximate date you last changed a document, click the Date Modified header. That places your newest files atop the list, making them easy to locate. (Clicking Date Modified again reverses the order, a handy way to weed out old files you may no longer need.)

✔ **Type:** This header sorts files by their contents. All your photos group together, for example, as do all your Word documents. It's a handy way to find a few stray photos swimming in a sea of text files.

✔ **Size:** Sorting here places your 45-page thesis on one end, with your grocery list on the other.

✔ **Authors:** Microsoft Word and other programs tack your name onto your work. A click on this label alphabetically sorts the files by their creators' names.

✔ **Tags:** Windows 8 often lets you assign tags to your documents and photos, a task I describe later in this chapter. Adding the tag "Moldy Cheese" to that pungent photo session lets you retrieve those pictures by either typing its tag or sorting a folder's files by their tags.

Whether you're viewing your files as thumbnails, icons, or filenames, the column headers always provide a handy way to sort your files quickly.

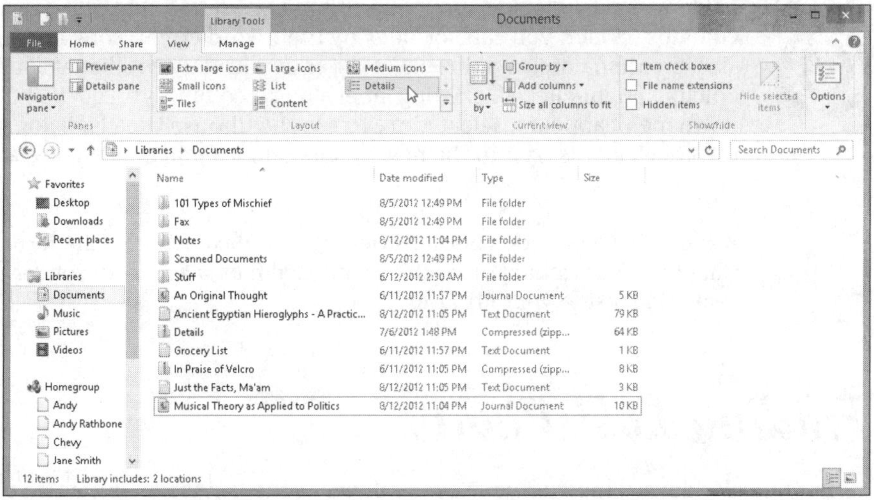

Figure 7-6:
Details view lets you sort your files by name, making them easier to find.

Deep sort

A folder's Details view (shown in Figure 7-6) arranges your files into a single column, with oodles of detail columns flowing off to the right. You can sort a folder's contents by clicking the word atop any column: Name, Date Modified, Author, and so on. But the sort features in Windows 8 go much deeper, as you'll notice when clicking the little downward-pointing arrow to the right of each column's name.

Click the little arrow by the words *Date Modified,* for example, and a calendar drops down. Click a date, and the folder quickly displays files modified on that particular date, filtering out all the rest. Beneath the calendar, check boxes also let you view files created Today, Yesterday, Last Week, Earlier This Month, Earlier This Year, or simply A Long Time Ago.

Similarly, click the arrow next to the Authors column header, and a drop-down menu lists the

authors of every document in the folder. Select the check boxes next to the author names you'd like to see, and Windows 8 immediately filters out files created by other people, leaving only the matches. (This feature works best with Microsoft Office documents.)

These hidden filters can be dangerous, however, because you can easily forget that you've turned them on. If you spot a check mark next to any column header, you've left a filter turned on, and the folder is hiding some of its files. To turn off the filter and see *all* that folder's files, deselect the check box next to the column header and examine the drop-down menu. Click any selected check boxes on that drop-down menu; that removes their check marks and removes the filter.

Folders usually display about five columns of details, but you can add more columns. In fact, you can sort files by their word count, song length, photo size, creation date, and dozens of other details. To see a list of available detail columns, right-click an existing label along a column's top. When the drop-down menu appears, select More to see the Choose Details dialog box. Click to put check marks next to the new detail columns you'd like to see and then click OK.

Folders living outside your libraries *aren't* indexed. (I explain libraries in Chapter 5.) Searching through nonindexed files takes *much* longer than searching inside your libraries.

Finding Lost Photos

Windows 8 indexes your e-mail down to the last word, but it can't tell the difference between photos of your cat and photos of your office party. When it comes to photos, the ID work lies in *your* hands, and these four tips make the chore as easy as possible:

✓ **Tag your photos.** When you connect your camera to your PC, as described in Chapter 17, Windows 8 graciously offers to copy your photos to your PC. Before copying, Windows 8 asks you to *tag* those pictures. That's your big chance to type a few words describing your photo session. Windows 8 indexes those words as a single tag, making the photos easier to retrieve later.

✓ **Store shooting sessions in separate folders.** The Windows 8 photo importing program automatically creates a new folder to store each session, named after the current date and the tag you choose. But if you're using some other program to dump photos, be sure to create a new folder for each session. Then name the folder with a short description of your session: Dog Walk, Kite Surfing, or Truffle Hunt. (Windows indexes the folders' names.)

View

✓ **Sort by date.** Have you stumbled onto a massive folder that's a huge mishmash of digital photos? Try this quick sorting trick: Click the View tab (shown in the margin) and choose Large Icons; the photos morph into identifiable thumbnails. Then, from the View tab menu, choose Sort By and select Date Taken. That sorts the photos by the date you snapped them, turning chaos into organization.

✓ **Rename your photos.** Instead of leaving your Tunisian vacation photos with their boring camera-given names like DSC_2421, DSC_2422, and so on, give them meaningful names: Select all the files in your Tunisia folder by clicking the Home tab on the Ribbon and clicking the Select All button. Then right-click the first picture, choose Rename, and type **Tunisia**. Windows names them as Tunisia, Tunisia (2), Tunisia (3), and so on. (If you messed up, press Ctrl+Z to undo the renaming.)

Following those four simple rules helps keep your photo collection from becoming a jumble of files.

Be *sure* to back up your digital photos to a portable hard drive, CDs, DVDs, or another backup method I describe in Chapter 13. If they're not backed up, you'll lose your family history when your PC's hard drive eventually crashes.

Finding Other Computers on a Network

A *network* is simply a group of connected PCs that can share things, such as your Internet connection, files, or a printer. Most people use a network every day without knowing it: Every time you check your e-mail, your PC connects to another PC on the Internet to grab your waiting messages.

Much of the time, you needn't care about the other PCs on your network. But when you want to find a connected PC, perhaps to grab files from the PC in your family room, Windows 8 is happy to help.

In fact, the Windows Homegroup system makes it easier than ever to share files with other Windows PCs. Creating a Homegroup is as simple as entering the same password on every connected PC.

To find a PC on your Homegroup or traditional network, open any folder and look at the bottom of the Navigation Pane along the folder's left edge, as shown in Figure 7-7.

Click Homegroup in the Navigation Pane to see a list of other Windows PCs in your Homegroup; click Network to see every PC that's connected to your own PC in a traditional (but more difficult to set up) network. To browse files on any of those PCs in either category, just double-click their names.

Figure 7-7:
To find computers connected to your PC through a network, click the Navigation Pane's Network category.

I walk through the steps of creating both your own Homegroup and home network in Chapter 15.

Finding Information on the Internet

The Charms bar's handy Search pane lets you quickly search for bits of information on your PC. But when you want to search the Internet, fire up your web browser. Windows 8 comes with two versions of Internet Explorer.

The Start screen's full-screen Internet Explorer works fine for quick searches. To search the web when it fills the screen, summon the Charms bar, click the Search icon, type your search into the search box at the top, and press Enter; Microsoft's Bing appears, listing the search results.

TECHNICAL STUFF

Rebuilding the index

When the Windows 8 Search pane slows down considerably or doesn't seem to find files you _know_ are in the pile, tell Windows 8 to rebuild the index from scratch.

Although Windows 8 re-creates its index in the background while you keep working, avoid slowing down your PC by sending a rebuild command in the evening. That way, Windows 8 can toil while you sleep, ensuring that you'll have a complete index the next morning.

Follow these steps to rebuild your index:

1. **From anywhere within Windows 8, right-click in the screen's bottom-left corner and choose Control Panel.**

The desktop's Control Panel appears.

2. **Click the Indexing Options icon.**

Don't spot it? Type **Indexing Options** in the Search box until its icon appears; then click the icon.

3. **Click the Advanced button and then click the Rebuild button.**

Windows 8 warns you, just as I do, that rebuilding the index takes a _long_ time.

4. **Click OK.**

Windows 8 begins indexing anew, waiting until it's finished with the new index before it deletes the old one.

The desktop's Internet Explorer, by contrast, offers many more options. It lets you save a particularly interesting webpage as a file, for example, or print only the interesting portions from a particularly lengthy web page.

To search using the desktop's Internet Explorer, type your query into the Address Bar — the place where you normally type in a web address. Press Enter, and Microsoft's Bing search engine displays the results. (I explain more about Internet Explorer, including how to change Bing to your favorite search engine, in Chapter 9.)

Chapter 8

Printing Your Work

· ·

· ·

*O*ccasionally you'll want to take text or an image away from your PC's whirling electrons and place it onto something more permanent: a piece of paper.

This chapter tackles that job by explaining all you need to know about printing. Here, you find out how to make that troublesome document fit on a piece of paper without hanging off the edge.

You'll discover how to print from the Start screen's gang of apps as well as from the desktop's programs.

I explain how to print just the relevant portions of a website — without the other pages, the ads, the menus, and the printer-ink-wasting images.

And should you find yourself near a printer spitting out 17 pages of the wrong thing, flip ahead to this chapter's coverage of the mysterious *print queue*. It's a little-known area that lets you cancel documents *before* they waste all your paper. (I explain how to set up a printer in Chapter 12.)

Printing from a Start Screen App

The new, tile-filled Start screen in Windows 8 behaves much differently than the traditional Windows desktop. Designed mostly for portable, touchscreen gadgets, the Start screen and its gang of apps works best for gathering informational tidbits while you're on the go.

Many of the apps can't print at all, and those that do allow printing don't offer many ways to tinker with your printer's settings. Nevertheless, when you *must* print something from a Start screen's app, follow these steps:

1. **From the Start screen, load the app containing information you want to print.**

   Not every app can print, unfortunately, and the apps don't disclose their limitations upfront. You might follow these steps only to find your hopes dashed by an obstinate app.

2. **Open the Charms bar and click the Devices icon.**

   Summon the Charms bar's Devices icon by using the spellcasting tools at your disposal:

   - **Mouse:** Point at the screen's top- or bottom-right corners; when the Charms bar appears, click Devices.

   - **Keyboard:** Press ⊞+K to jump straight to Devices.

   - **Touchscreen:** Slide your finger inward from the screen's right edge; when the Charms bar appears, tap the Devices icon.

   Windows 8 lists all the devices capable of working with your app, including, hopefully, any connected printers.

3. **Click the printer to receive your work.**

   Click your printer icon, shown in the margin. If you spot several printer icons, choose the one that should handle the job. (The icons are labeled.)

   Don't see a printer listed? Then that particular app won't let you print. (Until you try the next tip, that is.)

   If you have a keyboard, press ⊞+PrtScrn to save an image of the current screen as a file called `Screenshot.png` in your Pictures library. To print your screenshot, visit your desktop's Pictures library, right-click that file, and choose Print.

4. **Make any final adjustments.**

   The Printer window, shown in Figure 8-1, offers a preview of what you're printing, with the total number of pages listed beneath. Hover your mouse pointer over the preview page and click the little arrows to flip through the preview, page by page.

   On a touchscreen, flip through the pages by sliding your finger across the preview image.

   Not enough options? Then click the More Settings link. The Pages per Sheet setting lets you shrink several pages onto a single sheet of paper, which is handy for printing small photos on a color printer.

5. **Click the Print button.**

   Windows 8 shuffles your work to the printer of your choice, using the settings you chose in Step 4.

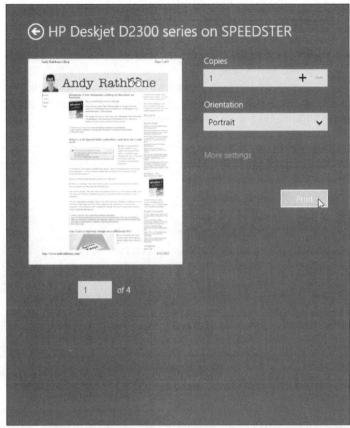

Copies

1   **+**

Orientation

Portrait

More settings

Print

1   of 4

Figure 8-1:
Choose
your print-
ing options
or click
the More
Settings
link for
additional
options.

Although you can print from apps, you'll eventually run against its limitations:

- ✔ Many apps can't print. You can't print a day's itinerary from your Calendar app, for example, or even a monthly calendar.

- ✔ When printing web pages with these steps, you're stuck printing the entire page; on some sites, that can mean printing a dozen pages to grab the single page you want. If you want to print only portions of a website, head for this chapter's later section, "Printing a web page."

- ✔ The More Settings link, described earlier in Step 4, lets you choose between Portrait and Landscape mode, as well as choose a printer tray. However, you won't find more detailed adjustments, such as choosing margins or adding headers and footers.

In short, although you *can* print from apps, your results will rarely match the experience of printing from the traditional Windows desktop, described in the rest of this chapter.

Printing Your Masterpiece from the Desktop

Built for power and control, the desktop offers much more control over printing your work. But that power and control often mean wading through a sea of options.

When working from the desktop, Windows 8 shuttles your work off to the printer in any of a half-dozen different ways. Chances are good that you'll be using these methods most often:

✔ Choose Print from your program's File menu.

✔ Click the program's Print icon, usually a tiny printer.

✔ Right-click your document icon and choose Print.

✔ Click the Print button on a program's toolbar.

✔ Drag and drop a document's icon onto your printer's icon.

If a dialog box appears, click the OK or Print button, and Windows 8 immediately begins sending your pages to the printer. Take a minute or so to refresh your coffee. If the printer is turned on (and still has paper and ink), Windows handles everything automatically, printing in the background while you do other things.

If the printed pages don't look quite right — perhaps the information doesn't fit on the paper correctly or it looks faded — then you need to fiddle around with the print settings or perhaps change the paper quality, as described in the next sections.

✔ If you stumble upon a particularly helpful page in the Windows Help system, right-click inside the topic or page and choose Print. (Or click the page's Print icon if you spot one.) Windows prints a copy for you to tape to your wall or stick in this book.

✔ For quick-'n'-easy access to your printer, add a printer shortcut to your desktop: Right-click the desktop's bottommost-left corner and choose Control Panel from the pop-up menu. From the Hardware and Sound category, choose View Devices and Printers. Finally, right-click your printer's icon and choose Create Shortcut. An icon for your printer appears on the desktop. To print a file, drag and drop its icon onto your printer's new desktop shortcut.

✔ To print a bunch of documents quickly, select *all* their icons. Then right-click the selected icons and choose Print. Windows 8 quickly shuttles all of them to the printer, where they emerge on paper, one after the other.

✔ Still haven't installed a printer? Flip to Chapter 12, where I explain how to plug one into your computer and make Windows 8 notice it.

Peeking at your printed page *before* it hits paper

Printing often requires a leap of faith: You choose Print from the menu and wait for the paper to emerge from the printer. If you're blessed, the page looks fine. But if you're cursed, you've wasted yet another sheet of paper.

The Print Preview option, found on nearly every program's File menu, foretells your printing fate *before* the words hit paper. Print Preview compares your current work with your program's page settings and then displays a detailed picture of the printed page. That preview makes it easy to spot off-kilter margins, dangling sentences, and other printing fouls.

Different programs use slightly different Print Preview screens, with some offering more insight than others. But almost any program's Print Preview screen lets you know whether everything will fit onto the page correctly.

If the preview looks fine, choose Print to send the work to the printer. If something looks wrong, however, click Close to return to your work and make any necessary adjustments.

Adjusting how your work fits on the page

In theory, Windows *always* displays your work as if it were printed on paper. Microsoft's marketing department calls it *What You See Is What You Get*, forever disgraced with the awful acronym WYSIWYG and its awkward pronunciation: "wizzy-wig." If what you see onscreen *isn't* what you want to see on paper, a trip to the program's Page Setup dialog box, shown in Figure 8-2, usually sets things straight.

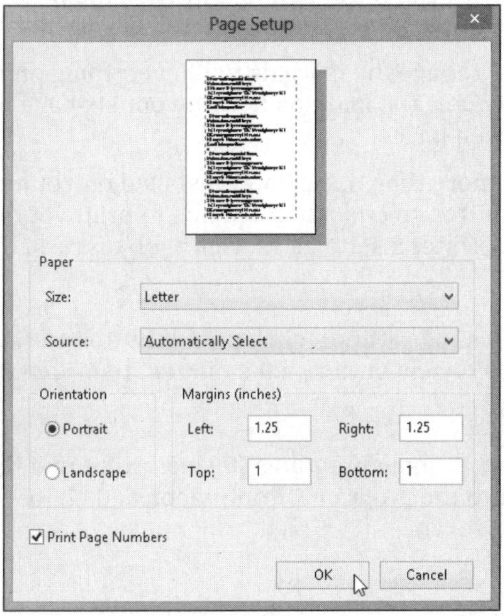

Figure 8-2: The Page Setup dialog box allows you to adjust the way your work fits onto a piece of paper.

Page Setup, found on nearly any program's File menu, offers several ways to flow your work across a printed page (and subsequently your screen). Page Setup dialog boxes differ among programs and print models, but the following list describes the options that you'll find most often and the settings that usually work best:

- ✔ **Size:** This option lets your program know what size of paper lives inside your printer. Leave this option set to Letter for printing on standard, 8.5-x-11-inch sheets of paper. Change this setting if you're using legal-size paper (8.5 x 14), envelopes, or other paper sizes. (The nearby sidebar, "Printing envelopes without fuss," contains more information about printing envelopes.)

- ✔ **Source:** Choose Automatically Select or Sheet Feeder unless you're using a fancy printer that accepts paper from more than one printer tray. People who have printers with two or more printer trays can select the tray containing the correct paper size. Some printers offer Manual Paper Feed, making the printer wait until you slide in that single sheet of paper.

- ✔ **Header/Footer:** Type secret codes in these boxes to customize what the printer places along the top and bottom of your pages: page numbers, titles, and dates, for example, as well as their spacing. Unfortunately, different programs use different codes for their header and footer. If you spot a little question mark in the Page Setup dialog box's top-right corner, click it; then click inside the Header or Footer box for clues to the secret codes.

- ✔ **Orientation:** Leave this option set to Portrait to print normal pages that read vertically like a letter. Choose Landscape only when you want to print sideways, which is a handy way to print wide spreadsheets. (If you choose Landscape, the printer automatically prints the page sideways; you don't need to slide the paper sideways into your printer.)

- ✔ **Margins:** Feel free to reduce the margins to fit everything on a single sheet of paper. Or *enlarge* the margins to turn your six-page term paper into the required seven pages.

- ✔ **Printer:** If you have more than one printer installed on your computer or network, click this button to choose which one to print your work. Click here to change that printer's settings as well, a job discussed in the next section.

When you're finished adjusting settings, click the OK button to save your changes. (Click the Print Preview button, if it's offered, to make sure that everything looks right.)

To find the Page Setup box in some programs (including Internet Explorer), click the little arrow next to the program's Printer icon and choose Page Setup from the menu that drops down.

Printing envelopes without fuss

Although clicking *Envelopes* in a program's Page Setup area is fairly easy, printing addresses in the correct spot on the envelope is extraordinarily difficult. Some printer models want you to insert envelopes upside down, but others prefer right side up. Your best bet is to run several tests, placing the envelope into your printer's tray in different ways until you finally stumble on the magic method. (Or you can pull out your printer's manual, if you still have it, and pore over the "proper envelope insertion" pictures.)

After you've figured out the correct method for your particular printer, tape a successfully printed envelope above your printer and add an arrow pointing to the correct way to insert it.

Should you eventually give up on printing envelopes, try using Avery's mailing labels. Buy your preferred size of Avery labels and then download the free Avery Wizard software from Avery's website (www.avery.com). Compatible with Microsoft Word, the wizard places little boxes on your screen that precisely match the size of your particular Avery labels. Type the addresses into the little boxes, insert the label sheet into your printer, and Word prints everything onto the little stickers. You don't even need to lick them.

Or do as I did: Buy a little rubber stamp with your return address. It's much faster than stickers or printers.

Adjusting your printer's settings

When you choose Print from many programs, Windows offers one last chance to spruce up your printed page. The Print dialog box, shown in Figure 8-3, lets you route your work to any printer installed on your computer or network. While there, you can adjust the printer's settings, choose your paper quality, and select the pages (and quantities) you'd like to print.

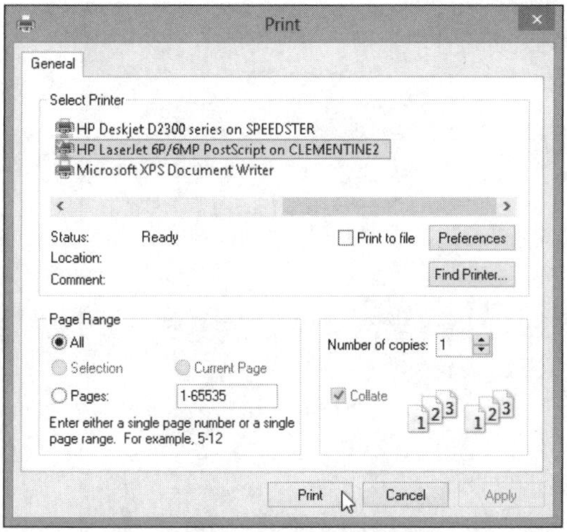

Figure 8-3: The Print dialog box lets you choose your printer and adjust its settings.

You're likely to find these settings waiting in the dialog box:

✔ **Select Printer:** Ignore this option if you have only one printer because Windows chooses it automatically. If your computer has access to several printers, click the one that should receive the job. Click Fax to send your work as a fax through Windows Fax and Scan program.

The printer called Microsoft XPS Document Writer sends your work to a specially formatted file, usually to be printed or distributed professionally. Chances are good that you'll never use it.

✔ **Page Range:** Select All to print your entire document. To print just a few of its pages, select the Pages option and enter the page numbers you want to print. For example, enter **1-4, 6** to leave out page 5 of a 6-page document. If you've highlighted a paragraph, choose Selection to print that particular paragraph — a great way to print the important part of a web page and leave out the rest.

✔ **Number of Copies:** Most people leave this set to 1 copy, unless everybody in the boardroom wants their own copy. You can choose Collate only if your printer offers that option. (Most don't, leaving you to sort the pages yourself.)

✔ **Preferences:** Click this button to see a dialog box like the one in Figure 8-4, where you can choose options specific to your own printer model. The Printing Preferences dialog box typically lets you select different grades of paper, choose between color and black and white, set the printing quality, and make last-minute corrections to the page layout.

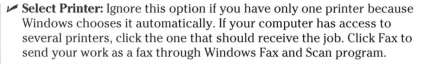

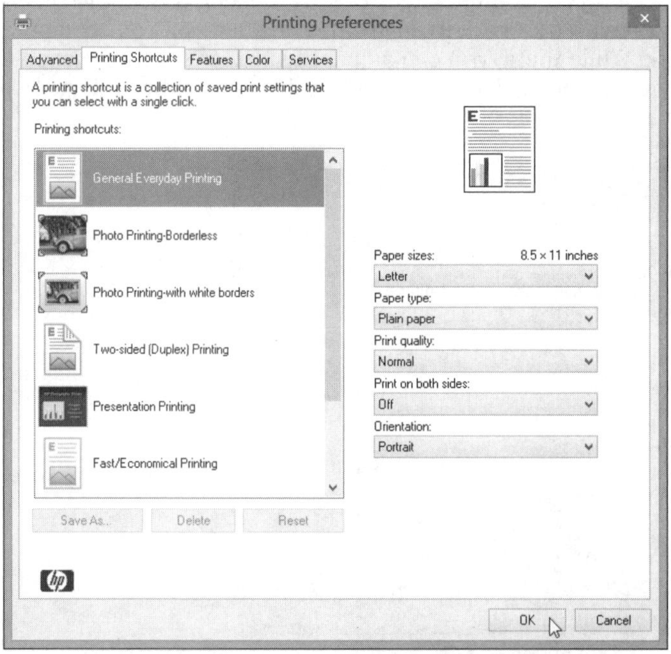

Figure 8-4: The Printing Preferences dialog box lets you change settings specific to your printer, including the paper type and printing quality.

Canceling a print job

Just realized you sent the wrong 26-page document to the printer? So you panic and hit the printer's off button. Unfortunately, many printers automatically pick up where they left off when you turn them back on, leaving you or your co-workers to deal with the mess.

To purge the mistake from your printer's memory, follow these steps:

1. **From the Start screen, click the Desktop tile.**

2. **Choose your printer's name or icon from the taskbar; when the Devices and Printers window appears, right-click your printer and choose See What's Printing.**

   The handy *print queue* appears, as shown in Figure 8-5.

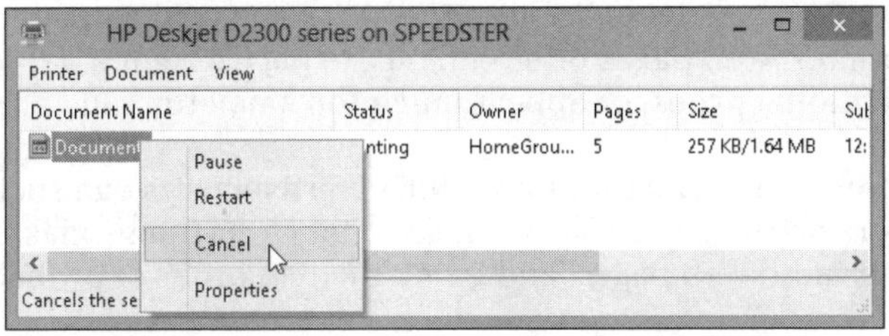

Figure 8-5:
Use the
print queue
to cancel a
print job.

3. **Right-click your mistaken document and choose Cancel to end the job. Repeat with any other listed unwanted documents.**

Your printer queue can take a minute or two to clear itself. (To speed things up, click the View menu and choose Refresh.) When the print queue is clear, turn your printer back on; it won't keep printing that same darn document.

✔ The print queue, also known as the print *spooler,* lists every document waiting patiently to reach your printer. Feel free to change their printing order by dragging and dropping them up or down the list. (You can't move anything in front of the currently printing document, though.)

✔ Sharing your printer on the network? Print jobs sent from other PCs end up in *your* computer's print queue, so *you'll* need to cancel the botched ones. (And networked folks who share *their* printer will need to delete your botched print jobs, as well.)

✔ If your printer runs out of paper during a job and stubbornly halts, add more paper. Then to start things flowing again, open the print queue, right-click your document, and choose Restart. (Some printers have an Online button that you push to begin printing again.)

✔ You can send items to the printer even when you're working in the coffee shop with your laptop. Later, when you connect the laptop to your printer, the print queue notices and begins sending your files. (Beware: When they're in the print queue, documents are formatted for your specific printer model. If you subsequently connect your laptop to a *different* printer model, the print queue's waiting documents won't print correctly.)

Printing a web page

Although information-stuffed web pages look awfully tempting, *printing* those web pages is rarely satisfying because they look so awful on paper. When sent to the printer, web pages often run off the page's right side, consume zillions of additional pages, or appear much too small to read.

To make matters worse, all those colorful advertisements can suck your printer's color cartridges dry fairly quickly. Only four things make for successfully printed web pages, and I rank them in order of probable success rate:

✔ **Use the web page's built-in Print option.** Some websites, but not all, offer a tiny menu option called Print This Page, Text Version, Printer-Friendly Version, or something similar. That option tells the website to strip out its garbage and reformat the page so that it fits neatly onto a sheet of paper. This option is the most reliable way to print a web page.

✔ **Choose Print Preview from your browser's File or Print menu.** After 15 years, some web page designers noticed that people want to print their pages, so they tweaked the settings, making their pages *automatically* reformat themselves when printed. If you're lucky, a clean look in the Print Preview window confirms that you've stumbled onto one of those printer-friendly sites.

✔ **Copy the portion you want and paste it into WordPad.** Try selecting the desired text from the web page, copying it, and pasting it into WordPad or another word processor. Delete any unwanted remnants, adjust the margins, and print the portion you want. I explain how to select, copy, and paste in Chapter 6.

✔ **Copy the entire page and paste it into a word processor.** Although it's lots of work, it's an option. Right-click a blank portion of the web page and choose Select All. Right-click again and choose Copy. Next, open Microsoft Word or another full-featured word processor and paste the web page inside a new document. By hacking away at the unwanted portions, you can sometimes end up with something printable.

These tips may also come in handy for moving a web page from screen to paper:

✔ If you spot an E-Mail option but no Print option, e-mail the page to yourself. You may have better success printing it as an e-mail message.

✔ To print just a few paragraphs of a web page, use the mouse to select the portion you're after. (I cover selecting in Chapter 6.) Choose Print from Internet Explorer's Tools menu (shown in the margin) to open the Print dialog box, shown earlier in Figure 8-3. Then, in the Page Range box, choose the Selection option.

✔ If a web page's table or photo insists on vanishing off the paper's right edge, try printing the page in Landscape mode rather than Portrait. See the "Adjusting how your work fits on the page" section, earlier in this chapter, for details on Landscape mode.

Troubleshooting your printer

When you can't print something, start with the basics: Are you _sure_ that the printer is turned on, plugged into the wall, full of paper, and connected securely to your computer with a cable?

If so, try plugging the printer into different outlets, turning it on, and seeing whether its power light comes on. If the light stays off, your printer's power supply is probably blown.

Printers are almost always cheaper to replace than repair. But if you've grown fond of your printer, grab an estimate from a repair shop — if you can find one — before discarding it.

If the printer's power light beams brightly, check these things before giving up:

✔ Make sure that a sheet of paper hasn't jammed itself inside the printer. (A steady pull usually extricates jammed paper; sometimes opening and closing the printer's lid starts things moving again.)

Choosing the right paper for your printer

If you've strolled the aisles at an office-supply store lately, you've noticed a bewildering array of paper choices. Sometimes the paper's packaging lists its application: Premium Inkjet Paper, for example, for high-quality memos. Here's a list of different print jobs and the types of paper they require. Before printing, be sure to click the Printer's Preferences section to select the grade of paper you're using for that job.

✔ **Junk:** Keep some cheap or scrap paper around for testing the printer, printing quick drafts, leaving desktop notes, and printing other on-the-fly jobs. Botched print jobs work great here; just use the paper's other side.

✔ **Letter quality:** Bearing the words Premium or Bright White, this paper works fine for letters, reports, memos, and other things designed for showing to others.

✔ **Photos:** You can print photos on any type of paper, but they look like photos only on actual *photo-quality paper*— the expensive stuff. Slide the paper carefully into your printer tray so that the picture prints on

the glossy, shiny side. Some photo paper requires placing a little cardboard sheet beneath it, which helps glide the paper smoothly through the printer.

✔ **Labels:** They've never sent me a T-shirt, but I still say that Avery's Wizard program (www.avery.com) makes it easy to print Avery labels and cards. The wizard teams up with Microsoft Word to mesh perfectly with Avery's preformatted mailing labels, greeting cards, business cards, CD labels, and many others.

✔ **Transparencies:** For powerful PowerPoint presentations, buy special transparent plastic sheets designed to be used with your type of printer. Make sure the transparency is compatible with your printer, be it laser or inkjet.

Before plunking down your money, make sure that your paper is designed specifically for your printer type, be it laser or inkjet. Laser printers heat the pages, and some paper and transparencies can't take the heat.

✔ Does your inkjet printer still have ink in its cartridges? Does your laser printer have toner? Try printing a test page: From the desktop, right-click in the bottom-right corner and choose Control Panel. From the Hardware and Sound category, choose Devices and Printers. Right-click your printer's icon, choose Printer Properties, and click the Print Test Page button to see whether the computer and printer can talk to each other.

✔ Try updating the printer's *driver*, the little program that helps it talk with Windows 8. Visit the printer manufacturer's website, download the newest driver for your particular printer model, and run its installation program. (I cover drivers in Chapter 13.)

Finally, here are a couple of tips to help you protect your printer and cartridges:

✔ Turn off your printer when you're not using it. Inkjet printers, especially, should be turned off when they're not in use. The heat tends to dry the cartridges, shortening their life.

✔ Don't unplug your inkjet printer to turn it off. Always use the on/off switch. The switch ensures that the cartridges slide back to their home positions, keeping them from drying out or clogging.

Part III
Getting Things Done on the Internet

The 5th Wave   By Rich Tennant

"Face it Vinnie—you're gonna have a hard time getting people to subscribe online with a credit card to a newsletter called, 'Felons Interactive.'"

In this part . . .

The Internet used to be clean, quiet, and helpful, just like a library. You could find detailed information about nearly anything, read newspapers and magazines from around the world, listen to music in the media section, or quietly browse the card catalogs.

Today, this wonderful global library has been bombarded with noisy people who toss ads in front of what you're trying to read. Some won't even let you close that book you inadvertently opened — the book keeps opening back up to the wrong page. Pickpockets and thieves stalk the halls.

This part of the book helps you turn the Internet back into that quiet, helpful library it once was. It shows how to avoid browser hijackers, and spyware. It explains how to send and receive e-mail so that you can keep in touch with friends.

It explains how to stock your contacts list with people listed in your Facebook, Twitter, LinkedIn, and other accounts, as well as how to send and receive e-mail.

Finally, it shows you how to stay safe using the Windows 8 User Account Protection, firewall, security center, and other tricks to help bring back the Internet you love.

Chapter 9

Cruising the Web

· ·

In This Chapter

▶ Finding out about Internet service providers

▶ Connecting to the Internet wirelessly

▶ Navigating the web from the Start screen

▶ Navigating the web from the desktop

▶ Finding information on the Internet

▶ Understanding plug-ins

▶ Saving information from the Internet

▶ Troubleshooting Internet Explorer problems

· ·

*E*ven when being installed, Windows starts reaching for the Internet, hungry for any hint of a connection. After connecting, Windows kindly downloads updates to make your PC run more smoothly. Other motives are less pure: Windows 8 also checks in with Microsoft to make sure that you're not installing a pirated copy.

Windows 8 is so web-dependent that it comes with two web browsers, both confusingly named Internet Explorer. One runs on the Start screen, naturally; the other hugs its traditional window on the desktop.

But no matter which of the two browsers you prefer, this chapter explains how to connect with the Internet, visit websites, and find all the good stuff online.

For ways to keep out the bad stuff, be sure to visit Chapter 11. It's a primer on safe computing that explains how to avoid the web's bad neighborhoods, viruses, spyware, hijackers, and other Internet parasites.

What's an ISP, and Why Do I Need One?

Everybody needs three things to connect with the Internet: a computer, web browser software, and an Internet service provider (ISP).

You already have the computer, be it a tablet, laptop, or desktop PC. And Windows 8 comes with a pair of web browsers. The Start screen's Internet Explorer browser works for full-screen, quick information grabs; the desktop's Internet Explorer browser offers more in-depth features.

That means most people need to find only an ISP. Although music wafts through the air to your car radio for free, you must pay an ISP for the privilege of surfing the web. When your computer connects to your ISP's computers, Internet Explorer automatically finds the Internet, and you're ready to surf the web.

Choosing an ISP is fairly easy because you're often stuck with whichever ISPs serve your particular geographical area. Ask your friends and neighbors how they connect and whether they recommend their ISP. Call several ISPs serving your area for a rate quote and then compare rates. Most bill on a monthly basis, so if you're not happy, you can always switch.

- ✔ Although ISPs charge for Internet access, *you* don't always have to pay. Some places share their Internet access for free, usually through a wireless connection. If your laptop or tablet includes wireless support, and most do, you can browse the Internet whenever you're within range of a free wireless signal. (I cover wireless in the next section.)

- ✔ Although a few ISPs charge for each minute you're connected, most charge from $30 to $100 a month for unlimited service. Make sure that you know your rate before hopping aboard or else you may be unpleasantly surprised at the month's end.

- ✔ ISPs let you connect to the Internet in a variety of ways. The slowest ISPs require a dialup modem and an ordinary phone line. Faster still are *broadband* connections: special DSL or ISDN lines provided by some phone companies, and the even faster cable modems, supplied by your cable television company. When shopping for broadband ISPs, your geographic location usually determines your options.

- ✔ You need to pay an ISP for only *one* Internet connection. By setting up a network, you can share that single connection with any other computers, cellphones, TVs, and other Internet-aware gadgetry in your home or office. (I cover networks in Chapter 15.)

Connecting Wirelessly to the Internet

Windows *constantly* searches for a working Internet connection. If it finds one that you've used previously, you're set: Windows passes the news along to Internet Explorer, and you're ready to visit the web.

When you're traveling, however, the wireless networks around you will often be new, so you'll have to authorize these new connections. Whenever you want to connect with a new network, you need to tell Windows that you want to connect, please.

To connect to a nearby wireless network for the first time, either one in your own home or in a public place, follow these steps:

1. **Summon the Charms bar and click or tap the Settings icon.**

   Any of these three tricks summons the Charms bar and its Settings screen, which I cover in Chapter 2:

   - **Mouse:** Point at the screen's top- or bottom-right edge; when the Charms bar appears, click the Settings icon.

   - **Keyboard:** Press ⊞+I to head straight for the Charms bar's Settings screen.

   - **Touchscreen:** Slide your finger inward from the screen's right edge; when the Charms bar appears, tap the Settings icon.

2. **Click or tap the wireless network icon.**

   Among the Settings screen's six bottom icons, the one in the top left represents wireless networks. The icon changes shape, depending on your surroundings:

   - **Available:** When the icon says Available, like the one in the margin, you're within range of a wireless network. Start salivating and move to the next step.

   - **Unavailable:** When the icon says Unavailable, like the one in the margin, you're out of range. Time to head for a different seat in the coffee shop or perhaps a different coffee shop altogether. Then return to Step 1.

3. **Click or tap the Available icon if it's present.**

   Windows lists all the wireless networks within range of your PC, as shown in Figure 9-1. Don't be surprised to see several networks listed; if you're at home, your neighbors probably see your network listed, too.

4. **Choose to connect to the desired network by clicking its name and clicking the Connect button.**

   If you select the adjacent Connect Automatically check box before clicking the Connect button, Windows automatically connects to that network the next time you're within range, sparing you from connecting manually each time.

   If you're connecting to an *unsecured network* — a network that doesn't require a password — you've finished. Windows warns you about connecting to an unsecured network, but a click or tap of the Connect button lets you connect, anyway. (Don't do any shopping or banking on an unsecured connection.)

Figure 9-1:
Windows
lists every
wireless
network
within
range.

5. Enter a password if needed.

If you try to connect to a *security-enabled* wireless connection, Windows asks you to enter a *network security key* — technospeak for *password.* If you're at home, here's where you type in the same password you entered into your router when setting up your wireless network.

If you're connecting to somebody *else's* password-protected wireless network, ask the network's owner for the password. If you're in a hotel, pull out your credit card. You probably need to buy some connection time from the people behind the front desk.

6. Choose whether you want to share your files with other people on the network.

If you're connecting on your own home or office network, choose "Yes, turn on sharing and connect to devices." That lets you share files with others and use handy devices, like printers.

If you're connecting in a public area, by contrast, choose "No, don't turn on sharing or connect to devices." That keeps out snoops.

If you're still having problems connecting, try the following tips:

✔ When Windows says that it can't connect to your wireless network, it offers to bring up the Network Troubleshooter. The Network Troubleshooter mulls over the problem and then says something about the signal being weak. It's really telling you this: "Move closer to the wireless transmitter."

✔ If you can't connect to the secured network you want, try connecting to one of the unsecured networks. Unsecured networks work fine for casual browsing on the Internet.

✔ Cordless phones and microwave ovens, oddly enough, interfere with wireless networks. Try to keep your cordless phone out of the same room as your wireless PC, and don't heat up that sandwich when web browsing.

✔ If your desktop's taskbar contains a wireless network icon (shown in the margin), click it to jump to Step 3. While you're working on the Windows 8 desktop, that wireless network icon provides a handy way to connect wirelessly in new locations.

What's the difference between the two web browsers?

Windows 8 comes with *two* web browsers. Adding to the confusion, each bears the name Internet Explorer. Although they look completely different, the Start screen's browser is really just a stripped-down version of the desktop's browser.

Because they're basically the same beast, they share your browsing history, cookies, saved passwords, and temporary files. Deleting those items from one browser also deletes them from the other.

The browsers differ in a few other ways, but most obviously through the limitations of the Start screen's browser. The Start screen's browser shows sites only in full-screen view; you can't place two sites side by side to compare them. It also won't let you save a Home screen; instead, the browser always opens to the last site you visited.

The Start screen's browser can only display Flash on a list of Microsoft-approved websites, so on some sites, you'll miss out on not only some movies but some advertisements. (Not that you'll miss those.)

If you find yourself needing a more powerful browser while in the Start screen, perhaps to watch something in Flash, right-click a blank portion of the currently viewed website. (On a tablet, swipe your finger inward from the top or bottom.) When the app's menu rises up from the screen's bottom edge, click the wrench icon and choose View in Desktop.

Browsing Quickly from the Start Screen

Built for quick, on-the-fly browsing, the Start screen's browser works quickly. Part of its speed comes from its limitations, though. Every site fills the screen, making it easy to read. But the browser shows the sites in their full glory only by hiding its own menus, making navigation challenging.

To open Internet Explorer from the Start screen, click its tile, shown in the margin. The browser opens, filling the screen with your last-viewed site.

When you want to visit someplace else, fetch the browser's hidden menus with any of these commands:

- ✔ **Mouse:** Right-click a blank portion of the web page, away from any words or pictures.
- ✔ **Keyboard:** Press ⊞+Z.
- ✔ **Touchscreen:** From the screen's top or bottom edge, slide your finger toward the screen's center.

The browser's top and bottom menus appear, shown and neatly labeled in Figure 9-2.

- ✔ **Currently open sites:** Your last-visited sites appear here, letting you revisit them with a click. (Or, you can close them by clicking the X in their upper-right corner.)

- ✔ **New Tab:** Clicking this icon fetches a blank screen with an Address Bar along the bottom. Type in the address of the website you'd like to visit.

- ✔ **Tab Tools:** Clicking this icon brings a drop-down list with two options: New InPrivate Tab and Close Tabs. Select the New InPrivate Tab option to open a new tab for visiting a website *privately;* the browser will conveniently forget you've visited that site. The other menu option, Close Tabs, removes the thumbnails of all your previously viewed sites from along the browser's top.

- ✔ **Back:** This icon on the bottom left lets you revisit the page you just visited.

- ✔ **Address Bar:** Type in the address of a website you'd like to visit in this box. Or just type in a subject, and your browser will search for it, displaying possible matches. *Tip:* Click inside the Address Bar to see a list of your frequently visited sites, as well as sites you've pinned to the Start screen.

- ✔ **Refresh:** Handy for viewing news sites, this icon reloads the currently viewed page, gathering the latest material available.

- ✔ **Pin to Start:** Take note of this one: When you find a website you like, click this icon to add the page to your Start screen as a tile. That gives you one-click access for a return visit.

New InPrivate window/Close tabs

Currently open websites

Open new blank tab

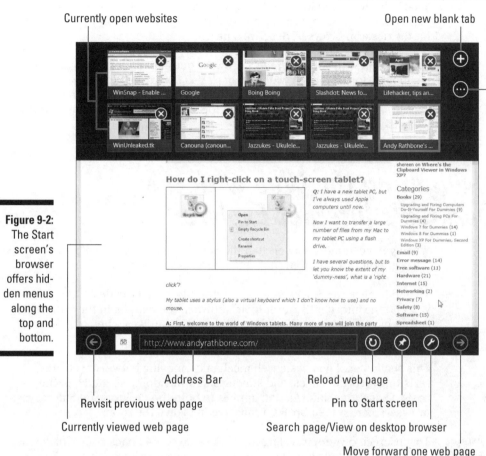

Figure 9-2:
The Start
screen's
browser
offers hid-
den menus
along the
top and
bottom.

Address Bar

Reload web page

Revisit previous web page

Pin to Start screen

Currently viewed web page

Search page/View on desktop browser

Move forward one web page

✔ **Page Tools:** This icon fetches a menu with two main options: Find On Page lets you search for text on the current page, whereas View on the Desktop lets you view that page on your desktop's Internet Explorer, which is handy when the Start screen's browser can't display something correctly. A third option, Get App for This Site, appears only when the site offers an app for direct access. (Accessing some sites is easier with an app than the browser.)

✔ **Forward:** Just as in the desktop browser, this icon lets you return to the page you just left.

You can also search for items through the Charm bar's Search icon. I cover the Charms bar in Chapter 2, but here's a hint: Point your mouse at the screen's top- or bottom-right corner to fetch the Charms bar; then click the Search icon and type a name for what you're hankering.

When you're on the go and looking for quick information, the Start screen's speedy browser and its simple menus might be all you need. When you need more control, though, or if a website doesn't seem to display properly, head for the desktop browser, described next.

 On many sites, the Start screen's browser doesn't support *Flash,* a popular technology for displaying web videos. If you find a site that says you need a Flash plug-in, ignore it. Instead, click the Page Tools icon (shown in the margin) and choose View on the Desktop. That loads the desktop's browser, which shows the site properly.

Navigating the Web with the Desktop's Internet Explorer

When you need more power than the Start screen's simplified browser has to offer, Internet Explorer awaits on the Windows 8 desktop.

 To find it, click the Start screen's Desktop tile. When the desktop appears, you find the Internet Explorer icon, shown in the margin, in the bottom-left corner of your screen. (Windows old-timers say it lives where the Start button once lived.)

This section explains basic web mechanics: moving between websites, revisiting favorite places, and staying safe while doing so. Much of the basic navigational information applies to both the desktop and Start screen browser; Start screen browser fans needn't leave the room.

 Touchscreen owners traveling to the desktop should pack a portable mouse and keyboard. Large fingertips can't easily maneuver through a desktop's tightly packed features. Fingertips work best on the Windows 8 Start screen and its simple, large buttons.

 If you've clicked or tapped the wrong button but haven't yet lifted your finger, stop! Command buttons don't take effect until you *release* your finger. Keep holding down the mouse button or your finger, but slide the pointer or finger away from the wrong button. Move safely away from the button and *then* lift your finger.

Moving from one web page to another

Web pages come with specific addresses, just like homes do. *Any* web browser lets you move between those addresses. You can use Internet Explorer from the Start screen or desktop, or even use a competing browser such as Firefox (www.getfirefox.com) or Chrome (www.google.com/chrome).

No matter which browser you use, they all let you move from one page to another in any of three different ways:

✔ By pointing and clicking a button or link that automatically whisks you away to another page

✔ By typing a complicated string of code words (the web address) into the Address Bar of the web browser and pressing Enter

✔ By clicking the navigation buttons on the browser's toolbar, which is usually at the top of the screen

Clicking links

The first way is by far the easiest. Look for *links* — highlighted words or pictures on a page — and click them.

 For example, see how the mouse pointer turned into a hand (shown in the margin) as it pointed at the word *Books* in Figure 9-3? Click that word to see a web page with more information about that subject. The mouse pointer morphs into a hand whenever it's over a link. Click any linked word to see pages dealing with that link's particular subject.

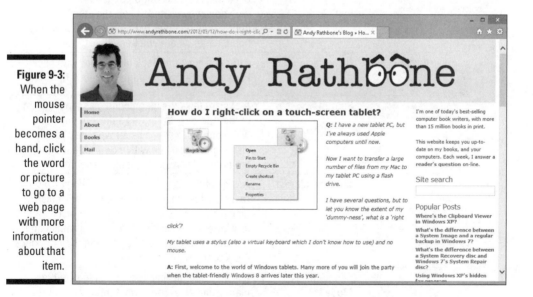

Figure 9-3: When the mouse pointer becomes a hand, click the word or picture to go to a web page with more information about that item.

Typing web addresses in the Address Bar

The second method is more difficult. If a friend gives you a napkin with a cool web page's address written on it, you need to type the website's address into your browser's *Address Bar* — the text-filled bar across the top. You'll do fine, as long as you don't misspell anything.

See the address for my website along the top of Figure 9-3? I typed **www. andyrathbone.com** into the Address Bar. When I pressed Enter, Internet Explorer scooted me to my web page. (You don't need to type the `http://` part, thank goodness.)

Using Internet Explorer's toolbar

Finally, you can maneuver through the Internet by clicking various buttons on Internet Explorer's newly stripped-down toolbar, which sits at the top of the screen. Table 9-1 offers a handy reference of the important navigation buttons.

Hover your mouse pointer over a confusing Internet Explorer button to see its purpose in life.

Table 9-1	Navigating with Internet Explorer's Buttons	
This Button . . .	**Is Called This . . .**	**And It Does This . . .**
←	Back	Pointed and clicked yourself into a dead end? Click this big Back button to head for the last web page you visited. If you click the Back button enough times, you wind up back at your home page, where you began.
→	Forward	After you click the Back button, you can click Forward to revisit the page you just left.
Q	Search	A click of this little magnifying glass to the right of the Address Bar brings a drop-down menu with your *History* — a list of websites you've visited previously — with a Search bar along the bottom for typing in sought-after items.
▼	Autocomplete	A click of this tiny downward-pointing arrow reveals sites that Internet Explorer will finish typing for you, as soon as you enter just a few letters. Click a site to revisit it; remove an unwanted site by pointing at it and then clicking the X to the right of its name.
▣	Compatibility Mode	If a site's menus, images, or text look out of place, click this icon to shift Internet Explorer into Compatibility Mode, which placates cranky old websites.
↻	Refresh	If a site doesn't load or doesn't load the latest updates, click the Refresh button to load the site once more.

This Button . . .	Is Called This . . .	And It Does This . . .
🏠	Home	If you get lost while exploring the Internet, return to familiar territory by clicking the Home button along the program's top. That returns you to the page that always appears when you first load Internet Explorer.
☆	Favorites	Clicking the Favorites button along the top reveals the Favorites list, a list of links that often lead to your favorite websites. From the Favorites list, you can click the Add to Favorites button to add your currently viewed site to the list.
⚙	Tools	This button opens a menu that's chock-full of Internet Explorer tweaks, including Print. Head for the menu's Safety option to delete your browsing history, browse in private (handy for bank sites), or check suspicious websites for danger.

Making Internet Explorer open to your favorite site

When you open the desktop's web browser, it needs to show you *something* right away. Well, that something can be any website you want. In computer terms, that's called your *home page,* and you can tell Internet Explorer to use any site you want for your home page by following these steps:

1. **Visit your favorite website.**

   Choose any web page you like. If you choose Google News (http:// news.google.com), for example, Internet Explorer always opens with the latest headlines.

 2. **Right-click the Home Page icon and choose Add or Change Home Page.**

   The new, security-conscious Internet Explorer asks whether you'd like to use that web page as your only home page or add it to your home page tabs. (You can have several home pages, each with its own tab along the page's top.)

3. **Click Use This Webpage As Your Only Home Page and click Yes.**

   When you click Yes, shown in Figure 9-4, Internet Explorer always opens to the page you're currently viewing.

But I *want* to see some pop-ups!

Early versions of Internet Explorer had no way to stop pop-up advertisements from exploding across your screen. Internet Explorer now offers a pop-up ad blocker that stops 90 percent of them.

If a site tries to send a pop-up ad or message, Internet Explorer places a strip along its bottom edge saying, Internet Explorer blocked a pop-up from *<name of site>*. The strip offers two buttons. Choose Allow Once button to see the blocked pop-up. If you're at a site that relies on pop-ups, click the Options for This Site button; that lets you add the website to a safe-sites list so its pop-ups won't be blocked.

Clicking No sticks with your current home page. Coincidentally, Microsoft initially assigns everybody's home page to be the advertisement-stuffed Microsoft Network (www.msn.com).

After Internet Explorer remembers your chosen home page, you can move around the Internet, searching for topics in Bing (www.bing.com), Google (www.google.com) or other search engines, simply pointing and clicking different links.

Figure 9-4:
Click
Use This
Webpage
As Your
Only Home
Page, and
Internet
Explorer
always
opens to
that same
page.

▶ Just as your browser's home page is the site you see when your browser opens, a website's home page is its "cover," like the cover of a magazine. Whenever you navigate to a website, you usually start at the site's home page and begin browsing from there.

▶ If your browser's home page is suddenly changed to a different site and these instructions don't fix it, then it's probably been hijacked by evil forces. Head to Chapter 11 and read the section on staying safe on the Internet, especially the portions on removing hijackers and spyware.

✔ Internet Explorer lets you choose several pages as home pages, simultaneously loading each one and placing a tab atop each page for switching between them. To add home pages to your collection, choose Add This Webpage to Your Home Page Tabs in Step 3 of the preceding list. (It's shown in Figure 9-4.)

Revisit favorite places

Sooner or later, you'll stumble across a web page that's indescribably delicious. To make sure that you can find it again later, add it to Internet Explorer's built-in list of favorite pages by following these steps:

1. **Click the Favorites icon (shown in the margin) on Internet Explorer's toolbar.**

   A little menu drops down.

2. **Choose Add to Favorites.**

   A box appears, offering to name the web page by its title — the words that appear on the tab at the page's top.

3. **Click the Add button to add the page to your Favorites list.**

Whenever you want to return to that page, click Internet Explorer's Favorites button. When the Favorites menu drops down, click your favorite site's name.

Librarian-types like to organize their menu of favorite links: Click the Favorites button, click the arrow by the Add to Favorites button, and choose Organize Favorites. That lets you create folders for storing similar and group-related links in single folders.

Don't see your favorites on the drop-down menu when you click the Favorites button? Click the Favorites tab at the menu's top to switch to them. (You may be looking at the History tab, covered in the sidebar, or the RSS feeds tab, which lists a site's headlines.)

Finding things on the Internet

When searching for a book in a library, you usually head straight for the computerized index. The same holds true for the Internet because you need an index to ferret out that piece of information you're after.

To help you out, Internet Explorer lets you consult a *search engine,* a service that contains a vast index of Internet sites. Previous versions of Internet Explorer offered a Search box, a special place along the top to type in a few words about what you're seeking.

Internet Explorer's secret history of your web visits

Internet Explorer keeps a record of every website you visit. Although Internet Explorer's History list provides a handy record of your computing activities, it's a spy's dream.

To keep tabs on what Internet Explorer is recording, click your Favorites button and click the History icon on the drop-down menu. Internet Explorer lists every website you've visited in the past 20 days. Feel free to sort the entries by clicking the little arrow to the right of the word History. You can sort them by date, alphabetically, most visited, or by the order you've visited on that particular day — a handy way to jump back to that site you found interesting this morning.

To delete a single entry from the history, right-click it and choose Delete from the menu. To delete the entire list, exit the Favorites area. Then choose Internet Options from the Tools menu and click the Delete button in the Browsing History section. A menu appears, letting you delete your History and other items.

To turn off the History, click the Settings button instead of the Delete button. Then in the History section, change the Days to Keep Pages in History option to 0.

Deleting your History in the Internet Explorer's desktop version also deletes it in the Start screen's version of Internet Explorer.

Both versions of Internet Explorer in Windows 8 remove the Search box. Instead, type your search term — **exotic orchids**, for example — directly into the Address Bar and press Enter.

Internet Explorer fires your search off to Bing, Microsoft's own search engine, and spits out websites dealing in exotic orchids.

Don't like Bing handling your search needs? You can change that search engine to Google (www.google.com) or any other search engine you like.

Follow these steps to customize Internet Explorer's searches to your liking:

1. **Click the Tools icon, which looks like a little gear in Internet Explorer's top-right corner.**

   A drop-down menu appears.

2. **Choose Manage Add-ons, choose Search Providers from the Add-On Types section, and choose Find More Search Providers from the page's bottom-left corner.**

   Internet Explorer visits Microsoft's website and lists a few dozen search engines.

3. **Click your favorite search engine and click the Add to Internet Explorer button.**

   A dialog box opens, asking whether you want to add that search provider.

If you want your searches to all go to one search engine — Google, for example — select the check box labeled Make This My Default Search Provider before you go to Step 4. That option tells Internet Explorer to automatically send all your searches to that provider.

4. Click the Add button.

Internet Explorer replaces Bing with your newly selected search provider. Changing the search engine in the *desktop* version of Internet Explorer also applies the change the *Start screen's* version of Internet Explorer.

The Web Page Says It Needs a Weird Plug-In Thing!

Years ago, computer programmers abandoned their boring old TV sets and turned to their exciting new computers for entertainment. Now, they're trying to turn their computers back into TV sets. To add sound and video onto websites, they're using fancy programming techniques called Java, Flash, RealPlayer, QuickTime, Silverlight, and others.

Programmers create little software tidbits called *plug-ins* that allow your computer's web browser to display these flashy items. You'll know when you're installing a plug-in when Internet Explorer sticks a threatening notice in your face, as shown in Figure 9-5.

Figure 9-5: A site asks to install software.

What's the problem? If Internet Explorer says it needs a plug-in or the latest version of the software, click the Install or Yes button — *only if you can trust the program.* Although it's often difficult to tell the good programs from the evil ones, I explain in Chapter 11 how to judge a plug-in's trustworthiness. Meanwhile, the following plug-ins are both free and safe:

✔ **QuickTime** (`www.apple.com/quicktime`)**:** The free version of QuickTime plays some sound and video formats that Microsoft's Media Player can't handle.

✔ **Adobe Flash** (`www.adobe.com/products/flashplayer`)**:** This double-edged download plays the most distracting advertisements on websites as well as most online videos and animations.

✔ **Adobe Acrobat Reader** (`www.adobe.com/products/reader`)**:** Another popular freebie, Acrobat Reader lets you view documents as if they're printed on paper. The Start screen's Reader program can also handle some formats used by Adobe Acrobat Reader, but not as well.

✔ **Microsoft Silverlight** (`www.silverlight.net`)**:** Microsoft's challenge to the hugely popular Flash, this software also plays movies and ads.

Beware of sites that try to slip in other programs when you download the plug-in. For example, some programs try to sneak in their partner's browser toolbar along with their plug-in. Examine the check boxes carefully and deselect any that you don't want, need, or trust before you click the Install or Download button. In case it's too late, I describe how to remove unwanted add-ons in the "Removing Unneeded Plug-Ins" section, later in this chapter.

Saving Information from the Internet

The Internet places a full-service library inside your house, with no long checkout lines. And just as every library comes with a copy machine, Internet Explorer provides several ways for you to save interesting tidbits of information for your personal use.

This section explains how to copy something from the Internet onto your computer, whether it's an entire web page, a single picture, a sound or movie, or a program.

I explain how to print a web page (or a snippet of information it contains) in Chapter 8.

Saving a web page

Hankering for a handy Fahrenheit/Centigrade conversion chart? Need that Sushi Identification Chart for dinner? Want to save the itinerary for next month's trip to Norway? When you find a web page with indispensable information, sometimes you can't resist saving a copy onto your computer for further viewing, perusal, or even printing at a later date.

When you save a web page, you're saving the page as it *currently exists* on your screen. To see any subsequent changes, you must revisit the actual site.

Saving your currently viewed web page is easy:

1. **Click Internet Explorer's Tools button, choose File, and choose Save As from the overly packed menu.**

   When the Save Webpage box appears, Internet Explorer enters the web page's name in the File Name text box, as shown in Figure 9-6.

   To save the entire page as a single file in your Documents folder, click Save. But if you want to save the file in a different place or in a different format, move to Step 2.

2. **Select a location in the Navigation Pane to save the file.**

   Internet Explorer normally saves the web page in your Documents folder, which is accessible from the Navigation Pane that hitches itself to every folder's left edge. To save the web page in a different place, perhaps Downloads, click the Downloads item in the Navigation Pane's Favorites section.

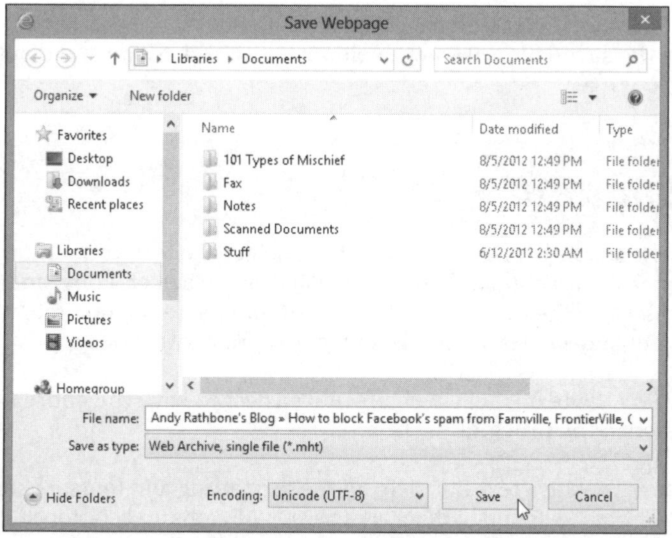

Figure 9-6:
Internet
Explorer's
Web
Archive for-
mat saves
the page to
a single file.

3. **Choose how you want to save the page in the Save As Type drop-down list.**

   Internet Explorer offers *four* different ways to save the web page:

- **Web Archive, Single File (*.mht):** This default choice saves an exact copy of the web page packed neatly into a single file named after the web page's title. Unfortunately, only Internet Explorer can open this type of file, ruling out its use by people who use other web browsing programs.

- **Webpage, Complete (*.htm;*.html):** More awkward but more compatible, this option saves the web page in two separate pieces: a folder containing the page's images and a link that tells the computer to display that folder's contents. It's unwieldy, but any web browser can open it.

- **Webpage, HTML Only (*.htm;*.html):** This option saves the page's text and layout but strips away the images. It's handy for stripping pictures and advertisements from tables, charts, and other formatted chunks of text.

- **Text File (*.txt):** This option scrapes all the text off the page and dumps it into a Notepad file without taking many pains to preserve the formatting. It's handy for saving very simple lists, but not much else.

   4. Click the Save button when you're done.

To revisit your saved web page, open the folder where you saved it and choose the saved file. Internet Explorer leaps back to life and displays the page.

Saving text

To save just a little of a web page's text, select the text you want to grab, right-click it, and choose Copy. (I explain how to select, copy, and paste text in Chapter 6.) Open your word processor and paste the text into a new document and save it in your Documents folder with a descriptive name.

To save *all* the text from a website, it's easiest to save the entire web page, as described in the previous section.

To save a website's text but strip all the formatting and fonts, paste the copied text into Notepad, found in the Start screen's All Apps area. Notepad immediately strips out the formatting. Then copy the text from Notepad and paste it into the word processor of your choice.

Saving a picture

As you browse through web pages and spot a picture that's too good to pass up, save it to your computer: Right-click the picture and choose Save Picture As, as shown in Figure 9-7.

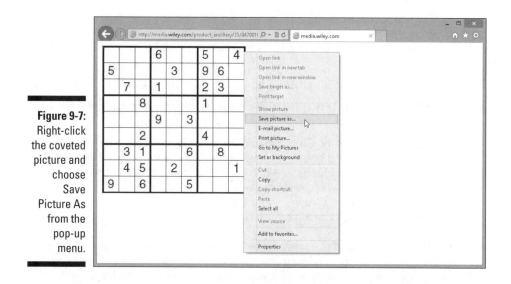

Figure 9-7:
Right-click
the coveted
picture and
choose
Save
Picture As
from the
pop-up
menu.

The Save Picture window appears, letting you choose a new filename for the picture or stick with the filename used by the web page. Click Save to place your pilfered picture in your Pictures folder.

The crowded pop-up menu shown in Figure 9-7 offers other handy options, as well, letting you choose to print or e-mail the picture or even set it as your desktop's background.

Remember the little picture by your name on the Windows 8 Welcome screen? Feel free to use any picture from the Internet. Right-click the new picture and save it to your Pictures folder. Then use the Start screen's equivalent of the desktop's Control Panel — the PC Settings screen (see Chapter 2) — to transform that picture into your new user account picture.

Downloading a program, song, or other type of file

Sometimes downloading is as easy as clicking a website's Click to Download Now button. When the website asks where to save your file, choose your Downloads folder for easy retrieval. The file usually arrives within a few seconds.

But when a website lacks a Click to Download Now button, you need to take a few extra steps:

1. **Right-click the link pointing to your desired file and choose Save Target As.**

For example, to download a song from a website, right-click its link (a song title, for example). Then choose Save Target As from the pop-up menu, similar to the menu shown earlier in Figure 9-7.

When you try to download a program, Windows asks whether you want to Save the File or Run It from Its Current Location. Choose Save the File.

2. **Navigate to your Downloads folder, if necessary, and click the Save button.**

Windows 8 normally offers to save the incoming file into the same folder your last download landed in, saving you the trouble of navigating to it. (You can see Downloads listed in the folder's Navigation Pane in Figure 9-8.) But if you prefer to download it to a different place — your Music library, for example, when downloading a song — navigate to that location and click the Save button.

No matter what type of file you're downloading, Windows 8 begins copying the file from the website to your hard drive. A window appears to tell you when it finishes downloading, and you can click the Open Folder button to open the folder harboring your downloaded file.

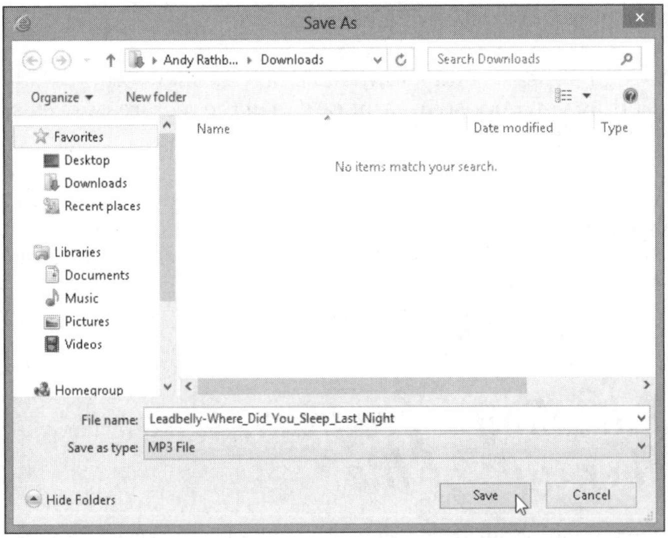

Figure 9-8:
Navigate to
a folder or
library and
click the
Save button.

Many downloaded files come packaged in a tidy folder with a zipper on it, known as a *Zip file*. Windows 8 treats them like normal folders; just double-click them to see inside them. (The files are actually compressed inside that folder to save download time, if you care about the engineering involved.) To extract copies of the zipped files, right-click the zipped file and choose Extract All.

It Doesn't Work!

If something doesn't work, don't feel bad. The Internet has been around for a while, but this whole web thing is relatively complicated, and changing quickly. It's not supposed to work as smoothly as a television yet, and it isn't something you can figure out overnight. This section explores common problems and possible solutions.

The person holding the Administrator account — usually the computer's owner — is the only one who is authorized to make some of the changes I describe in this section. If a mean message pops up, waving its finger and mumbling about administrator permissions, you're locked out. Better find the computer's owner to proceed.

Here are some general tips that you may want to try before you explore the following sections:

✔ When a website gives you problems on the desktop version of Internet Explorer, try emptying Internet Explorer's wastebasket. Click Internet Explorer's Tools button, choose Internet Options, and click the Delete button. Put a check mark in the check box called Temporary Internet Files, remove check marks from items you *don't* want to delete, and click the Close button. Revisit the problematic site and try again.

✔ If your connection settings seem askew, try setting up your Internet connection again. Described in the "Setting Up Internet Explorer the First Time" section, earlier in this chapter, the steps guide you through your current settings, letting you change things that look suspicious.

✔ Think you've messed up the desktop's Internet Explorer beyond repair? When all seems lost, return the program to its original settings with this trick: Click Tools, choose Internet Options, click the Advanced tab, and click Reset. This wipes out *all* of your settings, including your list of favorite sites. But it also removes any evil that may have attached itself to your browser.

✔ If you can't connect to the Internet at all, your best bet is to call your ISP's tech support number and ask for help. (Be sure to call your Internet service provider, not Microsoft.)

✔ If a page doesn't seem to display correctly on the desktop's Internet Explorer, look for a warning strip along the page's top. Click the strip and tell Internet Explorer *not* to block what it's trying to block.

Removing Unneeded Plug-Ins

Lots of websites install little programs inside Internet Explorer to help you navigate the web or to add features to some websites. Not all of those little programs are well behaved. To help you pry off the leeches, Internet Explorer lets you see a list of all the currently installed little programs, called *add-ons*.

You won't find any plug-ins in the Start screen's version of Internet Explorer. No, plug-ins can be installed only in the more full-featured (and hence more trouble-prone) desktop version of Internet Explorer.

 To see what's hanging onto your copy of Internet Explorer, click the program's Tools button and choose Manage Add-Ons. Internet Explorer's Manage Add-Ons window appears, as shown in Figure 9-9, letting you see all add-ons, toolbars, search engines, and more.

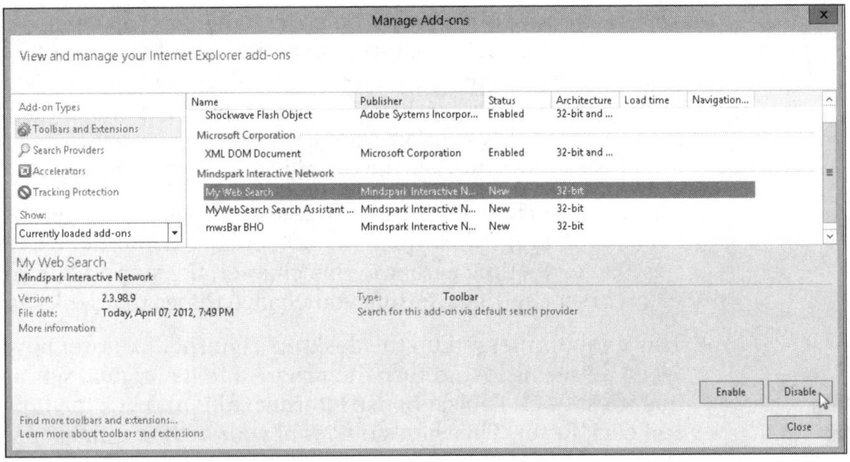

Figure 9-9: Select an unwanted add-on and click the Disable button.

Most add-ons listed in the Manage Add-Ons window are fine. (The ones from Microsoft are generally harmless.) But if you spot an add-on that you don't recognize or that you think is causing problems, look up its name in Google (www.google.com) to see what most people say about it. If you find one that seems bad, click its name and click the Disable button.

If disabling the add-on keeps something from working correctly, return to the Manage Add-Ons window, click the add-on's name, and click the Enable button.

Managing add-ons sometimes turns into a game of trial and error, but it's a handy way to disable a rogue add-on installed by a nasty website.

Chapter 10

Being Social: Mail, People, Calendar, and Messaging

- -

In This Chapter

▶ Adding your accounts

▶ Setting up e-mail

▶ Sending and receiving files and photos

▶ Managing your contacts

▶ Managing your calendar

▶ Sending and receiving instant messages

- -

*T*hanks to the Internet's never-fading memory, your friends and acquaintances never disappear. Old college chums, business pals, and even those elementary school bullies are all waiting for you online. Toss in a few strangers you may have swapped messages with on websites, and the Internet has created a huge social network.

Windows 8 helps you stay in touch with friends you enjoy and avoid those you don't. To manage your online social life, Windows 8 includes a suite of intertwined social apps: Mail, People, Calendar, and Messaging. You can pretty much guess which app handles what job.

The apps work together, vastly simplifying the chore of tracking your contacts and appointments. Tell Windows 8 about your Facebook account, for example, and Windows 8 automatically stuffs your Facebook friends' information into the People app, adds birthdays and appointments to your Calendar app, and sets up your Mail and Messaging app.

This chapter describes the Windows 8 suite of social apps and how they work with Facebook, Google, Twitter, LinkedIn, and other accounts. It explains how to set them up, keep the communications flowing, and when necessary, turn them off when you're feeling information overload.

Adding Your Social Accounts to Windows 8

For years, you've heard people say, "Never tell *anybody* your user account name and password." Now, it seems Windows 8 wants you to break that rule.

When you first open your People, Mail, or Messaging apps, Windows 8 may ask you to enter your account names and passwords from Facebook, Google, Twitter, LinkedIn, Hotmail, and other services.

It's not as scary as you think, though. Microsoft and the other networks have agreed to share your information, *only if you approve it.* And should you approve it, Windows connects to your social network — Facebook, for example — where you can tell Facebook it's okay to share your information with the People app in Windows 8.

And, frankly, approving the information swap is a huge timesaver. When you link those accounts to Windows 8, your computer signs in to each service, imports your friends' contact information, and stocks your apps.

To fill in Windows 8 about your online social life, follow these steps:

1. **From the Start screen, open the Mail app.**

   The tile-filled Start screen, covered in Chapter 2, appears when you first turn on your computer. If it's not onscreen, fetch it with these steps:

   - **Mouse:** Point at the top- or bottom-right corners to summon the Charms bar. Then click the Start icon that appears.

   - **Keyboard:** Press the ⊞ key.

   - **Touchscreen:** Slide your finger inward from the screen's right edge to fetch the Charms bar and then tap the Start icon.

   Click the Mail tile, and the app opens. If you haven't yet signed up for a Microsoft account, a prompter appears, reminding you that you need one. (I explain how to sign up for a Microsoft account in Chapter 2.)

   When the Mail app first appears, it usually contains at least one e-mail: a welcoming message from Microsoft, shown in Figure 10-1. (Mail also asks you to Allow or Decline the sending of error messages to Microsoft, so the company can improve its products.)

2. **Enter your accounts into the Mail app.**

   To add accounts, summon the Charms bar, click the Settings icon, click Accounts, and click Add an Account. Mail lists the accounts you can add: Hotmail, Outlook, Google, or Exchange.

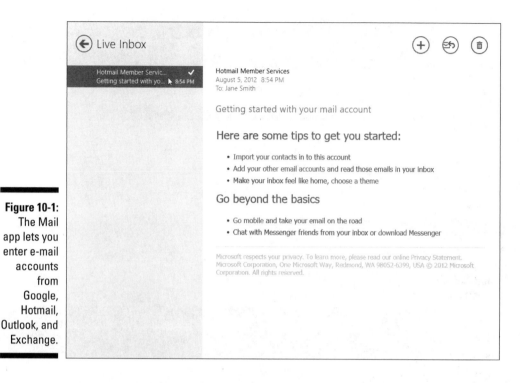

Live Inbox

Hotmail Member Servic...
Getting started with yo... 8:54 PM

Hotmail Member Services
August 5, 2012 8:54 PM
To: Jane Smith

Getting started with your mail account

Here are some tips to get you started:

- Import your contacts in to this account
- Add your other email accounts and read those emails in your inbox
- Make your inbox feel like home, choose a theme

Go beyond the basics

- Go mobile and take your email on the road
- Chat with Messenger friends from your inbox or download Messenger

Microsoft respects your privacy. To learn more, please read our online Privacy Statement.
Microsoft Corporation, One Microsoft Way, Redmond, WA 98052-6399, USA © 2012 Microsoft
Corporation. All rights reserved.

Figure 10-1:
The Mail
app lets you
enter e-mail
accounts
from
Google,
Hotmail,
Outlook, and
Exchange.

To add a Google account, for example, click the word *Google*. Windows 8 takes you to a secure area on Google's website where you can authorize the transaction by entering your Gmail e-mail address and password and then clicking Connect.

Repeat these steps for other listed accounts, authorizing each of them to share information with your Windows account.

I explain how to add e-mail addresses besides Hotmail, Outlook, and Google in this chapter's "Adding other e-mail accounts to Mail" sidebar.

3. **Return to the Start screen, click the People tile, and enter your other accounts.**

   Now's your chance to tell Windows about your friends: Click the People tile on the Start screen. When it appears, you may spot friends listed in the address books associated with the e-mail accounts you entered in Step 1.

   Continue adding contacts by entering your usernames and passwords from accounts from Facebook, Twitter, LinkedIn, and others.

   For example, choose Facebook, click Connect, and a window appears (shown in Figure 10-2) for you to enter your Facebook name and password.

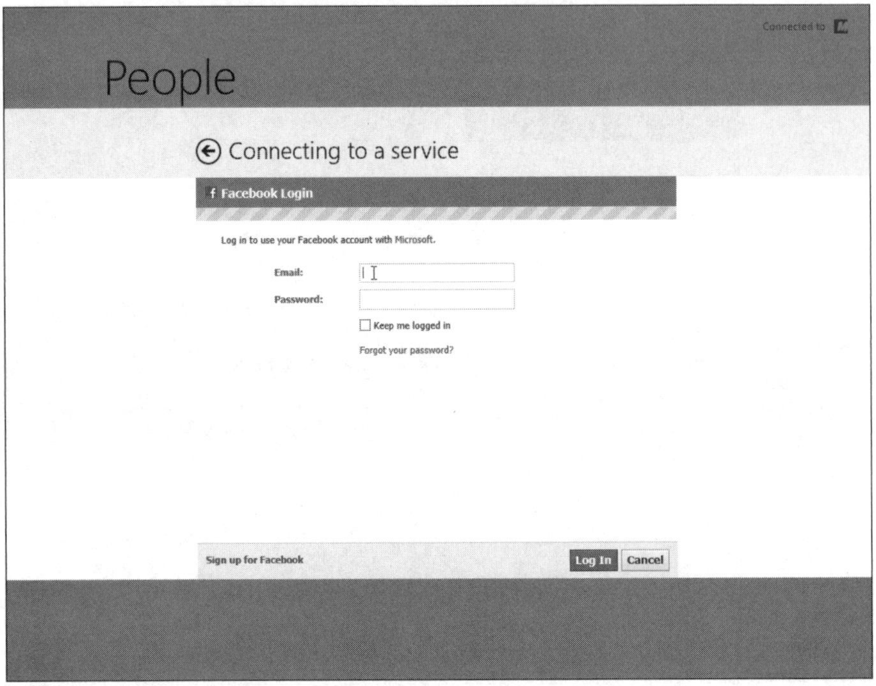

People

(←) Connecting to a service

f **Facebook Login**

Log in to use your Facebook account with Microsoft.

Email: | I

Password:

☐ Keep me logged in

Forgot your password?

Sign up for Facebook   Log In   Cancel

Figure 10-2:
Enter your
Facebook
e-mail
account and
password to
import your
friends
into your
People app.

After you've entered your accounts, Windows 8 automatically fetches your e-mail through your Mail app, fills the People app with your friends' contact information, and adds any appointments in your Calendar app.

Although it might seem frightening to give Windows 8 your coveted usernames and passwords, it enriches Windows 8 in many ways:

- ✔ Instead of typing in your contacts by hand, they're waiting for you automatically, whether they're from Facebook, Twitter, or LinkedIn or they're connected with your Google, Hotmail, Outlook, or Windows Live account.

- ✔ Windows 8 apps work well with apps and programs from other companies. For example, if a friend wants to chat with you from Facebook, the Windows 8 Messaging program opens, letting you swap messages. You don't need to open Facebook; Windows Messaging app talks with Facebook's messaging app.

- ✔ You can view your friends' Facebook, Twitter, and LinkedIn messages and photos directly from the People app. You no longer need to make the rounds of all your social networks to see what everybody's doing.

 ✔ Don't like these new-fangled Windows 8 apps? Then ignore them and spend your time on the Windows 8 desktop. There, you can visit Facebook and your other accounts from your web browser, the same way you've always done.

Removing social accounts from Windows 8

If your People app's a little crowded with the 2,835 people you follow on Twitter, you can remove them. In fact, you can remove *any* or *all* of the social accounts that you've added to Windows 8.

To remove any account, follow these steps:

1. **Open the app containing the accounts you'd like to delete, either Mail or People.**

2. **Fetch the Charms bar and click the Settings icon.**

3. **Click the Accounts setting; when the Accounts pane appears, click the name of the account you want to delete.**

   The Accounts pane changes to show the settings of your chosen account. (You can't delete your Windows account, but others are fair game.)

4. **When the pane displays the account's settings, click the Remove Account button at the pane's bottom edge.**

For some accounts, Step 4 takes you to yet another settings area. When removing Facebook from the People app, for example, Step 4 takes you to a site online where you can choose exactly what types of Facebook information you want to share with the People app. (Or you can sever ties by clicking the Remove This Connection Completely link.)

When you delete an account with these steps, you're nixing any interaction. Removing Facebook, for example, removes your Facebook friends from the People app and deletes any of their birthdays or invited events from your Calendar app. Your account on Facebook stays intact; it simply stops sharing information with Windows 8 apps.

Changed your mind about severing ties? Add the account back by following the steps in this chapter's "Adding Your Social Accounts to Windows 8" section.

Understanding the Mail App

Unlike Windows 7, Windows 8 comes with a built-in app for sending and receiving your e-mail. Not only is the Mail app free, but it also comes with a spell checker.

Considered a *live* app, the Mail app automatically updates its Start screen's tile. A glance at the Start screen's Mail tile quickly shows you the senders' names and subjects of your latest e-mails.

However, like many free things, the Mail app carries a cost in convenience, as described by these limitations:

✔ You need a Microsoft account to use the Mail app, as well as to use the bundled People, Calendar, and Messaging apps. I describe how to sign up for a free Microsoft account in Chapter 2.

✔ The Mail app works only with Hotmail accounts, Windows Live accounts (including outlook), and Google's Gmail accounts. (It also works with Exchange accounts, but those require special equipment usually found in larger businesses, not homes.)

If you need to add a different type of e-mail account, you need to do it through Internet Explorer on the Windows desktop. There you can visit your Microsoft or Google account and add your other e-mail accounts, should you need them. I explain more about that process in this chapter's "Adding other e-mail accounts to Mail" sidebar.

The rest of this section describes how to find the Mail app's hidden menus, as well as how to send and receive e-mail and files.

Switching among the Mail app's views, menus, and accounts

To load Windows' Mail app, open the Start screen with a press of your Windows key (⊞) and then click the Mail app tile. The Mail app quickly fills the screen, shown in Figure 10-3.

The Mail app lists your e-mail accounts in its bottom-left corner. Figure 10-3, for example, shows a Hotmail account at the top and a Google account beneath it. (If you've only set up one account, you see only one account listed.)

To see the mail sent to your account, click the account's name. For example, see how the name Hotmail is listed in the top-left corner in Figure 10-3? That's because it's the currently viewed account; accordingly, the Mail app shows the Hotmail account's newest e-mail on the screen's right side.

Beneath the names of your e-mail accounts, the Mail app lists its main folders:

✔ **Inbox:** Shown when you first load the Mail app, the Inbox folder lists your waiting e-mail. Mail automatically checks for new e-mail, but if you tire of waiting, click Sync, shown in the margin. That immediately grabs any waiting Mail. (Right-click a blank portion of the Mail app to reveal its menu, including the Sync icon, alon the bottom edge.)

✔ **Drafts:** When you're midway through writing an e-mail and want to finish it later, click the Close icon shown in the margin and choose Save Draft from the drop-down menu. The e-mail then waits in this folder for retrieval later. (I explain how to send e-mail in this chapter's next section.)

Mail app folders

Currently viewed e-mail account

Number of unread messages   Latest e-mail from currently viewed account

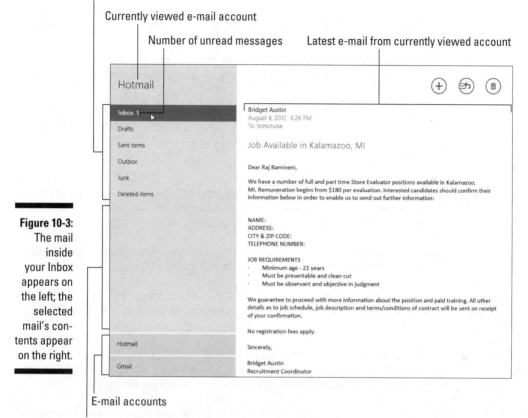

Figure 10-3:
The mail
inside
your Inbox
appears on
the left; the
selected
mail's con-
tents appear
on the right.

E-mail accounts

Folders on other accounts like Gmail appear here

Adding other e-mail accounts to Mail

The Mail app can fetch e-mail only from Hotmail, Outlook, or Gmail accounts. So, to add other accounts, you need to visit the Windows desktop, open Internet Explorer, and visit either Hotmail (www.hotmail.com), Outlook (www.outlook.com), or Gmail (www.google.com/mail).

From there, open the website's Options menu and look for an area where you can add other accounts. You'll need to enter your account's username and password.

When your Hotmail or Google accounts begin importing your mail from your other accounts, that mail will be waiting for you in your Mail app.

✔ **Sent Items:** *Every* piece of e-mail you've sent lingers in this folder, leaving a permanent record. (To kill any embarrassing e-mail from any folder, select the offending e-mail with a click and click the Delete icon shown in the margin.)

✔ **Junk:** The Mail app sniffs out potential junk mail and drops suspects into this folder. Peek in here every once in a while to make sure nothing falls in by mistake.

✔ **Deleted Items:** The Deleted Items folder serves as the Mail app's Recycle Bin, letting you retrieve mistakenly deleted e-mail. To delete something permanently from the Deleted Items folder, select it and choose the Delete icon.

✔ **Outbox:** When you send or reply to a message, the Mail app immediately tries to connect to the Internet and send it. If Mail can't find the Internet, your message lingers here. When you connect to the Internet again, click the Sync button, if necessary, to send it on its way.

To see the contents of any folder, click it. Click any e-mail inside the folder, and its contents appear in the pane to the far right.

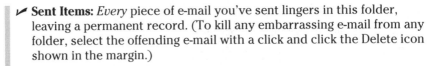

Created folders in your Gmail account? When you click your Google account, the Mail app lists those folders beneath the Map app's own folders, as shown in Figure 10-3.

But where are the Mail app's menus? Like *all* Start screen apps, the Mail app hides its menus on an App bar along the screen's bottom edge. You can reveal the App bar in Mail and *any* Windows app with a few tricks.

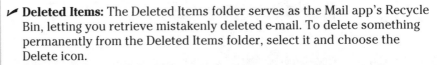

To summon the App bar along the bottom of any app, choose one of these options:

✔ **Mouse:** Right-click on a blank portion inside the app.

✔ **Keyboard:** Press ⊞+Z.

✔ **Touchscreen:** From the screen's bottom, slide your finger upward.

When the App bar rises from the screen's bottom edge, shown in Figure 10-4, it reveals icons to help you maneuver through the Mail app.

Composing and sending an e-mail

When you're ready to send an e-mail, follow these steps to compose your letter and drop it in the electronic mailbox, sending it through virtual space to the recipient's computer:

1. **From the Start screen, open the Mail app's tile and click the New icon in the program's top-right corner.**

Return to folder view

Currently viewed e-mail account

Currently viewed e-mail

Delete currently viewed e-mail

Respond to currently viewed e-mail

Create new e-mail

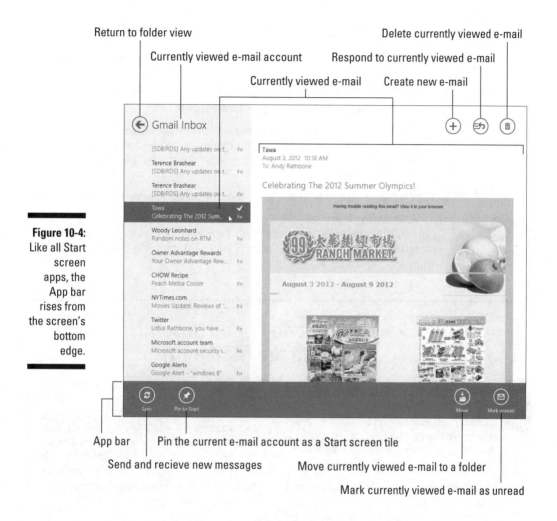

Figure 10-4:
Like all Start
screen
apps, the
App bar
rises from
the screen's
bottom
edge.

App bar

Pin the current e-mail account as a Start screen tile

Send and recieve new messages

Move currently viewed e-mail to a folder

Mark currently viewed e-mail as unread

A New Message window appears, empty and awaiting your words.

If you've added more than one e-mail account to the Mail app, choose your return address by clicking the downward-pointing arrow in the From box — the box currently listing your e-mail address. Then select the account you want to use for sending that particular mail.

2. **Type your friend's e-mail address into the To box.**

As you begin typing, the Mail app scans your People app's list for both names and e-mail addresses, listing potential matches below the To box. Spot a match on the list? Click it, and the Mail app automatically fills in the rest of the e-mail address.

To send an e-mail to several people, click the plus sign to the right of the To box. The People app appears, listing your contacts' names and e-mail addresses. Click the name — or names — of the people you want to receive your e-mail and then click the Add button. The Mail app addresses your e-mail, just as if you'd typed it in manually.

3. **Click in the Subject line and type in a subject.**

   Click the words Add a Subject at the top of the message and type in your own subject. In Figure 10-5, for example, I've added the subject Memorandum for Success. Although optional, the Subject line helps your friends sort their mail.

4. **Type your message into the large box beneath the Subject line.**

   Type as many words as you want. As you type, the Mail app underlines potentially misspelled words in red. To correct them, right-click the underlined word and choose the correct spelling from the pop-up menu, shown in Figure 10-5.

Exactly what do I need to send e-mail with the Mail app?

To send e-mail to a friend or foe with the Mail app, you need three things:

✔ **A Microsoft account:** You need to create this special type of e-mail address before the Mail app will run. I describe how to create a Microsoft account in Chapter 2.

✔ **An e-mail account:** Your Microsoft account can serve as an e-mail account if you use a Live, Hotmail, or Outlook account, or an IMAP account used by some businesses. Most ISPs (Internet service porviders, covered in Chapter 9) also give you a free e-mail address along with your Internet access, but that e-mail address probably won't work with the Mail app.

✔ **Your friend's or foe's e-mail address:** Find out your friends' e-mail addresses by simply asking them. Or import your friends' addresses from Facebook, Twitter, or LinkedIn, as I describe in this chapter's "Adding Your Social Accounts to Windows 8"

section. An address consists of a *username* (which occasionally resembles the person's real name), followed by the @ sign, followed by the name of your friend's ISP. The e-mail address of an America Online user with the username of JeffW8435 would be jeffw8435@aol.com. (Unlike your local post office, e-mail doesn't tolerate any spelling errors. Precision is a must.)

✔ **Your message:** Here's where the fun finally starts: typing your letter. After you enter the person's e-mail address and your message, click the Send button. The Mail app routes your message in the right direction.

If you misspell part of an e-mail address, your sent message bounces back to your own Inbox, with a confusing *undeliverable* message attached. Check the spelling of the address and try again. If it bounces again, humble yourself: Pick up the phone and ask the person to confirm his or her e-mail address.

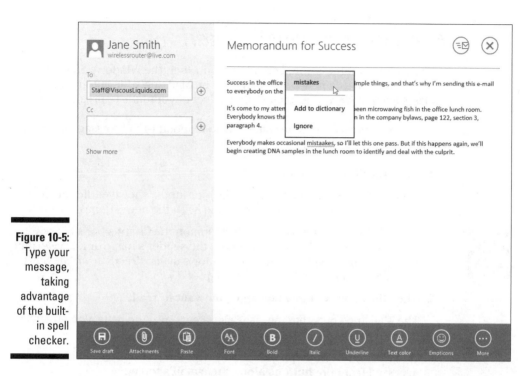

Figure 10-5:
Type your
message,
taking
advantage
of the built-
in spell
checker.

You can also change formatting by fetching the App bar along the app's bottom edge by right-clicking, by pressing ⊞+Z, or by swiping upward on a tablet. Shown in Figure 10-5, the App bar along the bottom lets you add bulleted lists, change fonts, add italics, and more.

5. **If you want, attach any files or photos to your e-mail.**

   I describe how to attach files in the "Sending and receiving files through e-mail" section, but if you're feeling savvy, you can attach them by clicking the Attachments icon on the Mail app's App bar.

   Most ISPs balk at sending files larger than about 5MB, which rules out nearly all movies and more than a few files containing digital music or photos.

6. **Click the Send button along the top-right corner.**

   Whoosh! The Mail app whisks your message through the Internet to your friend's mailbox. Depending on the speed of your Internet connection, mail can arrive anywhere from 5 seconds later to a few days later, with a few minutes being the average.

   Don't want to send the message? Then click the Close button, shown in the margin. When a drop-down menu appears, choose Delete to delete the message or choose Save Draft to keep a copy in your Drafts folder for later polishing.

Reading a received e-mail

When your computer is connected to the Internet, the Windows Start screen tells you as soon as a new e-mail arrives. The Mail app's tile automatically updates itself to show the sender and subject of your latest unread e-mails.

To see more information than that — or to respond to the message — follow these steps:

1. **Click the Start screen's Mail tile.**

   Mail opens to show the messages in your Inbox, shown earlier in Figure 10-3. Each subject is listed, one by one, with the newest one at the top.

   To find a particular e-mail quickly, summon the Charms bar's Search pane by pressing ⊞+Q and then type the sender's name or a keyword in the search box. (You can also search for e-mails directly from the Start screen's Search pane, covered in Chapter 7.)

2. **Click the subject of any message you want to read.**

   The Mail app spills that message's contents into the pane along the window's right side.

3. **From here, the Mail app leaves you with several options, each accessed from the buttons along the e-mail's top edge:**

   • **Nothing:** Undecided? Don't do anything, and the message simply sets up camp in your Inbox folder.

   • **Respond:** Click the Respond button in the top-right corner and choose Reply from the drop-down menu. A new window appears, ready for you to type in your response. The window is just like the one that appears when you first compose a message but with a handy difference: This window is preaddressed with the recipient's name and the subject. Also, the original message usually appears at the bottom of your reply for reference.

   • **Reply All:** Some people address e-mails to several people simultaneously. If you see several other people listed on an e-mail's To line, you can reply to all of them by clicking Respond and choosing Reply All from the drop-down menu.

   • **Forward:** Received something that a friend simply must see? Click Respond and choose Forward from the drop-down menu to kick a copy of the e-mail to your friend's Inbox.

   • **Delete:** Click the Delete button to toss the message into your Deleted Items folder. Your deleted messages sit inside that folder until you open the Deleted Items folder, click all the messages and click the Delete button again.

To print your currently viewed e-mail, summon the Charms bar, click the Devices icon, choose your printer from the list of devices, and click the Print button.

The Mail app works for basic e-mail needs. If you need more, you can find a more full-featured e-mail program, or you open Internet Explorer, go online to Hotmail (`www.hotmail.com`), Outlook (`www.outlook.com`), or Google (`www.google.com/gmail`), and manage your e-mail from there.

If you ever receive an unexpected e-mail from a bank, eBay, or any other website involving money, don't click any of the e-mail's web links. A criminal industry called *phishing* sends e-mails that try to trick you into entering your name and password on a phony website. That gives your coveted information to the evil folk, who promptly steal your money. I write more about phishing in Chapter 11.

Sending and receiving files through e-mail

Like a pair of movie tickets slipped into the envelope of a thank-you note, an *attachment* is a file that piggybacks onto an e-mail message. You can send or receive any type of file as an attachment.

This section describes how to both send and receive a file through the Mail app.

Saving a received attachment

When an attachment arrives in an e-mail, you'll recognize it: It's a large rectangle at the top of your e-mail; the rectangle lists the file's name with the word Download listed directly beneath it.

Saving the attached file or files takes just a few steps.

1. **Click the word Download next to the attached file.**

   This tells the Mail app to actually download the file. Until you click the rectangle, the Mail app tells you only the attached file's name and file size. When the download completes, the rectangle turns into an icon representing the newly downloaded file.

2. **When the file downloads to the Mail app, click the attached file's icon and choose Save.**

   That tells the Mail app to copy the file from your e-mail and save it to a folder in your computer.

3. **Choose a folder to receive the saved file.**

   The Windows 8 File Picker appears, shown in Figure 10-6, letting you navigate to a folder.

4. **Click the word Files in the File Picker's top-left corner and then choose which library to receive the incoming file: Documents, Pictures, Music, or Videos.**

   Saving the file inside one of your four libraries is the easiest way to ensure you'll find it later. I describe files, folders, and libraries in Chapter 5.

5. **Click the Save button in the File Picker's bottom-right corner.**

   The Mail app saves the file in the library of your choosing.

After you've saved the file, the Mail app returns to the screen. And, if you notice, the attachment still remains inside the e-mail. That's because saving attachments always saves a *copy* of the sent file. That's handy because, if you accidentally delete your saved file, you can return to the original e-mail and save the file yet again.

The built-in virus checker in Windows 8, Windows Defender, automatically scans your incoming e-mail for any evil file attachments. I explain more about Windows Defender in Chapter 11.

Sending a file as an attachment

Sending a file through the Mail app works much like saving an attached file, although in reverse: Instead of grabbing a file from an e-mail and saving it into a folder or library, you're grabbing a file from a folder or library and saving it in an e-mail.

To send a file as an attachment in the Mail app, follow these steps:

1. **Open the Mail app and create a new e-mail, as described earlier in this chapter's "Composing and sending an e-mail" section.**

2. **Open the Mail app's App bar, and click the Attachments icon.**

   Open the App bar by right-clicking on a blank part of the e-mail. When you click the Attachment icon, the Windows 8 File Picker window appears, shown earlier in Figure 10-6.

3. **Navigate to the file you'd like to send.**

   For easy browsing, click the word Files. That fetches a drop-down menu, shown earlier in Figure 10-6, listing your computer's major storage areas. Most files are stored in your Documents, Pictures, Music and Videos libraries. (I cover libraries in Chapter 5.)

   Click a folder's name to see the files it contains. Not the right folder? Click the File Picker's Go Up link to move back out of the folder and try again.

4. **Click the filenames you want to send and click the Attach button.**

   Selected too many files? Deselect unwanted files by clicking their names yet again. When you click the Attach button, the Mail app adds the file or files to your e-mail.

5. **Click the Send button.**

   The Mail app whisks off your mail and its attachment to the recipient.

Finding lost mail

Eventually, an important e-mail will disappear into a pile of folders and filenames. To retrieve it, rely on the same trick you use to search within *any* app in Windows 8: Summon the Search pane. From within Windows Mail, click the account holding the e-mail you want to search through and then follow these steps:

✔ **Mouse:** Point in the screen's top- or bottom-right corners; when the Charms bar appears, click the Search icon.

✔ **Keyboard:** Press ⊞+Q.

✔ **Touchscreen:** Slide your finger inward from the screen's right edge and tap the Search icon.

When the Search pane appears, type in a word from the lost e-mail or the person's name and then press Enter to see all your matching e-mail.

Note: If you have more than one account in Mail, you must search each account separately.

Managing Your Contacts in the People App

When you let Windows 8 eavesdrop on your online social networks, as described in this chapter's first section, you've conveniently stocked the People app with your online friends from Facebook, Twitter, and other networks.

To see everybody in your People app, click the Start screen's People tile. The People app appears, listing all your online friends, as shown in Figure 10-7.

Figure 10-7: The People app automatically stocks itself with friends listed in your online social networks like Facebook and Twitter.

The People app handles much of its upkeep automatically, axing people you've unfriended on Facebook, for example, and slyly removing contacts who've unfriended *you,* as well.

But friends who don't share their lives online through social networks won't appear in the People app. And some privacy-concerned Facebook friends may have told Facebook to withhold their information from other programs — and that includes Windows 8.

TIP

Keeping track of your friends' updates

For the most fun in the People app, click the words What's New in the People app's bottom-left corner, shown in Figure 10-7. The app lists all of your friends' status updates, whether they're posted on Facebook, Twitter, LinkedIn, or any other social network you've added.

Updated and frozen in place when opened, the What's New page presents a snapshot of social media information, offering you new ideas and information about your friends and their activities. Not seeing enough updates? Then you're not following enough people on Twitter.

You can also check on a particular friend by clicking his name in the People app. His contact information appears, but to the right, you can see his latest status updates.

That means you'll need to edit some People entries manually. This section explains the occasional pruning needed to keep up with our constantly evolving social networks.

Adding contacts

Although the People app loves to reach its fingers into any online crevice you toss its way, you can easily add people the old-fashioned way, typing them in by hand.

To add somebody to the People app, which makes those names available in your Mail and Messaging apps, follow these steps:

1. **Click the People tile on the Start screen.**

2. **Right-click on a blank part of the People app, and the App bar rises from the program's bottom edge. Then click the New icon.**

   A blank New Contact form makes its appearance.

3. **Fill out the New Contact form.**

   Shown in Figure 10-8, most of the choices are self-explanatory fields such as Name, Address, Email, and Phone. Click the Other Info button on the right to add items such as a job title, website, significant other, or notes.

   The biggest challenge comes with the Account field, an option seen only by people who've entered more than one e-mail account into the Mail app. Which e-mail *account* should receive the new contact?

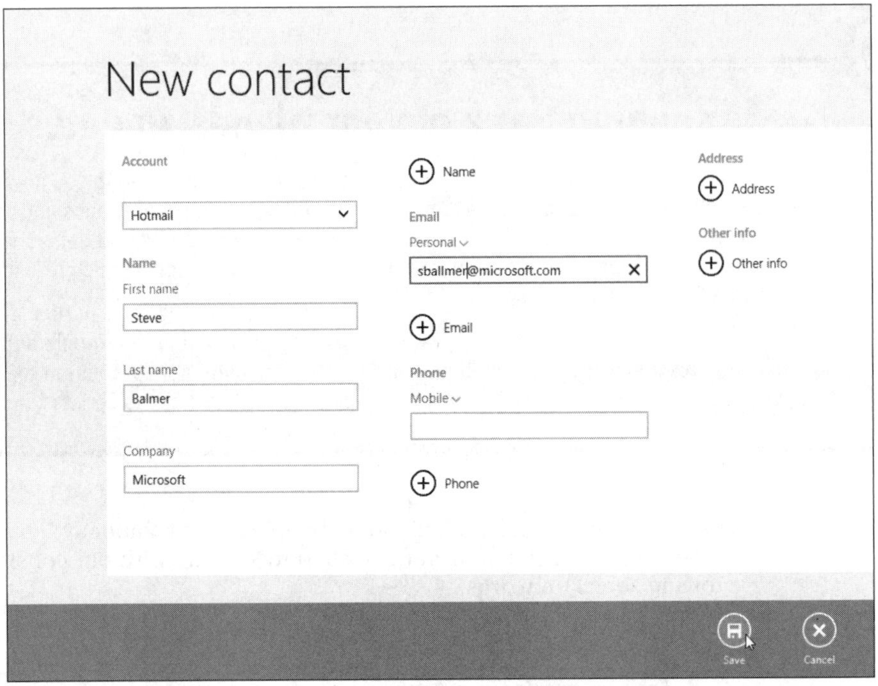

New contact

Account

Hotmail ⌄

Name
First name
Steve

Last name
Balmer

Company
Microsoft

⊕ Name

Email
Personal ⌄
sballmer@microsoft.com   ✕

⊕ Email

Phone
Mobile ⌄

⊕ Phone

Address
⊕ Address

Other info
⊕ Other info

Save   Cancel

Figure 10-8:
Add as
much infor-
mation as
you want
about your
new con-
tact. Then
click Save.

The answer hinges mainly on which cellphone you own. Choose your Google account if you use an Android phone, so your newly added account will appear on your Android phone's contacts list.

Choose the Microsoft account if you use a Microsoft phone, so the contact will appear there.

4. **Click the Save button.**

The People app dutifully saves your new contact. If you spot a mistake, however, you may need to go back and edit the information, described in the next section.

Deleting or editing contacts

Has somebody fallen from your social graces? Or perhaps just changed a phone number? Either way, it's easy to delete or edit a contact by following these steps:

1. **Click the People tile on the Start screen.**

The People app appears, as shown earlier in Figure 10-7.

2. **Click a contact.**

   The contact's page appears full-screen.

3. **Right-click a blank part of the contact's page to summon the App bar.**

   The App bar appears as a strip along the screen's bottom.

4. **Click Delete to delete the contact or click Edit to update a contact's information. Then click Save.**

Clicking Delete removes the person completely. However, the Delete button appears only for contacts you've added *by hand*. If they've been added through Facebook or another online social media site, you have to delete them by removing them from your contacts on that site. Unfriend them on Facebook or unfollow them on Twitter, for example, to remove them from the People app.

Clicking Edit fetches the screen shown back in Figure 10-8, where you can update or delete any information before clicking Save to save your changes.

Designed for best friends, the Pin to Start button turns that person into a Start screen tile, giving you easy access to her contact information and latest status updates.

To send a quick message to a contact in your People app, click her name. When her contact information appears, click the Send Email button. The Mail app calls up a handy, pre-addressed New Message window, ready for you to type your message and click Send. (This trick works only if you have that contact's e-mail address.)

Managing Appointments in Calendar

After you enter your social networking accounts such as Facebook and Google, as described in this chapter's first section, you've already stocked the Calendar app with appointments entered by both you and your online friends.

The Calendar displays your Facebook friends' birthdays, for example — if your Facebook friends have chosen to share that information. You can also find any appointments you've made in Google's calendar, a handy perk for owners of Android phones.

To see your appointments, click the Start screen's Calendar tile. The Calendar app appears, listing all your online appointments, as shown in Figure 10-9.

	Sunday	Monday	Tuesday	Wednesday	Thursday	Friday	Saturday
	25	26	27	28 3 events	29	30	1
	9:30a Point Lom...	6:30a Empty Tra...	Free Tuesday	9:30a Brownie T...	Janis Durelle's bir...	Luis Xum Garde...	9a Little Italy F:
		11:30a Ukulele q...	6:30p Happy Str...	3p Andy me...		10a Critique Gro...	
	2	3	4 3 events	5 3 events	6	7	8
	9:30a Point Lom...	11:30a Ukulele q...	Free Tuesday	Marsha Collier's...		Luis Xum Garde...	9a Little Italy F:
	3p Bird tour		Marsha Collier's...	3p Andy meets...		5p Friday Night...	
	9	10	11	12 3 events	13	14	15
	9:30a Point Lom...	6:30a Empty Tra...	Free Tuesday	9:30a Brownie T...		Luis Xum Garde...	9a Little Italy F:
		11:30a Ukulele q...	6:30p Happy Str...	3p Andy me...		Merri Miles's birt...	
	16	17	18	19	20	21	22
	9:30a Point Lom...	11:30a Ukulele q...	Free Tuesday	3p Andy meets...	Eric Warren's birt...	Luis Xum Garde...	9a Little Italy F:
	3p Bird tour		6:30p Happy Str...	4p Farmer's Ma...			
	23	24 3 events	25 4 events	26 3 events	27	28	29
	Glen Carlson's bi...	Christmas Eve	Free Tuesday	9:30a Brownie T...		Luis Xum Garde...	9a Little Italy F:
	9:30a Point Lom...	6:30a Empty Tra...	Christmas	3p Andy me...		10a Critique Gro...	
	30	31 3 events	1 3 events	2	3	4 4 events	5
	9:30a Point Lom...	New Year's Eve	Free Tuesday	3p Andy meets...	Ian Barnard's Birt...	Dierdre's Birthday	My Wedding A
		New Year's Eve	New Year's Day	4p Farmer's Ma...		Luis Xum Garde...	9a Little Italy F:

December 2012

Figure 10-9: The Calendar app stocks itself with appointments added from your online social networks.

Very few people keep all their appointments online, though, so you'll occasionally need to edit some entries, add new ones, or delete those you can no longer attend. This section explains how to keep your appointments up-to-date.

The Calendar opens to show a monthly view, shown earlier in Figure 10-9. To switch to other views, right-click the calendar app to fetch the App bar; then click the Day, Week, or Month button.

No matter which view the Calendar app displays, you can flip through the appointments by clicking the little arrows near the screen's top corners. Click the right arrow to move forward in time; click the left arrow to move backward.

The Calendar app grabs whatever appointments it can find from your online social networks. But you can still add or edit appointments manually when needed.

To add an appointment to your Calendar app, follow these steps:

1. **Click the Calendar tile on the Start screen.**

   The Calendar appears, shown earlier in Figure 10-9.

2. **Load the Apps bar and click the New icon.**

   I explain how to load any app's menu bar earlier in this chapter. (*Hint:* Right-click anywhere on the Calendar.)

3. **Fill out the Details form.**

   Shown in Figure 10-10, most of the choices are self-explanatory fields.

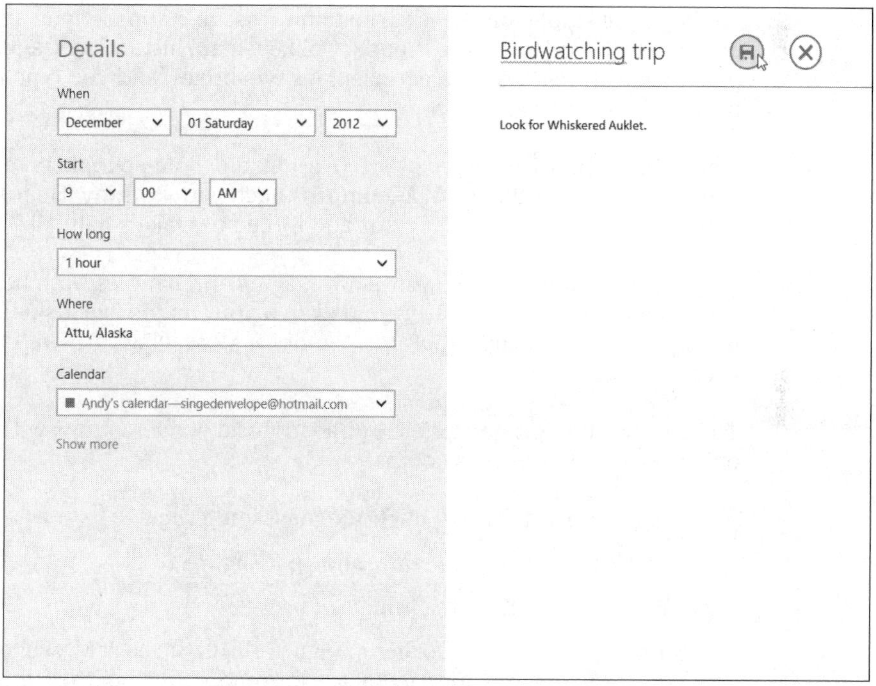

Figure 10-10: Add your appointment's date, start time, duration, and other details.

The biggest challenge comes with the Calendar field, an option available only if you've entered more than one e-mail account into your Mail app. Which e-mail *account* should receive the new calendar appointment?

As with the Contacts app, your answer depends primarily on which cellphone you own. Choose your Google account if you use an Android phone, so your newly added account will appear on Gmail's calendar, as well as your Android phone. Choose Microsoft if you own a Microsoft phone.

Microsoft's apps don't coordinate well, if at all, with Apple products.

4. Click the Save button.

   The Calendar app adds your new appointment to the Windows 8 Calendar, as well as to whichever account you chose in Step 3.

   To add or delete an appointment, open it from the calendar. Right-click the Calendar to summon the App bar and then click the Delete button to delete the appointment. To edit it, choose the Edit icon, and your appointment appears, shown earlier in Figure 10-10.

Chatting through Messaging

A computing staple for decades, instant messaging apps let you exchange messages with other online friends. Unlike e-mail, instant messaging takes place, well, *instantly*: the screen displays two boxes, and you type messages back and forth at each other.

Messaging apps spawn a love/hate relationship. Some people love the convenience and intimacy of keeping in touch with faraway friends. Others hate feeling trapped in an elevator and forced to make small talk.

But love it or hate it, the Windows Messaging app handles both heartfelt conversations and idle chatter. And even if your online friends use different messaging services and programs, Windows Messaging can swap messages with them all.

To begin swapping small talk, er, philosophical conversations with your online friends, follow these steps:

   1. From the Start screen, click the Messaging tile.

   The Messaging app appears, shown in Figure 10-11.

   2. Click the New Message link.

   Shown in the top-left corner of Figure 10-10, the New Message link lets you see which of your friends are currently online in their messaging programs. If a friend doesn't appear here, she's either not online or she's not listed in your People app.

   3. Click the person you'd like to chat with.

   When the messaging window appears, begin typing, as shown in Figure 10-12. Your friend will see a notice from his or her own messaging program, whether it's on Facebook, a cellphone, or a different system.

   When you press Enter, your message appears in their messaging program. And that's it. When you're done typing messages at each other, just say goodbye. The next time you visit the Messaging app, your conversation will still be there, waiting to be continued, if you wish.

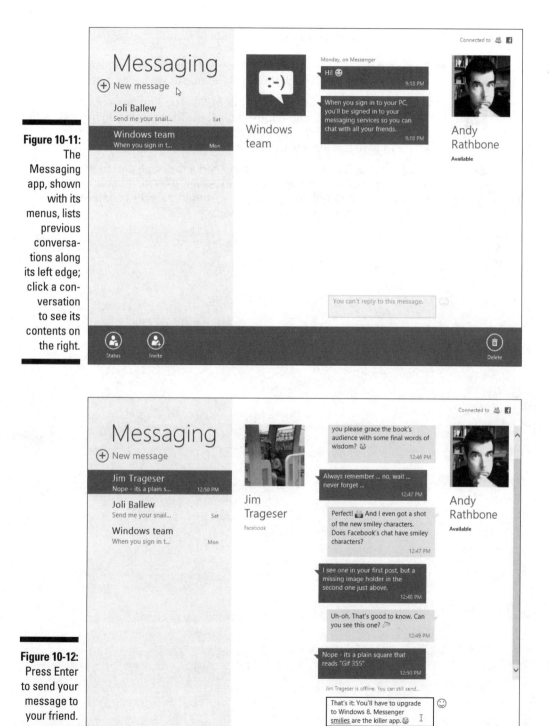

Figure 10-11:
The Messaging app, shown with its menus, lists previous conversations along its left edge; click a conversation to see its contents on the right.

Figure 10-12:
Press Enter to send your message to your friend.

Which brings this section to the finer points of instant messaging:

✔ To delete a conversation, right-click inside the Messaging app to fetch the App bar and then click the Delete icon, shown in the margin.

✔ Don't want to be bothered for awhile? Click the App bar's Status icon, shown in the margin, and choose Invisible. That keeps you from showing up as available in your friends' messaging programs. To reappear to your circle of friends, click the Status icon and choose Online.

✔ Messaging usually works best if you send a message and then wait for a response before sending another message. Too many quick messages make for a disjointed conversation, sort of like a press conference where everybody calls out questions at once.

Chapter 11

Safe Computing

. . . .

In This Chapter

▶ Dealing with permission warnings

▶ Assessing your safety in Action Center

▶ Staying safe on the Internet

▶ Removing browser add-ons

▶ Avoiding phishing scams

▶ Setting Family Safety controls

. . . .

*L*ike driving a car, working with Windows is reasonably safe, as long as you avoid bad neighborhoods, obey traffic signals, and don't steer with your feet while you stick your head out the sunroof.

But in the world of Windows and the Internet, there's no easy way to recognize a bad neighborhood, find a traffic signal, or even distinguish between your feet, the steering wheel, and the sunroof. Things that look innocent — a friend's e-mail or a program found on the Internet — may be a virus that infects your computer.

This chapter helps you recognize the bad streets in virtual neighborhoods and explains the steps you can take to protect yourself from harm and minimize any damage.

Note: The Windows 8 Start screen, although protected against threats by Windows Defender, lacks any adjustable security settings, so everything in this chapter takes place through the desktop.

Understanding Those Annoying Permission Messages

After more than 20 years of development, Windows is still pretty naive. Sometimes when you run a program or try to change a setting on your PC, Windows can't tell whether *you're* doing the work or a *virus* is trying to move in.

The Windows solution? When Windows 8 notices anybody (or anything) trying to change something that can potentially harm Windows or your PC, it darkens the screen and flashes a security message asking for permission, like the one shown in Figure 11-1.

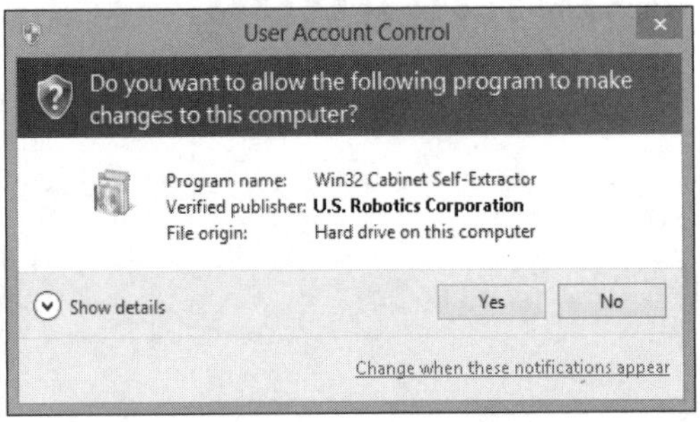

Figure 11-1:
Click No or
Don't Install
if a message
like this
appears out
of the blue.

User Account Control

Do you want to allow the following program to make changes to this computer?

Program name: Win32 Cabinet Self-Extractor
Verified publisher: **U.S. Robotics Corporation**
File origin: Hard drive on this computer

Show details   Yes   No

Change when these notifications appear

If one of these security messages appears out of the blue, Windows 8 may be warning you about a bit of nastiness trying to sneak in. So click No or Don't Install to deny it permission. But if *you're* trying to do something specific with your PC and Windows 8 puts up its boxing gloves, click Yes or Install, instead. Windows 8 drops its guard and lets you in.

If you don't hold an Administrator account, however, you can't simply approve the deed. You must track down an Administrator account holder and ask her to type her password.

Yes, a rather dimwitted security robot guards the front door to Windows 8, but it's also an extra challenge for the people who write the viruses.

Assessing Your Safety in the Action Center

 Take a minute to check your PC's safety with the desktop's Action Center. Part of the Control Panel, the Action Center displays any problems it notices with the Windows 8 main defenses, and it provides handy, one-button fixes for the situations. Its taskbar icon, the white flag shown in the margin, always shows the Action Center's current status.

The Action Center window, shown in Figure 11-2, color codes problems by their severity; a blood red band shows critical problems requiring immediate action, and a yellow band means the problem needs attention soon.

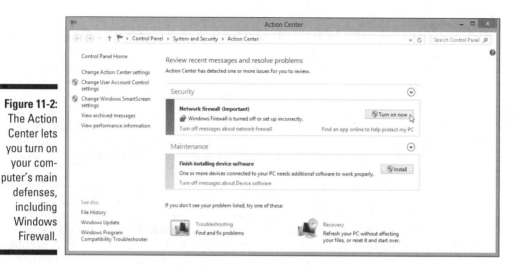

Figure 11-2:
The Action Center lets you turn on your computer's main defenses, including Windows Firewall.

For example, Figure 11-2 shows a red band by the first item in the Security category: Network Firewall (Important). In the Maintenance category, the Install Software for your Devices entry wears a yellow band.

Every defense in the Security category should be up and running for maximum safety because each protects you against different things.

If any of your computer's big cannons aren't loaded and pointing in the right direction, the Action Center's tiny taskbar icon, shown in the margin, appears with a red X across the flag.

When you spot that red-flagged icon on your taskbar, follow these steps to visit the Action Center and fix the problem:

1. **Click the taskbar's red-flagged Action Center icon and choose Open Action Center from the pop-up menu.**

   The Action Center, shown earlier in Figure 11-2, hops onscreen to display your computer's status in both security and maintenance. Normally, it doesn't list anything. But if you see an item listed in either the Security or Maintenance category, something's wrong.

2. **Click the button next to flagged items to fix any potential security problems.**

   Whenever you notice that one of the Windows 8 defenses is turned off in the Action Center, click the button next to the item. For example, in Figure 11-2, clicking the button named Turn on Now will either fix the problem automatically or head you to a one-click switch that sets things straight.

By following the two preceding steps, your computer will be as safe as possible.

Avoiding Viruses with Windows Defender

When it comes to viruses, *everything* is suspect. Viruses travel not only through e-mail messages, programs, files, networks, and flash drives, but also in screen savers, themes, toolbars, and other Windows add-ons.

To combat the problem, Windows 8 includes a new version of Windows Defender that incorporates Microsoft Security Essentials, a security and antivirus program Microsoft formerly offered as a free download.

Windows Defender scans everything that enters your computer, whether through downloads, e-mail, networks, messaging programs, flash drives, or discs. If Windows Defender notices something evil trying to enter your computer, it lets you know with a message, as shown in Figure 11-3. (That same message can appear on the Start screen or the desktop.) Then Windows Defender quarantines the virus, rendering it unable to infect your computer.

Figure 11-3: When Windows Defender notices an intruder, it lets you know immediately with this message and then begins removing the intruder.

Windows Defender constantly scans your PC in the background. But if your PC acts strangely, tell Windows Defender to scan your PC immediately by following these steps:

1. **While you're viewing the Start screen, type** Windows Defender **and press Enter.**

   When you type your first letter, the Start screen switches to the Search screen and begins listing apps that match the letters you type. When you finish typing **Windows Defender**, that word will be alone on the list, so pressing Enter launches it.

   Or, to speed things up, when you spot Windows Defender's name on the list, stop typing. Then click the adjacent Windows Defender icon, shown in the margin, to launch the program.

2. **Click the Scan Now button.**

   Windows Defender immediately performs a quick scan of your PC.

Windows Defender normally doesn't scan flash drives and portable hard drives. To include them, click the program's Settings tab, click Advanced, and put a check mark in the box called Scan Removable Drives. Click Save Changes to save the changes. The program's scans will take slightly longer, but the results are worth it.

But even with Windows Defender watching your back, follow these rules to reduce your risk of infection:

- ✔ Updates for Windows Defender arrive automatically through Windows Update. That's why it's important to connect with the Internet often, so Windows Update can keep Windows Defender working at the top of its game.

- ✔ Only open attachments that you're _expecting_. If you receive something unexpected from a friend, don't open it. Instead, e-mail or phone that person to see whether he or she _really_ sent you something.

- ✔ Don't install _two_ virus checkers because they often quarrel. If you want to test a different program, first uninstall your existing one from the Control Panel's Programs area. (You may need to restart your PC afterward.) It's then safe to install another virus checker that you want to try.

Staying Safe on the Internet

The Internet is not a safe place. Some people design websites specifically to exploit the latest vulnerabilities in Windows — the ones Microsoft hasn't yet had time to patch. This section explains some of Internet Explorer's safety features, as well as other safe travel tips when navigating the Internet.

Avoiding evil add-ons and hijackers

Microsoft designed Internet Explorer to let programmers add extra features through *add-ons*. By installing an add-on program — toolbars, stock tickers, and program launchers, for example — users can wring a little more work out of Internet Explorer.

Unfortunately, dastardly programmers began creating add-ons that *harm* users. Some add-ons spy on your activities, bombard your screen with additional ads, or redirect your home page to another site. Worst yet, some renegade add-ons install themselves as soon as you visit a website — without asking your permission.

Windows 8 packs several guns to combat these troublemakers. First, if a site tries to sneak a program onto your computer, Internet Explorer quickly blocks it. Then Internet Explorer places a warning message across the bottom of Internet Explorer's screen, shown in Figure 11-4. Sure you want the program? Then click the Install button to install the program. Then click the Enable button, shown in Figure 11-5, to turn on your new Internet Explorer add-on.

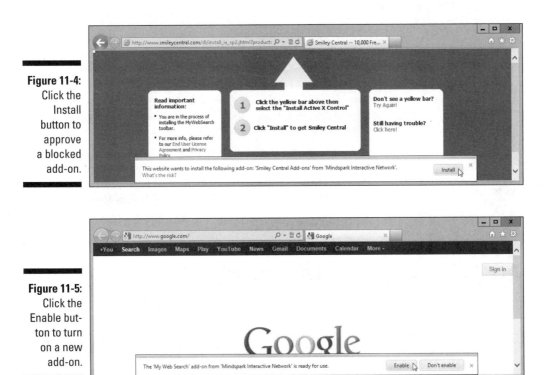

Figure 11-4: Click the Install button to approve a blocked add-on.

Figure 11-5: Click the Enable button to turn on a new add-on.

Unfortunately, Internet Explorer can't tell the good downloads from the bad, leaving the burden of proof to you. So, if you see a message like the one shown in Figure 11-4 and you *haven't* requested a download, chances are good that the site is trying to harm you: Don't click the Install button. Instead, click one of your Favorite links or your Home icon to quickly move to a new website.

If a bad add-on creeps in somehow, you're not completely out of luck. Internet Explorer's Add-On Manager lets you disable it. To see all the add-on programs installed in Internet Explorer (and remove any that you know are bad, unnecessary, or just plain bothersome), follow these steps:

1. **Click Internet Explorer's Tools menu and choose Manage Add-Ons.**

   The Manage Add-Ons window appears, as shown in Figure 11-6, letting you see all currently loaded add-ons.

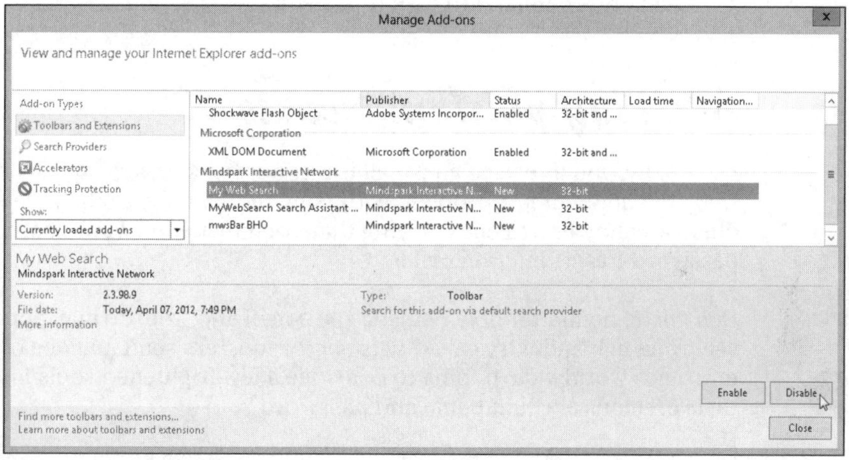

Figure 11-6: Internet Explorer's Manage Add-Ons window lets you see all installed add-ons and disable the ones you don't like.

2. **Click the add-on that gives you trouble and click the Disable button.**

   Can't find the unwanted add-on? Click the Show drop-down list to toggle between seeing All Add-Ons, Currently Loaded Add-Ons, Run Without Permission, and Downloaded Controls.

   When you spot the name of an unwanted toolbar or other bad program, purge it by clicking its name and clicking the Disable button.

3. **Repeat the process for each unwanted add-on and then click the Close button.**

   You may need to restart Internet Explorer for the change to take effect.

Not all add-ons are bad. Many good ones let you play movies, hear sounds, or view special content on a website. Don't delete an add-on simply because it's listed in the Add-On Manager.

✓ In the rare instance that disabling an add-on prevents an important website from loading, click that add-on's name in Step 2 of the preceding steps and click the Enable button to return it to working order.

✓ How the heck do you tell the good add-ons from the bad? Unfortunately, there's no sure way of telling, although the name listed under Publisher provides one clue. Do you recognize the publisher or remember installing its program? Instead of scratching your head later, think hard before installing things Internet Explorer has tried to block.

✓ Make sure that Internet Explorer's pop-up blocker runs by choosing Pop-Up Blocker from the Tools menu. If you see Turn Off Pop-Up Blocker in the pop-up menu, you're all set. If you see Turn On Pop-Up Blocker, click the command to turn it back on.

Avoiding phishing scams

Eventually, you'll receive an e-mail from your bank, eBay, PayPal, or a similar website announcing a problem with your account. Invariably, the e-mail offers a handy link to click, saying that you must enter your username and password to set things in order.

Don't do it, no matter how realistic the e-mail and website may appear. You're seeing an ugly industry called *phishing:* Fraudsters send millions of these messages worldwide, hoping to convince a few frightened souls into typing their precious account name and password.

How do you tell the real e-mails from the fake ones? It's easy, actually, because *all* these e-mails are fake. Finance-related sites may send you legitimate history statements, receipts, or confirmation notices, but they will *never, ever* e-mail you a link for you to click and enter your password.

If you're suspicious, visit the company's *real* website — by typing the web address by hand into Internet Explorer's Address Bar. Chances are good that the real site won't list anything as being wrong with your account.

Windows 8 employs several safeguards to thwart phishing scams:

✓ When you first run Internet Explorer, make sure its SmartScreen filter is turned on by clicking the Tools icon (shown in the margin) and choosing Safety from the top menu. When the Safety menu appears, look for an entry called Turn *on* SmartScreen Filter. If you spot it, select it. That turns the important filter back on.

✔ Internet Explorer compares a website's address with a list of known phishing sites. If it finds a match, the SmartScreen filter keeps you from entering, as shown in Figure 11-7. Should you ever spot that screen, close the web page.

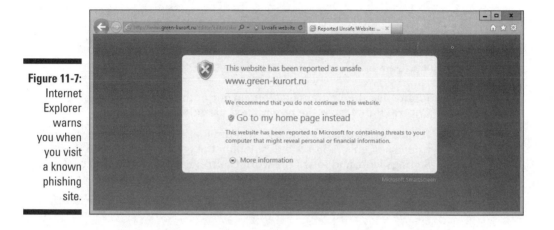

Figure 11-7: Internet Explorer warns you when you visit a known phishing site.

So, why can't the authorities simply arrest those people responsible? Because Internet thieves are notoriously difficult to track down and prosecute. The reach of the Internet lets them work from any place in the world.

✔ If you've already entered your name and password into a phishing site, take action immediately: Visit the *real* website and change your password. Then contact the company involved and ask it for help. It may be able to stop the thieves before they wrap their electronic fingers around your account.

✔ If you've entered credit card information, call the card's issuer immediately. You'll almost always find a toll-free, 24-hour phone number on the back of your credit card.

✔ You can warn Microsoft if you spot a site that smells suspiciously like phish. Choose Tools⇨Safety⇨Report Unsafe Website from Internet Explorer's menu bar. Internet Explorer takes you to Microsoft's SmartScreen Filter website to report the evil doer. Telling Microsoft of suspected phishing sites helps the company warn other visitors.

Setting Up Family Safety Controls

A feature much-welcomed by parents and much-booed by their children, Windows Family Safety area offer several ways to police how people can access the computer, as well as the Internet. In fact, people who share their PC with roommates should drop by Family Safety, as well.

Family Safety controls work best with these conditions:

✔ You must hold an Administrator account. (I explain the types of accounts in Chapter 14.) If everybody shares one PC, make sure that the other account holders — especially children or your roommates — have Standard accounts.

✔ If your children have their own PCs, create an Administrator account on their PCs for yourself. Then change their accounts to Standard.

To set up Family Safety, follow these steps:

1. **Right-click the bottommost-left corner of the screen and choose Control Panel from the pop-up text menu.**

   From the Start screen, tap the Desktop tile. Then slide a finger inward from a screen's right edge to summon the Charms bar. Touch the Settings icon, and touch the word Control Panel from the top of the Settings pane.

2. **From the User Accounts and Family Safety section, click the Set Up Family Safety For Any User link.**

   The Family Safety window appears.

3. **Click the user account you want to restrict.**

   Windows lets you add Family Safety restrictions to only one user account at a time, a laborious process for large families.

   When you choose a User account, the Family Safety screen appears, as shown in Figure 11-8. The next steps take you through each section of the controls.

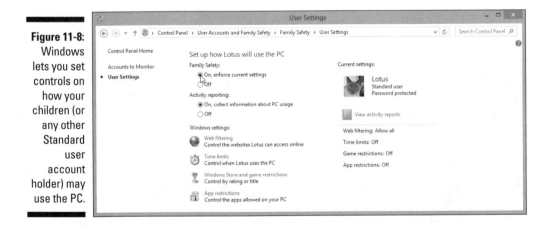

Figure 11-8: Windows lets you set controls on how your children (or any other Standard user account holder) may use the PC.

4. **Turn the Family Safety settings on or off.**

   The Family Safety area first presents two switches, letting you toggle the controls between On and Off. Turn them On to enforce the rules you'll be setting up; click Off to temporarily suspend them.

5. **Choose the categories you'd like to enforce and set the limits.**

   Click any of these four categories and make your changes:

   - **Web Filtering:** To supervise small children, turn this on. Then visit the Set Web Filtering Level window and click the Allow List Only button. On that same page, choose the link called Click Here to Change Allow List.

     When the Allow or Block Specific Websites window appears, type in *only* the sites that your child's user account may access, then click the Allow button. That makes *all* other sites off-limits.

   - **Time Limits:** This option fetches a grid, letting you click the hours when your child should be restricted from using the PC. (The clicked squares darken, representing forbidden hours. The remaining squares are fair game.) This offers an easy way to make the PC off-limits after bedtime, for example, or limit PC time to a set number of hours per day.

   - **Windows Store and Game Restrictions:** You may allow or ban *all* games here, restrict access to games with certain ratings (ratings appear on most software boxes), and block or allow individual games.

   - **App Restrictions:** Remember, Windows 8 now uses the term *apps* for both desktop programs *and* Start screen apps. Accordingly, this section lets you keep the kids out of your desktop's checkbook program, for example, as well as any Start screen apps you choose. You can block *all* programs, or you can allow access to only a handful of programs by selecting the boxes next to their names in a long list.

6. **When you're through, close the Family Safety window.**

   Your changes take place immediately.

Although the Family Safety controls work well, few things in the computer world are foolproof. If you're worried about your children's computer use, cast an occasional eye their way.

Encrypting your PC with BitLocker

The Windows 8 BitLocker feature scrambles the contents of your PC's hard drive. Then it quickly unscrambles it whenever you enter your user account's password. Why bother? It's a precaution against your information falling into the hands of thieves. If they steal your PC or even its hard drive, they won't be able to access your data, and its stash of passwords, credit-card numbers, and other personal information.

Unfortunately, BitLocker provides more protection than most people need. It's difficult for non-techies to set up, and if you ever lose your password, you've lost all your data, as well. BitLocker also requires your PC to be set up in a special way, with an extra *partition* — a separate storage area — on your hard drive.

If you're interested in BitLocker, take your PC to your office's information technology person and ask for help and advice on setting it up. Or, as a start, set up BitLocker on a portable flash drive, and keep your sensitive files on that. Because many flash drives live in pockets and keychains, they're much more likely to fall into a stranger's hands. If you're comfortable using your flash drive only on PCs running Windows 8, Windows 7, or Windows Vista, follow these steps to encrypt your flash drive with BitLocker:

1. **Insert your flash drive into your PC's USB port, open File Explorer from the Desktop, and navigate to your flash drive's icon.**

2. **Right-click the drive's icon and choose Turn On BitLocker from the pop-up menu.**

3. **When the BitLocker Drive Encryption window appears, click the Use a Password to Unlock the Drive check box, enter a password, and click Next.**

   The program offers tips for choosing a strong password. When you click next, the window asks how you want to back up your recovery key.

4. **Click the Print the Recovery Key option and click Next.**

   This important step prints a sequence of characters to type in should you lose your password. Alternatively, you can save the recovery key to a file or SkyDrive.

5. **Click the Encrypt Used Disk Space Only (best for larger drives) option, or the Encrypt Entire Drive (best for smaller drives) option. Then click Next.**

6. **Click the Start Encrypting button.**

The next time you insert your flash drive into a PC running Windows 8, Windows 7, or Windows Vista, you — or the thief — must enter the password entered in Step 3, or the drive's contents will stay encrypted and inaccessible. (*Warning:* Drives encrypted with BitLocker can't be opened on any Apple computers or PCs running Windows XP or earlier Windows versions.)

Part IV
Customizing and Upgrading Windows 8

The 5th Wave   By Rich Tennant

"We're much better prepared for this upgrade than before. We're giving users additional training, better manuals, and a morphine drip."

In this part . . .

When your life changes, you want Windows 8 to change with it, and that's where this part of the book comes in. Here's where you discover the Windows 8 Control Panel, which lets you change nearly everything but your computer's disposition.

Chapter 13 describes easy click-through tune-ups you can perform to keep your computer in top shape, backed up, and running smoothly. If you're sharing your computer with others, you discover how to dish out user accounts to each of them, with *you* deciding who can do what.

Finally, when you're ready to buy that second (or third, fourth, or fifth) computer, a chapter walks you through linking them all to create a home network, where they can all share the same Internet connection, printer, and files.

Chapter 12

Customizing Windows 8 with the Control Panel

*M*ost science fiction movies include a close-up of a smoking control panel, ready to burst into flames. If that happens in Windows, grab an extra fire extinguisher: Windows 8 contains *two* switch-packed control panels.

The Start screen's control panel, the PC Settings screen, which is full of oversized buttons, helps mostly with simple chores, such as changing your account photo or turning on the spell checker's autocorrect option. The desktop's mammoth set of switches, called simply *Control Panel,* carries the more powerful settings found in earlier Windows versions.

Although separate, the two panels often join forces. Sometimes a click on the desktop's Control Panel whisks you back to the Start screen's PC Settings screen for you to flip the final switch.

But no matter which bank of switches you face, they both let you customize the look, feel, behavior, and vibe of Windows 8. This chapter explains the switches and sliders you'll want to tweak, and it steers you away from the ones that are prone to causing fires.

One word of caution: Some of the Control Panel's settings can be changed only by the person holding the almighty Administrator account — usually the computer's owner. If Windows 8 refuses to open the Control Panel's hatch, call the PC's owner for help.

Finding the Right Switch

Windows 8 comes with hundreds of settings, sprinkled between two completely different control panels. You'll rarely stumble randomly across the setting you need. So, instead of clicking aimlessly at menus, let Windows do the hunting.

Follow these steps to find the setting you need:

1. **From the Start screen, summon the Charms bar's Search pane.**

   You can summon the Charms bar's Search pane in any of three ways:

   - **Mouse:** Point the cursor at the screen's top- or bottom-right corner; when the Charms bar appears, click the Search icon.

   - **Keyboard:** Press ⊞+Q.

   - **Touchscreen:** Slide your finger from the screen's right edge inward and then tap the Search icon.

2. **In the Search pane, click the word *Settings*.**

   That tells Windows to search through its *settings,* rather than your apps or files.

3. **In the search box, type a word describing your desired setting.**

   When you type the first letter, every setting containing that letter appears in a list. If you don't know the exact name of your setting, begin typing a keyword: **display**, **mouse**, **user**, **privacy**, or something similar.

   Don't see the right setting? Press the Backspace key to delete the letters you've typed and then try again with a different word.

4. **Click your desired setting on the list.**

   Windows takes you directly to that setting on the appropriate control panel.

   When searching for a setting, always try the Search pane first. A few minutes spent at the Search pane yields better results than scouring the hundreds of settings stuffed in the two Windows 8 control panels.

The Start Screen's PC Settings Screen

The Start screen's mini control panel — the PC Settings screen — would make more sense if it simply offered mini tweaks, such as changing colors or other cosmetic fluff.

But oddly enough, Microsoft stuffed it with some of the most powerful commands in Windows 8. To open the Start screen's PC Settings screen, follow these steps:

1. **Summon the Charms bar's Settings pane.**

   You can summon the Charms bar's Settings pane any of three ways:

   - **Mouse:** Point the cursor at the screen's top- or bottom-right corner; when the Charms bar appears, click the Settings icon.
   - **Keyboard:** Press ⊞+I.
   - **Touchscreen:** Slide your finger from the screen's right edge inward and then tap the Settings icon.

2. **Choose the words *Change PC Settings* with a mouse click or tap of a finger.**

The PC Settings screen appears, as shown in Figure 12-1.

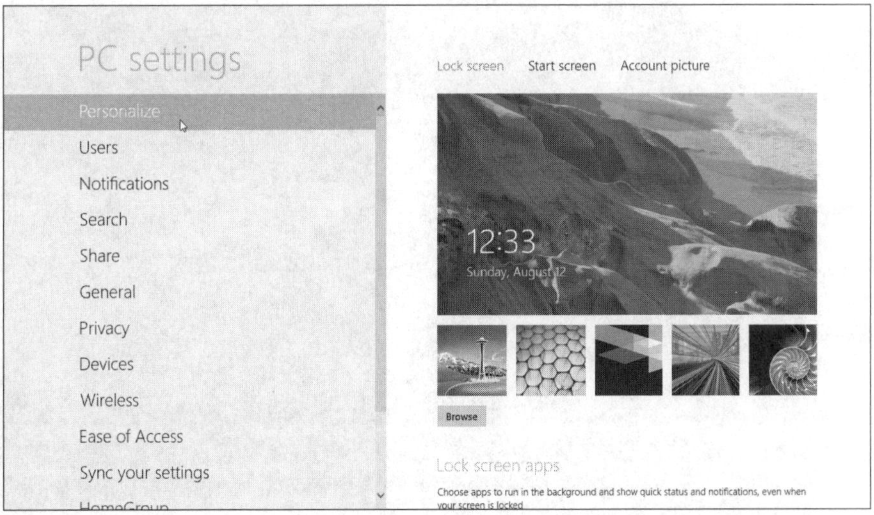

Figure 12-1: The Start screen's easy-to-touch PC Settings screen offers many common settings.

PC settings

Lock screen   Start screen   Account picture

Personalize
Users
Notifications
Search
Share
General
Privacy
Devices
Wireless
Ease of Access
Sync your settings
HomeGroup

12:33
Sunday, August 12

Browse

Lock screen apps

Choose apps to run in the background and show quick status and notifications, even when your screen is locked

Like the desktop's large Control Panel, the PC Settings screen breaks its settings down into categories, each described here:

✔ **Personalize:** This lets you choose a new picture for your Start screen and lock screen, described in Chapter 2. The Account Picture area lets you change the thumbnail photo assigned to your user account.

Don't overlook the Lock Screen Apps section, found at the bottom of the Lock Screen page of the PC Settings screen, shown in Figure 12-1. This section lets you choose which tiles should automatically update on your lock screen. Click the Calendar app, for example, and the lock screen displays your next appointment's time and date.

✔ **Users:** This category lets you change your password or authorize another person to use your computer. I cover both of those chores in Chapter 14.

✔ **Notifications:** Sometimes called *toast notifications,* these little strips of text appear on your screen's top-right corner, shown in Figure 12-2. If you find them informative, you needn't visit here. But if you find some of them to be distracting, head here to choose which programs, if any, are allowed to display onscreen notifications.

✔ **Search:** You can safely ignore this settings category, unless you want to prevent an app or its contents from being indexed. You usually want Windows to index *everything,* making everything easier to find.

Figure 12-2: Unless told to stop, the Messenger program places notifications about instant messages in your screen's upper-right corner.

✔ **Share:** Designed for social networkers who enjoy sharing what they see on their computer screens, this lets you choose apps that can share information. Windows 8 starts with your Mail and People apps for e-mailing items to friends. As you install other apps, they may appear as options here, as well.

✔ **General:** This catch-all category offers a way to turn off the spell checker and to make Windows ignore Daylight Savings Time. Don't ignore the General category completely, though, because three important troubleshooting tools live here: Refresh Your PC, Remove Everything, and Advanced Startup. I cover these three Get Out of Trouble Free cards in Chapter 18.

✔ **Privacy:** The Privacy category lets you prevent apps from knowing your geographic location and from sharing your name and account picture. If you're concerned about privacy, though, look for the Delete History buttons sprinkled in the General, Share, and Search categories.

✔ **Devices:** This simply lists all of your computer's *devices* — things you've plugged into your computer. That usually includes things like a mouse, monitor, printer, camera, speakers, and other gadgetry. (It doesn't let you adjust any of their settings, though.) To remove a device, click the gadget and then click the little icon in its top-right corner. To add a device, click the Add a Device button at the page's top.

✔ **Ease of Access:** This includes settings to make Windows more navigable by people with challenges in vision and hearing.

✔ **Sync Your Settings:** If you've signed in to Windows 8 with a Microsoft account, this category lets you pick and choose which settings should link to your account. Then, when you sign in to a different Windows 8 computer, that computer automatically changes to reflect your favorite colors, background, language preferences, app settings, and other personal details tied to your Microsoft account.

✔ **Homegroup:** Covered in Chapter 14, this lets you choose which libraries to share with other computers in your *Homegroup* — a simplified way to share files between connected computers.

✔ **Windows Update:** This settings category lets you know at a glance if Windows Update isn't working. Click the Check For Updates Now button to see whether Microsoft has released any fixes for your computer today.

The Big Guns: The Desktop's Control Panel

When the Start screen's PC Settings screen isn't enough, head for the big guns: The desktop's Control Panel lets you while away an entire workweek opening icons and flipping switches to fine-tune Windows 8. Part of the attraction comes from the Control Panel's magnitude: It houses nearly *50* icons, and some icons summon menus with dozens of settings and tasks.

Don't be surprised, though, when you flip one of the desktop Control Panel's switches and wind up in the Start screen's PC Settings screen to finish the job. The two control panels can't seem to leave each other alone.

To open the desktop's Control Panel, point your mouse cursor in the screen's bottom-left corner and right-click. (Or press ⊞+X.) When the text menu pops up in the bottom-left corner, choose Control Panel.

To save you from searching aimlessly for the right switch, the Control Panel lumps similar items together in its Category view, as shown in Figure 12-3.

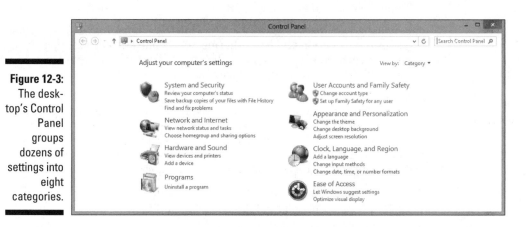

Figure 12-3:
The desktop's Control Panel groups dozens of settings into eight categories.

Below each category's name, shortcuts list that category's most popular offerings. The System and Security category icon in Figure 12-3, for example, offers shortcuts to review your computer's maintenance and security status, turn on the File History backup, and access troubleshooting tools.

Some controls don't fall neatly into categories, and others merely serve as shortcuts to settings found elsewhere. To see these and every other icon the Control Panel offers, choose either Large Icons or Small Icons from the View By drop-down list, shown in the top-right corner of Figure 12-3. The window quickly displays *all* umpteen-zillion Control Panel icons, as shown in Figure 12-4. (To return to the Category view in Figure 12-3, select Category from the View By drop-down list.)

Don't think something's astray if your Control Panel differs from the one in Figure 12-4. Different programs, accessories, and computer models often add their own icons to the Control Panel. Different versions of Windows 8, which I describe in Chapter 1, also have slightly different icons.

Figure 12-4:
Designed
for experi-
enced PC
owners with
good eye-
sight, the
Small Icons
view dis-
plays *every*
icon in the
Control
Panel.

All Control Panel Items

Adjust your computer's settings   View by: Small icons ▾

▶ Action Center	Administrative Tools	AutoPlay	BitLocker Drive
Color Management	Credential Manager	Date and Time	Default Programs
Desktop Gadgets	Device Manager	Devices and Printers	Display
Ease of Access Center	Family Safety	File History	Flash Player (32-bit)
Folder Options	Fonts	HomeGroup	Indexing Options
Internet Options	Keyboard	Language	Location Settings
Mouse	Network and Sharing Center	Notification Area Icons	Performance Information and Tools
Personalization	Phone and Modem	Power Options	Programs and Features
Recovery	Region	RemoteApp and Desktop Connections	Sound
Speech Recognition	Storage Spaces	Sync Center	System
Taskbar	Troubleshooting	User Accounts	Windows 7 File Recovery
Windows Defender	Windows Firewall	Windows Update	

Rest your mouse pointer over any confusing icon or category in the Control Panel, and Windows 8 thoughtfully explains its meaning in life. (Add this perk to the list of reasons why touchscreen owners will want a mouse when visiting the Windows desktop.)

The desktop's Control Panel gathers all the main switches in Windows 8 into one well-stocked panel, but it's certainly not the only way to change the settings. You can almost always jump to these same settings by right-clicking the item you want to change — be it your desktop, an icon, or a folder — and choosing Properties from the pop-up menu.

The rest of this chapter lists the Control Panel's categories shown in Figure 12-3, the reasons you'd ever want to visit them, and any shortcuts that jump straight to the setting you need.

System and Security

Like an old car or a new friendship, Windows 8 needs occasional maintenance. In fact, a little bit of maintenance can make Windows 8 run so much more smoothly that I devote the best of Chapter 13 to that subject. There, you discover how to speed up Windows, free up hard drive space, back up your data, and create a safety net called a restore point.

This category's security section contains a full brigade of soldiers, and I've written field manuals for them in Chapter 11. The new backup program in Windows 8, File History, gets its due in Chapter 13.

User Accounts and Family Safety

I explain in Chapter 14 how to create separate accounts for other people to use your PC. That lets them use your PC but limits the amount of damage they can do to Windows and your files.

If you want to create a user account for a visitor, here's a refresher so you needn't flip ahead to Chapter 14: Fetch the Charms bar, click the Settings icon, and click Change PC Settings. Choose Users and then choose Add a User.

The Control Panel's User Accounts and Family Safety category also includes a link to the Security section's Family Safety area, where you can place limits on how and when your kids access your PC. I explain Family Safety controls in Chapter 11.

Network and Internet

Plug an Internet connection into your PC, and Windows 8 quickly starts slurping information from the web. Connect it with another PC, and Windows 8 wants to connect the two with a Homegroup or another type of network. (I explain Homegroups in Chapter 14.)

But should Windows 8 botch the job, the Control Panel's Network and Internet category has some troubleshooting tools.

I devote Chapter 15 completely to networking; the Internet gets its due in Chapter 9.

Changing the Windows 8 Appearance (Appearance and Personalization)

One of the most popular categories, Appearance and Personalization lets you change the look, feel, and behavior of Windows 8 in a wide variety of ways. Inside the category await these six icons:

✔ **Personalization:** Pay dirt for budding interior designers, this area lets you stamp your own look and feel across Windows. Hang a new picture or digital photo across your desktop, choose a fresh screen saver, and change the colors of the Windows 8 window frames. (To head quickly to this batch of settings, right-click a blank part of your desktop and choose Personalize.)

✔ **Display:** Whereas personalization lets you fiddle with colors, the Display area lets you fiddle with your computer's screen. For example, it lets you enlarge the text to soothe tired eyes, adjust the screen resolution, and adjust the connection of an additional computer screen.

✔ **Taskbar:** Head here to add program shortcuts to your taskbar, the strip living along your desktop's bottom edge. I cover this easy way to avoid a trip the Start screen in Chapter 3. (To jump quickly to this area, right-click the taskbar and choose Properties.)

✔ **Ease of Access:** Designed to help people with special needs, this short-cut contains settings to make Windows more navigable by the blind, the deaf, and people with other physical challenges. Because Ease of Access exists as its own category, I describe it in its own section later in this chapter.

✔ **Folder Options:** Visited mainly by experienced users, this area lets you tweak how folders look and behave. (To jump quickly to Folder Options, open any folder, click the View tab, and click the Options icon.)

✔ **Fonts:** Here's where you preview, delete, or examine fonts that spruce up your printed work.

In the next few sections, I explain the Appearance and Personalization tasks that you'll reach for most often.

Changing the desktop background

A *background,* also known as wallpaper, is simply the picture covering your desktop. To change it, follow these steps:

1. **Right-click your desktop and choose Personalize.**

2. **When the Personalization window appears, select Desktop Background from the windows' bottom left.**

   The window shown in Figure 12-5 appears.

3. **Click a new picture for the background.**

   Be sure to click the drop-down list, shown in Figure 12-5, to see all the available photos and colors that Windows offers. To rummage through folders not listed, click the adjacent Browse button. Feel free to search your own Pictures library for potential backgrounds.

   Background files can be stored as BMP, GIF, JPG, JPEG, DIB, or PNG files. That means you can choose a background from nearly any photo or art found on the Internet or shot from a digital camera.

   When you click a new picture, Windows immediately places it across your desktop. If you're pleased, jump to Step 5.

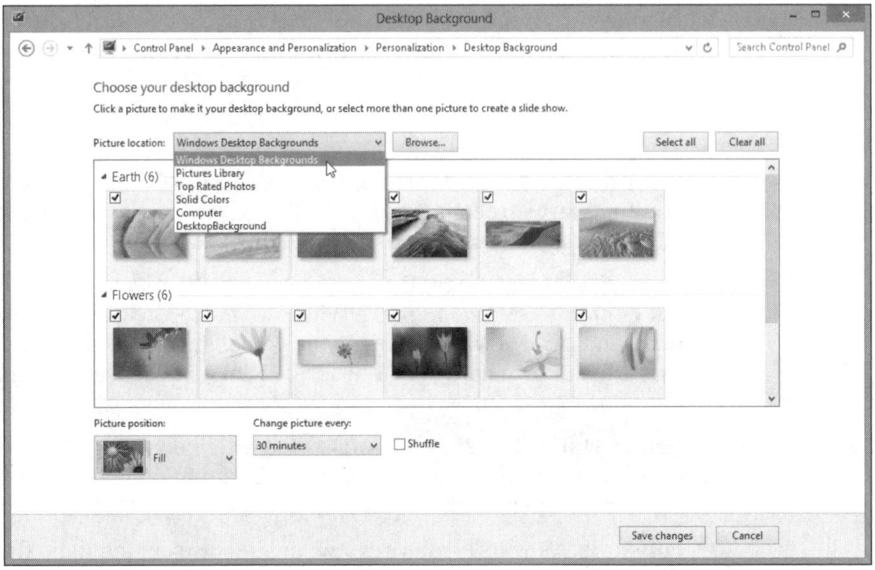

Figure 12-5:
Click the
drop-down
list to
find more
pictures
to splash
across your
desktop
as the
background.

4. **Decide whether to fill, fit, stretch, tile, or center the picture.**

   Not every picture fits perfectly across the desktop. Small pictures, for
   example, need to be either stretched to fit the space or spread across
   the screen in rows like tiles on a floor. When tiling and stretching still
   look odd or distorted, try the Fill or Fit option to keep the perspective.
   Or try centering the image and leaving blank space around its edges.

   You can automatically switch between images by choosing more than
   one photo. (Hold down Ctrl while clicking each one.) The picture then
   changes every 30 minutes unless you change the time in the Change
   Picture Every drop-down list.

5. **Click the Save Changes button to save your new background.**

   Windows saves your new background across your screen.

Did you happen to spot an eye-catching picture while web surfing with
Internet Explorer? Right-click that website's picture and choose Set As
Background. Sneaky Windows copies the picture and splashes it across your
desktop as a new background.

Choosing a screen saver

In the dinosaur days of computing, computer monitors suffered from *burn-
in:* permanent damage when an oft-used program burned its image onto the
screen. To prevent burn-in, people installed a screen saver to jump in with a
blank screen or moving lines. Today's computer screens no longer suffer from
burn-in problems, but people still use screen savers because they look cool.

Windows comes with several built-in screen savers. To try one out, follow these steps:

1. **Right-click your desktop and choose Personalize to open the Personalization window. Then select the Screen Saver link from the window's bottom-right corner.**

   The Screen Saver Settings dialog box appears.

2. **Click the downward-pointing arrow in the Screen Saver box and select a screen saver.**

   After choosing a screen saver, click the Preview button for an audition. View as many candidates as you like before making a decision.

   Be sure to click the Settings button because some screen savers offer options, letting you specify the speed of a photo slide show, for example.

3. **If desired, add security by selecting the On Resume, Display Logon Screen check box.**

   This safeguard keeps people from sneaking into your computer while you're fetching coffee. It makes Windows ask for a password after waking up from screen saver mode. (I cover passwords in Chapter 14.)

4. **When you're done setting up your screen saver, click OK.**

   Windows saves your changes.

If you *really* want to extend the life of your display (and save electricity), don't bother with screen savers. Instead, put your computer to Sleep before stepping away: Press ⊞+I with a keyboard, click the Power icon, and choose Sleep from the pop-up menu.

Changing the computer's theme

Themes are simply collections of settings to spruce up your computer's appearance: You can save your favorite screen saver and desktop background as a *theme,* for example. Then, by switching between themes, you can change your computer's clothes more quickly.

To try one of the built-in themes in Windows 8, right-click your desktop and choose Personalize. Windows 8 lists its token bundled themes shown in Figure 12-6, as well as an option to create your own. Click any theme, and Windows 8 tries it on immediately.

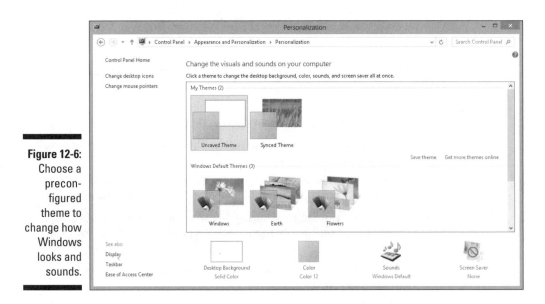

Figure 12-6:
Choose a
precon-
figured
theme to
change how
Windows
looks and
sounds.

The window offers these themes, with options listed along the window's
bottom.

- ✔ **My Themes:** Themes you've personally created appear here. If you have
  a Microsoft account, you'll see a Synced Theme, which is the theme
  you'll see on every PC you log into with that account.

- ✔ **Windows Default Themes:** This category includes the bundled themes
  in Windows 8, including its original one, called simply Windows.

- ✔ **Basic and High Contrast Themes:** This features high-contrast themes
  for the visually impaired.

Instead of choosing from the built-in themes, feel free to make your own by
clicking the buttons (shown along the bottom of Figure 12-6) for changing
the Desktop Background, Window Color, Sounds, and Screen Saver. After
creating the perfect look for your computer, save your work by clicking Save
Theme and typing a name.

Changing the screen resolution

One of Windows' many change-it-once-and-forget-about-it options, *screen
resolution* determines how much information Windows 8 can cram onto your
computer screen. Changing the resolution either shrinks everything to pack
more stuff onscreen, or it enlarges everything at the expense of desktop real
estate.

To find your most comfortable resolution — or if a program or game mutters something about you having to change your *screen resolution* or *video mode* — follow these steps:

1. **Right-click a blank part of your desktop and choose Screen Resolution.**

   The Screen Resolution window appears, as shown in Figure 12-7.

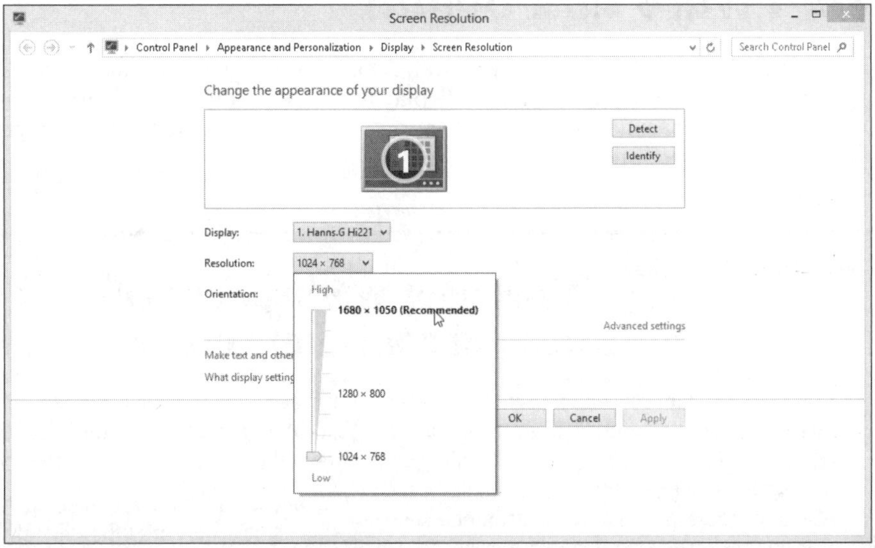

Figure 12-7:
The higher the screen resolution, the more information Windows can squeeze onto your computer screen.

2. **To change the screen resolution, click the Resolution drop-down list and use your mouse to drag the little bar between High and Low.**

   Watch the little preview screen near the window's top change as you move the mouse. The more you slide the bar upward, the larger your computer screen grows. Unfortunately, the more information Windows 8 can pack onto your computer screen, the smaller that information appears.

   There's no right or wrong choice here, but choosing Windows' recommended setting makes for the clearest text and images.

   Windows 8 only lets you snap an app to the side of your desktop at resolutions of 1366 x 768 or higher. (I cover snapping apps in Chapter 3.)

3. **View your display changes by clicking the Apply button. Then click the Keep Changes button to authorize the change.**

   When Windows 8 makes drastic change to your display, it gives you 15 seconds to approve the change by clicking a Keep Changes button. If a technical glitch renders your screen unreadable, you won't be able to see or click the onscreen button. After a few seconds, Windows notices that you didn't approve, and it reverts to your original, viewable display settings.

4. **Click OK when you're done tweaking the display.**

   After you change your video resolution once, you'll probably never return here unless you buy a new, larger monitor. You'll also want to revisit here if you plug a second computer screen into your PC, which I describe in the sidebar.

Hardware and Sound

 The Windows 8 Hardware and Sound category, shown in Figure 12-8, shows some familiar faces. The Display icon, for example, also appears in the Appearance and Personalization category, described in this chapter's previous section.

Doubling your workspace with a second computer screen

Have you been blessed with an extra computer screen, perhaps a leftover from a deceased PC? Connect it to your PC, place it beside your first computer screen, and you've doubled your Windows desktop: Windows 8 stretches your workspace across both computer screens. That lets you view the online encyclopedia in one computer screen while writing your term paper in the other.

To perform these video gymnastics, your PC needs a video card with two *ports,* and those ports must match your computer screen's *connectors.* This poses no problem to most newer computers, laptops, tablets, and monitors. Many tablets include an HDMI port for plugging in a second monitor.

After you plug the second computer screen into your computer, right-click a blank part of your desktop and choose Screen Resolution. The Screen Resolution window shows a second onscreen computer screen next to your first. (Click the Detect button if the second computer screen doesn't appear onscreen.)

Drag and drop the onscreen computer screens to the right or left until they match the physical placement of the *real* computer screens on your desk. Then click OK. (That bit of clickery lets Windows expand your newly widened desktop in the correct direction.)

To configure your second display from the Start screen, fetch the Charms bar and click the Devices icon (or press ⊞+K), and click the Second Screen icon. From there, you can choose any of these icons: PC Screen Only (ignore the second monitor), Duplicate (show the same thing on *both* screens), Extend (stretch Windows to fit across both screens), or Second Screen Only (switch completely to the second screen).

Figure 12-8:
The
Hardware
and Sound
category
lets you
control the
physical
aspects of
your PC:
its display,
sound, and
attached
gadgets.

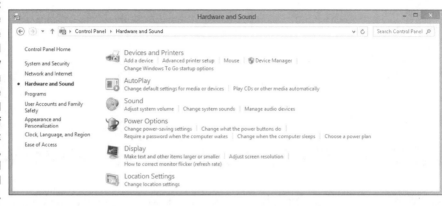

This category controls the parts of your PC you can touch or plug in. You can adjust the settings of your display here, as well as your mouse, speakers, keyboard, printer, telephone, scanner, digital camera, game controllers, and, for you graphic artists out there, digital pen.

You won't spend much time here, though, especially coming in through the Control Panel's doors. Most settings appear elsewhere, where a click will bring you directly to the setting you need.

Whether you arrive at these pages through the Control Panel or a shortcut, the following sections explain the most popular reasons for visiting here.

Adjusting volume and sounds

The Sound area lets you adjust your PC's volume, a handy commodity when trying to sneak in a computer game on a Windows tablet during a boring business meeting.

Most Windows 8 tablets come with toggle-switch volume controls mounted along their left or right edge. The top button turns up the volume; the lower button decreases the volume. Experiment with them a bit before playing Angry Birds in the board room.

To turn down your PC's volume from the desktop, shown in Figure 12-9, click the little speaker by your clock and slide down the volume. No speaker on your taskbar? Restore it by right-clicking the taskbar's clock, choosing Properties, and turning the Volume switch to On.

Figure 12-9:
Click the
speaker
icon and
move the
sliding con-
trol to adjust
your PC's
volume.

To mute your PC, click the little speaker icon at the bottom of the sliding control, shown in Figure 12-9. Clicking that icon again lets your computer blare
music again.

Click the word *Mixer* at the bottom of the sliding volume bar to set different
volumes for different desktop programs. You can quietly detonate explosives
in your favorite game while still allowing your desktop's e-mail program
to loudly announce any new messages. (*Note:* The volume levels for Start
screen apps won't appear here, unfortunately.)

To adjust the sound quickly from the Start menu on a touchscreen, summon
the Charms bar by sliding a finger inward from the screen's right edge. When
the Charms bar appears, tap the Settings icon and then tap the Sound icon. A
sliding control appears, letting you slide it up or down to adjust the volume.
(Slide the control to the bottom to mute the speakers.)

Installing or setting up speakers

Most PCs come with only two speakers. Others come with four, and PCs
that double as home theaters or gaming rigs sometimes have up to eight.
To accommodate the variety of setups, Windows 8 includes a speaker setup
area, complete with a speaker test.

If you're installing new speakers, or you're not sure your old ones are working, follow these steps to introduce them properly to Windows 8:

1. **From the desktop, right-click your taskbar's Speaker icon and choose
   Playback Devices.**

2. **Click your speaker or speaker's icon and then click the Configure
   button.**

   The Speaker Setup dialog box appears, as shown in Figure 12-10.

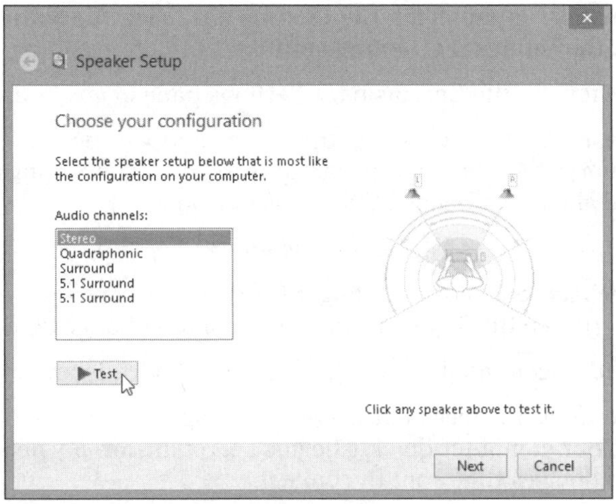

Figure 12-10:
Click the
Test button
to hear your
speakers,
one at a
time.

3. **Click the Test button, adjust your speaker's settings, and click Next.**

   Windows 8 walks you through selecting your number of speakers and their placement and then plays each one in turn so that you can hear whether they're in the correct locations.

4. **Click the tabs for any other sound devices you want to adjust. When you're through adjusting, click the OK button.**

While you're here, check your microphone volume by clicking the Recording tab, as well as tabs for any other sound gadgetry you've been able to afford.

If your speakers and microphone don't show up as devices, Windows 8 doesn't know they're plugged into your computer. That usually means you need to install a new *driver,* an annoying journey I walk you through in Chapter 13.

Adding a Bluetooth gadget

Bluetooth technology lets you connect gadgets wirelessly to your computer, removing clutter from your desktop. On a tablet, it lets you add a mouse and keyboard without hogging one of your coveted USB ports.

Bluetooth can also connect your computer, laptop, or tablet with some cell-phones for wireless Internet access — if your wireless provider allows it, of course.

To add a Bluetooth item to a computer, laptop, or tablet, follow these steps:

1. **Make sure your Bluetooth device is turned on.**

   Sometimes you can simply flip a switch. Other devices make you hold down a button until its little light begins flashing.

2. From the Start screen, fetch the Charms bar, click the Settings icon, and click the Change PC Settings button.

You can summon the Charms bar's Settings pane in any of three ways:

- **Mouse:** Point the cursor at the screen's top- or bottom-right corner; when the Charms bar appears, click the Settings icon, and then click the Change PC Settings button.

- **Keyboard:** Press ⊞+I and press Enter.

- **Touchscreen:** Slide your finger from the screen's right edge inward, tap the Settings icon, and then tap Change PC Settings.

3. From the Devices category, click the Add a Device icon.

The PC Settings' Devices pane appears, listing all your connected devices. Your computer quickly begins searching for any nearby Bluetooth devices that want to connect.

If your device doesn't appear, head back to Step 1 and make sure your Bluetooth gadget is still turned on. (Many give up and turn off after 30 seconds of waiting to connect.)

4. When your computer lists your device's name in the Devices pane, choose the name with a tap or mouse click.

5. Type in your device's code if necessary and, if asked, click the Pair button.

Here's where things get sticky. For security reasons, you need to prove that you're sitting in front of your *own* computer and that you're not an adjacent stranger trying to break in. Unfortunately, devices employ slightly different tactics when making you prove your innocence.

Sometimes you need to type a secret string of numbers called a *passcode* into both the device and your computer. (The secret code is usually hidden somewhere in your device's manual.) But you need to type quickly before the other gadget stops waiting.

On some gadgets, particularly Bluetooth mice, you hold in a little push button on the mouse's belly at this step.

Cellphones sometimes make you click a Pair button if you see matching passcodes on both your computer and phone.

When in doubt, type **0000** on your keyboard. That's often recognized as a universal passcode for frustrated Bluetooth devices owners who are trying to connect their gadgets.

After a gadget successfully pairs with your computer, its name and icon appear in the Devices category of the PC Settings screen.

To add a Bluetooth device from the Windows 8 desktop, click the taskbar's Bluetooth icon (shown in the margin), choose Add a Bluetooth Device, and then jump to Step 3 in the preceding list. Don't see the taskbar's Bluetooth icon? Then click the upward-pointing arrow that lives a few icons to the left of the taskbar's clock. The Bluetooth icon appears in the pop-up menu, ready for your click.

Adding an Xbox 360 game console

The Control Panel lets you add or tweak most computer accessories, but the Xbox 360 game console begs for an exception. If you own one of Microsoft's game machines, you instead grant your *Xbox* permission to connect with your computer.

To let Windows 8 and Xbox communicate, grab your Xbox 360 controller, sit in front of your TV, and follow these steps:

1. **Turn on your Xbox 360, signing in with the same account you've used to sign in to Windows 8.**

   If you've signed in to both your Xbox and computer with *different* Microsoft accounts, you're not left in the lurch. Sign out of that account and create *another* user account in Windows 8 using your Xbox 360 account name and password. (That's a Microsoft account, too.)

   Sign in to that account on Windows 8 whenever you want to use one of the Windows 8 Xbox apps.

2. **On your Xbox 360, go to System Settings, Console Settings, Xbox Companion.**

   There, you see two switches: Available and Unavailable.

3. **Switch from Unavailable to Available.**

4. **Open one of the Windows 8 Xbox apps and choose Connect.**

   After a few moments, the word *Connecting* appears on your television screen, and you're through. Your Xbox apps will find your Xbox in Windows 8.

Adding a printer

Quarrelling printer manufacturers couldn't agree on how printers should be installed. As a result, you install your printer in one of two ways:

✔ Some printer manufacturers say simply to plug in your printer by pushing its rectangular-shaped connector into a little rectangular-shaped USB port on your PC. Windows 8 automatically notices, recognizes, and embraces your new printer. Stock your printer with any needed ink cartridges, toner, or paper, and you're done.

✔ Other manufacturers take an uglier approach, saying you must install their bundled software *before* plugging in your printer. And if you don't install the software first, the printer may not work correctly.

Unfortunately, the only way to know how your printer should be installed is to check the printer's manual. (Sometimes this information appears on a colorful, one-page Quick Installation sheet packed in the printer's box.)

If your printer lacks installation software, install the cartridges, add paper to the tray, and follow these instructions to put it to work:

1. **With Windows 8 up and running, plug your printer into your PC and turn on the printer.**

   Windows 8 may send a message saying that your printer is installed successfully, but follow the next step to test it.

2. **Load the desktop's Control Panel.**

   Summon the desktop's Control Panel with the tools at your disposal:

   • **Mouse:** Right-click the screen's bottom-left corner and choose Control Panel from the pop-up menu.

   • **Keyboard:** From the desktop, press ⊞+I, scroll up to the words *Control Panel* and then press Enter.

   • **Touchscreen:** From the desktop, slide your finger from the screen's right edge inward, tap the Settings icon, and tap the words *Control Panel*.

3. **From the Hardware and Sound category, click the View Devices and Printers link.**

   The Control Panel displays its categories of devices, including your printer, if you're lucky. If you spot your USB printer listed by its model or brand name, right-click its icon, choose Printer Properties, and click the Print Test Page button. If it prints correctly, you're finished. Congratulations.

   Test page *didn't* work? Check that all the packaging is removed from inside your printer and that it has ink cartridges. If it still doesn't print, your printer is probably defective. Contact the store where you bought it and ask who to contact for assistance.

   Windows 8 lists a printer named Microsoft XPS Document Writer. It's not really a printer, so it can be safely ignored.

That's it. If you're like most people, your printer will work like a charm. If it doesn't, I've stuffed some tips and fix-it tricks in the printing section in Chapter 8.

If you have two or more printers attached to your computer, right-click the icon of your most oft-used printer and choose Set As Default Printer from the pop-up menu. Windows 8 then prints to *that* printer automatically, unless you tell it otherwise.

   ✔ To remove a printer you no longer use, right-click its name in Step 3 and then choose Delete from the pop-up menu. That printer's name no longer appears as an option when you try to print from a program. If Windows 8 asks to uninstall the printer's drivers and software, click Yes — unless you think you may install that printer again sometime.

   ✔ You can change printer options from within many programs. Choose File in a program's menu bar (you may need to press Alt to see the menu bar) and then choose Print Setup or choose Print. The window that appears lets you change things such as paper sizes, fonts, and types of graphics.

   ✔ To share a printer quickly over a network, create a Homegroup, which I describe in Chapter 14. Your printer immediately shows up as an installation option for all the computers on your network.

   ✔ If your printer's software confuses you, try clicking the Help buttons in its dialog boxes. Many buttons are customized for your particular printer model, and they offer advice not found in Windows 8.

Clock, Language, and Region

Microsoft designed this area mostly for travelers to different time zones and locations. Desktop computer owners will see this information only once — when first setting up your computer. Windows 8 subsequently remembers the time and date, even when your PC is turned off.

Portable computers owners will want to drop by here when visiting different time zones; bilingual computer owners will also appreciate settings allowing characters from different languages.

To visit here, right-click the screen's bottom-left corner; choose Control Panel from the pop-up menu; and click the Clock, Language, and Region category. Three sections appear:

   ✔ **Date and Time:** This area is fairly self-explanatory. (Clicking your task-bar's clock and choosing Change Date and Time Settings lets you visit here, as well.)

   ✔ **Language:** If you're bilingual or multilingual, visit this area when you're working on documents that require characters from different languages.

✓ **Region:** Traveling in Italy? Click this category's icon and, on the Formats tab, select Italian from the Formats drop-down list. Windows switches to that country's currency symbols and date format. While you're at the Region window, click the Location tab; and from the Home location drop-down list, select Italy — or whatever country you're currently visiting.

Adding or Removing Programs

Whether you've picked up a new program or you want to purge an old one, the Control Panel's Programs category handles the job fairly well. One of its categories, Programs and Features, lists your currently installed programs, shown in Figure 12-11. Click the one you want to discard or tweak.

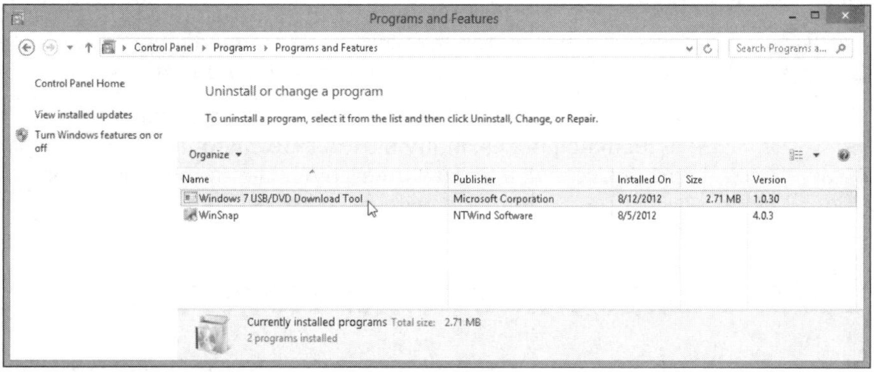

Figure 12-11:
The Uninstall or Change a Program window lets you remove any of your currently installed programs.

	Programs and Features	

Control Panel ▸ Programs ▸ Programs and Features

Control Panel Home

View installed updates

Turn Windows features on or off

Uninstall or change a program

To uninstall a program, select it from the list and then click Uninstall, Change, or Repair.

Organize ▼

Name	Publisher	Installed On	Size	Version
Windows 7 USB/DVD Download Tool	Microsoft Corporation	8/12/2012	2.71 MB	1.0.30
WinSnap	NTWind Software	8/5/2012		4.0.3

Currently installed programs Total size: 2.71 MB
2 programs installed

This section describes how to remove or change existing programs and how to install new ones.

Removing apps and programs

Removing an app from your computer doesn't take much effort. Right-click the app's tile from the Start screen; when the App bar rises from the Start screen's bottom edge, click the Uninstall icon, shown in the margin.

To remove an unwanted desktop program or change its settings, head for the desktop's Control Panel by following these steps:

1. **Right-click in the screen's bottom-left corner and choose the Control Panel from the pop-up menu.**

2. **When the Control Panel appears, choose Uninstall a Program from the Programs category.**

   The Uninstall or Change a Program window appears, as shown in Figure 12-11, listing your currently installed programs, their publisher, size, installation date, and version number.

   To free up disk space, click the Installed On or Size column header to find old or large programs. Then uninstall those forgotten programs you never or rarely use.

3. **Click the unloved program and then click its Uninstall, Change, or Repair button.**

   The menu bar above the programs' names always displays an Uninstall button, but when you click certain programs, you may also see buttons for Change and Repair. Here's the rundown:

   - **Uninstall:** This completely removes the program from your PC. (Some programs list this button as Uninstall/Change.)

   - **Change:** This lets you change some of the program's features or remove parts of it.

   - **Repair:** A handy choice for damaged programs, this tells the program to inspect itself and replace damaged files with new ones. You may need to have the program's original CD or DVD handy, though, because you'll need to insert it into your computer.

4. **When Windows asks whether you're *sure,* click Yes.**

   Depending on which button you've clicked, Windows 8 either boots the program off your PC or summons the program's own installation program to make the changes or repair itself.

   After you delete a program, it's gone for good unless you kept its installation CD. Unlike other deleted items, deleted programs don't linger inside your Recycle Bin.

Always use the Control Panel's Uninstall or Change a Program window to uninstall unwanted programs. Simply deleting their files or folders won't do the trick. In fact, doing so often confuses your computer into sending bothersome error messages.

Installing new programs

Today, most programs install themselves automatically as soon as you slide their discs into your PC's drive or double-click their downloaded installation file.

If you're not sure whether a program has installed, go to the Start screen and look for its tile, usually toward the far right edge. If it's listed there, the program has installed.

But if a program doesn't automatically leap into your computer, here are some tips that can help:

✔ You need an Administrator account to install programs. (Most computer owners automatically have an Administrator account.) That keeps the kids, with their Limited or Guest accounts, from installing programs and messing up the computer. I explain user accounts in Chapter 14.

✔ Downloaded a program? Windows 8 usually saves them in your Downloads folder, accessible by clicking your username on the Start screen. Double-click the downloaded program's name to install it.

✔ Many eager, newly installed programs want to add a desktop shortcut, a Start screen tile, *and* a Quick Launch toolbar shortcut. Say "yes" to all. That way you can start the program from the desktop, avoiding a trip to the Start screen. (Changed your mind? Right-click any unwanted short-cuts and choose either Delete or Unpin to remove them.)

✔ It's always a good idea to create a restore point before installing a new program. (I describe creating restore points in Chapter 13.) If your newly installed program goes haywire, use System Restore to return your com-puter to the peaceful state of mind it enjoyed before you installed the troublemaker.

Modifying Windows 8 for the Physically Challenged

Nearly everybody finds Windows 8 to be particularly challenging, but some people face special physical challenges, as well. To assist them, the Control Panel's Ease of Access area offers a variety of welcome changes.

If your eyesight isn't what it used to be, you may appreciate the ways to increase the text size on your computer screen.

Follow these steps to modify the settings in Windows 8:

1. Load the desktop's Control Panel.

You can fetch the Control Panel any of several ways:

• **Mouse:** Right-click the screen's bottom-left corner and choose Control Panel from the pop-up menu.

• **Keyboard:** From the desktop, press ⊞+I, scroll up to the words *Control Panel*, and then press Enter.

• **Touchscreen:** From the desktop, slide your finger from the screen's right edge inward, tap the Settings icon, and tap the words *Control Panel*.

2. **When the Control Panel appears, select the Ease of Access category, and choose the Ease of Access Center icon.**

   The Ease of Access Center appears, as shown in Figure 12-12. The ethereal voice of Windows 8 kicks in, explaining how to change its programs.

3. **Choose the Get Recommendations to Make Your Computer Easier to Use link.**

   Look for the link called Get Recommendations to Make Your Computer Easier to Use (shown with the mouse pointing to it in Figure 12-12). That makes Windows 8 give you a quick interview so that it can gauge what adjustments you may need. When it's through, Windows 8 automatically makes its changes, and you're done.

   If you're not happy with the changes, move to Step 4.

4. **Make your changes manually.**

   The Ease of Access Center offers these toggle switches to make the keyboard, sound, display, and mouse easier to control:

   - **Start Magnifier:** Designed for the visually impaired, this option magnifies the mouse pointer's exact location.

   - **Start Narrator:** The awful built-in narrator in Windows 8 reads onscreen text for people who can't view it clearly.

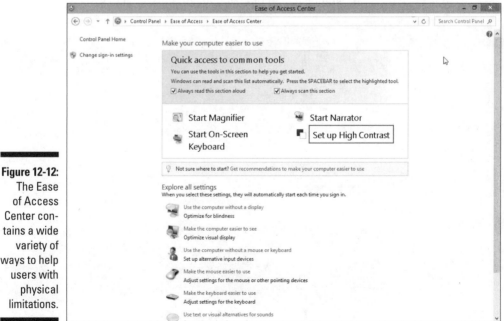

Figure 12-12:
The Ease of Access Center contains a wide variety of ways to help users with physical limitations.

- **Start On-Screen Keyboard:** This setting places a clickable keyboard along the screen's bottom, letting you type by pointing and clicking.

- **Set up High Contrast:** This setting eliminates most screen colors but helps vision-impaired people view the screen and cursor more clearly.

Choose any of these options to turn on the feature immediately. Close the feature's window if the feature makes matters worse.

If you're still not happy, proceed to Step 5.

5. **Choose a specific setting in the Explore All Settings area.**

Here's where Windows 8 gets down to the nitty gritty, letting you optimize Windows 8 specifically for the following things:

- Blindness or impaired vision

- Using an alternative input device rather than a mouse or keyboard

- Adjusting the keyboard and mouse sensitivity to compensate for limited movements

- Turning on visual alerts instead of sound notifications

- Making it easier to focus on reading and typing tasks

Some centers that assist physically challenged people may offer software or assistance for helping you make these changes.

Chapter 13

Keeping Windows from Breaking

*I*f something in Windows is already broken, hop ahead to Chapter 18 for the fix. (Windows 8 offers more and better quick fixes than ever before.) But if your computer seems to be running reasonably well, stay right here. This chapter explains how to keep it running that way for the longest time possible.

This chapter is a checklist of sorts, with each section explaining a fairly simple and necessary task to keep Windows running at its best. You discover how to turn on the automatic backup program in Windows 8, called *File History,* for example.

If somebody says your computer has a bad driver, it's not a personal insult. A *driver* is a little program that helps Windows talk to your computer's various parts. This chapter explains how to remove bad drivers by placing an updated driver behind the wheel.

In addition to the checklist this chapter offers, make sure that the Windows Update and Windows Defender programs are running on autopilot, a quick job I describe in Chapter 11. Those programs go a *long* way toward keeping your computer running safely and securely.

Creating a restore point

Windows 8 is moving away from restore points to its two new Refresh and Reset systems, covered in Chapter 18. But old-school System Restore fans can still create and use the trusty Windows restore points to return your PC to a time when it was feeling better.

To create a restore point, follow these steps:

1. **Open the Start screen, type** System Restore, **and click the word** *Settings* **in the Search pane on the right.**

   As you begin typing directly at the Start screen, the Search pane appears, listing matches. The Search pane normally searches for apps, so it won't find any matches. But when you click the word *Settings,* the Search pane lists all the *settings* containing the phrase "System Restore."

2. **Click the Create a Restore Point link.**

   The System Properties window appears, opened to the System Protection tab, which lists options for System Restore. Look for the Create button near the bottom.

3. **Click the Create button to fetch the System Protection window, type a name for your new restore point, and then click the System Protection window's Create button to save the restore point.**

   Windows 8 creates a restore point with your chosen name, leaving you some open windows to close.

By creating your own restore points on good days, you'll know immediately which ones to use on bad days. I describe how to resuscitate your computer from that restore point in the sidebar on System Restore in Chapter 18.

Tuning Up Windows 8 with Built-In Maintenance Tools

Windows 8 contains a slew of tools for keeping Windows 8 running smoothly. Several run automatically, limiting your work to checking their On switches. Others help you prepare for coming disasters by backing up your PC's files.

To check out your computer's survivalist tools, right-click your desktop's bottommost-left corner, choose Control Panel, and select the Control Panel's System and Security category.

From the desktop, slide your finger in from the screen's right edge, tap the Settings icon, and tap the word *Control Panel* link in the screen's top-right corner.

You need these tools most often:

- ✔ **File History:** The new backup program in Windows 8 drapes a safety net over every file in your four libraries, letting you retrieve backup copies should things go wrong. The free File History program leaves you no excuse not to turn it on. All hard drives eventually die, and you've stored lots of memories on yours.

- ✔ **System:** Technical support people thrive in this crawlspace. The System area lists your version of Windows 8, your PC's horsepower and networking status, and a scorecard rating of what Windows thinks of your PC's performance.

- ✔ **Windows Update:** This tool lets Microsoft automatically siphon security fixes into your PC through the Internet, usually a good thing. Here's where you can turn Windows Update back on, if it's not running.

- ✔ **Power Options:** Not sure whether your PC is sleeping, hibernating, or just plain turned off? Chapter 3 explains the difference, and this section lets you determine your PC's degree of lethargy when you press its Off button. (Or if you're a laptop owner, when you close its lid.)

- ✔ **Administrative Tools:** One gem lives in this complicated grab bag of tech tools: The Disk Cleanup program deletes your PC's garbage to give you more storage space.

I describe these tasks more fully in the next five sections.

Backing up your computer with File History

Your hard drive will eventually die, unfortunately, and it will take everything down with it: years of digital photos, music, letters, financial records, scanned memorabilia, and anything else you've created or stored on your PC.

That's why you must back up your files on a regular basis. When your hard drive finally walks off the stage, your backup copy lets you keep the show on the road.

Windows 8 includes a new backup solution called *File History*. After you turn it on, File History automatically backs up every file in your libraries every hour. The program is easy to turn on, is simple to figure out, runs automatically, and backs up everything you need.

Before File History can go to work, you need two things:

> ✔ **An external hard drive:** For dependable, automatic backups, you need a portable hard drive, which is simply a hard drive in a little box. A cord connects from the box to one of your computer's USB ports; when the drive is plugged in, Windows 8 recognizes the drive immediately. Keep the drive plugged into your computer, and you'll have completely automatic backups.
>
> A flash drive (those inexpensive, pocket-sized memory sticks) will also work with the Windows 8 File History program. But because they lack the storage capacity of a portable hard drive, they probably won't be able to back up all of your files.
>
> ✔ **Flip the On Switch:** The File History program comes free in every version of Windows 8. But it won't do anything until you tell it to begin running.

Follow these steps to tell your computer start backing up your work automatically every hour:

1. **Plug your drive or its cable into your USB port.**

   The rectangular shaped plug on the end of the drive or its cable plugs into the rectangular-shaped USB port on your computer.

2. **Click the pop-up notification that says, Tap to choose what happens with removable drives.**

   Shown in Figure 13-1, the notification appears whenever you plug in any new storage device, be it a flash drive or portable hard drive. (The notification appears on both the desktop and Start screen.)

Figure 13-1: Tap or click the pop-up notification.

Don't see the pop-up in Figure 13-1? Or do you want to tweak your existing File History settings? In either case, jump ahead to Step 4.

3. **Select the Configure this Drive for Backup option; when the File History window appears, click the Turn On button.**

   When the second notification appears, shown in Figure 13-2, select the Configure this Drive for Backup option. When the File History window appears, click the Turn On button.

Removable Disk (K:)

Choose what to do with removable drives.

- Speed up my system
  Windows ReadyBoost

- Configure this drive for backup
  File History

- Open folder to view files
  Windows Explorer

- Take no action

You may see a pop-up asking whether you'd like to recommend this drive to other members of your Homegroup. If it's a large drive meant for everybody on your computer to share, choose Yes. If you'd like to keep it for your personal backups, choose No.

File History begins saving copies of your files for the first time. Depending on the size and amount of your files, the process could take anywhere from a few minutes to a few hours.

If you don't see any pop-up messages when you plug in your drive, you're not left out. Move to Step 4.

4. **Open the Control Panel.**

   With a mouse, right-click in the screen's bottom-left corner; choose Control Panel from the pop-up menu.

   From the desktop, slide your finger inward from the screen's right edge, tap the Settings icon, and tap the Control Panel link in the screen's top-right corner.

5. **Select the System and Security category and click File History.**

   The File History program jumps to the screen. The program takes a guess as to which drive you want to begin filling with your backups. If it guessed correctly, go to Step 7. If it guessed incorrectly, you need Step 6.

6. **If you need to switch the drive, click the Select Drive link from the window's left side and select a different drive.**

7. **Click the Turn On button.**

   Click the Turn On button, shown in Figure 13-3, to start the backup process rolling.

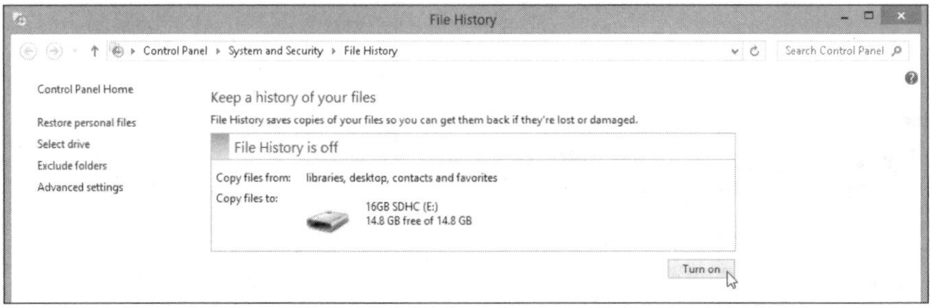

Figure 13-3:
Click the
Turn On
button to
create
automated
backups of
your impor-
tant files
every hour.

Although File History does a remarkable job at keeping everything easy to use and automatic, it comes with a few bits of fine print, described here:

- ✔ If you try to save to a networked drive on another PC, Windows 8 asks you to enter a username and password from an Administrator account on the other PC.

- ✔ File History backs up everything in your libraries: Documents, Music, Pictures, and Videos, as well as the Public folders. That's natural because that's where you store your files. To add new folders or exclude some libraries (perhaps exclude your Videos folder if you already have copies of your videos), choose the Exclude Folders link from the windows' left edge in Figure 13-3.

- ✔ Windows 8 normally backs up files automatically every hour. To change that schedule, click the Advanced Settings link from the windows' left edge in Figure 13-3. Then choose the backup frequency, which ranges from every 10 minutes to once a day.

- ✔ When you turn on File History, Windows 8 immediately starts its backup — even if one isn't scheduled yet. That's because the ever-vigilant Windows 8 wants to make sure that it grabs everything right now, before something goes wrong.

- ✔ I describe how to restore files from the File History backup in Chapter 18. That section's worth looking at now, though: not only does File History works in emergencies, but it also enables you to compare current files with versions you created just hours before. It lets you revive better versions of files that you've changed for the worse.

- ✔ Windows 8 saves your backup in a folder named FileHistory on your chosen drive. Don't move that folder, or else Windows 8 may not be able to find it again when you choose to restore it.

Finding technical information about your computer

If you ever need to look under Windows' hood, heaven forbid, head for the desktop's Control Panel: Right-click your screen's bottommost-left corner and choose System from the pop-up menu.

From the desktop, slide your finger in from the screen's right edge, tap the Settings icon, and tap the Control Panel link in the screen's top-right corner. When the Control Panel appears, select the System and Security category and choose System.

Shown in Figure 13-4, the System window offers an easily digestible technical briefing about your PC's viscera:

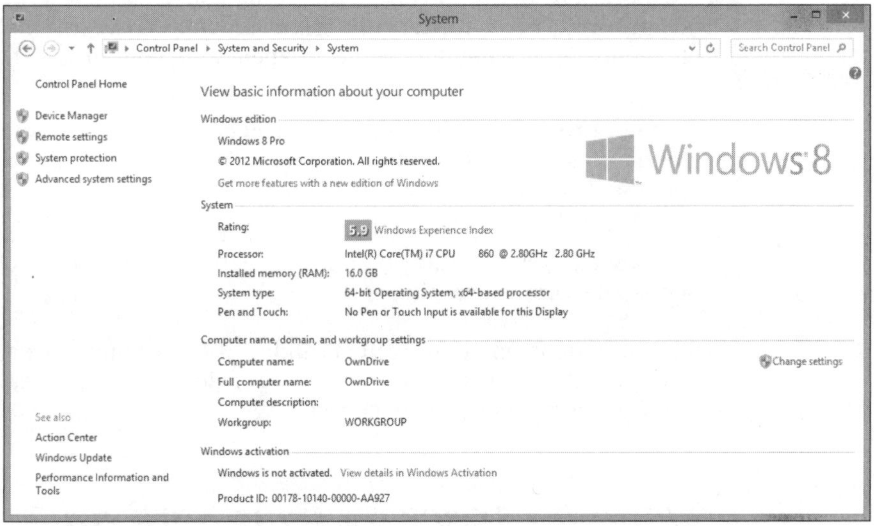

Figure 13-4: Clicking the System icon brings up technical information about your PC.

- ✔ **Windows Edition:** Windows comes in several versions, each described in Chapter 1. In this section, Windows lists the version that's running on your particular computer.

- ✔ **System:** Here, Windows rates your PC's strength — its *Windows Experience Index* — on a scale of 1 (frail) to 9.9 (powerhouse). Your PC's type of *Processor* — its brains, so to speak — also appears here, as well as its amount of memory.

✔ **Computer Name, Domain, and Workgroup Settings:** This section identifies your computer's name and *workgroup,* a term used when connecting to other computers in a network. (I cover networks in Chapter 15.)

✔ **Windows Activation:** To keep people from buying one copy of Windows 8 and installing it on several PCs, Microsoft requires Windows 8 to be *activated,* a process that chains it to a single PC.

The pane along the left also lists some more advanced tasks you may find handy during those panic-stricken times when something's going wrong with your PC. Here's the rundown:

✔ **Device Manager:** This option lists all the parts inside your computer, but not in a friendly manner. Parts with exclamation points next to them aren't happy. Double-click them to see Windows' explanation of why they're not working correctly. (Sometimes a Troubleshoot button appears by the explanation; click the button to diagnose the problem.)

✔ **Remote Settings:** Rarely used, this complicated setup lets other people control your PC through the Internet, hopefully to fix things. If you can find one of these helpful people, let them walk you through this procedure.

✔ **System Protection:** This option lets you create restore points (described in this chapter's first section). You can also come here and use a restore point to take your PC back to another point in time — hopefully when it was in a better mood.

✔ **Advanced System Settings:** Professional techies spend lots of time in here. Everybody else ignores it.

Most of the stuff listed in the System window is fairly complicated, so don't mess with it unless you're sure of what you're doing or a technical support person tells you to change a specific setting.

Freeing up space on your hard drive

Windows 8 grabs quite a bit of space on your hard drive, although it's slimmer than some earlier Windows versions. If programs begin whining about running out of room on your hard drive, this solution grants you a short reprieve:

1. **Right-click your screen's bottom-left corner and choose Control Panel.**

   From the desktop, slide your finger in from the screen's right edge, tap the Settings icon, and tap the Control Panel link in the screen's top-right corner.

2. **Click the Control Panel's System and Security category. Then, in the Administrative Tools category (near the bottom), click the Free Up Disk Space link.**

   If your PC has more than one disk drive, Windows 8 asks which drive to clean up. The Disk Cleanup Drive Selection window appears.

3. **Leave the choice set to (C:) and click OK.**

   The Disk Cleanup program calculates how much disk space you can save and presents the Disk Cleanup dialog box shown in Figure 13-5. (The amount of disk space you can save is shown at the top of the dialog box.)

4. **Select the check boxes for all the items and then click OK.**

   As you select a check box, the Description section explains what's being deleted. When you click the OK button, Windows asks if you're *sure* you want to delete the files.

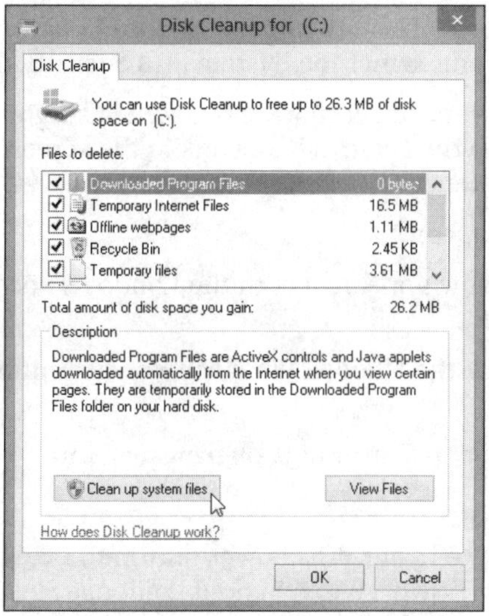

Figure 13-5: Make sure that all the check boxes are selected.

Disk Cleanup for (C:)
Disk Cleanup
You can use Disk Cleanup to free up to 26.3 MB of disk space on (C:).
Files to delete:
☑ Downloaded Program Files 0 bytes
☑ Temporary Internet Files 16.5 MB
☑ Offline webpages 1.11 MB
☑ Recycle Bin 2.45 KB
☑ Temporary files 3.61 MB
Total amount of disk space you gain: 26.2 MB
Description
Downloaded Program Files are ActiveX controls and Java applets downloaded automatically from the Internet when you view certain pages. They are temporarily stored in the Downloaded Program Files folder on your hard disk.
[Clean up system files] [View Files]
How does Disk Cleanup work?
[OK] [Cancel]

If you spot a Clean Up System Files button, click it, too. It deletes detritus created by your PC, not you.

5. **Click the Delete Files button to erase the unneeded files.**

   Windows 8 proceeds to empty your Recycle Bin, destroy leftovers from old websites, and remove other hard drive clutter.

Empowering your power button

Instead of reaching for your computer's power switch, you should turn off Windows 8 with its *own* power button, as described in Chapter 2. The power option offers three options: Sleep, Shut Down, and Restart.

Sleep, the most popular option, puts your computer into a low-power slumber, so it loads quickly when turned back on.

The built-in power switch in Windows takes quite a few steps to reach, however. To save time, tell your computer's *power button* how to react when pressed: Should it Sleep or Shut Down?

The same question applies to laptop owners: Should your computer sleep or shut down when you close the lid?

To answer that question, follow these steps:

1. **Right-click the desktop's bottom-left corner, choose Control Panel from the pop-up menu, and select the System and Security category.**

   From the desktop, slide your finger in from the screen's right edge, tap the Settings icon, and tap the Control Panel link in the screen's top-right corner. Then tap the System and Security category.

2. **Click the Power Options icon.**

   The Power Options window appears, set to the Windows normal setting: Balanced (Recommended).

3. **From the left panel, click the Choose What the Power Button Does link.**

   A window appears, shown in Figure 13-6, offering a menu.

4. **Select your changes.**

   Using the menu, you can tell your PC's power button to Do Nothing, Sleep, Hibernate, or Shut Down. (When in doubt, choose Sleep.)

   Laptops and tablets offer extra options on this window: You can make them behave differently according to whether they're plugged in or running on batteries. That lets you run them at full power when plugged in, but to conserve power when on batteries.

   Laptop owners also find a menu letting them choose their laptop's behavior when they close its lid or press its sleep button. (This menu also offers different behaviors depending on whether your laptop is plugged in or not.)

For extra security, select the Require a Password (Recommended) radio button so that anybody waking up your PC needs your password to see your information.

5. Click the Save Changes button.

Setting up devices that don't work (fiddling with drivers)

Windows comes with an arsenal of *drivers* — software that lets Windows communicate with the gadgets you plug in to your PC. Normally, Windows 8 automatically recognizes your new part, and it simply works. Other times, Windows 8 heads to the Internet and fetches some automated instructions before finishing the job.

But occasionally, you'll plug in something that's either too new for Windows 8 to know about or too old for it to remember. Or perhaps something attached to your PC becomes cranky, and you see odd messages grumble about "needing a new driver."

In these cases, it's up to you to track down and install a Windows 8 driver for that part. The best drivers come with an installation program that automatically places the software in the right place, fixing the problem. The worst drivers leave all the grunt work up to you.

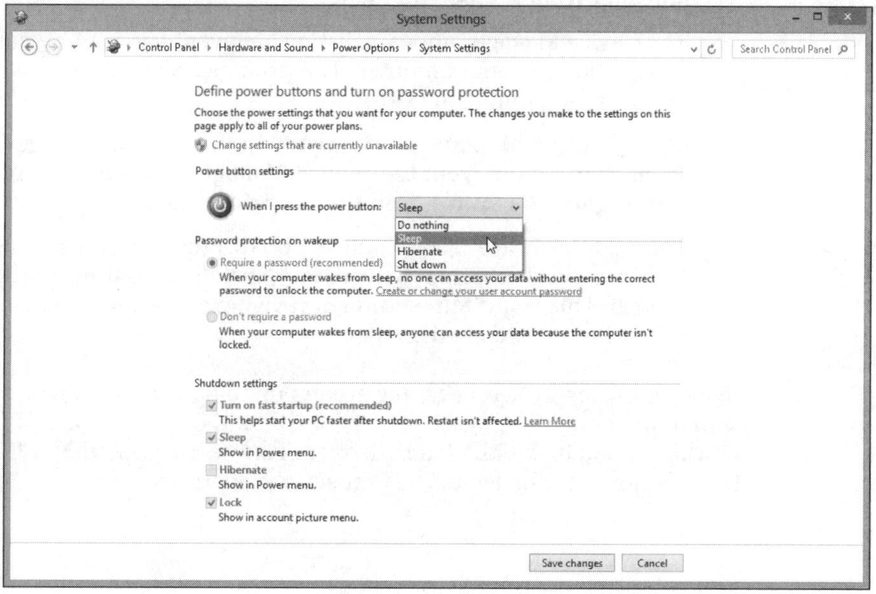

Figure 13-6:
Choose how your computer should behave when the power button is pressed.

If Windows 8 doesn't automatically recognize and install your newly attached piece of hardware — even after you restart your PC — follow these steps to locate and install a new driver:

1. **Visit the part manufacturer's website and download the latest Windows 8 driver.**

   You often find the manufacturer's website stamped somewhere on the part's box. If you can't find it, search for the part manufacturer's name on Google (www.google.com) and locate its website.

   Look in the website's Support, Downloads, or Customer Service area. There, you usually need to enter your part's name, its model number, and your computer's operating system (Windows 8) before the website coughs up the driver.

   No Windows 8 driver listed? Try downloading a Windows 7 or Windows Vista driver instead; they sometimes work just as well.

2. **Run the driver's installation program.**

   Sometimes clicking your downloaded file makes its installation program jump into action, installing the driver for you. If so, you're through. If not, head to Step 3.

   If the downloaded file has a little zipper on the icon, right-click it and choose Extract All to *unzip* its contents into a new folder that contains the files. (Windows 8 names that new folder after the file you've unzipped, making it easy to relocate.)

3. **Right-click in the screen's bottom-left corner and choose Device Manager from the pop-up menu.**

   The Device Manager appears, listing an inventory of every part inside or attached to your computer. The problematic one will have a yellow exclamation point icon next to it.

4. **Click your problematic device listed in the Device Manager window. Then click Action from the Device Manager's menu bar and choose Add Legacy Hardware from the drop-down menu.**

   The Add Hardware Wizard guides you through the steps of installing your new hardware and, if necessary, installing your new driver. Beware, though: This last-ditch method of reviving problematic parts can frustrate even experienced techies.

Avoid problems by keeping your drivers up-to-date. Even the ones packaged with newly bought parts are usually old. Visit the manufacturer's website, download, and install the latest driver. Chances are good that it fixes problems earlier users had with the first set of drivers.

Problems with a newly installed driver? Head back to Device Manager, double-click the troublesome part's name, and click the Driver tab on the Properties box. Keep your breathing steady. Then click the Roll Back Driver button. Windows 8 ditches the newly installed driver and returns to the previous driver.

Chapter 14

Sharing One Computer with Several People

*W*indows allows several people to share one computer, laptop, or tablet without letting anybody peek into anybody else's files.

The secret? Windows grants each person his or her own *user account,* which neatly isolates that person's files. When a person types in his user account name and password, the computer looks tailor-made just for him: It displays his personalized desktop background, menu choices, programs, and files — and it forbids him from seeing items belonging to other users.

This chapter explains how to set up a separate user account for everybody in your home, including the computer's owner, family members, roommates, and even occasional visitors who ask to check their e-mail.

You'll also discover how to break down some of those walls to share information between accounts, letting everybody see your vacation photos, for example, but keeping your love letters off-limits.

Understanding User Accounts

Windows 8 wants you to set up a *user account* for everybody who uses your PC. A user account works like a cocktail-party name tag that helps Windows recognize who's sitting at the keyboard. Windows 8 offers three types of user accounts: Administrator, Standard, and Guest. To begin playing with the PC, people click their account's name when the Windows 8 Start screen first loads, as shown in Figure 14-1.

Who cares? Well, Windows 8 gives each type of account permission to do different things on the computer. If the computer were a hotel, the Administrator account would belong to the desk clerk, each tenant would have a Standard account, and Guest accounts would belong to visitors trying to use the bathroom in the lobby. Here's how the different accounts translate into computer lingo:

- ✔ **Administrator:** The administrator controls the entire computer, deciding who gets to play with it and what each user may do on it. On a computer running Windows 8, the owner usually holds the almighty Administrator account. He or she then sets up accounts for each household member and decides what they can and can't do with the PC.

- ✔ **Standard:** Standard account holders can access most of the computer, but they can't make any big changes to it. They can't run or install new programs, for example, but they can run existing programs.

Figure 14-1:
Windows
8 lets
users sign
in under
their own
accounts.

✔ **Guest:** Guests can play with the computer, but the computer doesn't recognize them by name. Guest accounts function much like Standard accounts, but with no privacy: Anybody can sign in with the Guest account, and the desktop will look the way the last guest left it. It's great for web browsing, but not much else.

Here are some ways accounts are typically assigned when you're sharing the same computer under one roof:

✔ In a family, the parents usually hold Administrator accounts, the kids usually have Standard accounts, and the babysitter signs in using the Guest account.

✔ In a dorm or shared apartment, the computer's owner holds the Administrator account, and the roommates have either Standard or Guest accounts, depending on their trustworthiness level (and perhaps how clean they've left the kitchen that week).

To keep others from signing in under your user account, you must protect it with a password. (I describe how to choose a password for your account in this chapter's "Setting Up Passwords and Security" section.)

Sometimes somebody will be signed in to her account, but the computer will go to sleep if she hasn't touched the keyboard for a while. When the computer wakes back up, only that person's user account and photo will show up onscreen. To see *everybody's* account, click the arrow (shown in the margin) to the left of that person's account photo.

Guest accounts can't dial up the Internet. They can access the web only if your PC has a *broadband* connection — a connection that's always turned on and available.

Giving yourself a Standard account

Whenever an evil piece of software slips into your computer — and you're signed in as an administrator — that evil software holds as much power as you do. That's dangerous because Administrator accounts can delete just about anything. And that's why Microsoft suggests creating *two* accounts for yourself: an Administrator account and a Standard account. Then sign in with your Standard account for everyday computing.

That way, Windows 8 treats you just like any other Standard user: When the computer is about to do something potentially harmful, Windows 8 asks you to type the password of an Administrator account. Type your Administrator account's password, and Windows 8 lets you proceed. But if Windows 8 unexpectedly asks for permission to do something odd, you know something may be suspect.

This second account is inconvenient, no doubt about it. But so is reaching for a key whenever you enter your front door. Taking an extra step is the price of extra security.

Changing Your User Account or Adding a New Account

Being second-class citizens, Standard account holders lack much power. They can run programs and change their account's picture, for example, and even change their password. But the administrators hold the *real* power: They can create or delete any user account, effectively wiping a person's name, files, and programs off the computer. (That's why you should never upset a computer's administrator.)

If you're an administrator, create a Standard user account for everybody who's sharing your computer. That account gives the users enough control over the computer to keep them from bugging you all the time, yet it keeps them from accidentally deleting your important files or messing up your computer.

Adding another user to your computer

Administrator account holders can add another User Account through the Start screen's simple PC Settings screen by following these steps:

1. **Summon the Charms bar, click the Settings icon, and then click the words *Change PC Settings*.**

   You can fetch the new Charms bar by pointing your mouse cursor at the screen's top- or bottom-right corner, sliding a finger inward from a touchscreen's right edge, or pressing ⊞+C with a keyboard.

2. **From the PC Settings screen, click the Users category.**

   The Your Account screen appears, as shown in Figure 14-2, showing ways to change your own account, as well as how to add another person.

   While you're here, you can tweak your own account, changing your password or even switching from a Microsoft account to a Local account (both of which I explain in the next step).

3. **To add a new user account, click the words *Add a User* and then, in the Add a User window that appears, choose which type of account to create.**

   Microsoft complicates matters, as shown in the Add a User window in Figure 14-3, by forcing you to choose which *type* of account to create for the new person. You have two choices:

Figure 14-2:
Click the words *Add a User* to create a new user account.

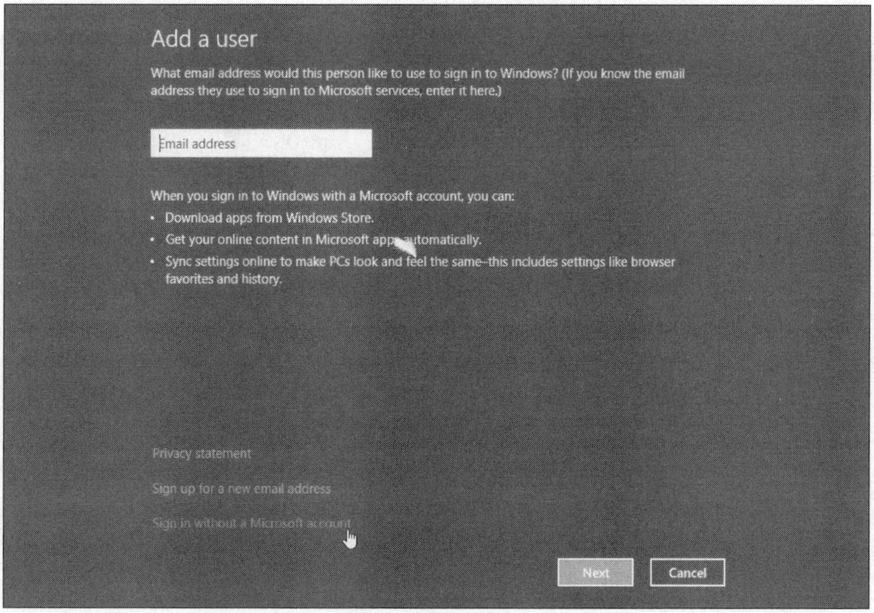

Figure 14-3:
Enter an e-mail address to sign up for a Microsoft account.

- **Local account:** Select this option for casual guests, family members, or people not interested in Microsoft accounts and their privileges. It lets the person use your computer with a generic account. To create a Local account, click the words *Don't Want this Person to Sign In With a Microsoft Account?* and then jump to Step 5.

- **Microsoft account:** Select this option when somebody *specifically asks for it.* Described in Chapter 2, a Microsoft account is an e-mail address that links to Microsoft, its computers, and its billing department. The account holder can then buy apps using his own credit card, for example, fetch personal files he has stored on an Internet storage space called SkyDrive, and access other perks offered by a Microsoft account. To create a Microsoft account, go to the next step.

Can't decide which type of account to create? Then create a Local account. The person can always turn it into a Microsoft account later, if he wants.

4. **To create a Microsoft account, enter the account's e-mail address in the Email Address text box, click Next, and then click Finish.**

   The account will be waiting on the Start screen.

   When the person wants to use the computer, he chooses the account bearing his e-mail address and then types in his Microsoft account password. Windows visits the Internet, and if e-mail address and password match, the account is ready for action. You've finished.

5. **Click the words Sign in without a Microsoft Account, shown at the bottom of Figure 14-3.**

   Alarmed that you'd consider choosing a lowly Local account over the wondrous Microsoft account, Microsoft displays a confirmation page with two buttons: Microsoft Account and Local Account.

6. **Click the Local Account button.**

   This tells Microsoft that yes, you really do want a Local account. (After all, you can always convert a Local account into a Microsoft account later on.)

   A new screen appears, asking for a name for the account (username), the account's password, and a password hint in case you forget the password.

7. **Enter a username, password, and password hint and then click Next.**

   Use the person's first name or nickname for the username. Choose a simple password and hint; the user can change them after he signs in.

8. **Click Finish.**

   Tell the person his new username and password. His username will be waiting at the Sign In screen for him to begin using the computer.

Unlike earlier Windows versions, Windows 8 creates Standard accounts for all new users. You can upgrade that later to an Administrator account if you want, by changing the account, described in the next section.

Changing an existing user's account

The Start screen's PC Settings screen (its mini-control panel) lets you create a new account for a friend or family member, as described in the previous section. And it lets you tweak your own account, changing your password or switching between a Microsoft or a Local account.

But if you want to change somebody *else's* account, either tweaking its settings or deleting it entirely, you need the power of the desktop's Control Panel.

To change an existing user's account, follow these steps:

1. **Right-click the screen's bottom-left corner and choose Control Panel from the pop-up menu.**

   From the desktop, slide your finger from the screen's right edge inward, tap the Settings icon, and tap the words *Control Panel* at the Setting's pane's top edge.

2. **Click to open the Control Panel's User Accounts and Family Safety category.**

3. **Click the User Accounts link and then click the Manage Another Account link.**

   The Manage Accounts window appears, as shown in Figure 14-4, listing all the accounts on your computer.

   While you're here, feel free to turn on the Guest account by selecting its name and clicking the Turn On button. A Guest account provides a handy and safe way to let visitors use your computer — without giving them access to your files or letting them do anything that might harm your computer.

4. **Click the account you'd like to change.**

   Windows 8 displays a page with the account's photo and lets you tweak the account's settings in any of these ways:

   • **Change the Account Name:** Here's your chance to correct a misspelled name on an account. Or feel free to jazz up your account name, changing Jane to Crystal Powers.

   • **Create/Change a Password:** Every account should have a password to keep out other users. Here's your chance to add one or change the existing one.

- **Set Up Family Safety:** An Easter egg for parents, Family Safety lets you choose the hours that an account holder may access the PC, as well as limit the programs and games the account holder may run. I cover Family Safety, known in Windows 7 and Vista as *Parental Controls*, in Chapter 11.

- **Change the Account Type:** Head here to promote a Standard user of high moral character to an Administrator account or bump a naughty administrator down to Standard.

- **Delete the Account:** Don't choose this setting hastily, because deleting somebody's account also deletes all her files. If you *do* choose it, also choose the subsequent option that appears, Keep Files. That places all of that person's files in a folder on your desktop for safekeeping.

- **Manage Another Account:** Save your current crop of changes and begin tweaking somebody else's account.

5. **When you're through, close the window by clicking the red X in its top-right corner.**

   Any changes made to a user's account take place immediately.

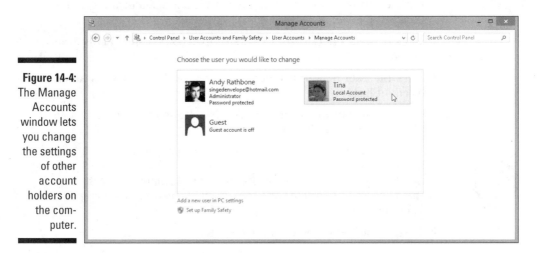

Figure 14-4:
The Manage Accounts window lets you change the settings of other account holders on the computer.

Switching Quickly between Users

Windows 8 enables an entire family, roommates, or employees in a small office to share a single computer or tablet. The computer keeps track of everybody's programs while different people use the computer. Mom can be playing chess and then let Jerry sign in to check his e-mail. When Mom signs back in a few minutes later, her chess match is right where she left it, pondering the sacrifice of her rook.

Known as *Fast User Switching,* switching between users works quickly and easily. When somebody else wants to sign in to his account for a moment, perhaps to check e-mail, follow these steps:

1. **Switch to the Start screen.**

   To return to the Start screen, press the keyboard's Windows key (▦); with a mouse, point in the screen's top- or bottom-left corner and then click the Start icon.

   On a touchscreen, slide your finger inward from the screen's right edge to summon the Charms bar and then tap the Start icon.

2. **Click your user account photo in the screen's top-right corner.**

   A menu drops down, as shown in Figure 14-5.

3. **Choose the name of the user account holder who wants to sign in.**

   Windows leaves you signed in, but immediately fetches the other person's account, letting him type in his password.

Figure 14-5: The menu lists the names of all user accounts authorized to use the computer.

When that person finishes with the computer, he can sign out just as you did in Step 2, by clicking his user account photo in the Start screen's upper-right corner. This time, however, he'll choose Sign Out. Windows closes down his session, letting you sign back in with your own password.

Keep these tips in mind when switching between other account holders on your PC:

✔ With all this user switching, you may forget whose account you're actually using. To check, open the Start screen. The current account holder's name and picture appear in the menu's top-right corner. Also, the Windows 8 opening screen lists the words "Signed In" beneath the picture of every user who's currently signed in.

✔ Don't restart the PC while another person is still signed in, or that person will lose any work he hasn't saved. (Windows 8 warns you before restarting the PC, giving you a chance to ask the other person to sign on and save his work.)

✔ If a Standard account owner tries to change a setting or install software, a window will appear, asking for Administrator permission. If you want to approve the action, just step over to the PC and type your password into the approval window. Windows 8 lets you approve the change, just as if you'd done it while signed in with your own account.

Sharing Files among Account Holders

Normally, the Windows user account system keeps everybody's files separate, effectively thwarting Jack's attempts to read Jill's diary. But what if you're co-writing a report with somebody, and you both want access to the same file? Sure, you can e-mail the file back and forth to each other, or you can store the file on a flash drive and carry the flash drive from PC to PC.

But for an easier way, head to the Windows desktop and use the Library system. Place a copy of that file in a *Public* folder in one of your libraries. When placed in a Public folder, that file then shows up in *everybody's* library, where anybody can view, change, or delete it. (Even visitors signing in with the Guest account can view, change, or delete items in a Public folder.)

Items placed in a Public folder even show up in the other computers connected through a Homegroup, a simple networking system I cover in Chapter 15.

Here's how to find the Public folders living in your libraries and copy files into them for sharing with others:

1. **From the desktop, open File Explorer.**

   If you're on the Start screen, click the Desktop tile. When on the desktop, click the File Explorer icon, which is shown in the margin.

   File Explorer appears, displaying your four libraries in its left pane: Documents, Music, Pictures, and Videos.

2. **Double-click the library where you want to share your files.**

   Double-click the Music library, for example, shown in Figure 14-6, and the Music library reveals the two folders living inside it: My Music and Public Music.

   To double-click on a touchscreen, tap twice in rapid succession.

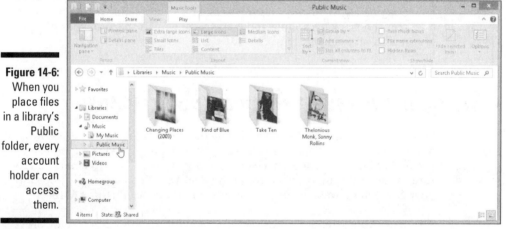

Figure 14-6: When you place files in a library's Public folder, every account holder can access them.

Every one of your four libraries constantly displays the contents of a Public folder, as well as the contents of your personal folder.

The beauty of Public folders is that their contents appear in *everybody's* library. If Nicole puts a music file into her Public Music folder, it automatically appears in Virginia's Public Music folder, as well.

3. **Copy the file or folder you want to share to the appropriate library's Public folder.**

   You can drag and drop the item directly into the Public folder's icon on the Navigation Pane along the folder's left edge. As soon as the item is in the Public folder, it automatically appears in everybody's library, where they can open, change, or even delete it. (Because it can be deleted, it's sometimes wiser to *copy* items into the Public folder rather than *move* them.)

Here are some other Public folder tips:

✔ To see exactly what items you're sharing, examine your own libraries, displayed in every folder's Navigation Pane. For example, to see what music you're sharing publicly, double-click the word *Music* in your library and then click Public Music. The contents of that folder can be accessed, changed, or deleted by anybody.

✔ If you find some things in your Public folder you don't want to share anymore, move them back into your own folder. For example, move that Beatles album from your Music library's Public Music folder to your Music library's My Music folder.

✔ If you connect your PCs through a network, which I describe in Chapter 15, you can create a *Homegroup* — a simple way of sharing files between PCs in the home or small office. After you create a Homegroup, everybody on any PC in your network can share *everything* in the libraries you choose. It's a simple and convenient way to share all your photos, music, and videos.

Changing a User Account's Picture

Okay, now the important stuff: changing the boring picture that Windows automatically assigns to your user account. For every newly created user account, Windows 8 chooses a generic silhouette. Feel free to change the picture to something more reflective of the Real You: You can snap a photo with your computer's webcam or choose any photo in your Pictures library.

To change your user account's picture, head for the Start screen and click your picture in the screen's top-right corner. When the menu drops down, choose Change Account Picture. Windows 8 presents the screen shown in Figure 14-7.

The Account Picture page offers three settings:

✔ **Browse:** To assign a picture already on your computer, click the Browse button. A new window appears, this time showing previous account photos you've chosen. To see photos in your Pictures library, click the word *Files* and choose Pictures from the drop-down menu. Select a desired picture from the folder and click the Choose Image button. Windows 8 quickly slaps that picture atop your Start screen.

✔ **Create an Account Picture:** This option, available only for people with a camera attached to their computers, lets you choose which app should handle the photo shoot. You can find the Windows 8 built-in Camera app listed here, as well as any other photo-snapping apps on your computer.

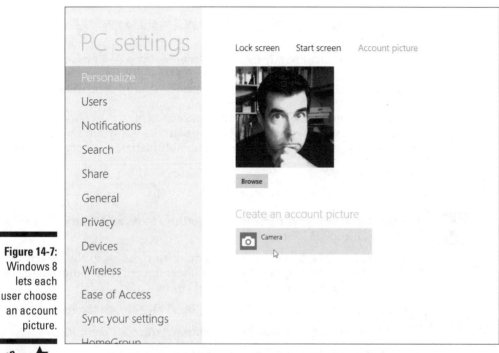

Figure 14-7:
Windows 8
lets each
user choose
an account
picture.

Here are a few more tips for choosing your all-important account photo:

✔ After you've chosen an account photo, it attaches to your Microsoft account and anything you sign into with that account: Your Microsoft phone, for example, Microsoft websites, and any Windows 8 computer you sign in to with your Microsoft account.

✔ You can grab any picture off the Internet and save it to your Pictures folder for use as your user account picture. (Right-click the Internet picture and, depending on your web browser, choose Save to Picture Library or Save Picture As.)

✔ Don't worry about choosing a picture that's too big or too small. Windows 8 automatically shrinks or expands the image to fit the postage-stamp-sized space.

✔ Only holders of Administrator and Standard accounts can change their pictures. (Guest accounts are stuck with the faceless gray silhouette.)

Setting Up Passwords and Security

There's not much point to having a user account if you don't have a password. Without one, Charles from the next cubicle can click your account on the sign-in screen, giving him free reign to snoop through your files.

Administrators, especially, should have passwords. If they don't, they're automatically letting anybody wreak havoc with the PC: When a permission's screen appears, anybody can just press Enter at the password screen to gain entrance.

To create or change a password, follow these steps:

1. **Summon the Charms bar, click the Settings icon, and then click the words** *Change PC Settings.*

   You can fetch the Charms bar by pointing your mouse at the screen's top- or bottom-right corner, sliding a finger inward from a touchscreen's right edge, or pressing ⊞+C with a keyboard.

2. **In the PC Settings screen, click the Users category on the left.**

   The Your Account screen appears, shown earlier in Figure 14-2.

3. **Click the Change Your Password button.**

   People who haven't created a password should instead click the Create a Password button.

4. **Make up an easy-to-remember password and type it into the New Password text box. Then retype the same characters into the Retype Password text box below it.**

   Retyping the password eliminates the chance of typos.

   Changing an existing password works slightly differently: The screen shows a Current Password text box where you must first type your existing password. (That keeps pranksters from sneaking over and changing your password during lunch hours.)

5. **In the Type a Password Hint text box, type a clue that helps you remember your forgotten password.**

   Make sure that the clue works only for you. Don't enter "My hair color," for example. If you're at work, enter **My cat's favorite food** or **The director of my favorite movie**. If you're at home, choose something only you — not the kids — know. And don't be afraid to change your password every once in a while, too.

   You can find out more about passwords in Chapter 2.

Although the password hint should remind you of your password, it doesn't hurt to create a Password Reset Disk, as well, as described in the sidebar.

Creating a Password Reset Disk

A Password Reset Disk serves as a key, letting you back into your computer in the event you've forgotten the password to your Local account. (You can't create a Password Reset Disk for a Microsoft account.) To create a Password Reset Disk, follow these simple steps:

1. **Fetch the Charms bar, click the Search icon, and click Settings in the Search pane.**

2. **In the Search box, type** Password Reset Disk **and press Enter.**

The Forgotten Password Wizard appears, walking you through the process of creating a Password Reset Disk from a memory card or a USB flash drive.

When you forget your password, you can insert your Password Reset Disk as a key. Windows 8 lets you in to choose a new password, and all will be joyous. Hide your Password Reset Disk in a safe place because it lets *anybody* into your account.

No matter how many times you change your password, your original Password Reset Disk still works, always providing a backup key to get into your account.

Chapter 15

Connecting Computers with a Network

*B*uying yet another PC can bring yet another computing problem: How can two or more PCs share the same Internet connection and printer? And how do you share your files between your two PCs?

The solution involves a *network*. When you connect two or more computers, Windows introduces them to each other, automatically letting them swap information, share an Internet connection, and print through the same printer.

Today, most computers can connect without anybody tripping over cables. Known as *Wi-Fi* or *wireless,* this option lets your computers chatter through the airwaves like radio stations that broadcast and take requests.

This chapter explains how to link a houseful of computers so that they can share things. Be forewarned, however: This chapter contains some pretty advanced stuff. Don't tread here unless you're running an Administrator account and you don't mind doing a little head-scratching as you wade from conceptualization to actualization to, "Hey, it works!"

Understanding a Network's Parts

A *network* is simply two or more computers that have been connected so that they can share things. Although computer networks range from pleasingly simple to agonizingly complex, they all have three things in common:

- ✔ **A router:** This little box works as an electronic traffic cop, controlling the flow of information between each computer. Most routers support both wired and wireless networks.

- ✔ **A network adapter:** Every computer needs its own *network adapter* — an electronic mouthpiece of sorts. A *wired* network adapter lets you plug in a cable; the cable's other end plugs into your router. A *wireless* network adapter translates your computer's information into radio signals and broadcasts them to the router.

- ✔ **Network cables:** Computers connecting wirelessly don't need cables, of course. But computers without wireless adapters need cables to connect them to the router.

When you plug a modem into the router, the router quickly distributes the Internet signal to every computer on your network.

Most home networks resemble a spider, as shown in Figure 15-1, with some computers' cables connecting to the router in the center. Other computers, laptops, tablets, and gadgets connect wirelessly to the same router.

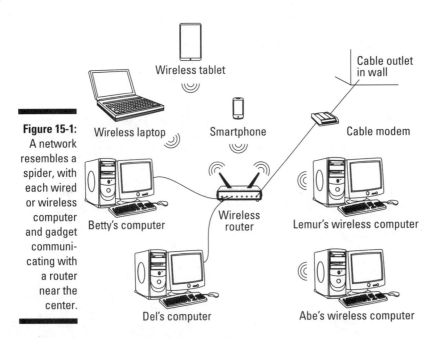

Figure 15-1: A network resembles a spider, with each wired or wireless computer and gadget communicating with a router near the center.

Wireless tablet

Cable outlet in wall

Wireless laptop   Smartphone   Cable modem

Betty's computer   Wireless router   Lemur's wireless computer

Del's computer   Abe's wireless computer

Choosing between wired and wireless networks

You can easily string cables between computers that sit on the same desk or live in one room. Beyond that, though, cables quickly become messy. To cut the clutter, most computers today include *wireless (Wi-Fi)* adapters, which let the computers chatter through the air.

But just as radio broadcasts fade as you drive out of the city, wireless signals also fade. The more they fade, the slower the connection becomes. If your wireless signals pass through more than two or three walls, your computers may not be able to communicate. Wireless networks are also more difficult to set up than wired networks.

Although wireless connections are popular, wired connections work more quickly, efficiently, securely, and inexpensively than wireless. But if your spouse wants the cables removed from the hallways, wireless may be your best option. For best results, combine the two: Connect adjacent computers with cables and use wireless for the rest.

The router divides its attention among networked computers efficiently, letting every computer simultaneously share a single Internet connection.

Windows lets every computer share a single printer, as well. If two people try to print something simultaneously, Windows stashes one person's files until the printer is free and then sends them automatically when the printer is ready for more work.

Wireless routers deliver an Internet signal to *all* connected wireless gadgets, not just Windows computers. After you set up your router, it also delivers your Internet signal to iPads and other tablets; Apple computers; smartphones; and even some home theater devices such as Blu-ray players, game consoles, and televisions.

Setting Up a Small Network

If you're trying to set up a lot of computers — more than ten — you probably need a more advanced book. Networks are fairly easy to set up, but sharing their resources can be scary stuff, especially if the computers contain sensitive material. But if you're just trying to set up a few computers in your home or home office, this information may be all you need.

So without further blabbing, here's a low-carb, step-by-step list of how to set up a small and inexpensive network. This section shows how to buy the three parts of a network, install the parts, and how to make Windows create a network out of your handiwork.

Buying parts for a network

Walk into the computer store, walk out with this stuff, and you're well on your way to setting up your network:

- ✔ **Network adapters (optional):** Because most newer computers and laptops include both wired *and* wireless adapters, you can probably cross this off your shopping list. But if you need to add wireless to an older computer, pick up an inexpensive wireless adapter that plugs into the computer's USB port.

- ✔ **Network cable (optional):** Not using wireless? Then buy *Ethernet* cables, which resemble phone cables but with slightly thicker jacks. Buy a cable for each computer you want to connect. The cables must be long enough to reach from the computer to the router, described next.

- ✔ **Router:** This little box does all the magic. Most routers today include built-in wireless; many also include a broadband modem for Internet access, as well. Look for a router supporting "802.11a/b/g/n," sometimes called 802.11n (Wireless-N). Those routers are compatible with nearly everything. Wireless routers usually include four jacks to accommodate any computers relying on cables.

Some ISPs will supply you with a wireless router/modem, and they'll even send a techie to your home to set up your network for you. It never hurts to ask.

Setting up a wireless router

Wireless connections bring a convenience felt by every cellphone owner. But with computers, a wireless connection also brings complication. You're basically setting up a radio transmitter that broadcasts to little radios inside your computers. You need to worry about signal strength, finding the right signal, and even entering passwords to keep outsiders from eavesdropping.

Unfortunately, different brands of wireless routers come with different setup software, so there's no way I can provide step-by-step instructions for setting up your particular router.

However, every router requires you to set up these three things:

- ✔ **Network name (SSID):** Enter a short, easy-to-remember name here to identify your particular wireless network. Later, when connecting to the wireless network with your computer, you'll select this same name to avoid accidentally connecting with your neighbor's wireless network.

✔ **Infrastructure:** Of the two choices, choose Infrastructure instead of the rarely used alternative, Ad Hoc.

✔ **Security:** To keep out snoops, this option uses a password to encrypt your data as it flies through the air. Most routers offer at least three types of password options: WEP is barely better than no password, WPA is much better, and WPA2 is better still. Choose the strongest security option available and create a short, memorable password with mixed characters, such as **One+One=2**.

Many routers include an installation program to help you change these settings; other routers contain built-in software that you access with Internet Explorer in Windows.

As you set each of the preceding three settings, write them on a piece of paper: You must enter these same three settings when setting up the wireless connection on each of your computers and other wireless gadgets, a job tackled in the next section. You'll also need to pass out that information to any houseguests who want to borrow your Internet connection.

Setting up Windows 8 to connect to a network

First, a word to the wired crowd: If you've chosen to connect a computer to your router with a cable, plug one end of the cable into your computer's network port. Plug the cable's other end into one of your router's network ports. (The ports are usually numbered; any number will do.) Then repeat with the other computer's cables.

If your Internet company didn't do it for you, plug a cable from your broadband modem's LAN or Ethernet port into your router's WAN port.

Turn on your router, and you've finished: You've discovered how easy it is to create a wired network.

Wireless is a different story. After you set up your router to broadcast your network wirelessly, you must tell Windows 8 how to receive it. Chapter 9 offers the full course in connecting to wireless networks, both your own, and those you'll find in public, but here's an abbreviated version for connecting to your own network:

1. **Summon the Charms bar and click the Settings icon.**

   You can tackle this step, which brings up the Start screen's Settings pane, in any of several ways.

Press ⊞+I to head straight for the Charms bar's Settings pane. Mouse owners can point at the screen's top- or bottom-right edge; when the Charms bar appears, click the Settings icon.

If you're a touchscreen user, slide your finger inward from the screen's right edge; when the Charms bar appears, tap the Settings icon.

2. **Click the network icon near the bottom of the Settings pane.**

The network icon changes shape depending on your surroundings and connection method:

- **Available (wireless):** When the icon says Available, like the one in the margin, you're within range of your wireless network. Start salivating and move to Step 3.

- **Unavailable (wireless):** When the icon says Unavailable, like the one in the margin, you're out of range of a wireless network. Move closer to your router until the icon says Available.

- **Connected (wired):** This icon means the cable is correctly connected between the router and the computer.

- **Unavailable (wired):** The cable isn't connected correctly, or the router hasn't had time to detect the connected computer.

If you've connected a wired network, and the icon shows Available, your network is up and running. If it's listed as Unavailable, turn off your router, modem, and computer. Then turn on your modem, router, and computer, in that order, waiting a minute before turning on the next one.

3. **Click the Wireless Available icon.**

Windows sniffs the airwaves and then lists all the wireless networks within range of your computer, including, hopefully, your own. (Your network will be the name — the *SSID* — that you chose when setting up your router, described in the previous section.)

4. **Choose the desired wireless network by clicking its name and then clicking the Connect button.**

If you select the adjacent Connect Automatically check box before clicking the Connect button, Windows automatically connects to that network the next time you're within range, sparing you from following all these steps again.

5. **Enter a password.**

Here's where you type in the same password you entered into your router when setting up your wireless network.

Or, if your router model allows it, you can press a button on the router to bypass the password and connect immediately.

6. **Choose whether you want to share your files with other people on the network.**

   When you see this question in Step 6, you know you've successfully set up your wireless network. All your networked computers should now have Internet access. Congratulations!

7 **Because you're connecting at home and not in a public place, select the option labeled Yes, Turn on Sharing and Connect to Devices.**

   That lets you share files and printers with others on the network.

If you're still having problems connecting, try the following tips:

✔ Cordless phones and microwave ovens interfere with wireless networks, oddly enough. Try to keep your cordless phone out of the same room as your wireless computer, and don't heat up that sandwich when web browsing.

✔ While you're working on the Windows 8 desktop, the taskbar's wireless network icon (shown in the margin) provides a handy way to connect wirelessly, as well. If your desktop's taskbar contains a wireless network icon, click it to jump to Step 3.

Setting Up or Connecting with a Homegroup

Creating a network between your computers makes it easier for them to share resources: an Internet connection, printers, and even your files. But how can you share some files while keeping others private?

Microsoft's solution is called a *Homegroup*. A simpler way of networking, a Homegroup lets every Windows PC in the house share the files nearly everybody wants to share: music, photos, movies, and the household printer. Set up a Homegroup, and Windows automatically begins sharing those items.

Homegroups aren't limited to Windows 8 computers, either — they work fine with any Windows 7 computers on your network, as well. (Homegroups *don't* work with Windows Vista and Windows XP, unfortunately.)

Here's how to set up a new Homegroup on a Windows 8 PC, as well as how to let Windows 8 join a Homegroup you may have already set up with your other networked computers:

1. **Summon the Charms bar, click the Settings icon, and click the words** *Change PC Settings.*

With a mouse, point at the screen's top- or bottom-right corners to summon the Charms bar. Click the Settings icon (shown in the margin) and click the words *Change PC Settings*.

On a touchscreen, slide your finger inward from the right edge, tap the Settings icon, and tap the words *Change PC Settings*.

2. **When the PC Settings screen appears, click the Homegroup category on the left and click either the Create or Join button.**

If you see a Create button, click it to begin creating a new Homegroup. Then move to Step 3.

If you see a Join button (as shown in Figure 15-2), somebody has already created a Homegroup on your network. To join it, type in the Homegroup's existing password and click the Join button.

Don't know the Homegroup's password? On a Windows 7 or Windows 8 computer, find the password by opening any folder, right-clicking the word *Homegroup* from the left pane, and choosing View the Homegroup Password.

Whether you click Join or Create, Windows asks what you'd like to share.

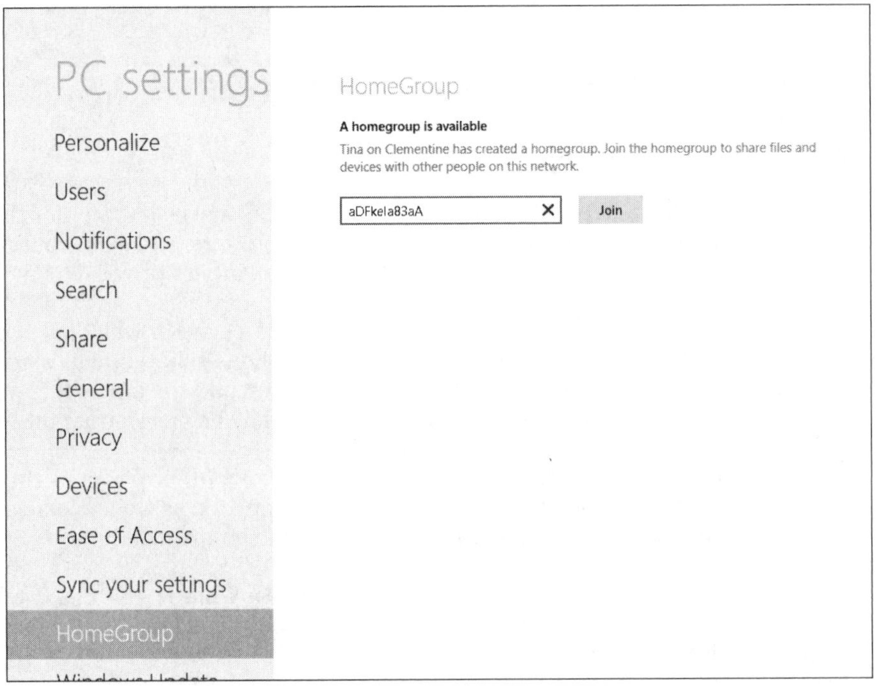

PC settings

HomeGroup

A homegroup is available

Tina on Clementine has created a homegroup. Join the homegroup to share files and devices with other people on this network.

aDFkela83aA   ✕   Join

Personalize

Users

Notifications

Search

Share

General

Figure 15-2:
Click Join
to join an
existing
Homegroup;
click Create
to cre-
ate a new
Homegroup.

Privacy

Devices

Ease of Access

Sync your settings

HomeGroup

3. **Choose the items you'd like to share.**

Shown in Figure 15-3, the window lets you select the items you want to share with your Homegroup brethren. To share an item, slide its toggle switch to the right. (The bar turns orange for shared items.) To keep items private, keep their switch slid to the left. (The bar stays gray for items not shared.)

Most people want to share their Music, Pictures, Videos, and Printers. Because the Documents library often contains more private material, it's usually left unshared. To share those folders with home theater components and game consoles, turn the Media Devices option on, as well, as shown at the bottom of Figure 15-3.

Sharing a folder simply lets other people access that folder's files — view the pictures or watch a video, for example. They can neither change nor delete those files, nor can they create or place any files in your folder.

If you're joining an existing Homegroup, you're finished.

4. **If you clicked the Create button, take note of the password listed at the screen's bottom.**

You must enter that same password into each computer you want to include in your Homegroup.

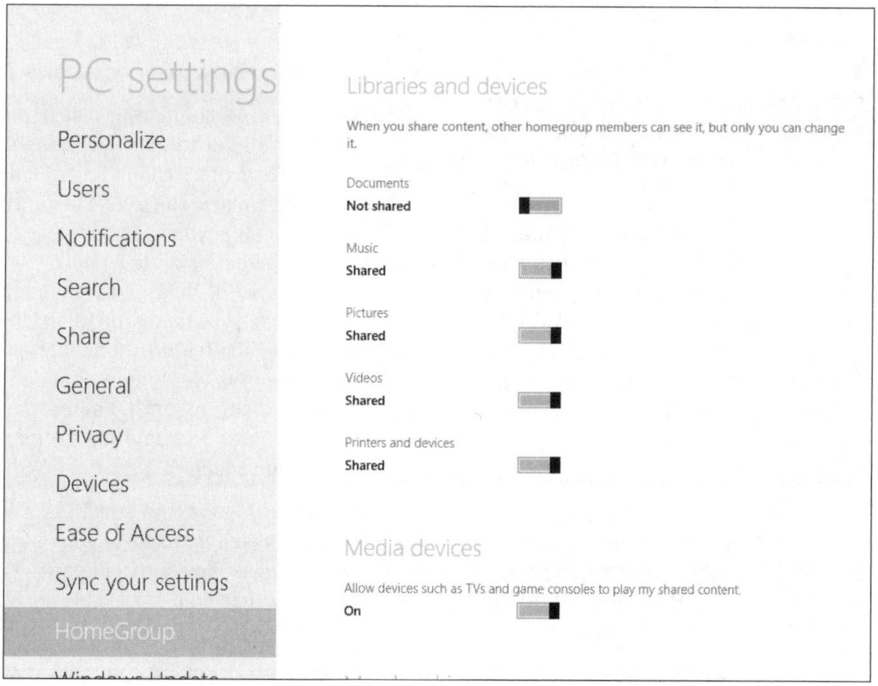

Figure 15-3:
Most people
share their
Music,
Pictures,
Videos,
Printers,
and Media
Devices,
leaving
Documents
unshared.

PC settings

Personalize

Users

Notifications

Search

Share

General

Privacy

Devices

Ease of Access

Sync your settings

HomeGroup

Windows Update

Libraries and devices

When you share content, other homegroup members can see it, but only you can change it.

Documents
Not shared

Music
Shared

Pictures
Shared

Videos
Shared

Printers and devices
Shared

Media devices

Allow devices such as TVs and game consoles to play my shared content.
On

When you're through with these steps, you've created or joined a Homegroup that's accessible from every Windows 8 and Windows 7 PC on your network. You've also set up your PC to allow its Music, Photos, and Videos libraries to be shared, something I describe in the next section.

- ✔ When you create or join a Homegroup, you're choosing which libraries to share only from your *own* account. If other account holders on that PC also want to share their libraries, they should do this: Open any folder, right-click Homegroup in the Navigation Pane, and choose Change HomeGroup Settings. There, they can add check marks to the items they want to share and then click Save Changes.

- ✔ Changed your mind about what to share with the Homegroup? Follow the preceding steps to change which libraries you'd like to share.

- ✔ Forgot the all-important Homegroup password? Open any folder, right-click the word *Homegroup* in the Navigation Pane, and then choose View the HomeGroup Password.

Can other people mess up my shared files?

When you share libraries on Homegroups, you want the benefits of sharing: You want your friends and family to marvel over your photos of Costa Rican tree frogs, for example. But you don't want anybody to delete or mess up your original files. Will sharing your files allow people to delete them or draw moustaches on your photos?

No. That's because Homegroups show the contents of a *library* (which I cover in Chapter 5). And libraries actually show the contents of at least *two* folders: your own folder and one that's called *Public*. The library displays the contents of both folders in one window, but it treats the two folders very differently. Here's the scoop:

- ✔ **Your own folder:** When you place a file or folder into one of your libraries, Windows automatically places the item in your *own* folder. If you've chosen to share that folder through the Homegroup, other people can *see* that folder's files, *view* the photos,

hear the music, or *watch* the videos. They can even make copies of them to do with as they please. But they can't change or delete any of your *original* files, thankfully.

- ✔ **Public:** In addition to displaying the contents of your folder, libraries display the contents of a second folder, known as the Public folder. The Public folder remains fair game for anybody and everybody. Anything you place inside the Public folder can be changed or deleted by anybody else. But because you made the decision to put it in the Public folder rather than in your own folder, you want that to happen: You *want* somebody to offer advice to your term paper, for example, or to touch up your photos and burn them to a DVD.

So, when you want to collaborate with others on a file, place that item in your library's Public folder, a task I explain in the section on letting others change your shared files in Chapter 14.

Accessing what others have shared

To see the shared libraries of other people on your PC and network, head for the desktop by clicking the Start screen's Desktop tile. When on the desktop, click the File Explorer icon, shown in the margin, from the taskbar.

Click the word *Homegroup*, found in the Navigation Pane of every folder. The right side of the window, shown in Figure 15-4, promptly lists the names and icons of every account holder who has chosen to share files.

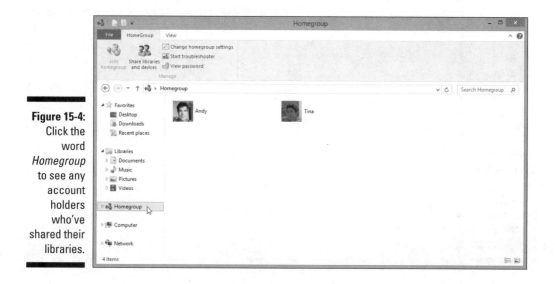

Figure 15-4: Click the word *Homegroup* to see any account holders who've shared their libraries.

You may also spot names of account holders on *networked* Windows PCs — PCs connected to your own PC either wirelessly or with cables — who've chosen to share their libraries.

To browse the libraries shared by another person within the Homegroup, double-click that person's name from the Homegroup window. The window promptly displays that person's shared libraries, as shown in Figure 15-5, ready to be browsed as if they were your own.

You can do more than browse those libraries, as described here:

✔ **Opening:** To open a file on a shared library, double-click its icon, just as you would any other file. The appropriate program opens it. If you see an error message, the sharing person created the file using a program you don't own. Your solution? Buy or download the program from the Internet or ask the person to save the file in a format that one of your programs can open.

✔ **Copying:** To copy a file from one person's Homegroup, drag it into your own library: Point at the file you want and, while holding down the mouse button, point at your own library. Let go of the mouse button, and Windows copies the file into your library. Alternatively, select the file and press Ctrl+C to copy it; then go into the folder where you want to put the copied file and press Ctrl+V to paste it.

✔ **Deleting or changing:** You can delete or change some, but not all, of the items in another person's Homegroup. I explain why in the sidebar "Can other people mess up my shared files?"

Figure 15-5:
Click a person's name to see her shared libraries.

Homegroups work only with Windows 7 and Windows 8 PCs, unfortunately. Holdouts still clinging to Windows Vista or Windows XP can still share files and folders through a network by copying them into their Public or Shared Documents folders.

Sharing a printer on the network

If you've turned on the Homegroups, covered earlier in this chapter, Windows makes sharing a printer extraordinarily easy. After you plug a USB printer — the kind with the connector shown in the margin — into one of your Windows 8 PCs, you're set: Windows automatically recognizes the newly plugged-in printer as soon as it's turned on.

Plus, your Windows 8 PC quickly spreads the news to all your networked Windows PCs. Within minutes, that printer's name and icon appear on all of those PCs and in all their programs' print menus.

To make sure, here's how to see that printer on your other networked Windows PCs:

- **Windows 8:** Right-click in the screen's bottom-left corner and choose Control Panel from the pop-up menu. From the Control Panel's Hardware and Sound category, click View Devices and Printers. The networked printer appears in the Printers section.

- **Windows 7:** Click the Start button and choose Devices and Printers. The networked printer appears in the Printers and Faxes section.

- **Windows Vista:** Click the Start button, choose Control Panel, and open the Hardware and Sound category. Click Printers to see the printer's icon.

- **Windows XP:** Click the Start button, choose Control Panel, and open the Printers and Hardware category. Click Printers and Faxes to see the new printer's icon.

Part V
Music, Photos, and Movies

In this part . . .

Up until now, the book has covered the boring-but-necessary stuff: adjusting your computer so that you can get your work done. This part of the book lets you turn your computer into an entertainment center:

- ✔ Show friends your photos from Facebook *and* your computer *from one program.*

- ✔ Create greatest hits CDs for your car stereo.

- ✔ Play digital movies on your computer or tablet.

- ✔ Organize a digital photo album from your digital camera.

When you're ready to play or be social for a while, flip to this part of the book for a helping hand.

Chapter 16

Playing and Copying Music in Media Player

*I*n keeping with the two-headed persona of Windows 8, your computer comes with two media players: one for the Start screen's tile-filled world, and the desktop's Windows Media Player, a Windows staple for years.

Like most items living in the Start screen's minimalist world, the Music player app offers the bare minimum necessary to play, pause, and skip between songs.

The desktop's Windows Media Player, by contrast, offers a huge bundle of buttons that organizes your music, creates playlists, transforms music CDs into files, and turns music files back into music CDs.

The Windows 8 Windows Media Player is virtually identical to the Windows 7 Windows Media Player, with one big exception: It can no longer play DVDs. To do that, you need to buy the *Windows Media Center add-on*, or *Windows Pro Pack:* upgrades to Windows 8 that I describe in Chapter 1.

This chapter explains how to play music with each player, as well as how to get the most from the player you prefer.

Playing Music from the Start Screen

The Start screen's Music app isn't as much of a music player as it is an online storefront. Shown in Figure 16-1, the program devotes most of its onscreen real estate to advertising: Billboard-like tiles promote the latest releases by the latest artists.

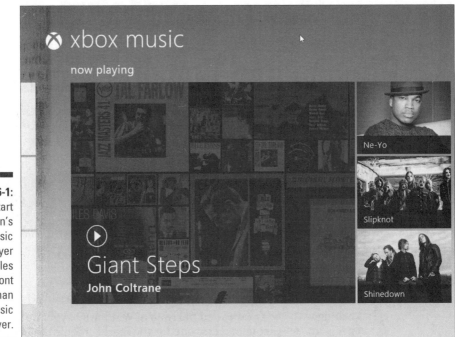

Figure 16-1:
The Start screen's music player resembles a storefront more than a music player.

And your *own* music? Scroll to the left, and you'll find tiles dedicated to music already on your computer. There's another surprise in the app's name. Although it's called Music, it calls itself *Xbox Music* once opened.

To launch the Music app and begin playing (or buying) music, follow these steps:

1. **Click the Start screen's Music tile.**

   The Start screen appears when you first turn on your computer. To find it from the desktop, press your keyboard's Windows key (⊞) or point your mouse cursor to the screen's bottom-left corner and click.

   On a touchscreen, slide your finger inward from any screen's right edge to summon the Charms bar; then tap the Start icon to return to the Start screen.

2. **Sign in with your Microsoft account or your Xbox Live account, if desired, or click Cancel.**

   Each time you open the Music app, Microsoft tries to link the Music app with your Microsoft account or Xbox Live account. Because those accounts can be linked to a credit card, you need one of those accounts to buy music. (I describe Microsoft accounts in Chapter 2.)

Don't want to buy music? The app still lets you listen to your own music, but you'll see the words *Can't Sign In* located in the screen's upper-right corner. If you change your mind and want to buy music, click the words *Can't Sign In*, and the app offers you a chance to sign in with a Microsoft account.

3. Scroll to the right to sample or buy new music.

The Music app, shown earlier in Figure 16-1, contains several screens, which you navigate by pressing the right-arrow key or pointing your mouse to the screen's right or left edges.

The opening screen shows either pictures of popular artists or a collage of the music stored on your computer. In the bottom-left corner, shown earlier in Figure 16-1, the opening screen lists the last song you heard. Click the Play button to hear it again.

The second screen to the right, called Xbox Music Store, lets you hear song previews from the latest CDs, and purchase the songs, if you wish.

One more screen to the right reveals Most Popular, yet another store-front for the latest popular tunes.

Click any tile to explore its category.

4. Scroll to the far left to see and play music stored on your computer.

To head straight for your own music, scroll to the far left; there, the My Music screen lists music stored on your own computer. Click an album's tile to see its songs.

To see *all* your stored music, click the words *My Music* at the screen's top; a list of your music appears, letting you sort it alphabetically by songs, albums, artists, or playlists.

5. To play an album or song, click its tile and then click Play.

Click a tile for an album or song, and the mini-player finally appears. Depending on the licensing agreements and your own equipment, you can choose to play it on your computer, play it on your Xbox, or add it to a playlist.

6. Adjust the music while it plays.

Right-click the screen (or tap it with a touchscreen) to bring up the con-trols on the App bar, shown in Figure 16-2. The App bar offers you five icons to control your music: Shuffle, Repeat, Previous (to move to the previous song), Pause, and Next (to move to the next song).

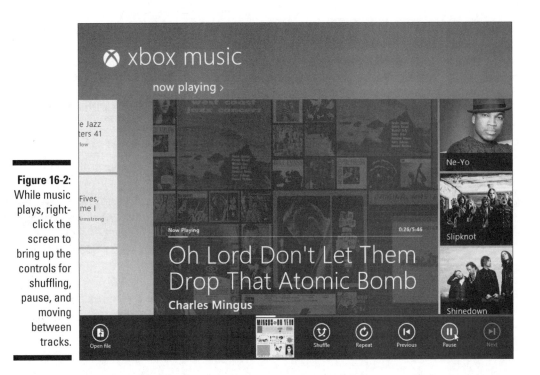

Figure 16-2:
While music
plays, right-
click the
screen to
bring up the
controls for
shuffling,
pause, and
moving
between
tracks.

As the music plays, the Music app shows a collage of your music's cover art, but it tosses in art from other artists in the hopes that it will inspire an impulse purchase.

To adjust the volume, summon the Charms bar by pressing ⊞+C or pointing your mouse cursor at the screen's bottom-right corner. Click the Settings icon, click the Sound icon, and slide the volume indicator up or down.

Most touchscreen tablets include a volume toggle switch built-in to one of their edges.

The Music app keeps playing music even if you begin working with other apps or switch to the desktop. To pause or move between tracks, you must return to the Music app and fetch its App bar, described in Step 7.

Handing Music-Playing Chores Back to Windows Media Player

Microsoft hopes that the Music app and its online store will be a big money-maker; accordingly, Windows 8 tries to shoehorn you into using the Music app. Open a music file from your desktop's Music library, for example, and the Start screen's Music app butts in to play the file.

To complicate matters, the desktop doesn't offer any icon to start the more full-featured Windows Media Player.

You can fix those quirks fairly easily, however. Follow the steps in this section to hand your music-playing chores back to Windows Media Player.

Note: The Windows RT version of Windows 8, described in Chapter 1, doesn't include Windows Media Player. If you don't like the built-in Music app, you can probably find one more to your liking in the Store app.

1. **Right-click the Start screen and choose All Apps from the App bar along the screen's bottom.**

   The Start screen lists *all* of your installed apps and programs.

   On a touchscreen, slide your finger up from the screen's bottom to see the App bar and its All Apps icon.

2. **Right-click the Windows Media Player tile and choose Pin to Taskbar from the bottom menu.**

   That places Windows Media Player's icon on your desktop's taskbar for easy access.

   If you're using a touchscreen, briefly slide the Windows Media Player icon downward and then lift your finger. Then choose Pin to Taskbar from the bottom menu.

3. **Load the Desktop app's Control Panel.**

   You can find the Desktop app's Control Panel's icon, shown in the margin, on the All Apps screen, a little to the right of the Windows Media Player icon.

4. **When the Control Panel opens, click the Programs category. Click Default Programs and then click Set Your Default Programs.**

5. **In the left pane, click Windows Media Player. Then click the Set This Program As Default option and click OK, as shown in Figure 16-3.**

   This step tells Windows Media Player to play *all* of your media, bypassing the Start screen's Music app.

After you follow these steps, Windows Media Player jumps into action whenever you double-click a music file on the desktop. You can also launch Windows Media Player directly by clicking its icon (shown in the margin) on your taskbar.

These steps don't permanently disable or uninstall the Start screen's Music app. To use the Music app, just click its tile from the Start screen; all the music listed in the app still plays through the Music app.

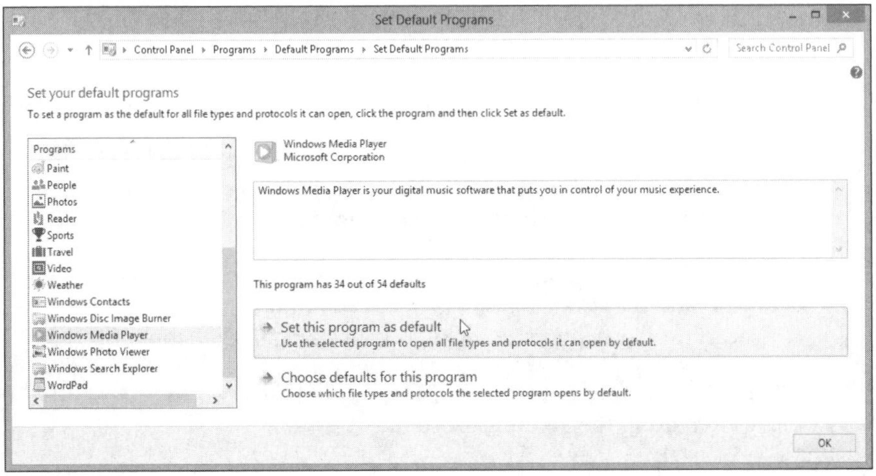

Figure 16-3:
Select
Set This
Program
as Default
to make
Windows
Media
Player
(instead of
the Start
screen's
Music app)
open your
music.

> Set Default Programs
>
> ← → ↑ 🖳 ▸ Control Panel ▸ Programs ▸ Default Programs ▸ Set Default Programs   ∨ 🖒   Search Control Panel 🔎
>
> Set your default programs
>
> To set a program as the default for all file types and protocols it can open, click the program and then click Set as default.
>
> Programs
> 🎨 Paint   ▶️ Windows Media Player
> 👥 People   Microsoft Corporation
> 🖼 Photos
> 📖 Reader   Windows Media Player is your digital music software that puts you in control of your music experience.
> 🏆 Sports
> 📑 Travel
> 🎞 Video
> ☀ Weather   This program has 34 out of 54 defaults
> 📇 Windows Contacts
> 💿 Windows Disc Image Burner
> ▶ Windows Media Player   → Set this program as default   ⬎
> 🖼 Windows Photo Viewer   Use the selected program to open all file types and protocols it can open by default.
> 🔍 Windows Search Explorer
> 📝 WordPad   → Choose defaults for this program
>   Choose which file types and protocols the selected program opens by default.
>
>   OK

Windows Media Player can open more than 50 types of music and video files.
To pick and choose which files it can open, select Choose Defaults for This
Program in Step 5 of the preceding step list. When the Set Associations For a
Program window appears, you can pick and choose exactly which files you
want Windows Media Player to open.

Running Windows Media Player for the first time

The first time you open the desktop's Windows
Media Player, an opening screen asks how to
deal with the player's settings for privacy, storage, and the music store. The screen offers two
options:

✔ **Recommended Settings:** Designed for the
impatient, this option loads Windows Media
Player with Microsoft's chosen settings in
place. Windows Media Player sets itself up
as the default player for most of your music
and video, but *not* your MP3 files. (The
Music app still holds title to those, the most
common digital music format.) Windows
Media Player will sweep the Internet to
update your songs' title information, and
it tells Microsoft what you're listening to
and watching. Choose Express if you're in
a hurry; you can always customize the settings some other time.

✔ **Custom Settings:** Aimed at the fine-tuners and the privacy-conscious folks, this
choice lets you micromanage Windows
Media Player's behavior. A series of
screens lets you choose the types of music
and video that the player can play, and you
can control how much of your listening
habits should be sent to Microsoft. Choose
this option only if you have time to wade
through several minutes of boring option
screens.

If you later want to customize any Windows
Media Player settings — either those chosen
for you in Express setup or the ones you've
chosen in Custom setup — click Windows
Media Player's Organize button in the top-left
corner and choose Options.

Stocking the Windows Media Player Library

 You can load Windows Media Player by clicking its icon in the taskbar, that strip along the desktop's bottom edge. No icon in the taskbar? The previous section explains how to put it here.

When you run Windows Media Player, the program automatically sorts through your computer's stash of digital music, pictures, videos, and recorded TV shows, automatically cataloging everything into the media player's *own* library.

But if you've noticed that some of your PC's media is missing from the Windows Media Player library, you can tell the player where to find any of those items by following these steps:

Organize ▼

1. **Click Windows Media Player's Organize button and choose Manage Libraries from the drop-down menu to reveal a pop-out menu.**

   The pop-out menu lists the four types of media that Windows Media Player can handle: Music, Videos, Pictures, and Recorded TV.

2. **From the pop-out menu, choose the name of the library that's missing files.**

   A window appears, shown in Figure 16-4, listing the folders monitored by your chosen library. For example, the player's Music library normally monitors the contents of your My Music folder and the Public Music folder.

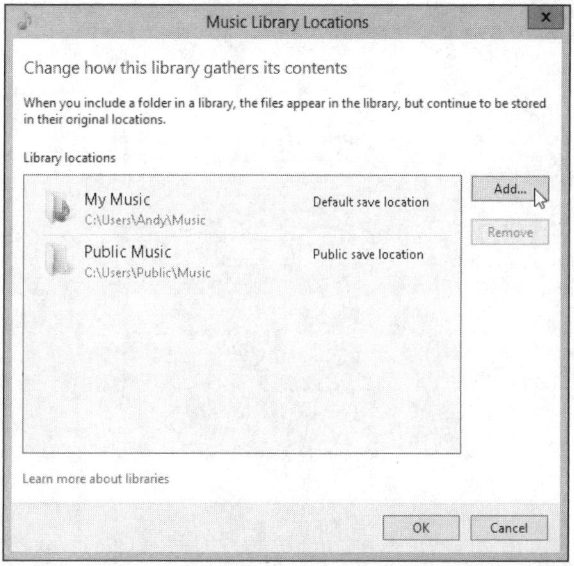

Figure 16-4: Click the Add button and browse to a new folder you want Windows Media Player to monitor.

Music Library Locations ✕

Change how this library gathers its contents

When you include a folder in a library, the files appear in the library, but continue to be stored in their original locations.

Library locations

🎵 My Music C:\Users\Andy\Music	Default save location	Add...
🎵 Public Music C:\Users\Public\Music	Public save location	Remove

Learn more about libraries

OK   Cancel

But if you're storing items elsewhere — perhaps on a portable hard drive, flash drive, or network location — here's your chance to give the player directions to that other media stash.

3. **Click the Add button, select the folder or drive containing your files, click the Include Folder button, and click OK.**

Clicking the Add button brings the Include Folder window to the screen. Navigate to the folder you'd like to add — the folder on your portable hard drive, for example — and click the Include Folder button. Windows Media Player immediately begins monitoring that folder, adding the folder's music to its library.

To add music from even more folders or drives — perhaps a folder on another networked PC or a flash drive — repeat these steps until you've added all the places Windows Media Player should search for media.

To stop the player from monitoring a folder, follow these steps, but in Step 3, click the folder you no longer want monitored and then click the Remove button shown earlier in Figure 16-4.

When you run Windows Media Player, the program shows the media it has collected (shown in Figure 16-5) and it continues to stock its library in the following ways:

Figure 16-5: Click an item from the left to see its contents on the right.

✔ **Monitoring your libraries:** Windows Media Player constantly monitors your Music, Pictures, and Videos libraries, as well as any other locations you've added. Windows Media Player automatically updates *its* library whenever you add or remove files from *your* libraries. (You can change what libraries and folders Windows Media Player monitors by following the three preceding steps.)

✔ **Monitoring the Public folder:** Windows Media Player automatically catalogs anything placed into your PC's Public folder by another account holder on your PC, or even by somebody on a networked PC.

✔ **Adding played items:** Anytime you play a music file on your PC or from the Internet, Windows Media Player adds the song or its Internet location to its library so that you can find it to play again later. Unless specifically told to, Windows Media Player *doesn't* add recently played items residing on other people's PCs, USB flash drives, or memory cards.

✔ **Ripped music from CD:** When you insert a music CD into your CD drive, Windows 8 offers to *rip* it. That's computereze for copying the CD's music to your PC, a task described in the "Ripping (Copying) CDs to Your PC" section, later in this chapter. Any ripped music automatically appears in your Windows Media Player library. (Windows Media Player won't copy DVD movies to your library, unfortunately, nor will it play the discs.)

✔ **Downloaded music and video from online stores:** Windows Media Player lets you shop from a variety of online stores (but not Apple's iTunes). When you buy a song, Windows Media Player automatically stocks its library with your latest purchase.

What are a song's tags?

Inside every music file lives a small form called a *tag* that contains the song's title, artist, album, and other related information. When deciding how to sort, display, and categorize your music, Windows Media Player reads those tags — *not* the songs' filenames. Nearly every digital music player, including the iPod, also relies on tags.

Tags are so important, in fact, that Windows Media Player visits the Internet, grabs song information, and automatically fills in the tags when it adds files to its library.

Many people don't bother filling out their songs' tags; other people update them meticulously. If your tags are already filled out the way you prefer, stop Windows Media Player from messing with them: Click the Organize button, choose Options, click the Library tab, and deselect the check box next to Retrieve Additional Information From the Internet. If your tags are a mess, leave that check box selected so that the player will clean up the tags for you.

If Windows Media Player makes a mistake, fix the tags yourself: Right-click the song (or, in the case of an album, the selected songs) and choose Find Album Info. When a window appears listing the player's guess as to the song or album, choose the Edit link. A new window appears, where you can fill in the album, artist, genre, tracks, title, contributing artist, and composer. Click Done when you're through tidying up the information.

Feel free to repeat the steps in this section to search for files whenever you want; Windows Media Player ignores the ones it has already cataloged and adds any new ones.

Windows Media Player 12 doesn't offer an advanced editor for changing a song's *tags,* which are described in the sidebar. Instead, the player edits them for you automatically from an online database.

Browsing Windows Media Player's Libraries

The Windows Media Player library is where the behind-the-scenes action takes place. There, you organize files, create playlists, burn or copy CDs, and choose what to play.

When first loaded, Windows Media Player displays your Music library, appropriately enough. But Windows Media Player actually holds several libraries, designed to showcase not only your music but photographs, video, and recorded TV shows as well.

All your playable items appear in the Navigation Pane along the window's left edge, shown in Figure 16-6. The pane's top half shows your own media collection, appropriately listed with your name at the top.

The bottom half, called Other Libraries, lets you browse the collections of other people using your PC, as well as people sharing their media from networked PCs.

Windows Media Player organizes your media into these categories:

- ✓ **Playlists:** Like playing albums or songs in a certain order? Click the Save List button atop your list of songs to save it as a playlist that shows up in this category. (I cover playlists in this chapter's Creating, Saving and Editing Playlists section.)

- ✓ **Music:** All your digital music appears here. Windows Media Player recognizes most major music formats, including MP3, WMA, WAV, and even 3GP files used by some cell phones. (It recognizes non-copy-protected AAC files, sold by iTunes, but it can't recognize lossless or uncompressed formats like FLAC, APE, or OGG.)

- ✓ **Videos:** Look here for videos you've saved from a camcorder or digital camera, or for videos you've downloaded from the Internet. Media

Library recognizes AVI, MPG, WMV, ASF, DivX, some MOV files, and a few other formats.

✔ **Pictures:** Windows Media Player can display photos individually or in a simple slide show, but your Pictures library, described in Chapter 17, handles photos better. (Windows Media Player can't correct upside-down photos, for example, a feat done easily from within your Pictures library.)

✔ **Recorded TV:** Recorded television shows appear here — if your PC has the equipment needed to record them. (The Windows 8 television recorder, Media Center, is available only as an add-on pack, described in Chapter 1.)

✔ **Other Media:** Items that Media Player doesn't recognize hide in this area. Chances are good that you won't be able to do much with them.

✔ **Other Libraries:** Here, you can find media appearing on other PCs in your *Homegroup* — a type of network I describe in Chapter 15.

✔ **Media Guide:** This opens the doors to Microsoft's online music stores.

After you click a category, Windows Media Player's Navigation Pane lets you view the files in several different ways. Click Artist in the Navigation Pane's Music category, for example, and the pane shows the music arranged alphabetically by artists' first names.

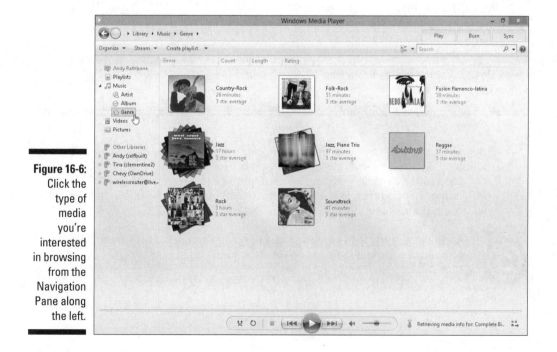

Figure 16-6:
Click the
type of
media
you're
interested
in browsing
from the
Navigation
Pane along
the left.

Yes, Windows Media Player spies on you

Just like your bank, credit card company, and grocery store club card, Windows Media Player spies on you. The player's 5,000-word online Privacy Statement boils down to this: Windows Media Player tells Microsoft every song, file, or movie that you play. Some people find that creepy, but if Microsoft doesn't know what you're playing, Windows Media Player can't retrieve that artist's profile information and artwork from the Internet.

If you don't care that Microsoft hums along to your CDs, don't bother reading any further. If you *do* care, choose your surveillance level: Click the Organize button in the top-left corner, choose Options, and click the Privacy tab. Here's the rundown on the Privacy tab options that cause the biggest ruckus:

✔ **Display Media Information from the Internet:** If this option is selected, Windows Media Player tells Microsoft what CD you're playing and retrieves doodads to display on your screen: CD covers, song titles, artist names, and similar information.

✔ **Update Music Files by Retrieving Media Info from the Internet:** Microsoft examines your files, and if it recognizes any, it fills in the songs' tags with the correct information. (For more information on tags, see the "What are a song's tags?" sidebar.)

✔ **Send Unique Player ID to Content Providers:** Known in the biz as *data mining*, this option lets other corporations track how you use Windows Media Player. To leave yourself out of their databases, leave this option blank.

✔ **Cookies:** Like many other programs and websites, Windows Media Player tracks your activity with little files called *cookies.* Cookies aren't necessarily bad because they help the player keep track of your preferences.

✔ **History:** Windows Media Player lists the names of your recently played files for your convenience — and for the possible guffaws of your co-workers or family. To keep people from seeing the titles of music and videos you've recently played, remove *all* the check marks from this section and click the two buttons called Clear History and Clear Caches.

Similarly, clicking Genre in the Music category separates songs and albums by different types of music, shown earlier in Figure 16-6. Instead of just showing a name to click — blues, for example — the player arranges your music into piles of covers, just as if you'd sorted your albums or CDs on your living room floor.

To play anything in Windows Media Player, right-click it and choose Play. Or to play all your music from one artist or genre, right-click the pile and choose Play All.

Playing Music Files (MP3s and WMAs)

Windows Media Player plays several types of digital music files, but they all have one thing in common: When you tell Windows Media Player to play a song or an album, Windows Media Player immediately places that item on your *Now Playing list* — a list of items queued up for playing one after the other.

You can start playing music through Windows Media Player in a number of ways, even if Windows Media Player isn't currently running:

- ✔ Click the File Explorer icon (shown in the margin) on your taskbar, right-click an album or a music-filled folder, and choose Play with Windows Media Player. The player jumps to the screen and begins playing your choice.

- ✔ While you're still viewing your own Music library, right-click items and choose Add to Windows Media Player List. Your computer queues them up in Windows Media Player, ready to be played after you've heard your currently playing music.

- ✔ Double-click a song file, whether it's sitting on your desktop or in any folder. Windows Media Player begins playing it immediately.

To play songs listed within Windows Media Player's own library, right-click the song's name and choose Play. Windows Media Player begins playing it immediately, and the song appears in the Now Playing list.

Here are other ways to play songs within Windows Media Player:

- ✔ To play an entire album in Windows Media Player's library, right-click the album from the library's Album category and choose Play.

- ✔ Want to hear several files or albums, one after the other? Right-click the first one and choose Play. Right-click the next one and choose Add to Now Playing list. Repeat until you're done. Windows Media Player queues them all up in the Now Playing list.

- ✔ To return to a recently played item, right-click Windows Media Player's icon in the taskbar. When the list of recently played items appears, click your item's name.

- ✔ No decent music in your music library? Then start copying your favorite CDs to your computer — a process called *ripping,* which I explain in the "Ripping (Copying) CDs to Your Computer" section, later in this chapter.

Controlling Your Now Playing Items

You can play music directly from the Windows Media Player's library: Just right-click a file, album, artist, or genre and then choose Play.

 But to summon a smaller, more manageable player, click the Library/Player toggle button shown in the margin and summon the Now Playing window shown in Figure 16-7. (The Library/Player toggle button lives in the library's bottom-right corner.)

Figure 16-7:
The window's bottom buttons work much like the buttons on a CD player.

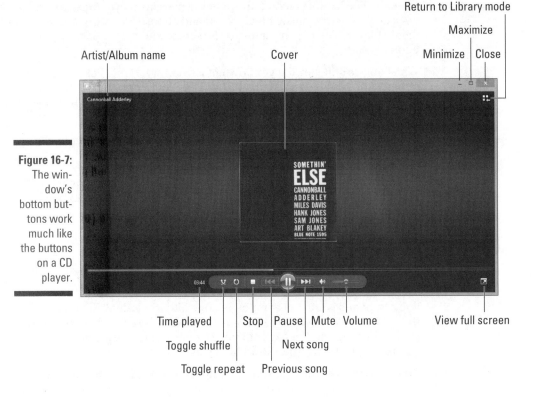

The minimalist Now Playing window shows what's currently playing, be it a video or artwork from your currently playing song. Onscreen controls let you adjust the volume, skip between listed songs or videos, or pause the action.

Windows Media Player offers the same basic controls when playing any type of file, be it a song, video, CD, or photo slide show. Figure 16-7 shows Windows Media Player open to its Now Playing window as it plays an album. The labels in the figure explain each button's function. Or rest your mouse pointer over an especially mysterious button, and Windows Media Player displays a pop-up explanation.

The buttons along the bottom work like those found on any CD player, letting you play, stop, rewind, fast-forward, and mute the current song or movie. For even more controls, right-click anywhere in the Now Playing window. A menu appears, offering to perform these common tasks:

- ✔ **Show List:** Shows the playlist along the right side, which is handy for jumping directly to different songs.

- ✔ **Full Screen:** Enlarges the window to fill the screen.

- ✔ **Shuffle:** Plays songs randomly.

- ✔ **Repeat:** Loops the same song.

- ✔ **Visualizations:** Choose between showing the album cover, wavy lines, groovy spirals, dancing waves, or other freaky eye games.

- ✔ **Enhancements:** Opens an equalizer, balance adjuster, playback speed, volume balancer, and other sound options.

- ✔ **Lyrics, Captions or Subtitles:** Display these items, if they're available, which come in handy when practicing for Karaoke night.

- ✔ **Shop for More Music:** Head to Microsoft's www.windowsmedia.com website to buy songs or albums from online stores.

- ✔ **Always Show Now Playing on Top:** Keeps the window above your other windows on the desktop.

- ✔ **More Options:** Brings up the Options page, where you can tweak Windows Media Player's habits when ripping CDs, stocking your Windows Media Player library, and other tasks.

- ✔ **Help with Playback:** Fetches the Help program to deal with head-scratchers.

The Now Playing controls disappear from the screen when you haven't moved the mouse for awhile. To bring them back, move your mouse pointer over the Now Playing window.

To return to the Windows Media Player library, click the Library/Player toggle icon in the window's top-right corner.

When you minimize Windows Media Player to the desktop's taskbar, hover your mouse pointer over the player's icon: a control pops up, letting you pause or jump between songs.

Playing CDs

As long as you insert the CD in the CD drive correctly (usually label-side up), playing a music CD is one of Windows Media Player's easiest tasks. You drop it into your CD drive, and the player jumps to the screen to play it, usually identifying the CD and its musicians immediately. In many cases, it even tosses a picture of the cover art on the screen.

The controls along the bottom, shown earlier in Figure 16-7, let you jump from track to track, adjust the volume, and fine-tune your listening experience.

If for some odd reason Windows Media Player doesn't start playing your CD, look at the Library item in Windows Media Player's Navigation Pane, along the left side of the window. You should spot either the CD's name or the words *Unknown Album.* When you spot the listing, click it and then click the Play button to start listening.

Press F7 to mute Windows Media Player's sound and pick up that phone call. Pressing Ctrl+P toggles the pause/play mode.

Want to copy that CD to your PC? That's called *ripping,* and I cover ripping in the "Ripping (Copying) CDs to Your PC" section, later in this chapter.

Playing DVDs

And now for a bit of bad news. The Windows 8 Windows Media Player can't play DVDs. That news comes as a bit of a shock, considering the Windows 7 Media Player *could* play DVDs. What gives?

According to Microsoft, DVDs are old-school technology that's no longer needed. Today's ultrathin laptops and tablets don't even have DVD drives. Most people watch movies by streaming them to their computers over the Internet, Microsoft says. Or, they watch their DVDs on TV.

Also, Microsoft no longer wanted to pay licensing fees to the companies owning the patents to the MPEG-2 decoder and Dolby Digital audio support required for playing back DVDs.

But although Windows Media Player can no longer play DVDs, Windows 8 can still play DVDs with any of these solutions:

✔ **Pay extra to buy either the Windows 8 Media Center Pack or the Windows 8 Pro Pack.** Described in Chapter 1, those packages add Windows *Media Center* to your computer. A separate program, Windows Media Center can play DVDs, as well as view and record television shows on computers with a TV tuner.

✔ **Use the third-party DVD players provided by your computer manufac-turer.** Most computer makers will toss in a free trial version of a DVD player. If you like it, you can pay to upgrade to the full version.

✔ **Download the free VLC media player from** www.videolan.org. Created by a nonprofit company based in France, it's not under United States jurisdiction.

Playing Videos and TV Shows

Many digital cameras can capture short videos as well as photos, so don't be surprised if Windows Media Player places several videos in its library's Video section.

Playing videos works much like playing a digital song. Click Videos in the Navigation Pane along Windows Media Player's left side. Double-click the video you want to see, and start enjoying the action, as shown in Figure 16-8.

Figure 16-8:
Move the mouse over the video to make the controls appear.

Playing Internet radio stations

Windows Media Player offers a few Internet radio stations through its website, www.windowsmedia.com, but offers no easy way to save them. Here are a few ways to tune into Internet radio stations with Windows Media Player:

✔ Head to Google (www.google.com) and search for "Internet radio station" to see what turns up. When you find a station broadcasting in MP3 or Windows Media Audio (WMA) format, click the website's Tune In or Listen Now button to load Windows Media Player and start listening.

✔ I like the stations at SomaFM (www.somafm.com). It offers about a dozen stations, in a variety of genres, all playable through Windows Media Player.

Windows Media Player lets you watch videos in several sizes. Make it fill the screen by holding down Alt and press Enter, for example. (Repeat those keystrokes to return to the original size.)

✔ To make the video adjust itself automatically to the size of your Windows Media Player window, right-click the video as it plays, choose Video from the pop-up menu, and select Fit Video to Player on Resize.

✔ You can also toggle full-screen mode by clicking the Full Screen toggle in the video's bottom-right corner, shown in Figure 16-8.

✔ When choosing video to watch on the Internet, your connection speed determines its quality. Broadband connections can usually handle high-definition videos; slower connections and slower computers often have problems. You can't damage your computer by choosing the wrong quality video; the video will just skip and pause while playing.

✔ Windows Media Player's Recorded TV area lists TV shows recorded by *Media Center,* an add-on available only with the Windows 8 Pro version. If you have the add-on pack, you can watch those recorded shows in either Windows Media Center or Windows Media Player.

Creating, Saving, and Editing Playlists

A *playlist* is simply a list of songs (and/or videos) that play in a certain order. So what? Well, the beauty of a playlist comes with what you can *do* with it. Save a playlist of your favorite songs, for example, and they're always available for playback with a single click.

You can create specially themed playlists to liven up long-distance drives, parties, special dinners, workouts, and other events.

To create a playlist, follow these steps:

1. **Open Windows Media Player and find the playlist.**

   Don't see the playlist hugging Windows Media Player's right edge? Click the Play tab near the top-right corner. Or when the player is in Now Playing mode, right-click a blank part of the Windows Media Player window and choose Show List from the pop-up menu: The list of currently playing items appears along Media Center's right edge.

2. **Right-click the album or songs you want, choose Add To, and select Play List.**

   Alternatively, you can drag and drop albums and songs onto the Playlist pane along Windows Media Player's right edge, as shown in Figure 16-9. Either way, Windows Media Player begins playing your playlist as soon as you add the first song. Your song choices appear in the right pane in the order you've selected them.

3. **Fine-tune your playlist to change the order or remove songs.**

   Added something by mistake? Right-click that item from the playlist and choose Remove from List. Feel free to rearrange your playlist by dragging and dropping items farther up or down the list.

   Check the line at the bottom of the playlist to see how many items you've added to the playlist, as well as your playlist's duration in minutes.

Figure 16-9: Choose items from the middle pane and then drag and drop them into the right-most pane.

4. **When you're happy with your playlist, click the Save List button at the list's top, type a name in the highlighted box, and press Enter.**

   Windows Media Player lists your new playlist in the library's Playlists section, ready to be heard when you double-click it.

After you save a playlist, you can burn it to a CD with one click, as described in the next tip.

Make your own Desert Island Disc or Greatest Hits playlists and then burn them to a CD to play in your car or on your home stereo. After you create a playlist of less than 80 minutes, insert a blank CD into your CD burner and click the Burn tab. Take up the player's offer to import your current playlist and then click the Start Burn button.

To edit a previously created playlist, double-click the playlist's name in the Library's Playlists area. Rearrange, add, or delete items in the playlist and then click the Save List button.

Ripping (Copying) CDs to Your PC

In a process known as *ripping,* Windows Media Player can copy your CDs to your PC as MP3 files, the industry standard for digital music. But until you tell the player that you want MP3 files, it creates *WMA* files — a format that won't play on iPods, nor many other music players.

To make Windows Media Player create songs with the more versatile MP3 format instead of WMA, click the Organize button in the top-left corner, choose Options, and click the Rip Music tab. Choose MP3 instead of WMA from the Format drop-down menu and nudge the audio quality over a tad from 128 to 256 or even 320 for better sound.

To copy CDs to your PC's hard drive, follow these instructions:

1. **Open Windows Media Player, insert a music CD, and click the Rip CD button.**

   You may need to push a button on the front or side of your computer's disk drive to make the tray eject.

   Windows Media Player connects to the Internet; identifies your CD; and fills in the album's name, artist, and song titles. Then the program begins copying the CD's songs to your PC and listing their titles in the Windows Media Player library. You're through.

   If Windows Media Player can't find the songs' titles automatically, however, move ahead to Step 2.

2. **Right-click the first track and choose Find Album Info, if necessary.**

   If Windows Media Player comes up empty-handed, right-click the first track and choose Find Album Info.

   If you're connected to the Internet, type the album's name into the Search box and then click Search. If the Search box finds your album, click its name, choose Next, and click Finish.

   If you're not connected to the Internet, or if the Search box comes up empty, right-click the first song, click Edit, and manually fill in the song title. Repeat for the other titles, as well as the album, artist, genre, and year tags.

Here are some tips for ripping CDs to your computer:

✔ Normally Windows Media Player copies every song on the CD. To leave Tiny Tim off your ukulele music compilation, however, remove the check mark from Tiny Tim's name. If Windows Media Player has already copied the song to your PC, feel free to delete it from within Windows Media Player. Click the Library button, right-click the song sung by the offending yodeler, and choose Delete.

✔ Some record companies add copy protection to their CDs to keep you from copying them to your computer. If you buy a copy-protected CD, try holding down the Shift key for a few seconds just before and after pushing the CD into the CD tray. That sometimes keeps the copy-protection software from working.

✔ Windows Media Player automatically places your ripped CDs into your Music library. You can also find your newly ripped music there as well as in the Windows Media Player library.

Burning (Creating) Music CDs

To create a music CD with your favorite songs, create a playlist containing the CD's songs, listed in the order you want to play them; then burn the playlist to a CD. I explain how to do that in the "Creating, Saving, and Editing Playlists" section, earlier in this chapter.

But what if you want to duplicate a CD, perhaps to create a disposable copy of your favorite CD to play in your car? No sense scratching up your original. You'll want to make copies of your kids' CDs, too, before they create pizzas out of them.

Unfortunately, neither Windows Media Player nor Windows 8 offers a Duplicate CD option. Instead, you must jump through the following five hoops to create a new CD with the same songs in the same fidelity as the original CD:

1. **Rip (copy) the music to your hard drive.**

   Before ripping your CD, change your burning quality to the highest quality: Click Organize, choose Options, click the Rip Music tab, and change the Format box to WAVE (Lossless). Click OK.

2. **Insert a blank CD into your writable CD drive.**

3. **In Windows Media Player's Navigation Pane, click the Music category and choose Album to see your saved CDs.**

4. **Right-click the album in your library, choose Add To, and choose Burn List.**

   If your Burn List already had some listed music, click the Clear List button to clear it; then add your CD's music to the Burn List.

5. **Click the Start Burn button.**

Now, for the fine print. Unless you change the quality to WAV (Lossless) when copying the CD to your PC, Windows Media Player compresses your songs as it saves them on your hard drive, throwing out some audio quality in the process. Burning them back to CD won't replace that lost quality. If you want the most accurate duplicates Windows Media Player can handle, change the Ripping Format to WAV (Lossless).

If you do change the format to WAV (Lossless) in order to duplicate a CD, remember to change it back to MP3 afterward, or else your hard drive will run out of room when you begin ripping a lot of CDs.

A simpler solution might be to buy CD-burning software from your local office supply or computer store. Unlike Windows Media Player, most CD-burning programs have a Duplicate CD button for one-click convenience.

The wrong player keeps opening my files!

You'd never hear Microsoft say it, but Windows Media Player isn't the only Windows program for playing songs or viewing movies. Many people use iTunes for managing their songs and movies because it conveniently drops items into their iPods for on-the-road enjoyment. Many Internet sounds and videos come stored in Real's (www.real.com) competing RealAudio or RealVideo format, which Windows Media Player can't handle, either.

And some people use Winamp (www.winamp.com) for playing their music, videos, and a wide variety of Internet radio stations.

With all the competing formats available, many people install several different media players — one for each format. Unfortunately, these multiple installations lead to bickering among each player because they all fight to become your default player.

Windows settles these arguments with its Default Programs area in the desktop's Control Panel. To choose the player that should open each format, head for this chapter's earlier section, "Handing Music-Playing Chores Back to Windows Media Player." There, you can divvy up format assignments among your favorite players.

Chapter 17

Fiddling with Photos (and Movies)

*T*oday's digital cameras are little computers in their own right, so it's natural that Windows 8 treats them like newfound friends. Plug a camera into your computer, turn on the camera, and Windows greets the newcomer, offering to copy your camera's photos onto your computer.

This chapter walks you through moving your digital photos from your camera into your computer, showing off photos to friends and family, e-mailing them to distant relatives, and saving them in places where you can easily find them again.

One final note: After you've begun creating a digital family album on your computer, please take steps to back it up properly by turning on File History, the automatic backup feature in Windows 8 that I describe in Chapter 13. (This chapter explains how to copy your photos to a CD or DVD, as well.) Computers will come and go, but your family memories can't be replaced.

Dumping a Camera's Photos into your Computer

Most digital cameras come with software that grabs your camera's photos and places them into your computer. But you needn't install that software or even bother trying to figure out its menus, thank goodness.

The built-in software in Windows 8 easily fetches photos from nearly any make and model of digital camera. It offers more control than earlier Windows versions, letting you group your camera's photo sessions into different folders, each named after the event.

To import your camera's photos into your computer, follow these steps:

1. **Plug the camera's cable into your computer.**

   Most cameras come with two cables: one that plugs into your TV set for viewing, and another that plugs into your computer. You need to find the one that plugs into your computer for transferring photos.

   Plug the transfer cable's small end into your camera, and the larger end (shown in the margin) into your computer's *USB port,* a rectangular-looking hole about 1/2-inch long and 1/4-inch high. USB ports live on the back of the older computers, along the front of newer computers, and along the sides of laptops and tablets.

2. **Turn on your camera (if it's not already turned on) and wait for Windows 8 to recognize it.**

   In your computer screen's top-right corner, a little announcement box (some manuals refer to these announcements as *toasts,* oddly enough) lists your camera's model and asks you to "Tap to choose what happens with this device."

   Tap the announcement with a finger (on a touchscreen tablet) or click it with a mouse; then move to the next step.

   If the announcement box fades away before you have a chance to open it, you're not lost. Turn your camera off. Wait a second; then turn it back on again. The announcement reappears.

   If Windows 8 doesn't recognize your camera, make sure that the camera is set to *display mode* — the mode where you can see your photos on the camera's viewfinder. If you still have problems, unplug the cable from your computer, wait a few seconds, and then plug it back in. Still having trouble? Head for this chapter's sidebar, "Windows 8 doesn't import my photos correctly!"

3. **Choose how to import your photos.**

   The announcement, shown in Figure 17-1, offers three options on how to handle your newly recognized digital camera:

   • **Import Photos and Videos:** Choose this option to import your photos with the Start screen's Photos app; then move to Step 4.

   • **Open Device to View Files:** Prefer the desktop? Then choose this option. It leaves you staring at your camera's contents as a little folder icon inside a window, where you can drag and drop your photos to a folder of your choice. To import the files from the desktop, jump ahead to Step 5.

• **Take No Action:** Changed your mind about importing your photos? Click this option to cancel and return later.

Windows remembers the choice you make here and repeats it automatically the next time you plug your camera into the computer.

4. **From the Photos app, choose your options; then click or tap Import to import your camera's photos and videos.**

The Photos app, shown in Figure 17-2, offers to import all your camera's photos and videos into a folder named after the current date. If those options meet your needs, click the Import button to begin. Or if you want to pick and choose the photos to import or store them in a differently named folder, the Photos app lets you change these options:

• **Pictures:** The Photos app normally selects *all* of your camera's photos and videos for importing. To leave a few behind, click the ones you *don't* want. Or, to just select a few photos, choose the words *Clear Selection* from the screen's top-right corner to deselect them all. Then click the ones you *want* to import.

• **Folder name:** The Photos app saves your camera's photos and videos in a folder named after the current day's date. To change that folder's name to something else, delete the current day's date from the bar along the app's bottom, and type in your preferred name for the folder.

Figure 17-1:
When you plug in a camera, Windows lets you import photos either through a Start screen app or through the Windows desktop.

Figure 17-2:
Click Import to import all your camera's photos and videos into a folder named after the current date.

Click or tap the Import button, and the Photos app imports your camera's photos and videos, placing them into your chosen folder.

When the Photos app announces that it's finished importing the photos, click the announcement box's Open Album button to see your photos. You're through.

5. **Manually copy your photos from the camera to the folders of your choosing.**

   Selecting the Open Device to Choose Files option in Step 3 leaves you at the desktop, staring at an icon representing your camera's memory card. Double-click the memory card to begin peeking inside its folders. Manually select the photos and videos you want and then copy or move them to the folders of your choice. (I explain files, folders, and memory cards in Chapter 5.)

   Or for an easier way to import your camera's photos, move to Step 6.

6. **Right-click your camera's icon, click Import Photos and Videos, and choose which way to import your photos.**

    Locate your camera's icon in the Navigation pane along the folder's left edge. Right-click the camera's icon and choose Import Photos and Videos from the pop-up menu. The Import Pictures and Videos dialog box appears, as shown in Figure 17-3.

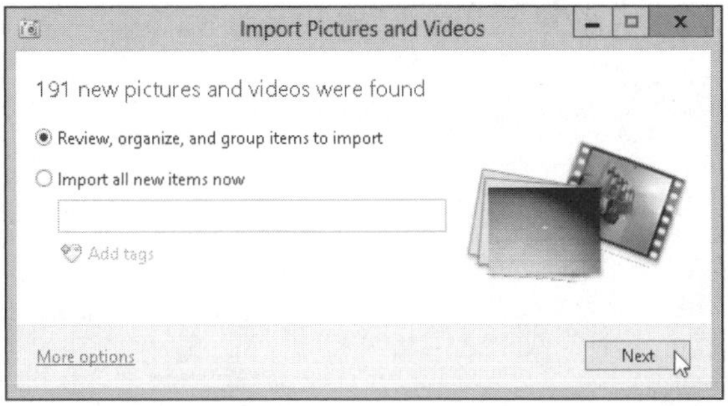

Figure 17-3:
The Import
Pictures
and Videos
dialog box
offers to
copy your
camera's
files to your
computer.

> **Import Pictures and Videos**
>
> 191 new pictures and videos were found
>
> ● Review, organize, and group items to import
>
> ○ Import all new items now
>
> ♡ Add tags
>
> More options   Next

Windows offers two options to match the two different ways people use their camera:

- **Review, Organize, and Group Items to Import:** Designed for cameras holding photos from several different sessions, this lets you sort your photos into groups, copying each group to a different folder. It takes more time, but it's a handy way to separate your Hawaiian vacation photos into folders named after each island. If you choose this option, move to Step 8.

- **Import All New Items Now:** Designed for cameras holding only one photo session, this much simpler approach copies every photo into one folder. If you choose this option, move to Step 7.

7. **Select the Import All New Items Now option, add a short description into the Add Tags box, and click Next.**

   Type a descriptive word into the Add Tags box — **Hawaii Trip**, for example — and click Next. Windows copies everything into a folder named after the date and the word "Hawaii Trip." It also names every file "Hawaii 001," Hawaii 002," and so on. You're done! To see your photos, open your Pictures library and look for your newly named folder.

8. **Select the Review, Organize, and Group option. Then click Next.**

   Clicking the words *More Options*, shown in the bottom left of Figure 17-3, lets you change how Windows 8 imports your photos. It's worth a look-see because it lets you undo any options you've mistakenly chosen when importing your first batch of photos.

   After you click Next at the Review, Organize, and Group window, Windows examines the time and date you snapped each of your photos. Then, the program tentatively separates your photos into groups for your approval, as shown in Figure 17-4.

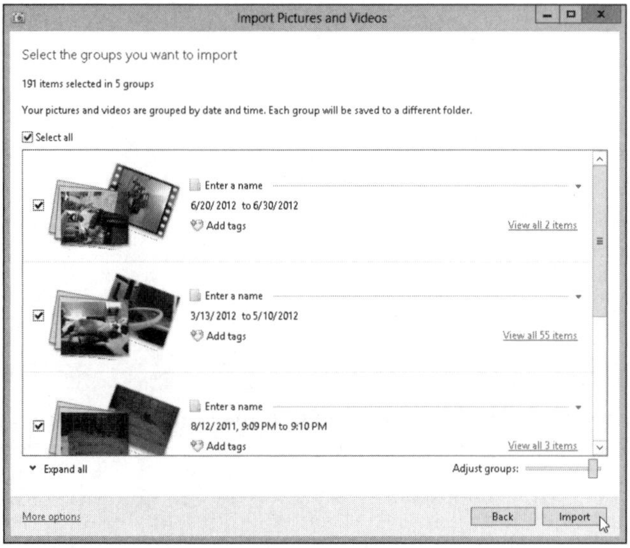

Figure 17-4:
Windows
offers
groups of
pictures
based on
the time
and date
you took
them. You
can review
and modify
the groups
before
importing.

Import Pictures and Videos

Select the groups you want to import

191 items selected in 5 groups

Your pictures and videos are grouped by date and time. Each group will be saved to a different folder.

☑ Select all

Enter a name
6/20/ 2012 to 6/30/2012
Add tags   View all 2 items

Enter a name
3/13/ 2012 to 5/10/2012
Add tags   View all 55 items

Enter a name
8/12/ 2011, 9:09 PM to 9:10 PM
Add tags   View all 3 items

▾ Expand all   Adjust groups:

More options   Back   Import

9. **Approve Windows' groups, name the groups' folders, add descriptive tags, and then click the Import button.**

   Name each group by clicking the words *Enter a Name* and then typing a descriptive title; that becomes the new folder's name.

   In the Add Tags area for each group, type in descriptive words about the photo session, separating each word with a semicolon. By tagging your photos, you can easily find them later with the Windows Search program, described in Chapter 7.

   Don't like the Windows choice of groups? Then change them by sliding the Adjust Groups bar to the left or right. Slide to the left for *lots* of small groups, sorted by every half hour you snapped a photo. Keep sliding to the right for *fewer* groups; slide to the farthest right, and Windows places everything into one group, meaning they all go into one folder.

   After you've named the groups and added tags, click the Import button to finish the job.

   If you don't delete your camera's photos after Windows 8 copies them into your computer, you won't have room to take more photos. As Windows 8 begins grabbing your photos, you can select the Erase After Importing check box, shown in Figure 17-5. That tells Windows 8 to erase the camera's photos, saving you the trouble of manually deleting them with your camera's awkward menus.

   When Windows finishes importing your photos, it displays the folder containing your new pictures.

Windows 8 doesn't import my photos correctly!

Although Windows 8 usually greets cameras as soon as you connect them to your computer, sometimes the two don't become friends immediately: Windows 8 may not display its Import Photos menu, or another program may intervene. If those problems occur, unplug your camera and wait 10 seconds before plugging it back in and turning it back on.

If that doesn't do the job, follow these steps:

1. **Right-click in the screen's bottom-left corner and choose Control Panel.**

2. **Click the Programs category and then click Change Default Settings for Media and Devices.**

3. **Scroll down to the Devices area near the window's bottom.**

4. **From the Devices area, click your camera's model. Then, from the drop-down list, choose how you'd like Windows to behave whenever you plug your camera into your computer.**

If Windows 8 *still* doesn't greet your camera when you plug it in, Windows 8 needs a translator to understand your camera's language. Unfortunately, that translator will have to be the camera's bundled software. If you no longer have the software, you can usually download it from your camera manufacturer's website.

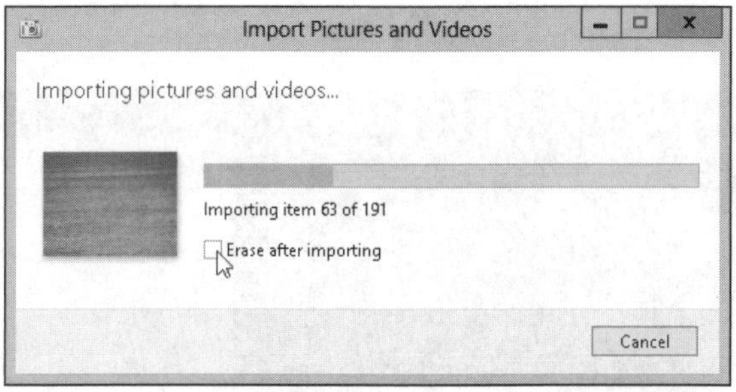

Figure 17-5:
If desired, select the Erase After Importing check box to free up space on your camera for more photos.

Import Pictures and Videos

Importing pictures and videos...

Importing item 63 of 191

☐ Erase after importing

Cancel

Taking Photos with the Camera App

Most tablets, laptops, and some desktop computers come with built-in cameras, sometimes called *webcams*. Their tiny cameras can't take high-resolution close-ups of that rare bird in the neighbor's tree, but they work fine for their main purpose: taking a quick photo to e-mail to friends or post on Facebook.

To take a photo through your computer's camera with the Camera app, follow these steps:

1. **From the Start screen, click the Camera tile to open the app.**

2. **If the app asks to use your camera and microphone, choose Allow.**

   As a security precaution, Windows asks permission to turn on your camera. That helps prevent sneaky apps from spying on you without your knowing.

   After you grant approval, the computer screen turns into a giant viewfinder, showing you exactly what the camera sees: your face.

3. **Adjust the settings, if desired.**

   Depending on your type of camera, the Camera's App bar offers different icons, as shown in Figure 17-6:

   • **Change camera:** Meant for laptops and tablets with front- and back-facing cameras, this button lets you toggle between the two.

   • **Camera Options:** Clicking this icon brings the pop-up menu similar to the one shown in the right of Figure 17-6. Here, you can choose your camera's resolution and toggle between different microphones attached to your computer. If you see More Options at the pop-up menu's bottom edge, choose it to tweak even more options offered by your particular camera.

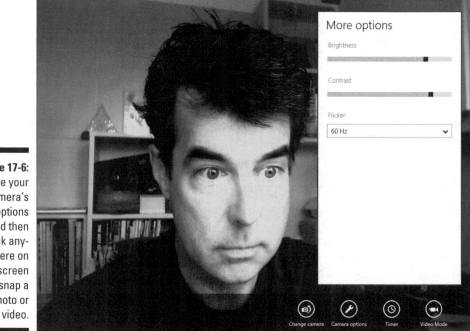

Figure 17-6: Choose your camera's options and then click anywhere on the screen to snap a photo or video.

- **Timer:** Helpful for setting up shots, this tells the camera to snap the photo three seconds *after* you click the screen. (When you click the icon, it turns white, letting you know it's turned on.)

- **Video mode:** Click this icon to shoot videos rather than still shots. Clicking the screen toggles the video on and off. (The video icon turns white when activated, so you know the camera's in video mode.) While recording, a small timer appears in the screen's bottom-right corner, letting you know the video's current length.

4. **To snap a photo, click anywhere on the screen.**

To see the photo you just snapped, click the arrow on the right edge of the screen; to return to the Camera app, click the arrow to the left of the screen.

The camera app saves all your snapped photos and videos in a folder called Camera Roll in your Pictures library.

Viewing Photos from the Start Screen

The two-headed beast of Windows 8 naturally includes *two* ways to view your digital photos on your computer: the Start screen's Photos app and the Desktop app's Photo Viewer.

The Start screen's Photos app works best for quickly showing off photos to visitors. It pulls in photos from your social networks such as Facebook and Flickr, making it easy to display *all* your photos from within one program.

What the Photos app lacks, however, are options. It won't rotate a sideways photo so it's right-side-up. You can't see the date you snapped a photo, or which camera snapped it. It's awkward for managing photos. It can't print, nor can it crop.

But when you want to show off your photos without a lot of fuss, follow these steps:

1. **From the Start screen, click the Photos tile.**

The Photos app quickly appears, shown in Figure 17-7, showing tiles representing your main photo storage areas:

- **Pictures Library:** These photos live in your *own* computer, inside your Pictures library. You can see these photos even if you're not connected to the Internet. Photos stored in the other areas, by contrast, can't usually be seen without an Internet connection.

- **SkyDrive:** These photos live on Microsoft's huge Internet-connected computers, but you can access them from any Internet-connected computer after you enter your Microsoft account and password. (I cover Microsoft accounts in Chapter 2 and SkyDrive in Chapter 5.)

- **Facebook:** This area shows all the photos you've uploaded to your Facebook account (`www.facebook.com`).

- **Flickr:** These photos come from your account on Flickr (`www.flickr.com`), one of many photo-sharing sites.

Depending on the social media accounts you've added to Windows 8, you may see other areas listed here, as well. (I explain how to add social media accounts to Windows in Chapter 10.)

2. **Click a storage area to see its photos; while inside any storage area, right-click the screen to see its App bar, which offers that screen's particular menus.**

Click or tap a storage area to see the photos and folders hidden inside. The Photos app shows photos in a long horizontal strip across your screen, as shown in Figure 17-8. The folder's name appears across the top.

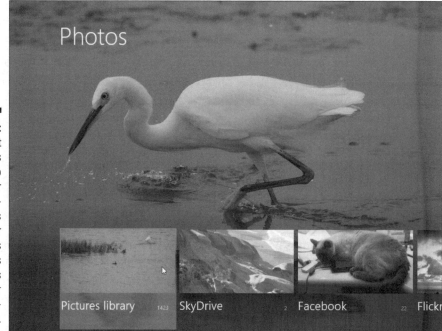

Figure 17-7:
The Start screen's Photos app lists your photo storage areas from your computer's Pictures library, as well as your online storage areas.

Return to previous folder

Location of current folder

Name of current folder

Number of files in current folder

Click any photo to view full screen

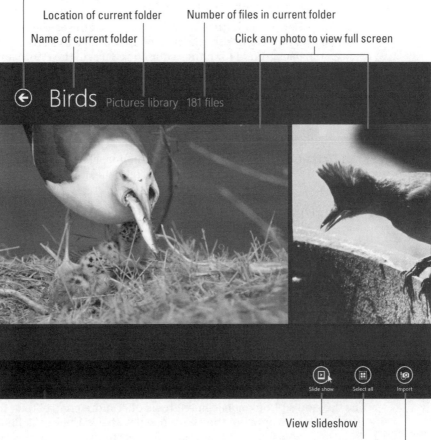

Birds Pictures library 181 files

Figure 17-8:
Scroll to
the left or
right to see
the photos,
right-click
to see
menus on
the App bar,
and click
a photo to
view it full
screen.

Slide show   Select all   Import

View slideshow

Select all photos in folder

Import photos from camera

On a touchscreen, slide your finger up from the screen's bottom edge to see the App bar, shown in Figure 17-6. Depending on what you're viewing, you'll see icons to Delete, Select All, Browse by Date, or see a Slide Show.

To navigate between folders, click the left-pointing arrow in the screen's top-left corner. (Click or tap the photo to bring a missing arrow into view.)

To delete a photo, right-click it and then click the Delete icon (shown in the margin) from the App bar along the screen's bottom edge.

3. **Click a photo to see it full-screen.**

When a photo fills the screen, an arrow appears on its left and right edges; click the arrow to move from photo to photo.

On a touchscreen, tap a photo to view it full screen and then tap the side arrows to navigate between photos.

When viewing a photo full screen, right-click to see the App bar. From the App bar, choose the Set As icon for options to set the current photo as the background for either your Lock Screen, the Photo app's Start screen tile, or the background for the Photo app itself. (For example, the snowy egret in Figure 17-7 is the current background for the Photo app.)

Viewing a photo that a friend *has* to see? E-mail it to them. I describe the details in Chapter 10, but here's the quick-and-dirty version: Fetch the Charms bar, click the Share icon (or press ⊞+H), and click Mail.

To return to the strip view of your photos, click the left-pointing arrow at the top-left corner. (You may need to click the photo to see the arrow.)

 4. **To view a slide show of the current folder, right-click any photo and then click the Slide Show icon on the App bar.**

The slideshow lacks any options for timing.

 5. **To exit the slide show, click any photo.**

To exit the Photos app, head for the Start screen: Press the ⊞ key or fetch the Charms bar and click the Start icon.

Viewing Photos from the Desktop

The desktop's photo-management tools offer more control than the Start screen's Photos app, but they have one drawback: Unlike the Photos app, the desktop's Photo Viewer shows only photos stored on your *own* computer. To see photos stored elsewhere, you need to visit that site, be it on Facebook, SkyDrive, or Flickr, for example.

This section describes how to browse photos stored in your Pictures library, rotate pictures until they're right side up, view them in a slide show, copy them to a disc, e-mail them to friends, and even print them if you're not tired of paying exorbitant prices for photo–quality ink cartridges.

To take advantage of the desktop's side of photo management, click the Desktop app's tile on the Start screen. That fires up the Desktop app and places its file management tools at your disposal.

There's one problem: When you double-click a photo from the desktop, the Start screen's Photos app butts in to open the photo. To let the desktop's Windows Photo Viewer program take over the job, follow these steps:

1. **From the desktop, load the Control Panel.**

   Right-click the screen's bottom-left corner and choose Control Panel from the pop-up menu.

2. **When the Control Panel opens, click the Programs category. Click Default Programs and then click Set Your Default Programs.**

   The Set Default Programs window appears.

3. **From the left pane, click Windows Photo Viewer. Then select Set This Program As Default and click OK.**

   That tells Windows Photo Viewer to open *all* of your photos, bypassing the Start screen's Photos app.

After following these steps, a double-click on a digital photo fetches Windows Photo Viewer, shown in Figure 17-9. The Start screen's Pictures app still handles your photo displays when you're visiting the Start screen. But while you're on the desktop, the desktop's Windows Photo Viewer takes over.

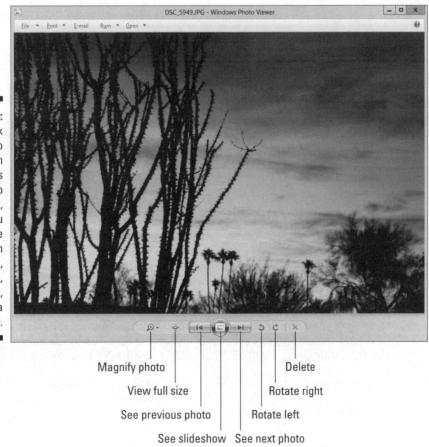

Figure 17-9: Double-click any photo to view it in Windows Photo Viewer, where you can cycle through photos, rotate them, delete them, or view a slide show.

Magnify photo

View full size

See previous photo

See slideshow

See next photo

Rotate left

Rotate right

Delete

Grabbing your camera's photos with a card reader

Windows 8 grabs photos from your camera fairly easily. But a *memory card reader* not only speeds up the job but it's your only option when you've lost your camera's transfer cable. A memory card reader is a little box with a cable that plugs into your computer's USB port — the same spot used by your camera.

To move your camera's pictures into your computer, remove the camera's memory card and carefully slide the card into the matching slot in the card reader. Windows 8 notices that you've inserted the card and treats it much like your camera, offering similar menus.

Or choose File Explorer from the desktop and double-click the card reader's drive letter to see all the photos. From there, you can select the photos you want and cut and paste them to a folder in your Pictures library.

Memory card readers are cheap (less than $20), easy to set up, fast at copying images, and super-convenient. Plus, you can leave your camera turned off while dumping the vacation photos, saving battery life. When buying a card reader, make sure that it can read the type of memory cards used by your camera — as well as several other types of memory cards. (That ensures it will work with the latest computer-related gadgets you might acquire around the holidays.)

Browsing your photos from the desktop's Pictures library

Your Pictures library, found on the strip hugging the left edge of every desktop folder, easily earns kudos as the best place in Windows 8 to store your digital photos. When Windows 8 imports your digital camera's photos, it automatically stuffs them there to take advantage of that folder's built-in viewing tools.

To peek inside any folder in your Pictures library, double-click the folder's icon, and the folder's contents appear, shown in Figure 17-10.

The Ribbon's View tab works best when you're viewing or organizing photos. Click the tab and then hover your mouse pointer over each option, from Extra Large Icons to Details. As you hover, the photos quickly cycle through the changes, letting you see how choice changes the view.

The Pictures library's Sort By option, shown in Figure 17-8, offers oodles of ways to sort quickly through thousands of photos by clicking different words, dates, and tags listed on the Sort By drop-down list.

Right-click any photo and choose Preview to see a larger view in Photo Viewer; return to the Pictures library by closing Photo Viewer with a click on the red X in Photo Viewer's upper-right corner.

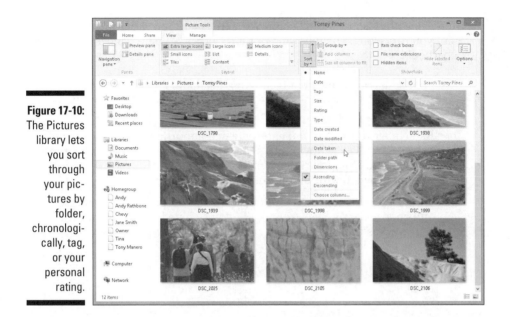

Figure 17-10:
The Pictures
library lets
you sort
through
your pic-
tures by
folder,
chronologi-
cally, tag,
or your
personal
rating.

The options in the Sort By drop-down list let you sort your photos in a variety of ways, including these:

- **Date taken:** Handy for viewing photos in a timeline, this sorts them by
  the order you snapped them. This works best when viewing large groups
  of photos in a single folder.

- **Tags:** If you've added *tags* — descriptive words — to your photos when
  importing them from your camera, you can find misplaced photos more
  easily by sorting them by their tags.

- **Date:** This option sorts the photos by the day you added them to your
  computer, a quick way to find photos added this week.

- **Dimensions:** This option sorts them by physical size, letting you know
  which ones hog the most disk space. (It's a handy way to find videos
  you've accidentally taken with your camera.)

Fixing rotated pictures

In the old days, it never mattered how you
tilted your camera when taking the photo; you
simply turned the printed photo to view it. Many
of today's computer screens don't swivel, so
Windows 8 rotates the photo for you — if you
figure out how.

The trick is to right-click any photo that shows
up sideways. Then choose Rotate Clockwise or
Rotate Counter Clockwise to turn your green
cliffs back into grassy meadows.

By sorting photos in different ways, you can usually ferret out the particular shot you're seeking. The following tips also increase your chances of locating a particular photo:

- ✔ Spot a blurred or ugly photo? Right-click it and choose Delete. Taking out the garbage with the Delete key makes the good photos easier to find.

- ✔ Remember those tags you entered when importing your photos from your camera? Type any photo's tag into the Pictures library's Search box, located in its top-right corner, and Windows 8 quickly displays photos assigned with that particular tag.

- ✔ Want to cover your entire desktop with a photo? Right-click the picture and choose Set As Background. Windows immediately splashes that photo across your desktop.

- ✔ Hover your mouse pointer over any photo to see the date it was taken, its rating, size, and dimensions.

Viewing a slide show

Windows 8 offers a simple slide slow that displays one photo after another. It's not fancy, but it's a built-in way to show photos to friends crowding around your computer screen. Start the photos flowing across the screen either of these two ways:

- ✔ When in your Pictures library or folder, click the Manage tab; then click the Slide Show icon (shown in the margin) from along the folder's top.

- ✔ When viewing a single photo in Windows Photo Viewer, click the large, round Play Slide Show button (shown in the margin) from along the folder's bottom center.

Windows immediately darkens the screen, fills the screen with the first picture, and then cycles through each picture in the folder.

Here are more tips for successful on-the-fly slide shows:

- ✔ Before starting the slide show, rotate any sideways pictures, if necessary, so that they all appear right-side up: Right-click the problem photo and choose Rotate Clockwise or Rotate Counterclockwise.

- ✔ The slide show includes only photos in your current folder; it won't dip into folders *inside* that folder and show their photos, too.

- ✔ Select just a few of a folder's pictures and click the Slide Show button to limit the show to just those pictures. (Hold down Ctrl while clicking pictures to select more than one.)

✔ Feel free to add music to your slide show by playing a song in Media Player, described in Chapter 16, before starting your show. Or, if you picked up a Hawaiian CD while vacationing on the islands, insert that in your CD player to play a soundtrack during your vacation slide show.

Copying digital photos to a CD or DVD

Your photos will be backed up automatically after you set up the Windows 8 File History backup program, covered in Chapter 13. But if you just want to copy some photos to a CD or DVD, perhaps to share with others, stick around.

Head to the computer or office-supply store and pick up a stack of blank CDs or DVDs. Most newer computers can handle any type of blank CD or DVD except for Blu-ray discs.

Then follow these steps to copy files in your Pictures library to a blank CD or DVD:

1. **Open your Pictures library from the desktop, select your desired photos, click the Share tab from the Ribbon along the top, and click the Burn to Disc icon.**

   Select the photos and folders you want to copy by holding down the Ctrl key and clicking their icons. Or, to select them *all,* hold down Ctrl and press the letter A. When you click the Burn to Disc icon, Windows 8 asks you to insert a blank disc into your drive.

2. **Insert a blank CD or DVD into your writable disc drive's tray and push the tray shut.**

   If you're copying a lot of files, insert a DVD into your DVD burner because DVDs can store five times as much information as a CD. If you're giving away a few photos to a friend, insert a blank CD instead because blank CDs cost less.

3. **Decide how you want to use the disc.**

   Windows offers two options for creating the disc:

   • **Like a USB Flash Drive:** Select this option when you intend for other computers to read the disc. Windows 8 treats the disc much like a folder, letting you copy additional photos to the disc later. It's a good choice when you're backing up only a few pictures because you can add more to the disc later.

   • **With a CD/DVD Player:** Select this option to create discs that play on CD and DVD players attached to TVs. After you write to the disc, it's sealed off so you can't write to it again.

4. **Type a short title for your backup disc and click Next.**

   Type something short but descriptive. When you click Next, Windows 8 begins backing up all of that folder's photos to the disc.

5. **Click the Burn or Burn to Disc button again, if necessary.**

   If you selected With a CD/DVD Player in Step 3, click Burn to Disc to start copying your photos to the disc.

   If you didn't select any photos or folders in Step 1, Windows 8 opens an empty window showing the newly inserted disc's contents: nothing. Drag and drop the photos you want to burn into that window.

Don't have enough space on the CD or DVD to hold all your files? Unfortunately, Windows 8 isn't smart enough to tell you when to insert the second disc. Instead, it whines about not having enough room and doesn't burn *any* discs. Try burning fewer files, adding more until you fill up the disc.

Keeping digital photos organized

It's tempting to create a folder called New Photos in your Pictures library and start dumping new pictures into it. But when it comes time to finding a particular photo days later, that system breaks down quickly. The Windows 8 importing tools do a fairly good job of naming each photo session after the date and the tag. These tips also help keep your pictures organized and easy to retrieve:

✔ Assign a few key tags, such as *Home, Travel, Relatives,* or *Holidays,* to photos. Searching for those tags makes it easy to see all the pictures taken at your own house, while traveling, when visiting relatives, or during holiday events.

✔ Windows assigns your chosen tag to each batch of photos you import. Spend a little time immediately afterward to assign more tags to each photo. (You can assign several tags to one photo by placing a semicolon between each tag.)

✔ If digital photography turns into a hobby, consider one of many free third-party photo programs like Google's Picasa (`http://picasa.google.com`). They provide more photo-management and -editing features, improving upon the basic tools in Windows 8.

Part VI
Help!

"Don't laugh. It's faster than our current system."

In this part . . .

Windows 8 can do hundreds of tasks in dozens of ways, which means that several thousand things can fail at any given time.

Some problems are easy to fix — if you know how to fix them, that is. For example, one misplaced click on the desktop makes all your icons suddenly vanish. Yet, one more click in the right place puts them all back.

Other problems are far more complex, requiring teams of computer surgeons to diagnose, remedy, and bill accordingly.

This part of the book helps you separate the big problems from the little ones. You'll know whether you can fix a mistake yourself with a few clicks and a kick. You also discover how to solve one of the biggest computing problems of all: how to copy your old PC's information to your *new* PC.

Chapter 18

The Case of the Broken Window

S ometimes you just have a vague sense that something's wrong. Your computer displays an odd screen that you've never seen before, or Windows starts running more slowly than Congress.

Other times, something's obviously gone haywire. Programs freeze, menus keep shooting at you, or Windows 8 greets you with a cheery error message every time you turn on your computer.

Many of the biggest-looking problems are solved by the smallest-looking solutions. This chapter points you to the right one.

New Magic Fixes in Windows 8

For years, System Restore was the Windows go-to fix when your computer began running rough. System Restore lives on in Windows 8, as I describe in the sidebar. But Windows 8 offers three powerful new tools that also bring an ailing computer back to health.

This section explains each new tool, when to reach for it, and how best to make it work its magic.

Refreshing your computer

When dealing with a particularly sick computer, sometimes reinstalling Windows is the only cure. In the past, reinstalling Windows took a lot of time and effort. When you add together the time spent installing and the time spent copying your files and programs back onto the computer, you could be looking at a half-day's work.

The new Windows 8 Refresh tool aims to solve that problem. By pushing a few buttons, you can tell Windows 8 to reinstall itself onto your computer. And while installing a fresh copy of itself, Windows 8 saves your user account, your personal files, your apps downloaded from the Windows Store, and some of your most important settings.

Choosing Refresh saves settings from your wireless network connections, as well as from your cellular connection, if you have one. It also remembers any BitLocker and BitLocker-To-Go settings, drive letter assignments, and personalization settings, including your lock screen background and desktop wallpaper.

When your computer wakes up feeling refreshed with its new copy of Windows 8, you only need to reinstall your desktop programs. (The program politely leaves a handy list of those programs on your desktop, complete with website links, so you know exactly what to reinstall.)

To refresh your ailing PC, follow these steps:

1. **Open the Charms bar and click the Settings icon (shown in the margin).**

   You can fetch the new Charms bar by pointing your mouse cursor at the screen's top- or bottom-right corner, sliding a finger inward from a touchscreen's right edge, or pressing ⊞+C with a keyboard.

   When you click the Settings icon, the Settings pane appears.

2. **At the bottom of the Settings pane, click the words *Change PC Settings* to open the PC Settings screen. Then click the word *General* from the PC Settings screen's left edge.**

3. **Scroll down the right side of the PC Settings screen's General section. When you reach the section called Refresh Your PC Without Affecting Your Files, click the Get Started button.**

   Windows displays the window shown in Figure 18-1, explaining what will happen to your computer.

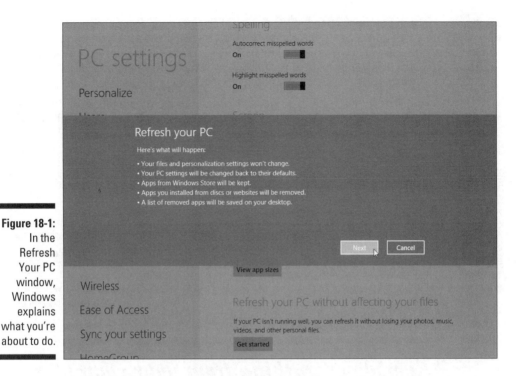

Figure 18-1:
In the
Refresh
Your PC
window,
Windows
explains
what you're
about to do.

4. Click Next to start the Refresh process.

5. If asked, insert your Windows 8 disc, flash drive, or whatever else you used to first install Windows.

When you insert the disc or drive, Windows 8 automatically grabs the files it needs.

Don't have a Windows 8 installation disc or drive? Then click Cancel. You can't use the Refresh option, unfortunately.

6. Click the Refresh button.

Windows 8 refreshes your computer, using any files it needs from the disc or drive you inserted in the previous step. It may restart a few times during the process, which usually takes less than a half hour.

When your computer wakes up, it should feel refreshed and ready to work again. Expect any or all of the following things to take place when refreshing your computer:

✔ If you've inserted a Windows 8 DVD into your computer in Step 5, be careful when your computer restarts. As it restarts, your computer may ask you to "Press any key to boot from disc." *Don't* press any key. That lets Windows 8 load itself from your computer's *hard drive* rather than the DVD.

✔ When your computer wakes up, you find an Internet Explorer link called Removed Apps waiting on your desktop. Click it, and your web browser displays a page with links to any programs and apps that you'll need to reinstall — if you decide you miss them, that is. (And if you *do* miss them, you'll need the program's installation discs to reinstall them.)

✔ Shortly after Windows 8 wakes up, it visits Windows Update to download and install oodles of security patches.

✔ After refreshing your computer, reinstall your programs one by one, restarting your computer after each new install. That gives you the best chance to weed out any misbehaving programs that may have caused the problems that messed things up.

✔ If you're connected to a network, you need to tell Windows 8 whether you're on a *home* network or a *public* network. You also have to rejoin your Homegroup, a simple task that I explain in Chapter 15.

Remove everything from your computer

The Windows 8 Refresh tool, described in the previous section, freshens up your PC by reinstalling Windows but saving much of your information. The new *Remove Everything* feature, by contrast, *doesn't* save it.

Choosing the Remove Everything tool completely erases your copy of Windows, your programs, your apps, and all your files. In other words, the program wipes your computer completely clean. Then, Windows 8 magically reinstalls itself, leaving you with a working computer, but without your programs, your files, or even your user account.

In fact, nobody will even recognize it as being your computer. Why bother? Well, the feature comes in very handy in two scenarios:

✔ **Starting from scratch:** Removing everything can be a magic fix when nothing else cures your computer. Although it leaves you with many things to reinstall, removing everything is a sure-fire, last-resort cure for an ailing version of Windows. In fact, many repair shops charge about $150 for this very task.

✔ **Wiping away your personal data:** After you've removed everything from your computer, you can safely give it away or donate it to charity without worrying that somebody will grab your personal information.

To remove everything from your computer, follow these steps:

1. **Open the Charms bar and click the Settings icon (shown in the margin).**

   You can fetch the Charms bar by pointing your mouse cursor at the screen's top- or bottom-right corner, sliding a finger inward from a touchscreen's right edge, or pressing ⊞+C with a keyboard.

   When you click the Settings icon, the Settings pane appears.

2. **At the bottom of the Settings pane, click the words *Change PC Settings* to open the PC Settings screen. Then click the word *General* from the PC Settings screen's left edge.**

3. **Scroll down the right side of the PC Settings screen's General section. When you reach the section called Remove Everything and Reinstall Windows, click the Get Started button.**

   The program warns you that it will remove all your personal files, programs, and apps, as shown in Figure 18-2, and that it will change your settings back to *default* — the way they were when Windows was first installed.

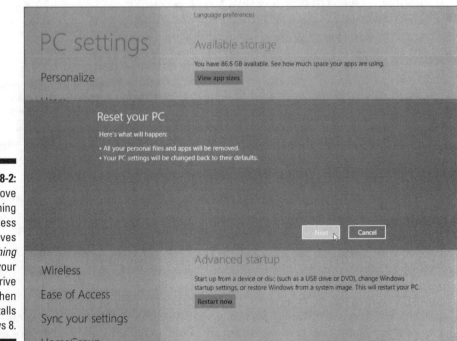

Figure 18-2: The Remove Everything process removes *everything* from your hard drive and then reinstalls Windows 8.

4. **If asked, insert your Windows 8 disc, flash drive, or whatever else you used to first install Windows.**

   When you insert the disc or drive, Windows 8 automatically grabs the files it needs.

   Don't have a Windows 8 installation disc or drive? Then click Cancel. You can't use the Remove Everything option, unfortunately.

5. **Click Next and choose how you want to remove your personal files.**

   The Remove Everything command offers two options:

   - **Just Remove My Files:** Select this option only when your computer will stay within your family. Although this option is relatively secure, somebody with the right tools may be able to extract some previously erased information.

   - **Fully Clean the Drive:** Select this option when you'll be giving away or donating your computer to strangers. This option removes your data and then scrubs the hard drive *extra* clean. That keeps out everybody but the most dedicated specialists who own expensive data recovery equipment.

6. **Choose your desired option and wait for the process to finish. Or click Cancel to return to the PC Settings screen.**

   Removing the files should finish in less than an hour. Fully cleaning the drive will take several hours.

When your computer wakes up, it's as if Windows 8 was freshly installed on a new computer. In fact, the Remove Everything feature leaves you looking at a freshly installed copy of Windows 8. At that point, you need to enter your *product key,* the long string of numbers and letters that links your copy of Windows 8 to your computer. I describe the process of upgrading in an article you can find at www.dummies.com/go/windows8. (You can find your product key on a sticker attached to your computer's case or inside your Windows 8 software box.)

- ✔ The Remove Everything feature leaves you with a newly installed version of Windows. That means you need to create new user accounts, reinstall all your programs, and restore all your files from a backup.

- ✔ If you've kept a backup of your files with File History, described in the next section, you can easily restore the files that once lived in your Documents, Music, Pictures, and Videos libraries.

- ✔ The Reset feature's Fully Clean the Drive option in Step 5 overwrites every bit of your computer's hard drive with random characters. That's enough to keep all but the most dedicated thugs away from your data.

Restoring backups with File History

The new Windows 8 backup program, File History, emphasizes saving your *own* data, not your apps and programs. After all, apps and programs can always be reinstalled. But many of the moments that inspired so many of your photos, videos, and documents can *never* be re-created.

To keep your files safe, File History automatically makes a copy of *every* file in your Documents, Music, Photos, and Videos libraries. It copies all the files on your desktop, as well. And File History automatically makes those copies *every hour.*

File History makes your backups easy to see and restore, letting you flip through different versions of your files and folders, comparing them to your current versions. Should you find a better version, a press of a button brings that older version back to life.

File History doesn't work until you turn it on, a process I describe in Chapter 13. Please turn it on now; the earlier you turn it on, the more backups you'll have to choose from when you need them.

To browse through your backed up files and folders, restoring the ones you want, follow these steps:

1. **From the desktop, open the folder containing the items you'd like to retrieve.**

   For example, to retrieve items that once lived in your Documents, Music, Pictures, or Videos libraries, open that particular library. (The left edge of every folder offers one-click access to those libraries.)

   To retrieve an item from a particular folder inside a library, open that particular folder.

   To see past versions of a particular file, click that file's name. (Don't *open* it; just select its name to highlight it.)

   Or, to restore *everything,* click the word *Libraries* in the left pane.

2. **Click the Home tab on the Ribbon atop your folder; then click the History button.**

   Clicking the History button, shown in the margin, fetches the File History program, shown in Figure 18-3. The program looks much like a plain old folder. Figure 18-3, for example, shows what happens if you click the word *Libraries* in any folder's left pane and then click the History button.

See newest version

Time and date of current view   Search box   Exit File History

Figure 18-3:
The File
History
program lets
you restore
backups
from any of
your librar-
ies, desktop,
contacts,
or Internet
Explorer
Favorites.

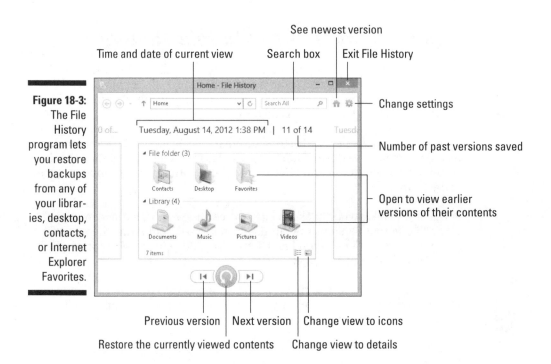

Change settings

Number of past versions saved

Open to view earlier
versions of their contents

Previous version | Next version | Change view to icons

Restore the currently viewed contents   Change view to details

The File History program shows you what it has backed up: your libraries, your desktop, your contacts, and your favorite websites.

Feel free to open the libraries and folders inside the File History window.
You can also peek inside the files you find there to see their contents.

3. **Choose what you'd like to restore.**

Point and click your way through the libraries, folders, and files until
you spot the item or items you'd like to restore.

- **Library:** To restore an entire library — perhaps your Documents
  library — open the Documents library in the File History window.

- **Folder:** To restore an entire folder, open the library where it lives.
  When you can see the folder, open it.

- **Files:** To restore a group of files, open the folder containing them,
  so the files' icons are onscreen.

- **One file:** To restore an earlier version of a file, open that file from
  inside the File History window; File History displays that file's
  contents.

When you're looking at what you want to restore, move to the next step.

4. Move forward or backward in time to find the version you'd like to restore.

To browse through different versions of what you're currently viewing, choose the left-pointing arrow along the bottom, shown in Figure 18-4. To see a newer version, choose the right-pointing arrow.

An older version of the document   A newer version of the same document

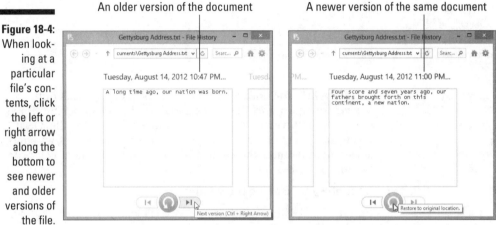

Figure 18-4: When looking at a particular file's contents, click the left or right arrow along the bottom to see newer and older versions of the file.

As you move forward and backward through time, feel free to click open libraries, folders, or individual files, peeking inside them until you're looking at the version that you want to retrieve.

5. Click the Restore button to restore your desired version.

Whether you're looking at an individual file, a folder, or an entire library's contents, clicking the Restore button places that item back in the place where it used to live.

That brings up a potential problem, however: What happens if you try to restore an older file named Notes into a place that already contains a file named Notes? Windows warns you of the problem with the window in Figure 18-5, which brings you to Step 6.

6. Choose how to handle the conflict.

If Windows notices a naming conflict with the item you're trying to restore, File History offers you three ways to handle the situation, as shown in Figure 18-5.

- **Replace the File in the Destination Folder.** Click this option only when you're *sure* that the older file is better than your current file.

- **Skip This File.** Click this if you don't want to restore the file or folder. This option returns you to File History, where you can browse other files.

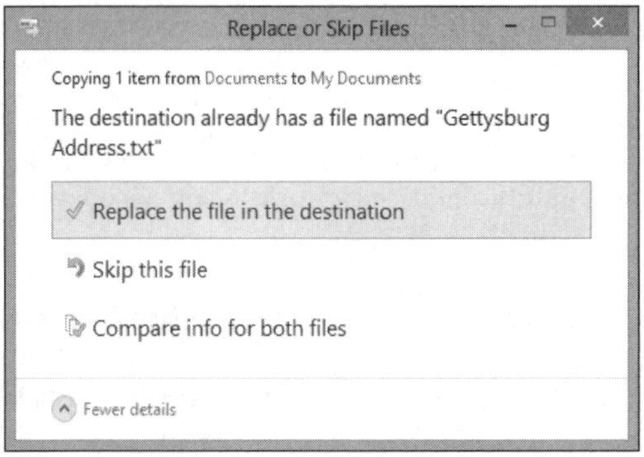

Figure 18-5:
Choose
whether to
replace the
existing file,
skip the file,
or choose
which file to
keep.

> **Replace or Skip Files** — □ ✕
>
> Copying 1 item from Documents to My Documents
>
> The destination already has a file named "Gettysburg Address.txt"
>
> ✓ Replace the file in the destination
>
> ↝ Skip this file
>
> ↳ Compare info for both files
>
> ⌃ Fewer details

- **Compare Info for Both Files.** Often the best choice, this option lets you compare the files' sizes and dates before choosing which one to keep, the incoming file or the currently existing file. Or, if you want, this choice also lets you keep *both* files: Windows simply adds a number after the name of the incoming file, naming it Notes (1), for example.

7. **Exit File History by closing the window.**

   You close the File History window just as you close any other window: Click the X in its top-right corner.

File History isn't just for the desktop side of Windows 8; your Start screen benefits from File History, as well. That's because your Start screen's Pictures, Music, and Videos apps all draw their files from the libraries on your desktop, all of which File History backs up.

Want to know more about File History? Read on:

- ✔ In addition to backing up everything in your libraries and on your desktop, File History stores a list of your favorite websites, listed earlier in Figure 18-3 as Favorites. It also stores the contents of your Contacts folder. (That's overkill if you're using your Start screen's People app to manage your contacts, as the People app automatically stocks itself with contacts from your list on Facebook, Google, and other sites.)

- ✔ Want to restore *everything* onto a newly Reset computer? Then open any folder, and click Libraries from the left pane. Choose History from the folder's Home tab. Then, when File History appears, shown earlier in Figure 18-3, click the green Restore button (shown in the margin).

- ✔ When buying a portable hard drive to create backups, don't skimp on size. The larger the hard drive you choose, the more backups you'll be able to save. You'll find that File History comes in *very* handy.

Restoring from a restore point

The new Refresh and Reset programs in Windows 8 work wonders in resuscitating an ailing computer, and they're more powerful than the older System Restore technology. But in case you've come to rely on the System Restore programs built into Windows XP, Windows Vista, and Windows 7, Windows 8 still includes System Restore — if you know where to find it.

To send your computer back to a restore point when it was working much better, follow these steps:

1. **Right-click the bottom-left corner of any screen and choose System from the pop-up menu. When the System window appears, click System Protection from the left pane. Finally, when the System Properties window appears, click System Restore.**

   The System Restore window appears.

2. **Click the Next button at the System Restore window.**

   The System Restore Point lists available restore points.

3. **Click a listed restore point.**

   You can see more available restore points by selecting the Show More Restore Points check box.

4. **Click the Scan for Affected Programs button to see how your chosen restore point will affect programs.**

   A handy touch, this lists programs you'll probably need to reinstall.

5. **Click Next to confirm your chosen restore point. Then click Finish.**

   Your computer grumbles a bit and then restarts, using those earlier settings that (hopefully) worked fine.

If your system is *already* working fine, feel free to create your own restore point, as I describe at the beginning of Chapter 13. Name the restore point something descriptive, such as Before Letting the Babysitter Use the Computer. (That way, you know which restore point to use if things go awry.)

Windows 8 Keeps Asking Me for Permission

Like Windows versions before it, Windows 8 serves up both Administrator and Standard user accounts. The Administrator account, meant for the computer's owner, holds all the power. Holders of Standard accounts, by contrast, aren't allowed to do things that might damage the computer or its files.

But no matter which of the two accounts you hold, you'll occasionally brush up against the Windows 8 version of a barbed-wire fence. When a program tries to change something on your computer, Windows 8 pokes you with a message like the one shown in Figure 18-6.

Figure 18-6:
The
Windows 8
permission
screens pop
up when
a program
tries to
change
something
on your PC.

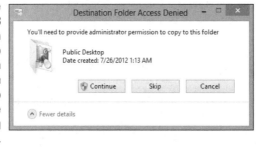

Standard account holders see a slightly different message that commands them to fetch an Administrator account holder to type in a password.

Of course, when screens like this one pop up too often, most people simply ignore them and give their approval — even if that means they've just allowed a virus to settle comfortably inside their PC.

So, when Windows 8 sends you a permission screen, ask yourself this question:

Is Windows 8 asking permission for something *I* did or requested? If your answer is yes, then give your approval so Windows 8 can carry out your bidding. But if Windows 8 sends you a permission screen out of the blue, when you haven't done anything, click No or Cancel. That keeps potential nasties from invading your PC.

If you don't have time for this bothersome security layer, and you're willing to suffer the consequences, you can find out how to turn off user account permissions by reading Chapter 11.

I Need to Retrieve Deleted Files

Everybody who's worked on a computer knows the agony of seeing hours of work go down the drain: You mistakenly delete a file.

The Windows 8 File History backup program, described earlier in this chapter, is a lifesaver here. But if you never turned on File History — an easy task I explain in Chapter 13 — Windows 8 offers another way to retrieve your deleted files: the Recycle Bin.

The Recycle Bin works because Windows doesn't *really* destroy your deleted files. Instead, Windows slips those files into your Recycle Bin (shown in the margin), which lives on your desktop.

Open the Recycle Bin with a double-click, and you'll find every file or folder you've deleted within the past few weeks. I cover the Recycle Bin in Chapter 3, but here's a tip: To restore a file from the Recycle Bin, right-click the file and choose Restore.

My Settings Are Messed Up

Sometimes you want to return to the way things were *before* you started messing around with them. Your salvation lies in the Restore Default button, which awaits your command in strategically placed areas throughout Windows 8. A click of that button returns the settings to the way Windows 8 originally set them up.

Here are a few Restore Default buttons you may find useful:

- ✔ **Libraries:** Every folder's Navigation Pane lists your *libraries* — collections of your files and folders that I cover in Chapter 5. But if one of your libraries is missing (say, the Music library), you can put it back. Right-click the word *Libraries* along the right side of any folder and choose Restore Default Libraries. Your default libraries — Documents, Music, Pictures, and Videos — all reappear.

- ✔ **Taskbar:** From the desktop, right-click a blank part of the taskbar and choose Properties. Click the Customize button and then click the words *Restore Default Icon Behaviors* at the bottom of the Properties window.

- ✔ **Internet Explorer:** When the desktop's Internet Explorer program seems clogged with unwanted toolbars, spyware, or just plain weirdness, take the last resort of bringing back its original settings: In Internet Explorer, click the Tools icon (shown in the margin) and choose Internet Options from the drop-down menu. Click the Advanced tab and click the Reset button.

  This action wipes out nearly *everything*, including your toolbars, add-ons, and search engine preference. If you also select Internet Explorer's Delete Personal Settings check box, clicking the Reset button even kills your browser history and saved passwords. Only your favorites, feeds, and a few other items remain. (For a complete list of what's deleted, click that page's How Does Resetting Affect My Computer option.)

- ✔ **Firewall:** If you suspect foul play within Windows Firewall, bring back its original settings and start over. (Some of your programs may need to be reinstalled.) From the desktop, right-click in the screen's bottom-left corner and choose Control Panel. When Control Panel opens, choose

System and Security, and open Windows Firewall. Click Restore Defaults in the left column.

✔ **Media Player:** When the Media Player library contains mistakes, tell it to delete its index and start over. In Media Player, press and release the Alt key, click Tools, choose Advanced from the pop-out menu, and choose Restore Media Library. (Or if you've accidentally removed items from the Media Player library, choose Restore Deleted Library Items instead.)

✔ **Colors:** Windows lets you tweak your desktop's colors and sounds, sometimes into a disturbing mess. To return to the default colors and sounds, right-click your desktop, choose Personalize, and choose Windows from the Windows Default Themes section.

✔ **Fonts:** Have you tweaked your fonts beyond recognition? Return them to normal by opening the desktop's Control Panel, clicking Appearance and Personalization, and then clicking Fonts. In the left pane, click Font Settings and then click the Restore Default Font Settings button.

✔ **Folders:** Windows 8 hides a slew of switches relating to folders, their Navigation Panes, the items they show, how they behave, and how they search for items. To mull over their options or return them to their default settings, open any folder and click the View tab on the Ribbon menu along the top. Click the Options icon; when the drop-down list appears, click Change Folder and Search Options. You can find a Restore Defaults button on each tab: General, View, and Search.

Finally, don't forget the new Refresh option in Windows 8, described at the beginning of this chapter. Although it's overkill for many problems, it resets most of your settings to the default.

I Forgot My Password

When Windows won't accept your password at the Sign In screen, you may not be hopelessly locked out of your own computer. Check all these things before letting loose with a scream:

✔ **Check your Caps Lock key.** Windows passwords are *case-sensitive,* meaning that Windows considers **OpenSesame** and **opensesame** to be different passwords. If your keyboard's Caps Lock light is on, press your Caps Lock key again to turn it off. Then try entering your password again.

✔ **Use your Password Reset Disk.** I explain how to create a Password Reset Disk in Chapter 14. When you've forgotten the password to your Limited account, insert that disk to use as a key. Windows lets you back into your account, where you can promptly create an easier-to-remember password. (Flip to Chapter 14 and create a Password Reset Disk now if you haven't yet.)

✔ **Let another user reset your password.** Anybody with an Administrator account on your computer can reset your password. Have that person head for the desktop's Control Panel (see Chapter 12), click User Accounts and Family Safety, and click User Accounts. There, she can click the Manage Another Account link to see a list of every account. She can click your account name, and click the Change the Password link to create a password you can remember more easily.

Note: If you've forgotten the password to your Microsoft account, open any web browser and visit www.live.com. The site leads you through the steps to reset your password.

If none of these options works, then you're in sad shape, unfortunately. Compare the value of your password-protected data against the cost of hiring a password recovery specialist. You can find a specialist by searching for **recover windows password** on Google (www.google.com).

My program is frozen!

Eventually one of your programs will freeze up solid, leaving you no way to reach its normal Close command. Should you find yourself facing this icy terrain, these four steps will extricate the frozen program from your computer's memory (and the screen, as well):

1. **Hold down the Ctrl, Alt, and Delete keys simultaneously.**

   Known as the "three finger salute," this combination almost always catches the attention of Windows 8, even when it's navigating arctic waters. When a gray, option-filled screen appears, move to Step 2.

   If Windows 8 *doesn't* respond, however, hold down your PC's power button until

your PC shuts down. After a few seconds, push the power button again to restart your PC and see whether Windows 8 is in a better mood.

2. **Select the Start Task Manager option.**

   The Task Manager program appears.

3. **Click the Task Manager's Processes tab, if necessary, and then right-click the frozen program's name.**

4. **Click the End Task button, and Windows 8 whisks away the frozen program.**

   If your computer seems a bit groggy afterward, play it safe by restarting it.

My Computer Is Frozen Solid

Every once in a while, Windows just drops the ball and wanders off somewhere to sit under a tree. You're left looking at a computer that just looks
back. None of the computer's lights blink. Panicked clicks don't do anything.
Pressing every key on the keyboard doesn't do anything, or worse yet, the
computer starts to beep at every key press.

When nothing onscreen moves (except sometimes the mouse pointer), the
computer is frozen up solid. Try the following approaches, in the following
order, to correct the problem:

- **Approach 1:** Press Esc twice.

  This action rarely works, but give it a shot anyway.

- **Approach 2:** Press Ctrl, Alt, and Delete simultaneously and choose Start
  Task Manager from the menu that appears.

  If you're lucky, the Task Manager appears with the message that it discovered an unresponsive application. The Task Manager lists the names
  of currently running programs, including the one that's not responding.
  On the Processes tab, click the name of the program that's causing the
  mess and then click the End Task button. You lose any unsaved work in
  that program, of course, but you should be used to that. (If you somehow stumbled onto the Ctrl+Alt+Delete combination by accident, press
  Esc to quit Task Manager and return to Windows.)

  If that still doesn't do the trick, press Ctrl+Alt+Delete again and click the
  Power icon (shown in the margin) in the screen's bottom-right corner.
  Choose Restart from the pop-up menu, and your computer will shut
  down and restart, hopefully returning in a better mood.

- **Approach 3:** If the preceding approaches don't work, turn off the computer by pressing its power button. (If that merely brings up the Turn
  Off the Computer menu, choose Restart, and your computer should
  restart.)

- **Approach 4:** If you keep holding down the computer's power button
  long enough (usually about 4 to 5 seconds), it eventually stops resisting
  and turns off.

Chapter 19

Strange Messages: What You Did Does Not Compute

In This Chapter

▶ Understanding notifications

▶ Deciphering security messages

▶ Responding to messages on the desktop

*E*rror messages in *real* life are fairly easy to understand. A blinking digital clock means you need to set the time. A car's beeping dashboard means that you've left your keys in the ignition. A spouse's stern glance means that you've forgotten something important.

But Windows 8 error messages may have been written by a Senate subcommittee, if only the messages weren't so brief. The error messages rarely describe what you did to cause the event or, even worse, how to fix the problem.

In this chapter, I've collected some of the most common Windows 8 error messages, notifications, and just plain confusing attempts at conversation. Find a message that matches what you're experiencing and then read how to handle the situation as gracefully as Windows 8 will allow.

Could Not Enable File History. The System Cannot Find the Path Specified.

Meaning: The message in Figure 19-1 tells you that the Windows 8 backup program, File History, isn't working anymore.

Probable cause: File History was saving your files on a portable hard drive, flash drive, or memory card that's no longer plugged in to your computer.

Solutions: Find the portable hard drive or flash drive, plug it back into one of your computer's USB ports, and turn on File History again, described in Chapter 11, to make sure the settings are correct.

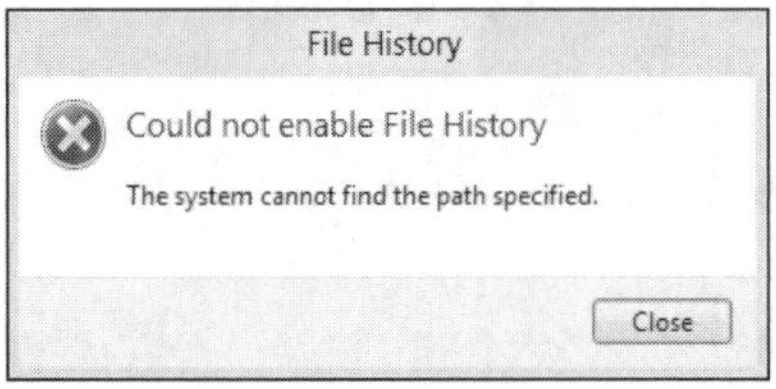

Figure 19-1:
Your backup drive isn't plugged in to your computer.

> **File History**
>
> ❌ Could not enable File History
>
> The system cannot find the path specified.
>
> [Close]

Do You Want to Install This Device Software?

Meaning: Are you sure that this software is free from viruses, spyware, and other harmful things?

Probable cause: A window similar to the one shown in Figure 19-2 appears when you try to install or update a driver for one of your computer's parts.

Figure 19-2:
Do you think this software is safe?

> **Windows Security** ✕
>
> Would you like to install this device software?
>
> Name: Model 5637 Voice Driver
> Publisher: U.S. Robotics Corporation
>
> ☐ Always trust software from "U.S. Robotics Corporation".   [Install] [Don't Install]
>
> ⓘ You should only install driver software from publishers you trust. How can I decide which device software is safe to install?

Solutions: If you're sure the file is safe, click the Install button. But if this message appears unexpectedly, or you think it may not be safe, click the Don't Install button. I cover safe computing in Chapter 11.

Do You Want to Save Changes?

Meaning: Figure 19-3 means you haven't saved your work in a program, and your work is about to be lost.

Probable cause: You're trying to close an application, sign out, or restart your computer before telling a program to save the work you've accomplished.

Solutions: Look in the window's title bar for the program's name. Then find that program on your desktop (or click its name on the taskbar to bring it to the forefront). Finally, save your work by choosing Save from the program's File menu (or tab) or clicking the program's Save icon. I cover saving files in Chapter 6. Don't want to save the file? Then click Don't Save to discard your work and move on.

Figure 19-3:
Do you want
to save your
work?

> Notepad ✕
>
> Do you want to save changes to
> C:\Users\Andy\Desktop\Shopping List.txt?
>
> Save   Don't Save   Cancel

How Do You Want to Open This Type of File?

Meaning: The dialog box in Figure 19-4 appears when Windows doesn't know which program created the file that you double-clicked.

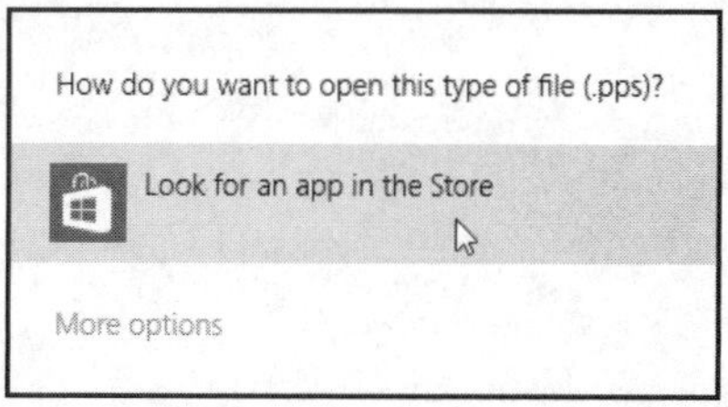

Figure 19-4:
Windows
doesn't
know what
program
should open
this file.

> How do you want to open this type of file (.pps)?
>
> 🔲 Look for an app in the Store
>
> More options

Probable cause: Windows programs add hidden secret codes, known as *file extensions,* onto the ends of filenames. When you double-click a Notepad file, for example, Windows spots the file's secret, hidden file extension and uses

Notepad to open the file. But if Windows doesn't recognize the file's secret code letters, this error message appears.

Solutions: If you know what program created the mysterious file, choose it from the list of programs offered in the message. (Click More Options to see other programs, but those programs will rarely be able to open the file.)

If Windows doesn't offer any valid suggestions, however, choose Look for an App in the Store. (I cover this problem in Chapter 6.) You may need to download or buy an app from the Start screen's Store app.

Insert Media

Meaning: The window in Figure 19-5 appears when your computer needs some of the original Windows 8 installation files.

Probable cause: You're trying to use some troubleshooting tools like the Windows 8 Reset or Remove Everything options, and the tools need original files to replace some missing ones.

Solutions: Rummage around for your original Windows 8 disc or flash drive and insert it into your computer. Windows will notice the incoming files and take over from there.

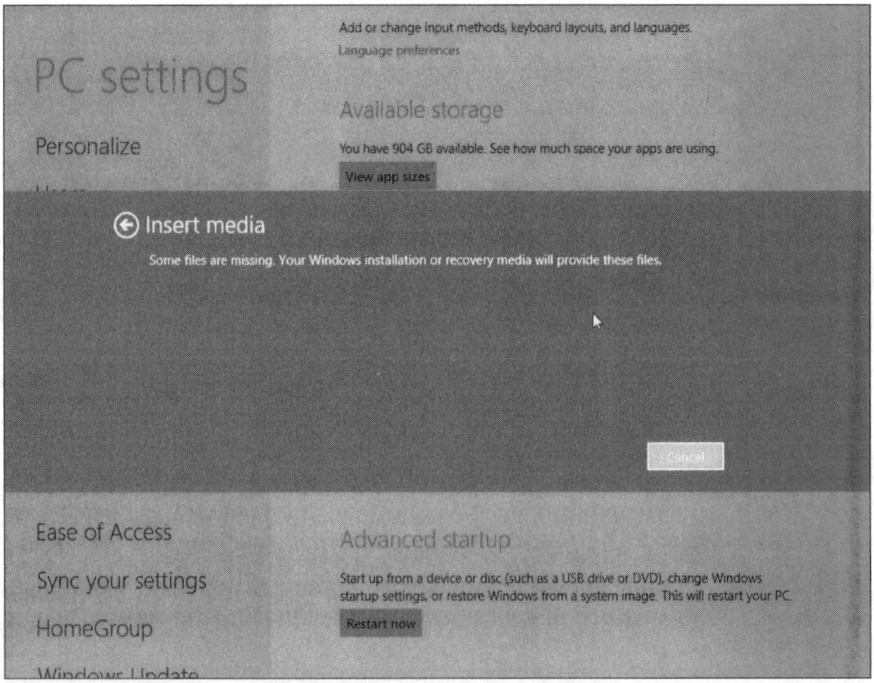

Figure 19-5: Insert your Windows 8 DVD or flash drive so your computer can grab the files it needs.

Malware Detected: Windows Defender Is Taking Action

Meaning: When the built-in Windows 8 antivirus program, Windows Defender, finds a potentially dangerous file on your computer, it lets you know with the message in Figure 19-6. Windows Defender then removes the file so it can't harm your computer or files.

Figure 19-6:
Windows Defender has found and removed a potentially dangerous file on your computer.

Malware Detected
Windows Defender is taking action to clean detected malware

This particular notification looks identical on both the desktop and the Start screen; it always appears in the screen's top-right corner.

Probable cause: A dangerous file — *malware* — probably arrived through e-mail, a flash drive, a networked computer, or a website. Windows is removing the file so it can't do any harm.

Solutions: You needn't do anything. Windows Defender has already caught and removed the evildoer.

Removable Disk: Choose What to Do with Removable Drives

Meaning: When the window in Figure 19-7 appears, tell Windows what to do with the flash drive or memory card you've inserted into your computer.

Probable cause: You've just slid a *flash drive* (a stick of memory) into your computer's USB port, or you've put a memory card, perhaps from a camera, into a card reader attached to your computer.

Solutions: Most of the time, you'll click the Open Folder to View Files option. That lets you see your stored files and copy or move them to other folders in your computer. But you have three other options:

- ✔ **Speed Up My System (Windows ReadyBoost).** Click this only if you plan on leaving the item permanently attached to your computer. On slower computers that need more memory, this option can speed them up.

- ✔ **Configure this Drive for Backup (File History).** Click this to leave the item permanently attached to store backups. With a large flash drive, it works fine with File History, described in Chapter 13.

- ✔ **Take no action.** Clicking this simply gets rid of the message. To access the item later, open File Explorer from the desktop, and open the card from there. *Tip:* See the letter listed after Removable Disk in the message? That's the letter of the drive Windows has assigned to your item.

Sign In with a Microsoft Account

Meaning: You must sign in with a Microsoft account to perform several tasks in Windows 8. If you don't have a Microsoft account, you'll see the message in Windows 19-8. As described in Chapter 2, Microsoft accounts let you reap the most benefits from Windows 8.

Probable cause: You may have tried to use the Mail, People, Calendar or Messenger app, which all require a Microsoft account. You also need one to download an app from the Microsoft Store.

Solutions: Sign up for a free Microsoft account, as I describe in Chapter 2.

Figure 19-8:
To take advantage of many Windows 8 features, you must create a Microsoft account.

Something Went Wrong: Couldn't Share Photo(s) with Mail

Meaning: The Mail app tried to send photos with your e-mail but failed. Your e-mail hasn't been sent. (See Figure 19-9.)

Probable cause: First, make sure your Internet connection is up and running. As long as your Internet connection isn't at fault, then this message usually appears after you've tried to send too many photos to a friend. E-mail programs choke on large files, and today's high-resolution cameras create photos too large to be sent more than two or three at a time.

Solutions: Send your photos no more than two at a time, creating a new e-mail for each one. Or, click the Send Using SkyDrive Instead link. That sends the photos to a safe storage spot on the Internet where the recipient can download them, bypassing the limitations of e-mail.

Figure 19-9:
Windows Mail couldn't send your e-mail, likely because you're trying to send too many attached photos.

There Is No Email Program Associated to Perform the Requested Action

Meaning: The particularly cryptic message in Figure 19-10 means you're trying to send e-mail from the desktop, but you haven't installed an e-mail program.

Probable cause: Unlike the Start screen and its Mail app, the Windows 8 desktop doesn't come with a built-in program to send or receive e-mail. (The desktop can't use the Mail app.) If you click any program's Send This or E-mail This option, this message appears until you choose and install an e-mail program.

Solutions: You can download and install an e-mail program or set up an e-mail program at one of many websites. I describe choosing and setting up e-mail in Chapter 10.

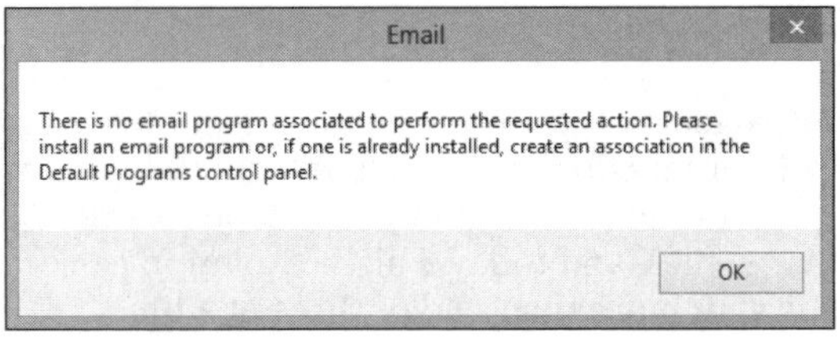

Figure 19-10:
You need to install an e-mail program onto the desktop.

Email

There is no email program associated to perform the requested action. Please install an email program or, if one is already installed, create an association in the Default Programs control panel.

OK

USB Device Not Recognized

Meaning: Figure 19-11 appears when you're trying to plug a new part into your computer's USB port, but something went wrong.

Probable cause: The part isn't compatible with Windows 8, or it simply hit a glitch.

Solutions: If you've plugged a cable or device into one of your computer's connectors, unplug it. Wait 30 seconds and then plug it back into a different USB port. No luck? Then leave it plugged in, but restart your computer.

If it *still* doesn't work, the answer is clear: You need to track down a *driver*, which is a special piece of software that lets your gadget talk to Windows. I cover the art of tracking down and installing drivers in Chapter 13.

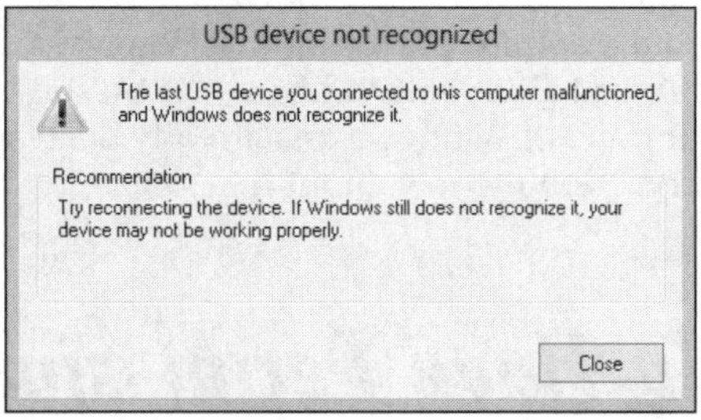

Figure 19-11:
Your new
part won't
work
until you
install its
necessary
software.

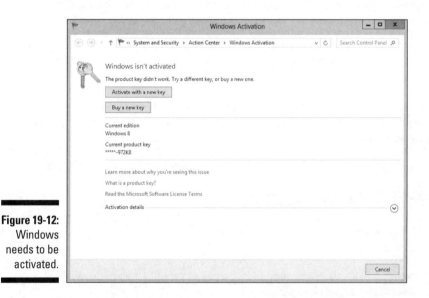

Windows Isn't Activated

Meaning: When Windows isn't activated, it nags you with the message shown in Figure 19-12.

Figure 19-12:
Windows
needs to be
activated.

Probable cause: Microsoft's copy-protection scheme requires every person to activate his or her Windows 8 copy. When activated, your copy of Windows 8 is linked to your particular computer so that you can't install it onto another computer, including a tablet or laptop.

Solutions: Choose the link called Learn More About Why You're Seeing this Issue. You may have been sold a counterfeit version of Windows. Look for the phone number where you can call Microsoft to discuss the issue. ***Note:*** If you never see this message, your copy of Windows has already been activated by your computer's manufacturer. Don't worry about it.

You Don't Currently Have Permission to Access This Folder

Meaning: If you see the dialog box in Figure 19-13, it means Windows won't let you peek inside the folder you're trying to open. (The folder's name appears in the message's title bar.) A similar message appears when Windows won't let you peek inside a file.

Probable cause: The file or folder belongs to somebody with a different user account.

Solutions: If you hold an Administrator account, you can open files and folders from other people's user accounts by clicking Continue. If you don't have an Administrator account, however, you're locked out.

If an account holder *wants* to let others see inside the file or folder, he or she should copy or move the item into the Public folder, an easy task described in Chapter 15.

Figure 19-13:
Find some-
body with
an Admin-
istrator
account to
open the
folder or file.

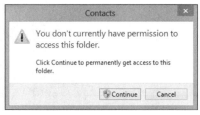

Chapter 20

Moving from an Old PC to a New Windows 8 PC

. . . .

In This Chapter

▶ Copying your old PC's files and settings into your new PC

▶ Using Windows Easy Transfer

▶ Transferring files through an easy transfer cable, network, or portable hard drive

. . . .

*W*hen you bring home an exciting new Windows 8 computer, it lacks the most important thing of all: your *old* computer's files. How do you copy your files from that drab old Windows PC to that shiny new Windows 8 PC? How do you even *find* everything you want to move?

To solve the problem, Microsoft stocked Windows 8 with a virtual moving van called Windows Easy Transfer. The Windows Easy Transfer program grabs not only your old computer's data but also settings from some of your programs: your browser's list of favorite websites, for example.

Not everybody needs Windows Easy Transfer. If you're upgrading a Windows XP, Windows Vista, or Windows 7 PC to Windows 8, for example, Windows 8 keeps your files in place.

But should you need to copy information from an older Windows PC to your new Windows 8 PC, this chapter introduces the program and walks you down the path.

Note: Windows Easy Transfer works only with Windows XP, Windows Vista, Windows 7, and Windows 8. It *doesn't* work with older Windows versions such as Windows Me or Windows 98.

Choosing How to Transfer Your Old Information

Like any other moving day, the event's success depends on your preparation. Instead of rummaging for boxes and duct tape, you must choose how to transfer the information to your new PC.

Windows Easy Transfer offers *three* different ways to copy your old PC's information into your new PC. Each method works at a different level of speed and difficulty. Here are the contenders:

- ✔ **Easy Transfer cable:** Your least-expensive and easiest solution, this special cable resembles a normal USB cable that has swallowed a mouse: The cable usually bulges in the middle, as shown in Figure 20-1. These cables cost less than $20 at most electronics stores or online. Plug one end into each PC's USB port, and you're ready to copy. (No, a normal USB cable won't work.)

  Older Easy Transfer cables made for Windows Vista or Windows 7 should still work fine with Windows 8.

- ✔ If you're transferring from a Windows XP or Vista PC through an Easy Transfer cable, shown earlier in Figure 20-1, be sure to install the Easy Transfer cable's bundled drivers. (You needn't worry about drivers in newer Windows versions because Windows 7 and Windows 8 automatically recognize the cable as soon as you plug it into a USB port.)

- ✔ **External hard disk:** Windows 8 calls it an *external hard disk,* but everybody else calls it a *portable hard drive.* But no matter what it's called, the little box costs between $75 and $150, and it makes copying your information quick and easy. Some portable drives plug into both a wall outlet and your PC's USB port; others draw their power right from the USB port.

- ✔ **Flash drive:** These little memory sticks, often spotted sprouting from nerds' key chains, plug into a computer's USB port. Unfortunately, they usually lack enough storage space to hold *all* your old computer's files. Flash drives work great, however, for copying the Windows 8 Easy Transfer program to your old Windows XP or Windows Vista PC.

- ✔ **Network:** If you've linked your two PCs through a *network* (a chore I cover in Chapter 15), the Windows Easy Transfer program can transfer your old PC's information that way.

If your PCs aren't connected through a network and they live more than a cable's reach apart, a portable hard drive is your best option. Choose one with as much capacity as the hard drive inside your new PC. After you've transferred the files, you can use the hard drive to back up your files automatically with the easy-to-use Windows 8 File History program, a simple task I describe in Chapter 13.

I can't copy Windows Easy Transfer to my old computer!

Windows 8 can pack a copy of Windows Easy Transfer onto a flash drive, portable hard drive, or network location, so you can grab that program with your older computer. But what if you have a cheap Easy Transfer cable, but you don't *have* a network, portable hard drive, or flash drive? Then head to your old computer and download the Windows Easy Transfer program from Microsoft's website at (www.microsoft.com/).

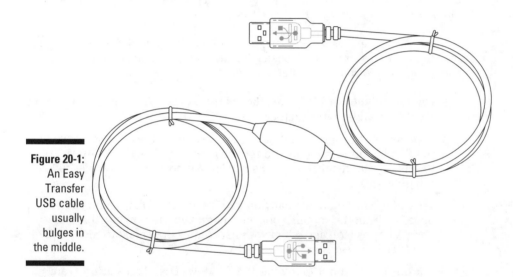

Figure 20-1: An Easy Transfer USB cable usually bulges in the middle.

Windows Easy Transfer can't transfer files from a 64-bit computer to a 32-bit computer. However, this rarely presents a problem because older computers are mostly 32-bit and newer computers are usually 64-bit.

Transferring Information Between Two PCs

Windows Easy Transfer works in just a few short steps or a lengthy series of leaps, depending on the method you choose to pipe your old PC's information into your new PC: cable, network, or portable drive.

This section walks you through how to transfer your old PC's information using each of the three methods. The section that follows aims at fine-tuners who want to pick and choose the type of information they want transferred from their old PC.

Depending on your transfer method and your computer's configuration, the steps listed here may be slightly different on your own computer. But the program does a pretty good job of walking you through moving your information from your old computer to your new one.

Be sure to sign in to your old and new PCs with an *Administrator* account; other accounts don't have the authority to copy files. And remember that you can take your time: You can always return to a previous screen by clicking the blue arrow in the window's top-left corner.

Before transferring files to or from a tablet or laptop computer, be sure to plug the computer into an outlet. Transferring files requires quite a bit of power, and it might drain your computer's batteries.

1. **On your Windows 8 PC, start the Windows Easy Transfer program and click Next at the introductory screen.**

   To launch the program, right-click a blank part of the Start screen; when the App bar appears along the screen's bottom, click the All Apps icon to see all your installed apps. Then click Windows Easy Transfer to load the program.

   To load the program manually on a touchscreen tablet, swipe your finger up from the screen's bottom to bring up the App bar. Tap the App bar's All Apps icon and when your list of apps appears, tap the words *Windows Easy Transfer.*

   Clicking the Next button moves the Windows Easy Transfer program past its introductory screen.

2. **Choose how you want to transfer items to your new PC.**

   The program offers the three options discussed earlier in this chapter: an Easy Transfer Cable, a network, or an external hard disk/flash drive.

3. **Now you need to choose whether you're running Windows Easy Transfer on your new PC or on your old PC — choose This Is My New PC.**

4. **Depending on your transfer method, choose your appropriate course of action.**

   Here's where the program differs depending on your transfer method:

   • **Easy Transfer Cable:** The program asks whether you need to install the Windows Easy Transfer program onto your old PC. If your old PC runs Windows XP or Windows Vista, the program walks you through transferring the Windows Easy Transfer program to the older PC using a portable drive.

Run the Windows Easy Transfer program on both PCs and then connect the Easy Transfer cable between the two PCs' USB ports. From your Windows 8 PC, select the files you'd like to transfer, as described in this chapter's "Picking and Choosing the Files, Folders, and Accounts to Transfer" section. When you click the Transfer button, the program copies the files to your Windows 8 PC, finishing the job.

- **A network:** The program asks whether you need to install the Windows Easy Transfer program onto your old PC. If your old PC runs Windows XP or Windows Vista, the program walks you through transferring the Windows Easy Transfer program to the older PC using a portable drive.

  From your *old* computer, run the Windows Easy Transfer program, following the steps and choosing to transfer by network. The program gives you a six-digit key for you to write down.

  Returning to your *new* PC, enter the same six-digit key, and the two PCs connect through the network. While still on your new PC, select what you'd like to transfer, as described in this chapter's "Picking and Choosing Files, Folders, and Accounts to Transfer" section. When you click the Transfer button, the program copies the files to your Windows 8 PC, finishing the job.

- **An external hard disk:** When the program asks whether you've already copied your old PC's files to the external hard disk, choose No. The program then asks whether you need to install the Windows Easy Transfer program onto your old PC. If your old PC runs Windows XP or Windows Vista, the program walks you through transferring the Windows Easy Transfer program to the older PC using a portable drive.

  From your *old* PC, run the Windows Easy Transfer program and plug in the portable drive, if it's not already plugged in. Follow the program's introductory steps, choose to transfer by external hard disk, and then select what you'd like to transfer, as described in this chapter's "Picking and Choosing Files, Folders, and Accounts to Transfer" section. (Type in an optional password, if asked, for extra security.)

  When the program finishes copying the information to the portable hard drive, unplug the drive from your old PC, and plug it into your new PC. On your new PC, browse to the saved files, click the Transfer button, and the program transfers them to your new PC. (If you entered the optional password, re-enter it before you can transfer the files.)

5. Finish up.

The program leaves you with these two options:

- **See What Was Transferred.** This rather technical report shows exactly what was transferred.

- **See a List of Apps You Might Want to Install on Your New PC.** Another overly technical report tells you what programs were installed on your old PC. You may need to install some of them on your new PC in order to open some of your transferred files.

Unplug your Easy Transfer cable from both PCs, if necessary, and save it for any later emergencies.

If you transferred files using a portable hard drive, keep the drive attached to your new PC and use it with the Windows 8 File History backup program, described in Chapter 13.

You're through!

Picking and Choosing Files, Folders, and Accounts to Transfer

No matter what route you choose to transfer your files, you'll eventually face the window similar to the one shown in Figure 20-2, along with the program's stern demand: Choose What to Transfer.

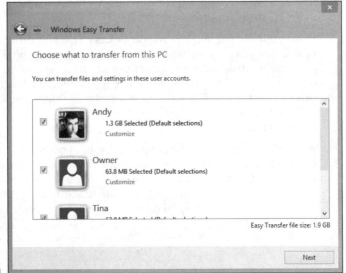

Figure 20-2: Click Transfer to transfer everything possible to your new PC.

This window appears on your *old* PC if you're transferring by portable drive; the window appears on your *new* PC if you're transferring by cable or network.

To transfer *everything* from *all* your old PC's user accounts to accounts on your new PC, simply click the Transfer button. If your new PC has enough space, the program copies everything from your old PC to your new PC. You can always delete unwanted items later from your new PC if you want.

But if your new PC doesn't have enough storage space or you don't want everything copied, here's how to choose which items to transfer:

- ✔ **User accounts:** Here's your chance to weed out user accounts you don't want to transfer: Windows Easy Transfer puts a check mark next to each user account it will transfer, as shown in Figure 20-2. Click to remove the check mark from the user accounts you *don't* want transferred.

- ✔ **Advanced Options:** Haven't set up accounts for everybody on your new PC? The Advanced Options area, just above the Transfer button, lets you create new accounts on your new PC and then fill them with the appropriate incoming files. This area also comes in handy for old PCs with two or more drives, as it lets you map which drive's contents go to which drive on your new PC.

- ✔ **Customize:** Sometimes you don't need it all. To pick and choose which categories of items should be transferred from each account, click the Customize link under each account's name, shown back in Figure 20-2. A window pops up, as shown in Figure 20-3, letting you exclude certain categories. Remove the check mark from My Videos, for example, to grab everything but your videos from your old PC. After customizing your transfer, click the little red X in the pop-up window's top-right corner to return to the Choose What to Transfer window.

- ✔ **Advanced:** The Advanced link, shown at the bottom of the pop-up list in Figure 20-3, is meant for techies who enjoy micromanaging. If you click it, you arrive at a tree of folder and filenames. This area lets you pick and choose individual files and folders to copy. It's overkill for most people, but it's an option, nevertheless. When you're done, click the Save button to return to the Choose What to Transfer window.

When you're through fine-tuning the process, click the Transfer button to begin copying your carefully selected files and settings to your new Windows 8 PC.

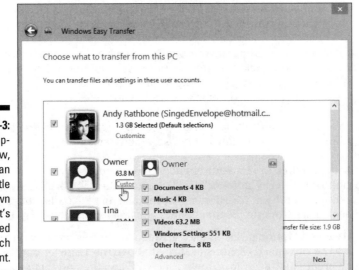

Figure 20-3:
In this pop-up window, you can whittle down what's transferred from each account.

Chapter 21

Help on the Windows 8
Help System

Don't bother plowing through this whole chapter for the nitty gritty: Here are the quickest ways to make Windows 8 dish out helpful information when you're stumped:

✔ **Press F1:** Press the F1 key from within Windows or any program.

✔ **Start screen:** Type the word **help** directly at the Start screen and then click Help and Support.

✔ **Question Mark:** If you spot a little blue question mark icon near a window's top-right corner, pounce on it with a quick click.

In each case, Windows 8 fetches its Help and Support program, beefed up with tables, charts, indexes, and step-by-step instructions for you to follow.

The Help program frequently grabs updated information from Microsoft's websites, so you'll find the most help when connected to the Internet.

This chapter explains how to wring the most help from Windows Help and Support.

Consulting a Program's Built-In Computer Guru

Almost every Windows program includes its own Help system. To summon a program's built-in computer guru, press F1, choose Help from the menu, or click the little blue question mark icon shown in the margin.

To find help and start asking pointed questions in Windows Media Player, for example, follow these steps:

1. **Choose Help from the program's menu and choose View Help. (Alternatively, press F1 or click the blue question mark icon.)**

   The Windows Help and Support program opens to its page dedicated to Windows Media Player. (See Figure 21-1.) There, the program lists the topics that give people the most headaches.

   The Search text box at the top of the window lets you search the Help program's index. Typing a few words describing your question often fetches the exact page you need, saving you a few steps.

2. **Click the topic where you need help.**

   For example, clicking the Rip Music From a CD link tells Windows 8 to explain more about copying a CD's music files to your computer.

3. **Click the subtopic that interests you.**

   After a brief explanation about the topic, the Help page offers several subtopics: You can see how to edit media information, such as the titles of your copied songs. Don't miss the topics listed at the page's bottom; they can fetch related information you may find helpful.

4. **Follow the listed steps to complete your task.**

   Windows 8 lists the steps needed to complete your task or fix your problem, sparing you from searching through the menus of your problematic program. As you scan the steps, feel free to look at the area below them; you often can find tips for making the job easier next time.

Try to keep the Help window and your problematic program open in adjacent windows. That lets you read each step in the Help window and apply the steps in your program without the distraction of the two windows covering each other up.

Figure 21-1: Choose the topic confusing you in Windows Media Player.

> Windows Help and Support
>
> Search
>
> Help home | Browse help | Contact support
>
> Windows Media Player: Recommended links
>
> You can use Windows Media Player to find and play digital media files on your PC or network, play CDs and DVDs, and stream media from the Internet. You can also rip music from audio CDs, burn CDs of your favorite music, sync media files to a portable device, and find and purchase content on the Internet through online stores.
>
> For more info, we recommend the following links:
>
> • Burn a CD or DVD in Windows Media Player
> • Rip music from a CD in Windows Media Player
> • Set up a device to sync in Windows Media Player
>
> Online Help ▼   100% ▼

The Windows 8 Help system is sometimes a lot of work, forcing you to wade through increasingly detailed menus to find specific information. Still, using Help offers a last resort when you can't find the information elsewhere. And it's often much less embarrassing than tracking down the neighbor's teenagers.

If you're impressed with a particularly helpful page, send it to the printer: Click the Printer icon (shown in the margin) at the page's top. Windows 8 shoots that page to the printer so that you can keep it handy until you lose it.

Finding the Information You Need in Windows Help and Support

When you don't know where else to start, fire up Windows Help and Support and begin digging at the top.

To summon the program from the Start screen, type the word **help**. As you begin to type the word, the Start screen clears immediately and begins displaying names of all matching apps. When the words Help and Support appear, click or tap the words to launch the program. The Help and Support window rises to the screen, as shown in Figure 21-2.

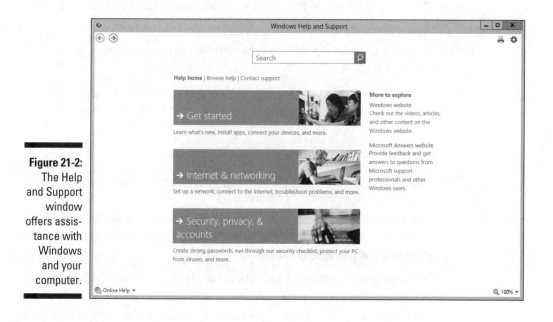

Figure 21-2:
The Help and Support window offers assistance with Windows and your computer.

The program offers three sections:

- ✔ **Get Started:** This section introduces the confusing new Windows 8 and then explains information about the basics: using a mouse and keyboard, running your fingers on a touchscreen tablet, installing programs, and adding new devices and printers to your computer.

- ✔ **Internet & Networking:** This section moves to the specifics of connections: connecting to the Internet, as well as to other computers through a network.

- ✔ **Security, Privacy, & Accounts:** Always trying to be more secure, Windows explains how to create strong passwords and avoid viruses and other malware.

Windows Help and Support works much like a website or folder. To move back one page, click the little Back arrow in the upper-left corner. That arrow helps you out if you've backed into a corner.

Summoning the Windows Troubleshooters

When something's not working as it should, the Troubleshooting section of the Windows Help and Support center may sleuth out a fix. Sometimes, it works like an index, narrowing down the scope of your problems to the one button that fixes it. Then it displays the button on the Help page for your one-click cure.

Other times, it interviews you about the problem, narrowing down the list of suspects until it finds the culprit — and your magic button to fix the situation.

Sometimes, unfortunately, a magic button isn't available. If your wireless Internet signal isn't strong enough, for example, the Troubleshooter tells you to stand up and move your laptop closer to the transmitter.

To summon the troubleshooters, follow these steps:

1. **Right-click the Action Center icon in your desktop's taskbar and choose Troubleshoot a Problem.**

   The Troubleshoot Computer Problems window, shown in Figure 21-3, is ready to tackle a wide variety of problems, from general to specific.

2. **Click the subject that troubles you.**

   The window offers these four topics that mimic their counterparts in Control Panel, which I cover in Chapter 12:

   - **Programs:** This guides you through running older programs that initially balked at running under Windows 8. It also takes a look at your web browser and tries to fix any problems it finds.

- **Hardware and Sound:** This area shows how to diagnose driver problems, the biggest cause of bickering between Windows 8 and things plugged into or inside your PC. It also helps diagnose problems with your printer, speakers, and microphone.

- **Network and Internet:** Head here for help with Internet connections, as well as common problems encountered when connecting two or more PCs in your home.

- **System and Security:** A catch-all section for everything else, this helps out with security and improving your PC's performance.

Click a topic, and Windows 8 whisks you to the page dealing with that subject's most common problems. Keep clicking the subtopics until you find the one dealing with your particular problem.

3. **Follow the recommended steps.**

Occasionally, you'll stumble onto numbered steps that solve your problem. Follow those steps one at a time to finish the job.

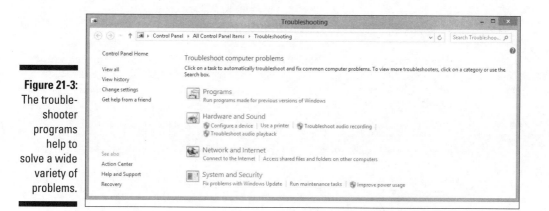

Figure 21-3: The troubleshooter programs help to solve a wide variety of problems.

When you right-click on a misbehaving icon, you may see Troubleshoot Problems listed on the pop-up menu. Click it to fetch the troubleshooter for that particular item, saving you some time.

At the window's bottom, be sure to select the check box called Get the Most Up-to-Date Troubleshooters From the Windows Online Troubleshooting Service. That feature lets Microsoft visit the Internet and grab any newly developed troubleshooters to beef up your computer's troubleshooting arsenal.

As with many portions of Windows Help system, you must be connected with the Internet to run some of the troubleshooters.

Part VII
The Part of Tens

"Jeez — I thought the Registry just defined the wallpaper on the screen."

In this part . . .

No *For Dummies* book is complete without a Part of Tens section: lists of ten easy-to-read informational nuggets. Of course, the lists don't always contain exactly ten, but you get the general idea.

The first list explains ten things you'll absolutely hate about Windows 8 (followed by ways to fix those problems).

The second list contains tips exclusively for tablet and laptop owners. It explains how to change how your laptop reacts when you close its lid, for example, as well as quick ways to switch in and out of Airplane Mode while flying.

I also throw in step-by-step instructions for tasks mobile computer owners repeat constantly: logging on to new wireless networks and setting the clock for a new time zone.

Chapter 22

Ten Things You'll Hate about Windows 8 (and How to Fix Them)

*Y*ou may find yourself thinking Windows 8 would be perfect if only . . . *(insert your pet peeve here)*.

If you find yourself thinking (or saying) those words frequently, read this chapter. Here, you find not only a list of ten or so of the most aggravating things about Windows 8, but also ways you can fix them.

I Want to Avoid the Start Screen!

If you find the mysterious new Start screen to be more startling than helpful, here's how to avoid it. This section explains how to stay on the desktop as long as possible.

Bringing back the Start button

Even before Windows 8 hit the stores, a cottage industry began creating ways to put the Start button and its menu back onto the desktop's taskbar, conveniently bypassing the new Start screen.

A Google search for *"Windows 8 Start Button"* turns up several programs, including Lee-Soft's ViSoft (`http://lee-soft.com/visoft`). Shown in Figure 22-1, the program restores the Start button and menu to Windows 8. Yet, the program leaves the Start screen in place, just in case you must revisit that strange land.

If you want the best of both worlds — desktop and apps — try Start8 by StarDock (`www.stardock.com/products/start8`). Start8 restores the Start button to its usual place. Clicking the Start button, however, fetches the Start screen showing icons for *all* your programs and apps.

I describe other Start screen–avoiding tactics in Chapter 3 in the section on making programs easier to find.

Knowing when the Start screen reappears unexpectedly

The Start screen and the desktop aren't self-contained entities. No, the two worlds intertwine, and one wrong click on the desktop tosses you back onto the Start screen's sharp-edged tiles.

Figure 22-1: Several Windows 8 programs and apps put the Start button and menu back onto the taskbar.

So, no matter how many Start screen–avoiding tactics you may employ, you'll still find yourself tossed back onto the Start screen when you do any of the following things:

✔ **Add user accounts.** The desktop's Control Panel lets you manage a user account. You can toggle a user account between Standard and Administrator, change its name, and even delete it completely. But if you need to *add* a user account — or even change your own account's picture — you're dropped off at the Start screen's PC Settings screen to finish the job.

✔ **Play a music file or view a photo.** Windows 8 sets itself up to use the Start screen's Music and Pictures apps. Open one photo or MP3 file on the desktop, and you'll find yourself back in Start screen land. (I explain how to fix that in Chapter 16, in the section on giving the music playing task back to Windows Media Player. Chapter 17 explains how to assign photo chores back to the desktop's Windows Photo Viewer.)

✔ **Troubleshoot.** Although the Start screen specializes in rather anemic faire, it also contains two of the most powerful troubleshooting tools in Windows 8: Refresh and Remove Everything. Described in Chapter 18, these two tools offer last-ditch cure-alls for ailing computers. You won't find any way to access these tools from the desktop, however.

In short, even adding a Start button back to the desktop won't keep you from being dropped off into the land of the Start screen. Be prepared for these occasional unavoidable journeys.

I Want to Avoid the Desktop!

On a touchscreen tablet, it's enticing to stay on the Start screen with its finger-sized tiles and easy-to-touch icons. Smartphone owners have enjoyed the app lifestyle for years. Easily downloadable apps offer help for nearly every niche, from bird watching to car repair.

The tablet's portable size and larger screen makes it easier to read digital books, newspapers, and magazines. And you can browse your favorite websites away from your desk.

But staying nestled within the Start screen's world of apps can be more difficult than it appears. No matter how hard you try to avoid the desktop and its pin-sized controls, you'll find yourself dragged there when you do any of the following things from the Start screen:

 ✔ **Click the Desktop tile.** This app brings you straight to the desktop zone. To hide this tile or any other Start screen tile, right-click the unwanted app to reveal the App bar and then click the Unpin from Start icon, shown in the margin.

✔ **Browse files.** The Start screen isn't sophisticated enough to browse your files. As soon as you plug in a flash drive or portable hard drive, the desktop's File Explorer leaps onscreen to handle the job.

✔ **Manage a user account.** You can *create* new accounts from the Start screen, but to *delete* or *change* an existing account, you need the desktop's Control Panel, covered in Chapter 12.

 ✔ **Watch Flash videos.** The Start screen's version of Internet Explorer handles most websites well. But on some websites, it can't play videos that employ Adobe Flash technology. When a video won't play, right-click a blank part of the website to reveal the App bar. Then click the Page Tool icon (shown in the margin) and choose View on the Desktop. The desktop's Internet Explorer jumps in to finish the task.

✔ **Manage gadgetry.** The Start screen's PC Settings screen lists all the devices connected to your computer, from printers to mice to portable hard drives. But it shows only their names; to change the *settings* of any of those devices requires a trip to the desktop's Control Panel.

✔ **Manage files.** You can access your photos and music files from the Start screen's Photos and Music apps, respectively. But *changing* those files in any way — renaming a file or folder, perhaps — requires a trip to the desktop. You'll find yourself there when looking for the date you snapped a photo, as well.

In short, the Start screen works well for most simple computing tasks. But when it comes to fine-tuning your computer's settings, performing maintenance work, or even browsing files, you'll find yourself returning to the desktop.

 If you find yourself constantly returning to the desktop for certain tasks, keep visiting the Windows Store to search for an app that can accomplish the same task. Microsoft stocks the store with more apps every day; as the apps fill more niches, you'll find yourself relying on the desktop less often.

But until the apps catch up with the desktop, tablet owners might want to pop a portable Bluetooth mouse (covered in Chapter 12) into their gadget bags for those inevitable trips to the desktop.

Windows Makes Me Sign In All the Time

The power-conscious Windows 8 normally blanks your screen when you haven't touched a key for a few minutes. And, when you belatedly press a key to bring the screen back to life, you're faced with the lock screen.

And to move past the lock screen, you need to type your password to sign back in to your account.

Some people prefer that extra level of security. If the lock screen kicks in while you're spending too much time at the water cooler, you're protected: Nobody can walk over and snoop through your e-mail.

Other people don't need that extra security, and they simply want to return to work quickly. Here's how to accommodate both camps:

If you don't *ever* want to see the lock screen, use a single user account without a password, which I describe in Chapter 14. That defeats all the security offered by the user account system, but it's more convenient if you live alone.

To keep Windows from asking for a password whenever it wakes back up, follow these steps:

1. **Right-click in any screen's bottom-left corner and then choose Control Panel.**

2. **From the Control Panel, click System and Security and then click Power Options.**

3. **From the screen's left edge, click Require a Password on Wakeup.**

   When the window appears, most of the options are *grayed out* — inaccessible.

4. **Select the option labeled Change Settings That Are Currently Unavailable.**

5. **Select the Don't Require a Password option and then click the Save Changes button.**

That leaves you with a more easy-going Windows. When your computer wakes up from sleep, you're left at the same place where you stopped working, and you don't have to enter your password anymore.

Unfortunately, it also leaves you with a less-secure Windows. Anybody who walks by your computer will have access to all your files.

To return to the safer-but-less-friendly Windows, follow these same steps, but in Step 5, select the Require a Password (Recommended) option. Then click the Save Changes button.

The Taskbar Keeps Disappearing

The taskbar is a handy Windows 8 feature that usually squats along the bottom of your desktop. Sometimes, unfortunately, it up and wanders off into the woods. Here are a few ways to track it down and bring it home.

If your taskbar suddenly clings to the *side* of the screen — or even the ceiling — try dragging it back in place: Instead of dragging an edge, drag the entire task-bar from its middle. As your mouse pointer reaches your desktop's bottom edge, the taskbar suddenly snaps back into place. Let go of the mouse and you've recaptured it.

Follow these tips to prevent your taskbar from wandering:

✔ To keep the taskbar locked into place so that it won't float away, right-click a blank part of the taskbar and select Lock the Taskbar. Remember, though, that before you can make any future changes to the taskbar, you must first unlock it.

✔ If your taskbar drops from sight whenever the mouse pointer doesn't hover nearby, turn off the taskbar's Auto Hide feature: Right-click a blank part of the taskbar and choose Properties from the pop-up menu. When the Taskbar Properties dialog box appears, deselect the Auto-Hide the Taskbar check box. (Or to turn on the Auto Hide feature, select the check box.)

I Can't Line Up Two Windows on the Screen

With its arsenal of dragging-and-dropping tools, Windows simplifies grabbing information from one window and copying it to another. You can drag an address from an address book and drop it atop a letter in your word proces-sor, for example.

However, the hardest part of dragging and dropping comes when you're lining up two windows on the screen, side by side, for dragging.

Windows 8 offers an easy way to align windows for easy dragging and dropping:

1. **Drag one window against a left or right edge.**

   When your mouse pointer touches the screen's edge, the window reshapes itself to fill half the screen.

2. **Drag the other window against the opposite edge.**

   When your mouse pointer reaches the opposite edge, the two windows are aligned side by side.

You can also minimize all the windows except for the two you want to align side by side. Then right-click a blank spot on the taskbar, and then choose Show Windows Side By Side. The two windows line up on the screen perfectly.

Try both to see which meets your current needs.

It Won't Let Me Do Something Unless I'm an Administrator!

Windows 8 gets really picky about who gets to do what on your computer. The computer's owner gets the Administrator account. And the administrator usually gives everybody else a Standard account. What does that mean? Well, only the administrator can do the following things on the computer:

- ✔ Install programs and hardware.
- ✔ Create or change accounts for other people.
- ✔ Start an Internet connection.
- ✔ Install some hardware, such as digital cameras and MP3 players.
- ✔ Perform actions affecting other people on the PC.

People with Standard accounts, by nature, are limited to fairly basic activities. They can do these things:

- ✔ Run previously installed programs.
- ✔ Change their account's picture and password.

Guest accounts are meant for the babysitter or visitors who don't permanently use the computer. If you have a broadband or other "always on" Internet account, guests can browse the Internet, run programs, or check their e-mail. (Guest accounts aren't allowed to *start* an Internet session, but they can use an existing one.)

If Windows says only an administrator may do something on your PC, you have two choices: Find an administrator to type his or her password and authorize the action; or convince an administrator to upgrade your account to an Administrator account, covered in Chapter 14.

I Don't Know What Version of Windows I Have

Windows has been sold in more than a dozen flavors since its debut in November 1985. How can you tell what version is installed on your computer?

Right-click in the bottom-left corner of any screen. When the pop-up menu appears, choose System. When the System window appears, look near the top to see which version of Windows 8 you own: Windows 8 (for consumers), Windows Pro (for businesses), Enterprise (for large businesses), or WinRT.

I describe the different Windows versions in Chapter 1.

My Print Screen Key Doesn't Work

Contrary to its name, the Print Screen key doesn't shuttle a picture of your screen to your printer. Instead, the Print Screen key (usually labeled PrintScreen, PrtScr, or PrtSc) sends the screen's picture to the Windows 8 memory.

From there, you can paste it into a graphics program, such as Paint, letting the graphics program send the picture to the printer.

Windows 8 introduces something new, though: If you want to capture an image of the entire screen and save it as a file, press ⊞+PrtScr.

That tells Windows to snap a picture of your current screen and save it in your Pictures library with the name *Screenshot*. (Windows saves those images in the PNG format, if you're interested, and it captures your mouse pointer, as well.) Subsequent screenshots include a number after the name, like Screenshot (2) and Screenshot (3).

When saved, your screenshot can head for your printer when you right-click the file and choose Print from the pop-up menu.

Chapter 23

Ten or So Tips for Touchscreen Owners

*F*or the most part, everything in this book applies to deskbound PCs, laptops, and tablets alike. Windows 8 offers a few settings exclusively for the portable crowd, however, and I cover those items here. I also throw in a few tips and quick references to make this chapter especially suited for laptop owners who need information in a hurry.

Switching to Airplane Mode

Most people enjoy working with their tablets or laptops during a long flight. Portable devices are great for watching movies, playing games, or catching up on some work.

But most airlines make you turn off your wireless connection while the plane is in flight, referred to in airport lingo as *Airplane Mode.*

To turn on Airplane Mode on either a laptop or tablet, follow these steps:

1. Launch the Charms bar and click the Settings icon.

On a laptop, press ⊞+I. On a touchscreen, slide your finger inward from the screen's right edge and tap the Settings icon (shown in the margin).

The Settings pane appears.

2. **Click or tap your wireless network icon (shown in the margin).**

   Drag or slide your Airplane Mode toggle to On, as shown in Figure 23-1.

   That immediately puts your computer into Airplane Mode. Your computer's wireless radio turns off, and the wireless network icon morphs into a tiny airplane, shown in the margin.

Figure 23-1:
Drag or slide the Airplane Mode toggle to the On position to put your computer in Airplane Mode while flying.

To turn off Airplane mode and reconnect to the Internet, repeat these steps. This time, however, you'll tap or click the little airplane icon because that's what represents your wireless connection.

Airplane Mode not only puts your tablet and laptop in compliance with airline safety rules but it conserves battery life, as well. Feel free to keep your computer in Airplane Mode even when you're not on an airplane.

Airplane Mode turns off not only your computer's wireless but its cellular gear, as well, if you have a cellular data plan. It's a handy way to shut *off* all your computer's radio activity with one switch.

Connecting to a Wireless Internet Network

Every time you connect to a wireless network, Windows 8 stashes its settings for connecting again the next time you visit. But when you're visiting one for the first time, you need to tell your computer that it's time to connect.

I explain wireless connections more thoroughly in Chapter 15, but here are the steps for quick reference:

1. **Turn on your laptop's wireless adapter, if necessary.**

   Some laptops offer a manual switch somewhere on the case; others leave it turned on all the time. (If your computer is in Airplane Mode, turn off Airplane Mode, as described in the previous section.)

2. **On the desktop, click your taskbar's network icon, shown in the margin. (From the Start screen, fetch the Charms bar, click the Settings icon, and click your Wireless icon.)**

   Windows 8 lists any wireless networks it finds within range.

3. **Connect to a wireless network by clicking its name and clicking the Connect button.**

   At many places, clicking Connect may connect your laptop to the Internet immediately. But if your laptop asks for more information, move to Step 4.

   Never connect to a wireless network listed as an *Ad Hoc* connection. Those connections are usually set up in public places by thieves hoping to rip off unsuspecting visitors.

4. **Enter the wireless network's name and security key/passphrase, if asked.**

   Some secretive wireless networks don't broadcast their names, so Windows lists them as Unnamed Network. If you spot that name or Windows asks for the network's security key, track down the network's owner and ask for the network's name and security key or passphrase to enter here.

   When you click the Connect button, Windows 8 announces its success. Be sure to select the two check boxes, Save This Network and Start This Connection Automatically, to make it easier to connect the next time you come within range.

Toggling Your Tablet's Screen Rotation

Most Windows tablets are meant to be held horizontally. But if you pick them up, they automatically rotate to keep your work right-side up.

Turn the tablet vertically, for example, and your desktop becomes long and vertically narrow.

Autorotation comes in handy when you're reading a digital book, for example, because the longer, thinner pages more closely resemble a printed book. But when the screen rotates unexpectedly, autorotate becomes a bother.

Most tablets come with a rotation lock button along one edge. (The rotation button is usually near the power button for some reason.) Pressing that button either locks the screen in place or lets it rotate automatically.

If your tablet lacks that button, or you can't find it, you can toggle autorotation directly from the desktop by following these steps:

1. **From the Start screen, click the Desktop tile.**

2. **Right-click a blank portion of your screen's background and choose Screen Resolution.**

3. **Select the check box labeled Allow the Screen to Auto-Rotate.**

   When the check mark appears, Windows allows the screen to rotate automatically, so it's always right-side up. Remove the check mark, and the screen stays fixed in its current position, no matter how you move the tablet.

Repeat these steps to toggle autorotate on or off.

Choosing What Happens When You Close Your Laptop's Lid

Closing the laptop's lid means that you're through working, but for how long? For the night? Until you get off the subway? For a long lunch hour? Windows 8 lets you tailor exactly how your laptop should behave when you latch your laptop's lid.

To start tweaking, follow these steps:

1. **From the desktop, right-click the screen's bottom-left corner and choose Control Panel from the pop-up menu.**

2. **Click System and Security, click Power Options, and then click Choose What Closing the Lid Does from the left pane.**

   Shown in Figure 23-2, Windows 7 offers three lid-closing options for whether your laptop is plugged in or running on its batteries: Do Nothing, Hibernate, or Shut Down.

Generally, choose Hibernate because it lets your laptop slumber in a low-power state, letting it wake up quickly so that you can begin working without delay. But if you'll be shutting down your laptop for the evening, turning it off is often a better idea. That option lets the laptop conserve its battery power and, if plugged in overnight, wake up with fully charged batteries.

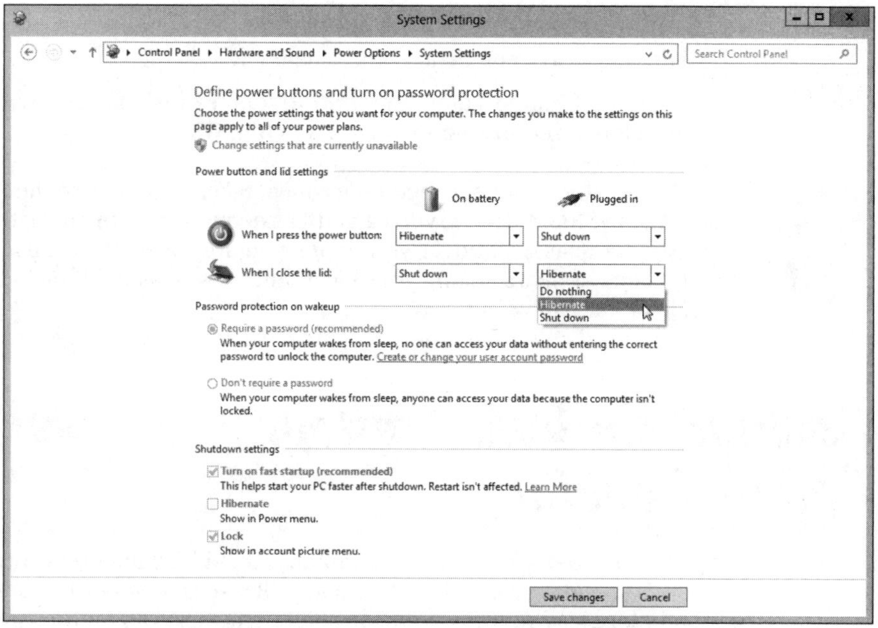

Figure 23-2:
Change your
laptop's
reactions
when
plugged in
or on
batteries.

Also, you can choose whether your computer should require you to
enter a password when it's turned back on. (Passwords are always a
good idea.)

3. Click the Save Changes button to make your changes permanent.

Adjusting to Different Locations

PCs don't move from a desktop, making some things pretty easy to set up.
You need only enter your location once, for example, and Windows 8 automatically sets up your time zone, currency symbols, and similar things that
change over the globe.

But the joy of a tablet or laptop's mobility is tempered with the agony of telling the thing exactly where it's currently located. This section supplies the
steps you need to change when traveling to a different area.

Follow these steps to let your laptop know you've entered a new time zone:

1. From the desktop, click the clock in the taskbar's bottom-right corner.

A calendar and clock appear in a small window.

2. **Click Change Date and Time Settings.**

   The Date and Time dialog box appears.

3. **Click the Change Time Zone button, enter your current time zone in the Time Zone drop-down list, and click OK twice.**

If you frequently travel between time zones, take advantage of the Additional Clocks tab in Step 3. There, you can add a second clock; to check the time quickly in Caracas, just hover your mouse pointer over the taskbar's clock. A pop-up menu appears, listing your local time as well as the time in the additional location you've entered.

Backing Up Your Laptop Before Traveling

I explain how to back up a PC in Chapter 13, and backing up a laptop works just like backing up a desktop PC. Please, please remember to back up your laptop before leaving your home or office. Thieves grab laptops much more often than desktop PCs. Your laptop can be replaced, but the data inside it can't.

Keep the backed up information at *home* — not in your laptop's bag.

Index